5 Steps to a 5

AP Computer Science

D1384615

Other books in McGraw-Hill's *5 Steps to a 5* Series include:

AP Biology
AP Calculus AB
AP Chemistry
AP English Language
AP English Literature
AP Microeconomics/Macroeconomics
AP Physics B and C
AP Psychology
AP Spanish Language
AP Statistics
AP U.S. Government and Politics
AP U.S. History
AP World History
Writing the AP English Essay

McGRAW-HILL

5 Steps to a 5

AP Computer Science

Kathleen A. Larson
David Levine

MCGRAW-HILL

New York   Chicago   San Francisco   Lisbon   London   Madrid   Mexico City
Milan   New Delhi   San Juan   Seoul   Singapore   Sydney   Toronto

1 2 3 4 5 6 7 8 9 0   QPD/QPD   0 9 8 7 6 5

ISBN 0-07-143711-8

⊗ This book is printed on recycled, acid-free paper containing a minimum of 50% recycled, de-inked fiber.

Library of Congress Cataloging-in-Publication Data

Larson, Kathleen A.
   AP computer science / Kathleen A. Larson, David Levine.—1st ed.
        p. cm.—(5 steps to a 5)
   ISBN 0-07-143711-8 (alk. paper)
1. Computer science—Examinations, questions, etc.   2. Advanced placement programs (Education)—Examinations—Study guides.   I. Levine, David (David B.)   II. Title   III. Series.
   QA76.28.L37 2005
   004—dc22

                             2005007564

Contents

Chapter 8   **Nonprogramming Issues / 155**

Chapter 9   **Asymptotic Analysis of Programs (Big-Oh) / 161**

Chapter 10   **Collections of Data / 172**

Chapter 11   **Dynamically Linked Structures / 188**

Preface

Computer science is a vast field that requires both broad understanding and specific knowledge if one is to master it. Different colleges (and high schools) have taken different approaches to introducing students to this field. There are probably more different introductory courses taught in computer science than in any other field. And yet, there is only one AP Computer Science curriculum. The AP Computer Science Development Committee has taken the time to poll a large number of colleges about which concepts of computer science they teach in the first year and has designed the curriculum to include those concepts which are most commonly included in college courses. What does this mean for you, the AP Computer Science student? No matter where you continue your education, it is likely that the introductory course there will not match your high school course exactly. Also, it is almost certain that you will have covered concepts in your high school course that will not be tested on the exam. (Getting input from the keyboard is one such concept; the exam will not test that, but it is unlikely that you didn't learn at least some way to accomplish this task.)

So what is the purpose of this book? It is meant to serve as a bridge between your previous preparation (your AP course and your other experiences) and the exam itself. It will draw attention to various concepts that you have already studied and will help you evaluate how well you understand them. You cannot master the concepts of AP Computer Science from this book alone, but it may present some of the concepts in a new way that will help you appreciate their usefulness and will help you master them before you take the exam. The book also contains some practice exams near the back. These exams should give you an idea of what to expect when you take the actual exam. We recommend that you take the practice exams under "game conditions." Wait until you are almost ready to take the regular exam, and then take the practice exams in one 3-hour session each. Use the Diagnostic Exam in Part II much earlier to help you identify areas of weakness, and the chapter review questions to help you address them.

There are actually two AP Computer Science exams: A and AB. The A curriculum is covered in the first eight chapters of this book. There are a few sections of those chapters that refer to more advanced material, but they are clearly marked. A student who is studying for the A exam need not study Chapters 9–12. The AB curriculum encompasses the entire book. There are two A and two AB practice exams. How do you know which exam to take? You might just look at the table of contents and see which topics are familiar. You might ask your teacher. You might try the AB exams and see how well you do. One word of warning, however: you must sign up in advance. You do not get to "change your mind" at the last minute. So, whatever your plan is, make sure that you discuss it with your teacher so that you are signed up for the correct exam.

Chapter 7 is of particular interest to students who are not formally enrolled in an AP Computer Science course. Both AP Computer Science exams will make use of a case study, a narrative and accompanying program with which it is assumed that students are familiar. One of the main purposes of including the case study in the curriculum (and on the exam) is to ensure that students have been exposed to large programs and the issues that surround them. Because of the nature of the exam, you will need to be familiar with this particular program. If you are not yet familiar with the case study, you may obtain a copy free of charge from the Web site mentioned in the Webliography. During the exam, you will be given a copy of the program, but if you have never seen it before, it would take a lot of time to understand what is necessary to answer the questions.

Once upon a time, we took our own AP exams (but not in computer science). It is an exciting, but also a nerve-wracking experience. We hope that this book helps with the excitement and calms the nerves. Good luck!

Kathleen A. Larson
David Levine

McGRAW-HILL

5 Steps to a 5

AP Computer Science

PART I

HOW TO USE THIS BOOK

THE BASICS

What Is Unique about This Book?

It is important that you understand this book prepares students for two separate examinations, Computer Science A and Computer Science AB. You can take only one of these exams in a year, so you must decide, based upon the level of your preparation, which exam is the right one for you. Topics tested on the A exam are found in Chapters 1 through 8. The AB exam covers all chapters, 1 through 12. If you are not well versed and comfortable with the AB topics (Chapters 9 through 12), you should pass up the AB exam, concentrate on the A topics, and plan to earn your very best score on the A exam.

Organization of the Book

Part I contains an introduction to the five-step program and three study plans for preparing for the AP Computer Science exam.

Part II discusses the AP exam and contains a diagnostic test for Computer Science A (which should be taken by all students) and an AB supplement (which should be taken only by students preparing for Computer Science AB). The diagnostic exam contains fewer questions than does a full-length AP Computer Science exam. Moreover, the questions are designed primarily to see if you need additional review on a topic rather than as a dry run for the exam.

Part III (Comprehensive Review) contains 12 chapters covering the topics that comprise the curriculum. Code examples demonstrate common algorithms with which you should be familiar. At the end of each chapter you will find a Rapid Review section that summarizes the content and the key terms, followed by a set of Practice Problems. Complete solutions are provided for each set of problems.

Part IV contains four full-length practice examinations, two for the A exam and two for the AB exam. Complete solutions and rubrics for grading the free-response questions are included.

In Part V the appendixes list additional resources and Web sites that will prove helpful to you. The glossary provides definitions and page references to more detailed explanations of the glossary terms.

This book is intended to serve as a resource and study guide for you throughout the year; but, if you have acquired it just before the exam, it can be an invaluable aid in reviewing and practicing for the test. Follow the five-step plan outlined in the next sections and you will be well on your way to a top score on this exam.

INTRODUCTION TO THE FIVE-STEP PROGRAM

The five-step plan is designed to provide you with knowledge, skills, and strategies to help lead you to the highest score you can earn on the AP exam. Each step is designed to provide you with the opportunity to get closer and closer to the "Holy Grail" score of 5.

Step One leads you through a brief process to help determine which type of exam preparation you want to commit to:

1. Month by month: September through May
2. The calendar year: January through May
3. Basic training: six weeks before the exam

2 *Step Two* helps you develop the knowledge you need to succeed on the exam:

1. A comprehensive review of exam topics
2. One diagnostic exam, which you can go through step by step and question by question to determine the areas in which you will need more work
3. Explanation of multiple-choice answers, and rubrics for free-response questions
4. A glossary of terms related to the AP Computer Science exam
5. A list of useful related Web sites
6. A guide to the Quick Reference and Case Study materials provided with the exam

3 *Step Three* helps you develop the skills necessary to take the exam and do well:

1. Practice multiple-choice questions
2. Practice free-response questions

4 *Step Four* helps you develop strategies for taking the exam:

1. Learning about the test itself
2. Learning to read multiple-choice questions
3. Learning how to answer multiple-choice questions, including whether or not to guess
4. Learning how to plan and write free-response answers

5 *Step Five* helps develop your confidence using the skills demanded on the AP Computer Science exam:

1. The opportunity to take a diagnostic exam
2. Time management techniques and skills
3. Practice exams (two A level and two AB level) that test how well honed your skills are

GRAPHICS USED IN THIS BOOK

To emphasize particular skills, strategies, and practice, we use seven sets of icons throughout this book.

The first icon is an hourglass, which indicates the passage of time during the school year. This hourglass icon will appear in the margin next to an item that may be of interest to one of the three types of students who are using this book (mode A, B, or C students).

 For the student who plans to prepare for the AP Computer Science exam during the entire school year, September through May, we use an hourglass that is full on the top.

 For the student who decides to begin preparing for the exam in January of the calendar year, we use an hourglass that is half full on the top and half full on the bottom.

 For the student who wishes to prepare during the final six weeks before the exam, we use an hourglass that is empty on the top and full on the bottom.

 The second icon is a footprint, which indicates which step in the five-step program is being emphasized in a given analysis, technique, or practice activity.

Plan   Knowledge   Skills   Strategies   Confidence Building

The third icon is a clock, which indicates a timed practice activity or a time management strategy. It will indicate on the face of the dial how much time to allow for a given exercise. The full gray dial will remind you that this is a strategy which can help you learn to manage your time on the test.

The fourth icon is an exclamation point, which indicates a very important idea, concept, or strategy point that you should not pass over.

The fifth icon is a checkmark, which will alert you to pay close attention. This activity will be most helpful if you go back and check your own work, your calendar, or your progress.

The sixth icon is a light bulb, which indicates strategies that you might want to try.

The seventh icon is the sun, which indicates a tip that you might find useful.

Boldfaced terms are included in the glossary at the back of the book.

THREE APPROACHES TO PREPARING FOR THE AP COMPUTER SCIENCE EXAM

No one knows your study habits, likes, and dislikes better than you. You are the only one who can decide which approach you want or need adopt to prepare for the Advanced Placement Computer Science Examination.

Look at the brief profiles below and determine which prep mode approach you will follow.

You're a full-year prep student (Approach A) if:

1. You are the kind of person who likes to plan for everything very far in advance.
2. You like to plan for a graduation party or vacation a year in advance.
3. You arrive at the airport three hours before your flight because you never know when something can happen.
4. You like detailed planning and everything in its place.
5. You feel you must be thoroughly prepared.
6. You are always early for appointments.
7. You hate surprises.

You're a one-semester prep student (Approach B) if:

1. You begin to plan for a graduation party or vacation four to five months before the event.
2. You get to the airport at least two hours before your flight is scheduled to leave.
3. You are willing to plan ahead to feel comfortable in stressful situations, but you are okay with skipping some details.
4. You feel more comfortable when you know what to expect, but a surprise or two is fine.
5. You are always on time for appointments.

You're a six-week prep student (Approach C) if:

1. You plan a graduation party or vacation a week before the big day.
2. You get to the airport gate just as final boarding for your plane is being announced.
3. You work best under pressure and tight deadlines.
4. You feel very confident with the knowledge and skills you've learned in your AP Computer Science class.
5. You decided late in the year to take the exam.
6. You feel okay if you arrive a little late for an appointment.
7. Surprises energize and please you.

CALENDAR FOR EACH PLAN

 Calendar for Approach A for the A-Level Student: Year-Long Preparation for the AP Computer Science Exam

Although its primary purpose is to prepare you for the AP Computer Science exam you will take in May, this book can enrich your study of computer science, your analytical skills, and your free-response writing skill.

SEPTEMBER–OCTOBER (Check off the activities as you complete them.)

_____ Carefully read Parts I and II of this book.
_____ Pay close attention to your walk through of the diagnostic exam.
_____ Get on the Internet and take a look at the AP Web sites listed in the appendix.
_____ Skim the Comprehensive Review section. (Reviewing the topics covered in this section will be part of your year-long preparation.)
_____ Buy a few color highlighters. Flip through the entire book. Break the book in. Write in it. Highlight it.
_____ Get a clear picture of your own school's AP Computer Science curriculum.
_____ Begin to use the book as a resource to supplement classroom learning.
_____ Read and study Chapter 1, Talking about Programs.
_____ Read and study Chapter 2, Object-Oriented Design.
_____ Download the PDF file of the Marine Biology Simulation (MBS) case study. (See appendix.) Study Chapters 1 and 2 of the MBS case study. Write answers to the analysis questions and code the exercises.

NOVEMBER (The first 10 weeks have elapsed.)

_____ Read and study Chapter 3, Statement-Level Java Programming.
_____ Practice object-oriented design by applying the principles to classroom assignments.
_____ Study Chapter 3 of the MBS case study. Answer the questions and code the exercises.

DECEMBER

_____ Read and study Chapter 4, Inheritance.
_____ Read and study Chapter 5, Lots of Data.
_____ Review Chapters 1–3 and answer the practice questions.

JANUARY (20 weeks have passed)

_____ Read and study Chapter 6, Algorithmic Techniques.
_____ Review Chapters 1–5.
_____ Study Chapter 4 of the MBS case study. Answer the questions and code the exercises.
_____ Read and study Chapter 7, Marine Biology Simulation Case Study. Remember, this is review. You have already covered the case study.

FEBRUARY

_____ Continue to study Chapter 7, Marine Biology Simulation Case Study. Answer all review questions.
_____ Review Chapters 1–6.

MARCH (30 weeks have elapsed)

_____ Read and study Chapter 8, Non-programming Issues. (Review the first chapter of your text book; it probably parallels this topic.)
_____ Review (and retake if necessary) the diagnostic test

APRIL

_____ Review all the chapters.

_____ Take Practice Exam A1 the first week in April.

_____ Score yourself. Evaluate your strengths and weaknesses.

_____ Study appropriate chapters to correct your weaknesses.

_____ If they are available, go over all the tests you took in your AP class.

_____ Highlight only those terms in the glossary about which you are still unsure. Ask your teacher for clarification.

MAY (THIS IS IT!)

_____ Review all the chapters again.

_____ If you have additional time, answer questions at the suggested Web sites that offer them.

_____ Take Practice Exam A2.

_____ Score yourself. Evaluate your strengths and weaknesses.

_____ Study appropriate pages to correct your weaknesses.

_____ Get a good night's sleep before the exam.

_____ Fall asleep knowing that you are well prepared.

Calendar for Approach B for the A-Level Exam: Semester-Long Preparation for the AP Computer Science Exam

Assuming that you have completed one semester of computer science studies, the following calendar will enable you to use the knowledge and the skills you've been practicing to help you prepare for the May exam.

JANUARY (Check off the activities as you complete them.)

- ✓ Carefully read Parts I and II of this book.
- _____ Take the diagnostic exam.
- _____ Determine your weaknesses.
- _____ Read and study Chapter 1, Talking about Programs. Answer all review questions.
- _____ Read and study Chapter 2, Object-Oriented Design. Answer all review questions.
- _____ Read and study Chapter 3, Statement-Level Java Programming. Answer all review questions.
- _____ Study Chapters 1 and 2 of the Marine Biology Simulation (MBS) case study (see appendix). Answer all questions and code the exercises.

FEBRUARY

- _____ Read and study Chapter 4, Inheritance. Answer all review questions.
- _____ Read and study Chapter 5, Lots of Data. Answer all review questions.
- _____ Study Chapter 3 of the MBS case study. Answer all questions and code the exercises.

MARCH

- _____ Look at the AP Web sites listed in the appendix.
- _____ Read and study Chapter 6, Algorithmic Techniques. Answer all review questions.
- _____ Study Chapter 4 of the MBS case study. Answer all questions and code the exercises.

APRIL

- _____ Read and study Chapter 7, Marine Biology Simulation Case Study. Answer all review questions.
- _____ Read and study Chapter 8, Nonprogramming Issues. Answer all review questions.
- _____ Review Chapters 1–6.
- _____ Take Practice Exam A1 in the third week of April.
- _____ Score yourself. Evaluate your strengths and weaknesses.
- _____ Study appropriate chapters to correct your weaknesses.

MAY (THIS IS IT!)

- _____ Take Practice Exam A2.
- _____ Score yourself. Evaluate your strengths and weaknesses.
- _____ Study appropriate pages to correct your weaknesses.
- _____ Get a good night's sleep before the exam.
- _____ Fall asleep knowing that you are well prepared.

Calendar for Approach C for the A-Level Exam: Six-Week Preparation for the AP Computer Science Exam

At this point we are going to assume that you have been building your computer science knowledge base for more than six months. You will, therefore, use this book primarily as a specific guide to the AP Computer Science exam.

Given the time constraints, now is not the time to expand your AP Computer Science curriculum. Rather, it is the time to limit and refine what you already do know.

APRIL

_____ Skim Parts I and II.

_____ Take the diagnostic exam and see how well you do.

_____ Carefully read the chapters containing any topics you did not cover in your computer science course.

_____ Focus on the Rapid Reviews at the end of each chapter, and then answer the chapter Practice Problems.

_____ Take Practice Exam A1.

_____ Score yourself. Evaluate your strengths and weaknesses.

_____ Study appropriate chapters to correct your weaknesses.

MAY (THIS IS IT!)

_____ Go over the glossary. Highlight any terms you don't know.

_____ Take Practice Exam A2.

_____ Score yourself. Evaluate your strengths and weaknesses.

_____ Go back to the glossary and review the highlighted terms.

_____ Study sections appropriate to your weaknesses.

_____ Get a good night's sleep before the exam.

_____ Fall asleep knowing you are well prepared.

Calendar for Approach A for the AB-Level Student: Year-Long Preparation for the AP Computer Science Exam

Although its primary purpose is to prepare you for the AP Computer Science exam you will take in May, this book can enrich your study of computer science, your analytical skills, and your free-response writing skill.

SEPTEMBER–OCTOBER (Check off the activities as you complete them.)

_____ Carefully read Parts I and II of this book.

_____ Pay close attention to your walk through of the diagnostic exam.

_____ Get on the Internet and take a look at the AP Web sites listed in the appendix.

_____ Skim the Comprehensive Review section. (Reviewing the topics covered in this section will be part of your year-long preparation.)

_____ Buy a few color highlighters. Flip through the entire book. Break the book in. Write in it. Highlight it.

_____ Get a clear picture of your own school's AP computer science curriculum.

_____ Begin to use the book as a resource to supplement classroom learning.

_____ Read and study Chapter 1, Talking about Programs.

_____ Read and study Chapter 2, Object-Oriented Design.

_____ Read and study Chapter 3, Statement-Level Java Programming.

_____ Practice object-oriented design by applying the principles to classroom assignments.

_____ Study Chapters 1 and 2 of the Marine Biology Simulation (MBS) case study. Write answers to the analysis questions and code the exercises.

NOVEMBER (The first 10 weeks have elapsed.)

_____ Study Chapter 3 of the MBS case study. Answer the questions and code the exercises.

_____ Read and study Chapter 4, Inheritance.

_____ Read and study Chapter 5, Lots of Data.

DECEMBER

_____ Review Chapters 1–5 and go over the practice questions.

_____ Read and study Chapter 6, Algorithmic Techniques.

_____ Study Chapter 4 of the MBS case study. Answer all questions and code the exercises.

JANUARY (20 weeks have elapsed)

_____ Study Chapter 5 of the MBS case study. Answer all questions and code the exercises.

_____ Read and study Chapter 7, Marine Biology Simulation Case Study. Answer the review questions.

_____ Read and study Chapter 8, Nonprogramming Techniques. Answer the review questions.

_____ Check Chapter 1 of your text for additional information on this topic.

_____ Review Chapters 1–6.

FEBRUARY

_____ Read and study Chapter 9, Asymptotic Analysis of Programs. Answer the review questions.

_____ Read and study Chapter 10, Collections of Data.

_____ Review Chapters 1–8.

MARCH (30 weeks have elapsed)

_____ Read and study Chapter 11, Dynamically Linked Structures. Answer the review questions.

_____ Read and study Chapter 12. Elementary Data Structures. Answer the review questions.

_____ Review all the chapters.

APRIL

_____ Take Practice Exam AB1 the first week in April.

_____ Score yourself. Evaluate your strengths and weaknesses.

_____ Study appropriate chapters to correct your weaknesses.

_____ If they are available, go over all the tests you took in your AP class.

_____ Highlight only those terms in the glossary about which you are still unsure. Ask your teacher for clarification.

_____ Review all the chapters again.

_____ If you have additional time, answer questions at the suggested Web sites that offer them.

MAY (THIS IS IT!)

_____ Take Practice Exam AB2.

_____ Score yourself. Evaluate your strengths and weaknesses.

_____ Study appropriate pages to correct your weaknesses.

_____ Get a good night's sleep before the exam.

_____ Fall asleep knowing that you are well prepared.

Calendar for Approach B for the AB-Level Exam: Semester-Long Preparation for the AP Computer Science Exam

Assuming that you have completed one semester of computer science studies, the following calendar will enable you to use the knowledge and the skills you've been practicing to help you prepare for the May exam.

JANUARY (Check off the activities as you complete them.)

_____ Carefully read Parts I and II of this book.
_____ Take the diagnostic exam. Determine your weaknesses.
_____ Read and study Chapter 1, Talking about Programs. Answer all review questions.
_____ Read and study Chapter 2, Object-Oriented Design. Answer all review questions.
_____ Read and study Chapter 3, Statement-Level Java Programming. Answer all review questions.
_____ Study Chapters 1, 2, and 3 of the Marine Biology Simulation (MBS) case study. (See appendix.) Answer all questions and code the exercises.

FEBRUARY

_____ Read and study Chapter 4, Inheritance. Answer all review questions.
_____ Read and study Chapter 5, Lots of Data. Answer all review questions.
_____ Read and study Chapter 6, Algorithmic Techniques. Answer all review questions.
_____ Study Chapters 4 and 5 of the MBS case study. Answer all questions and code the exercises.
_____ Read and study Chapter 7, Marine Biology Simulation Case Study.
_____ Review Chapters 1–3.

MARCH (Ten weeks to go!)

_____ Log on to the Internet and take a look at the AP Web sites listed in the appendix.
_____ Continue with Chapter 7, Marine Biology Simulation Case Study. Answer all review questions.

_____ Read and study Chapter 8, Nonprogramming Issues. Answer all review questions.
_____ Read and study Chapter 9, Asymptotic Analysis of Programs. Answer all review questions.
_____ Read and study Chapter 10, Collections of Data. Answer all review questions.
_____ Review Chapters 1–7.

APRIL

_____ Read and study Chapter 11, Dynamically Linked Structures. Answer all review questions.
_____ Read and study Chapter 12, Elementary Data Structures. Answer all review questions.
_____ Take Practice Exam AB1 in the third week of April.
_____ Score yourself. Evaluate your strengths and weaknesses.
_____ Study appropriate chapters to correct your weaknesses.

MAY (THIS IS IT!)

_____ Take Practice Exam AB2.
_____ Score yourself. Evaluate your strengths and weaknesses.
_____ Study appropriate pages to correct your weaknesses.
_____ Get a good night's sleep before the exam.
_____ Fall asleep knowing that you are well prepared.

Calendar for Approach C, for AB-Level Exam: Six-Week Preparation for the AP Computer Science Exam

At this point we are going to assume that you have been building your computer science knowledge base for more than six months. You will, therefore, use this book primarily as a specific guide to the AP Computer Science exam.

Given the time constraints, now is not the time to expand your AP Computer Science curriculum. Rather, it is the time to limit and refine what you already do know.

APRIL

———— Skim Parts I and II.
———— Take the diagnostic exam and see how well you do.
———— Carefully read the chapters of any topics you did not cover in your computer science course.
———— Focus on the Rapid Reviews at the end of each chapter, and then answer the chapter Practice Problems.
———— Take Practice Exam AB1.
———— Score yourself. Evaluate your strengths and weaknesses.
———— Study appropriate chapters to correct your weaknesses.

MAY (THIS IS IT!)

———— Go over the glossary. Highlight any terms you don't know.
———— Take Practice Exam AB2.
———— Score yourself. Evaluate your strengths and weaknesses.
———— Go back to the glossary and review the highlighted terms.
———— Study sections appropriate to your weaknesses.
———— Get a good night's sleep before the exam.
———— Fall asleep knowing you are well prepared.

Summary of the Three Study Plans for the A Exam

Month	Approach A: Year-Long Plan	Approach B: Semester-Long Plan	Approach C: Six-Week Plan
September–October	Diagnostic Exam Ch. 1 and 2		
November	Ch. 3		
December	Ch. 4 and 5 Review Ch. 1–3		
January	Ch. 6 and 7 Review Ch. 1–5	Diagnostic Exam Ch. 1, 2, and 3	
February	Ch. 7, continued Review Ch. 1–6	Ch. 4 and 5	
March	Ch. 8	Ch. 6	
April	Review all chapters Practice Exam A1	Ch. 7 and 8 Review Ch. 1–6 Practice Exam A1	Diagnostic Exam Practice Exam A1 Rapid Reviews
May	Review all chapters again Practice Exam A2	Practice Exam A2	Practice Exam A2 Glossary review

Summary of the Three Study Plans for the AB Exam

Month	Approach A: Year-Long Plan	Approach B: Semester-Long Plan	Approach C: Six-Week Plan
September–October	Diagnostic Exam Ch. 1, 2, and 3		
November	Ch. 4 and 5		
December	Ch. 6 Review Ch. 1–5		
January	Ch. 7 and 8 Review Ch. 1–6	Diagnostic Exam Ch. 1, 2, and 3	
February	Ch. 9 and 10 Review 1–8	Ch. 4, 5, and 6 Begin Ch. 7 Review Ch. 1–3	
March	Ch. 11 and 12 Review all chapters	Ch. 7, continued Ch. 8, 9, and 10 Review Ch. 1–7	
April	Practice Exam AB1 Review all chapters	Ch. 11 and 12 Practice Exam AB1 Review all chapters	Diagnostic Exam Rapid Reviews Practice Exam AB1
May	Practice Exam AB2	Practice Exam AB2	Practice Exam AB2 Glossary review

PART II

WHAT YOU NEED TO KNOW ABOUT THE AP COMPUTER SCIENCE EXAM

BACKGROUND ON THE AP COMPUTER SCIENCE EXAM

The AP Computer Science examination was first administered in 1984. The course was first taught using the Pascal language, then C++, and is currently taught using Java. Approximately 25,000 students took the exam in 2004, the first year that it was offered in Java. The focus of the course is not, strictly speaking, the language, but rather principles of computer science that transcend language. Java is the current language because it is the best vehicle for teaching current principles that guide problem solving through programming, as measured by a survey of colleges and universities. There are two exams: an A-level examination representing the first semester of college work, and an AB-level examination representing the first full year of college work. Students may choose to take either examination. Studying this book may help you to decide which examination you should take. That decision must be made by the beginning of March when the examinations are ordered by school districts.

What Is Covered in the AP Computer Science Exam?

The AP Computer Science exams cover the following six broad themes:

- **Object-oriented program design:** Specifying and designing a correct program that is also understandable, modifiable, and reusable.
- **Program implementation:** Choosing classes, data structures, and algorithms to carry out the objectives of object-oriented design.
- **Program analysis:** Examining and testing programs to determine whether they meet their specifications; analysis of time and space requirements.
- **Standard data structures:** Data abstraction and the development and application of data structures.
- **Standard algorithms:** Good solutions to standard problems; closely related to the choice of data structures; efficiency considerations.
- **Computing in context:** Hardware and software considerations; awareness of ethical and social implications.

The broad themes described above cover the following:

- Objects, classes, state, and behavior; using, modifying, and designing classes; reusability, full-program design (AB only); inheritance hierarchy; "IS-A" relationships; class composition; "HAS-A" relationships; libraries; instance variables; method signatures; public, private, extending a class; interface; implementing an interface; multiple class design and interaction (AB only); coupling; cohesion; super; this.
- Top-down design, encapsulation, information hiding, designing subclasses, super class, procedural abstraction, helper methods, cohesive units, variables, primitives, Boolean, int, double, object variables, reference, aliasing, identifier, constant, instance and static methods, parameter list, passing parameters by value, return type, control structures, method call, accessor and modifier (or mutator) methods, conditional and iterative control, recursion, polymorphism.
- Testing, correctness, efficiency, unit testing, integration testing, boundary cases, erroneous cases, debugging, error categories (compile-time, runtime, logic), recognize runtime exceptions, throw runtime exceptions (AB only), preconditions and postconditions, loop invariant, informal time and space efficiency comparisons, asymptotic analysis of algorithms (AB only), "big-oh," representations of numbers in different bases, imprecision of floating point, round-off error.
- Standard representations of integers, real numbers, and Boolean values; simple and complex classes; String and its methods; array; ArrayList and its methods; casting.

AB only: lists, stacks, queues, priority queues, sets, maps, two-dimensional arrays, linked lists, trees, heaps, hash tables, `List` interface, `LinkedList`, `Set` interface, `HashSet`, `TreeSet`, `Map` interface, `HashMap`, `TreeMap`, `Iterator` interface, `ListIterator` interface, asymptotic time relative to these data structures.

- Traversing, inserting into, and deleting from an array; sequential search; binary search; Selection sort; Insertion sort, Merge sort. AB only: analysis of algorithms, Quicksort, Heapsort, hash tables, asymptotic complexity.
- Primary and secondary memory, processors, peripheral devices, software components, interpreters, compilers, Java virtual machine, bytecode, operating system and its responsibilities, networks, social issues.

For a more detailed description of the topics covered in the AP Computer Science exam, visit the College Board's Web site at http://www.collegeboard.com/student/testing/ap/subjects.html.

What Is the Format of the AP Computer Science Exam?

The A and AB Computer Science exams follow exactly the same format. The AP Computer Science exam has two sections: Section I contains 40 multiple-choice questions. The time allowed for this section is 75 minutes. Section II contains four free-response questions. The time allowed for this section is 105 minutes.

The two sections of the test are completely separate and are administered in separate blocks of time as specified above. Please note that you are not expected to be able to answer all the questions in order to receive a grade of 5. The College Board's Web site has specific instructions for each part of the test.

You will be provided with an examination appendix booklet containing the following:

- A Java quick reference for either the A or AB exam
- Source code for the visible classes of the Marine Biology Simulation (MBS)
- Black box classes for the MBS case study
- A Java MBS quick reference
- Index for the MBS source code

Instructions for downloading these test materials are given in the appendix.

What Are the Advanced Placement Exam Grades?

Advanced placement grades are given on a 5-point scale, with 5 being the highest and 1 being the lowest. The grades are described below:

5 = Extremely well qualified
4 = Well qualified
3 = Qualified
2 = Possibly qualified
1 = No recommendation

There is no official "passing" grade on the exam. Many people consider 3 or better to be passing. Many colleges will give course credit for grades of 3 or better, although some schools require a 4 for credit. Some schools maintain different requirements for the A exam and for the AB exam.

How Is the AP Computer Science Grade Calculated?

The exam has a composite score of 100 points: 50 points for the 40 multiple-choice questions in Section I and 50 points for the 4 free-response problems in Section II.

In Section I, the weighted score is computed as follows:

[(number correct) − (1/4 (number wrong))] × 1.25 = Weighted Section I Score (minimum score = 0). (There is no deduction for blank answers.)

In Section II, each problem is scored according to a 9-point rubric. The distribution of points in this section is determined by the chief faculty consultant, the development committee, and exam and question leaders prior to the start of actual grading. A scoring rubric is developed by considering the concepts being tested and the expected, canonical solutions. The rubric is tested against a substantial number of randomly selected student responses to ensure that it can be applied whether a student's response fits the canonical solution or not. Sometimes points are divided into half-points. For example, there may be ½ point for an attempt to write the correct code and ½ point for correctness. In general, graders are generous with the first ½ point and strict with the second ½ point.

The sum of a student's points on the four free-response problems is then multiplied by 1.389 to calculate the Weighted Section II Score, which comprises the remaining 50 points.

The weighted scores for Sections I and II are combined to yield a composite score based on 100 (rounded to the nearest whole number).

The chief faculty consultant for the exam has the responsibility of turning the composite score into an AP exam grade. The cutoff points for each grade (1–5) vary from year to year, but approximate ranges (based on past exams) are shown in the following table.[1]

Raw Score	AP Grade
75–100	5
56–74	4
41–55	3
31–40	2
0–30	1

What Do I Need to Bring to the Exam?

- Several #2 pencils
- A good eraser and a pencil sharpener (or mechanical pencils)
- Two black or blue pens (possibly needed to fill out forms, although all questions on the exam are to be answered in pencil)
- A watch
- An admission card or a photo ID card if your school requires identification
- Your Social Security number
- Your school code number if the test site is not at your school
- A simple snack if your test site permits it
- A light jacket if you know the test site has strong air-conditioning

Do not bring White Out or scrap paper.

[1]Note that the A exam is scored on a scale of 80 points rather than 100.

TIPS FOR TAKING THE AP COMPUTER SCIENCE EXAM

The following suggestions represent some of the collective wisdom of many AP Computer Science teachers, who have guided thousands of students through the AP Computer Science exam since its inception in 1984. We urge you to take advantage of their expert advice.

What Should I Do to Prepare for the Exam?

- Practice writing legibly.
  - Write (or print) answers by hand.
  - Ask someone to critique your handwriting.
  - Even if your handwriting is beautiful, if it is so small that a grader would need a magnifying glass to read it, practice enlarging its size.
- Organize your solutions so that they are easy for another person (the grader) to follow.
  - Indent carefully, logically, and consistently.
  - Pay attention to identifiers that are given in the problem and use meaningful identifiers when you create your own variables or methods.
- Start reviewing for the exam early and review often. Don't wait until the last minute to ask for answers to your questions.
- Be familiar with the format and instructions for the exam beforehand so that there are no surprises the day of the exam.
- Review the course description for computer science provided by the College Board at its Web site http://www.collegeboard.com/student/testing/ap/subjects.html. In this valuable resource you will find the following.
  - The topic outline, which lists topics that are tested on the A and AB exams and other topics that are "useful but not tested."
  - The "commentary on the topic outline," which explains the topics more fully and provides some examples.
  - Sample multiple-choice and free-response questions and solution keys.
  - The AP Computer Science Java subset. This defines the features of Java that may appear on an AP Computer Science exam and, consequently, that students should understand.
  - Standard Java library methods that are required for the A or AB exam.
  - Implementation classes and interfaces for data structures tested on the AB exam.
- Familiarize yourself with the quick reference materials provided with the exam.
  - This includes the Java library methods and implementation classes and interfaces listed above.
  - Know this material so well that you do not waste time searching for information you need during the exam but know just where to turn to find it.
- Review the Marine Biology Simulation case study. The following information is provided with the exam.
  - All source code for the visible classes (Appendix B).
  - Summary class documentation for the `Environment` interface and the Marine Biology Simulation utility classes covered in Chapters 1–4 (Appendix C).
  - Source code for environment implementations covered in Chapter 5 (Appendix D) for AB only.
  - Index for source code found in Appendixes B and D (Appendix G).
  - Be familiar with these resources so that you can easily and quickly find whatever you are looking for without wasting test time.
- Review the tests, quizzes, and lab assignments from the course.

- Practice exam questions from previous years. These can be found at the College Board Web site. Also look at the scoring rubrics and sample student solutions to note how they were graded and common errors students make.
- Memorizing code, such as searching and sorting algorithms, will be of little value to you. You should be able to recognize and analyze common algorithms, but you will not be asked to reproduce them.
- Relax and get a good night's sleep before the exam.

WHAT ARE SOME TIPS THAT WILL HELP ME DURING THE EXAM?

Here are some helpful hints to keep in mind while you are taking the exam. They fall into three categories: tips to help you overall, tips specific to multiple-choice questions, and tips for the free-response questions.

General Tips

- First of all, rest assured that the people grading your examination (readers) are never "out to get you." In fact, they want you to do well. The idea is to give credit for how much you know, not to see how many points can be deducted.
- Questions usually progress from easier to more difficult. Try to get through the first few questions quickly to allow more time for later questions that may require more time.
- If your mind goes blank on a question, skip it. A later question may jog your memory and help you to answer one you skipped.
- Try to remain focused. Don't let your mind wander. Keep checking your watch to help you stay on task.
- Use the case study as a model for well-written code.
- Pay attention to examples, comments, and diagrams. They can help you understand the problem.

Multiple-Choice Questions

- If you can narrow the choices down to two or three, go ahead and guess. Otherwise, leave the question blank.
- Be careful to bubble in the correct place on the answer sheet, especially if you skip a question.
- Read all the answers before selecting one. You may find you have misinterpreted the question and need to rethink it by checking all the choices.
- Try working backward to eliminate some of the choices.
- Keep moving. You have 75 minutes to answer 40 questions.
- Be careful about questions that seem too obvious. You may be missing an important detail. Read the question again.
- Some questions are very long and require a great deal of reading. There may be two, but not more than two, questions based on a lengthy body of code. Read the questions before you read the code so that you know what you are looking for.
- Sometimes you can "see" what a recursive method is doing by analyzing the big picture rather than performing a complicated trace.
- Read method signatures carefully. The name of the method may tell you what it does. Check out the parameters and return type.
- You are permitted to write in the test booklet. If you need to list variables and trace some code, do it in the space next to the question.

Free-Response Questions

- You have 105 minutes to answer 4 questions. That's about 26 minutes per question. The first question will probably be the easiest. Try to complete it in less than 26 minutes (15 would be good) so you have extra time for the more difficult questions.
- You will be given two booklets containing the test questions: one with a pink cover and one that is green. The pink booklet is the one that will be graded; the green booklet is intended for planning or scrap work. Do not write your answers in the green booklet. You won't have time to write them there and then copy them into the pink booklet. You may want to use the green booklet for sketchy planning, but do all your coding in the pink one.
- Write your answers in pencil; you may erase and make changes. If you want to change your answer, make a single large X over the code you do not want graded, and write your new answer in the space provided. If you write two solutions but fail to cross out the one you do not want graded, the reader has no choice but to grade the first one on the page.
- If you run out of space, the blank pages in the back of the pink booklet may be used, but you should include a note to the reader on the page where the question is found directing the reader to look at the page where you wrote your answer. Otherwise, your answer could be overlooked.
- Write as neatly and legibly as you possibly can. A different reader will be grading each free-response question, and these readers don't know you the way your teacher does. They don't know your writing style, nor do they know your handwriting idiosyncrasies. Organize your work and make your code clear to anyone who reads it.
- Write *something* for all of the questions. Don't leave anything blank. Even if you aren't sure, try writing some code. You may be right, or you may receive partial credit.
- Be sure you answer the question that is asked. That is, don't misinterpret the problem by reading your own thoughts into it. Underline, circle, or highlight important words or phrases.
- Section II questions usually have two or three parts. If you don't know what to write for Part A, go on and try Parts B and C anyway. Sometimes Parts B and C say, "In writing Part B, you may use method <blah> that you wrote in Part A. You may assume <blah> works as intended regardless of what you wrote in Part A." This may help you past the stumbling block and allow you to earn points for Parts B and C.
- If some part of a question says that you "may" use code you wrote in an earlier part, take that as a very strong hint that you "should" use that code. It probably will make the solution much easier.
- If, in Parts B or C, you reimplement code that you wrote in an earlier part rather than invoking that code, you may be penalized.
- Do *not* code your answer so that it works for the specific examples given. The examples are there to illustrate general and special cases; your code should work for any situation that meets the preconditions.
- Read preconditions and postconditions very carefully. Be sure your code satisfies the postconditions.
- Read method signatures carefully:
  - The method name describes what the method is supposed to do.
  - Be sure, when you invoke a method, that your parameters match those of the method signature.
  - Be sure, when you write the body of a method, that its return statement matches the return type.
- Don't spend your time writing comments. Only code will be graded.
- This is not the time to write intricate or "tricky" code in order to test the grader or show how smart you are. If your code contains an error, you may outsmart yourself. Straightforward, readable code is the best bet.

- With the possible exception of a "design" question, you will not receive credit for writing a description of how to solve a problem or what you would do if you had time.
- If you are asked to "justify" your solution, you will need to write a sentence or two. Keep it brief and to the point.
- Avoid creating or using classes that aren't specified in the problem and aren't part of the Java standard language or the case study.
- For the case study question, use code within the case study as a model to help you write a new method or class. Don't forget to include a consistency check. (Do the fish and the environment agree? Especially if a fish is removed from the environment.)

Smile as you turn in your paper, knowing you have done the best job you could do.

2 DIAGNOSTIC TEST

A note to the student: The purpose of this "test" is to help you determine your strengths and weaknesses vis-à-vis the AP Computer Science curriculum. The questions below cover material in that curriculum, but do not mimic the style or format of a real AP exam. The balance of questions is different; the style of questions and answers is often different; and the amount of time that you would be expected to spend on various questions is also different. *In short, this is NOT a practice AP exam.* There are two practice exams each for the A and AB curricula in Part IV of this book.

You will make the best use of this test if you answer the questions in a single sitting and go over the answers immediately upon completion. The solutions include not just the answer, but also a reference to the portion of the book that you should study for a "refresher" on the material in question. Remember that the purpose of this test is to find your weaknesses, not to prove to yourself—or anyone else—how strong you are. Use the test to help you identify the areas in which you are most in need of review.

To best assess your preparedness for the exam, write the code in long-hand rather than implementing it on your computer. After you have completed the exam, you may wish to implement any solution about whose quality you are unsure, but defer this until you have examined your results carefully.

For questions involving the Marine Biology Simulation, it is expected that you will be looking at the code (but not the narrative) as you answer these questions.

(The astute reader will note that this diagnostic test does not cover any material from Chapter 8. Such material, while part of the official AP curriculum, does not translate well to "typical," diagnostic questions. The practice exams at the end of the book do include some such questions, but they are omitted here. In any case, the material tends to be tested much less than most other concepts in the curriculum.)

1. Consider the following method:

```java
public static int compute(int val)
{
    val = val * val;
    val = val * val;
    return val;
}
```

Which statement could replace the body of `compute` so that the result is the same?

A. `return Math.pow(val, 4);`
B. `return Math.pow(val, 8);`
C. `return 2 * Math.pow(val, 2);`
D. `return val * 4;`
E. `return val * 8;`

2. Consider the following class declaration:

```
public class Word
{
  private String myWord;
  // constructor not shown

  // modifier
  public void setWord(String newWord)
  { myWord = newWord; }

  // accessor
  public String getWord()
  { return myWord; }
}
```

Assume that Word object w has been defined in a client program as follows:

```
Word w = new Word();
```

Of the following statements, which will *not* result in an error if used in the client program?

A. `System.out.println(w.myWord);`
B. `System.out.println((new Word(w)).myWord);`
C. `System.out.println(w.setWord(myWord));`
D. `System.out.println(w.getWord());`
E. `System.out.println(getWord(w));`

3. In the game of Craps, a pair of dice is rolled, the sum of the dice is noted, and the player either wins (sum = 7 or 11), loses (sum = 2, 3, or 12), or neither wins nor loses and the game continues. If the game continues, the sum is called the player's "point," and the player continues to roll the dice until either the point is matched (a win) or a 7 is rolled (a loss). In designing a computer program to simulate Craps, Alex decides to include the following classes: Die, PairOfDice, and GameSim. List the principles of object-oriented design illustrated by Alex's decision.

4. Suppose that the PairOfDice class is (partially) written as follows:

```
public class PairOfDice
{
  public PairOfDice(int numSides)
    { /* Implementation not shown */ }

  public int roll() { /* Implementation not shown */ }

  // Other parts of class not shown
}
```

Write code that creates a pair of six-sided dice, rolls them until a 9 is rolled, and then prints a message stating how many rolls it took to achieve that value.

5. Consider the following code fragment:

```
public static final int YEAR = 2005;
```

Which of the following is (are) *not* legal code?

A. `if(maxYear != YEAR) //assume maxYear is an int`
B. `for(YEAR = 2005; YEAR < 2010; YEAR++) {...}`
C. `System.out.println("Double year = " + 2*YEAR);`
D. `YEAR = in.readInt(); //assume allows valid input`
E. None of the above is a legal use of YEAR

6. Consider the incomplete method below:

```
// precondition: x*y > 0
// postcondition: returns a value > 0
public int doSomething(int x, int y)
{ /* Implementation not shown */ }
```

For which values of x and y can the assumption be made that the postcondition has been met?

A. x = 1, y = 0
B. x = −1, y = 1
C. x = 0, y = 0
D. x = −1, y = −1
E. None of the above permits such an assumption

7. Owen has been asked to implement the class LockerCombination. The idea is that objects of this class hold the combination needed to open a school locker. These combinations consist of three ordered numbers in the range of 0–63. Objects of the class are expected to support a getNumber method which takes a parameter that specifies which number of the combination (first, second, or third) is desired and then reports that number. Owen has chosen to store the numbers in a single String. As a client of the class, what is your comment about this?

8. For the LockerCombination class described in question 7, write appropriate pre- and postconditions for the getNumber method, along with its signature.

9. Under what circumstances can a class have two or more methods with the same name?

10. What will be output by the following code fragment?

```
int a = 3;
int b = 6;
int c = 10;
System.out.println("Average = " + a + b + c / 3);
```

A. Average = 3610/3
B. Average = 363
C. Average = 6
D. Average = 6.33333333
E. A compile time error will be output

11. Consider the method classAverage shown below. Each of numStu students has taken a number of quizzes. The method is meant to return the average of all the student quiz averages. It contains several errors. Identify as many of them as you can.

```
public double classAverage(int numStu)
{
  for(int stu = 0; stu < numStu; stu++)
  {
    int grade = console.readInt(); //assume reads a grade
    while(grade >= 0)                //negative indicates end of input
    {
      sum += grade;
      count++;
    }
    double avg = grade/count;
  }
  double classAvg = avg/numStu;
}
```

12. Consider the following method:

```
// precondition: n > 0
public int doSomething(int n)
{
  int x = 0;
  for(int a = 0; a < n; a++)
  {
    for(int b = 0; b < n; b++)
    {
      x++;
    }
  }
  return x;
}
```

Which of the following is execution equivalent to the body of doSomething(n)?

A. return 2*n;
B. return n*(n - 1);
C. return Math.pow(n, 2);
D. return Math.pow(n, 2) - 1;
E. return Math.pow(2, n);

For questions 13 to 15, consider the following class hierarchy:

```
public class Base
{
  private String name;

  public Base(String s) { name = s; }

  public int doIt(int n)
  { /* Implementation not shown */ }

  public int compareTo(Object other)
  { /* Implementation not shown */ }

  public String getName() { return name; }

  // Other parts of class not shown
}
public class Derived extends Base
{
  private int secret;

  public Derived(String s, int n)
  { /* Implementation not shown */ }

  public int doIt(int x, int y)
  { /* Implementation not shown */ }

  public int getNum() { return secret; }
  // Other parts of class not shown
}
```

13. Write the constructor for the Derived class in such a way that the getName and getNum methods will return the parameters passed in the constructor.

14. For each of the following method invocations, indicate which block of code, if any, gets executed:

```
Derived item = new Derived("Batman", 7);
item.doIt(3,-28);          // (a)
item.doIt(48);             // (b)
item.doIt();               // (c)
```

```
Base foo = (Base) item;
foo.doIt(19);                  // (d)
foo.doIt(41,2);                // (e)
```

15A. True or False. Objects of type `Base` may be passed as a parameter to a method that expects a `Comparable` object.

15B. True or False. Objects of type `Derived` may be passed as a parameter to a method that expects a `Comparable` object.

16. Describe the key differences between an abstract class and an interface.

17. Consider an array, `nums`, containing integer values. Which of the following methods will return the sum of the values in `nums`? (In the case of III, assume that the second parameter is `nums.length` on the initial call.)

```
I.   public int addUp(int[] nums)
     {
       int sum = 0;
       for(int k=0; k<nums.length; k++)
         sum += nums[k];
       return sum;
     }

II.  public int addUp(int[] nums)
     {
       int len = nums.length;
       int sum = 0;
       int k = 0;
       while(k < len)
       {
         sum += nums[k];
         k++;
       }
       return sum;
     }

III. public int addUp(int[] nums, int len)
     {
       if(len == 0)
         return 0;
       else if(len == 1)
         return nums[len - 1];
       else
         return nums[len - 1] + addUp(nums, len - 1);
     }
```

A. I only
B. II only
C. I and II only
D. II and III only
E. I, II, and III

18. An array named a contains a group of `Objects`. We wish to copy these objects to the `ArrayList` named b. Consider the incomplete code below:

```
for (int i=0; i<a.length; i++)
{
     /* missing code */
}
```

Which of the following expressions will cause b to contain copies of the same objects, in the same order, as a?

A. `a[i].add( b );`
B. `a[i].add( 0, b );`
C. `b.add( a[i] );`
D. `b.add( a[i], 0 );`
E. `b.add( 0, a[i] );`

19. Given an array named `stuff`, of objects, write a code segment to determine how many of those objects are equivalent to their successor.

20. It is desired to write a recursive method that computes the square of a number. An outline of such a method is below:

```
public int square(int n)
{
  if(n = = 0)
    < missing code 1>
  else
    < missing code 2>
}
```

Which of the following replacements for the two missing code fragments would cause `square` to return the proper answer?

	missing code 1	missing code 2
A.	`return 0;`	`return n + square(n - 1);`
B.	`return 1;`	`return square(n - 1);`
C.	`return 0;`	`return n * square(n - 1);`
D.	`return 0;`	`return 2*n + square(n - 1) - 1;`

E. None of the above works; a recursive version of `square` requires two parameters

21. For which of the sorting algorithms below is it most difficult to reverse the order of the sort, i.e., to arrange the items from largest to smallest instead of the other way around:

A. Insertion sort is more difficult to reverse than either Selection sort or Merge sort.
B. Selection sort is more difficult to reverse than either Insertion sort or Merge sort.
C. Merge sort is the most difficult to reverse, followed by Insertion sort, and then Selection sort.
D. Insertion sort and Selection sort are equally easy to reverse but Merge sort is more difficult.
E. Insertion sort, Selection sort, and Merge sort are equally difficult to reverse.

22. When is sequential search more efficient than binary search?

A. When there are fewer then ten data items.
B. When the data are a primitive type.
C. When the data are sorted.
D. When the data are unsorted.
E. Sequential search is never more efficient than binary search.

23. Write code to find the largest element in an `ArrayList` of mutually `Comparable` elements named `items` if:

    A. The `ArrayList` is unsorted
    B. The `ArrayList` is sorted in ascending order

24. Suppose that an `ArrayList list` holds elements of type `Magic`. Suppose further that the class `Magic` contains a parameterless `boolean` method named `hasProperty`. Write code that splits `list` into two as yet undeclared `ArrayLists`, `has` and `hasNot`, such that all the elements of `has` have the property in question and all the elements of `hasNot` do not.

For questions concerning the Marine Biology Simulation (25–29), it is acceptable—even desirable—to have access to a code listing.

25A. Explain the movement algorithm for `DarterFish` and for `SlowFish`.

25B. Explain the implementation issues illustrated by the `DarterFish` class and by the `SlowFish` class.

26. Suppose there is one `Fish` with no nearby neighbors in the middle of an `Environment`. Suppose that on turn 7, it breeds. This means that there is now a `Fish` immediately south of the original `Fish`. Such a `Fish` would be expected to act some time after the original `Fish`, and yet it gets "skipped," i.e., does not act during turn 7. Explain why this is so. Express your answer in terms of code, not just by stating that "this is the way it works."

27. A `LeftFish` is similar to a `Fish` in all respects except that its default color is green and it moves as follows: A `LeftFish` always either moves forward or turns left. A `LeftFish` will never move forward twice in a row, but it will turn left any time that the space in front of it is occupied. Implement the necessary methods to add `LeftFish` to the Marine Biology Simulation.

End of Diagnostic Exam for A Students.
AB Students Should Continue.

28. `Fish` in an `UnboundedEnv` do not act in the same order as they would in a `BoundedEnv`. Why not?

29. It has been decided to modify the `UnboundedEnv` class so that it uses a `HashMap` rather than an `ArrayList` as its underlying data structure. The map will use the location of a given `Fish` as the key, and the `Fish` itself as the value. Implement this new version of the `UnboundedEnv` class.

30. After executing the following code, what does the matrix m contain?

```
int[][] m = new int[3][5];
for (int a=0; a<5; a++)
{
  for(int b=0; b<3; b++)
  {
    m[b][a] = b+a;
  }
}
```

A. 0 0 0 0 0
   1 1 1 1 1
   2 2 2 2 2

B. 0 1 2 3 4
   0 1 2 3 4
   0 1 2 3 4

C. 0 1 2 3 4
   1 2 3 4 5
   2 3 4 5 6

D. 0 1 2
   1 2 3
   2 3 4
   3 4 5
   4 5 6

E. The code causes an exception to be thrown prior to completion

31. quizScores is a matrix of integers such that quizScores[i][j] represents the score that student i earned on the jth quiz in a particular course.

A. Complete the method averageScore that returns the average score that all the students earned on a given quiz.

```
double averageScore(int quizNo)
{
```

B. The method aboveAverage returns the number of times that a given student scored at or above the class average on a given quiz. Complete that method below:

```
int aboveAverage(int studentNo)
{
```

32. For what data sets does Quicksort exhibit its worst case behavior, and what is the most descriptive big-oh bound for that behavior?

33. What is the best possible big-oh bound for the number of times the word "Wow" is printed by the code below?

```
for (int y=0; y<N; y+=4)
{
  System.out.println("Wow");
  for (int x=0; x<y; x++)
  {
    System.out.println("Wow");
  }
}
```

34. What is the best possible big-oh bound for the number of times the word "Wow" is printed by the code below?

```
for (int y=0; y<N; y*=2)
{
  for (int x=0; x<N; x+=2)
  {
    System.out.println("Wow");
  }
}
```

35. Jason has two choices for storing a list of data. He can use either an array (of fixed size) or an ArrayList. He does not know the exact amount of data that will be present, but does have an upper bound on the amount of data. If he declares the array large enough to ensure capacity for all the data, then it may be up to three times as large as necessary. In an asymptotic (big-oh) sense, how do the array and ArrayList compare in terms of memory usage?

36. What are the fundamental differences between a List and a Set?

37. What are the fundamental differences between a TreeSet and a HashSet?

38. Consider the code below that operates on a Map m:

```
Set keys = m.keySet();
Iterator it = keys.iterator();
while (it.hasNext())
{
  Something s = (Something) m.get(it.next());
  if (s.isSpecial())
  {
    s.applyBonus();
  }
}
```

Assuming that isSpecial and applyBonus each takes O(1) time to execute, what is the running time of this code if m is a HashMap? What if m is a TreeMap?

39. Write the method maxInSet that returns the largest item from within a Set of Comparable items.

```
// postcondition: returns any object in the Set s
//        that is at least as large as all other objects
//        in the set; returns null if the set is empty
public static Object maxInSet( Set s )
{
```

For Questions 40–44, you may examine the listings of the ListNode and TreeNode classes found in Chapter 11 while you are answering the questions.

40. What is the effect of executing the following code?

```
ListNode lonely = new ListNode( "Solo", null );
System.out.println( p.getNext().getValue() );
```

41. Consider the linked list of `ListNodes` shown below:

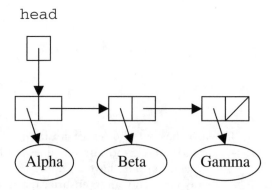

Draw a picture that shows the result of executing the following code:

```
ListNode extra = head.getNext();
extra.getNext().setData(head.getData());
head.setNext(extra.getNext());
extra.setNext(head);
head = extra;
```

42. Given a null-terminated, singly linked list (of `ListNodes`) whose first element is referenced by the variable `head`, write code to reverse the given list.

43. A certain binary search tree had its items printed using an in-order traversal. The items were printed in exactly the order in which they were inserted into the tree. What can you conclude about the structure of the tree?

44. A binary tree has been constructed out of `TreeNodes`. The data field of each `TreeNode` is a `Task` object as described below:

```
public class Task
{
  public int getValue();
  // Constructors and other methods not shown
}
```

A worker may complete any set of tasks that begins at the root of the tree and continues from there to a leaf. The worker will earn the total value of all tasks completed. (Completing no tasks, of course, results in earning nothing.) You are to write the method `maxValue` as described below:

```
// precondition: root refers to the root of a "task tree"
// postcondition: returns the value of the set of tasks
//        that will earn the most for a worker
public static int maxValue(TreeNode root)
{
```

45. Which of the following structures is defined by its LIFO (last in, first out) protocol?

    A. Stack
    B. Queue
    C. Priority Queue
    D. Set
    E. Map

46. What is printed by the following code fragment?

```
Stack s = new ListStack(); // ListStack implements Stack
s.push(new Integer(5));
System.out.println( s.pop() );
if (s.isEmpty())
{
  System.out.println("empty");
}
else
{
  System.out.println("not empty");
}
s.push(new Integer(21));
s.push(new Integer(34));
s.pop();
System.out.println( s.pop() );
s.push(new Integer(14));
if (s.isEmpty())
{
  System.out.println("empty at end");
}
else
{
  System.out.println("not empty at end");
}
```

47. Consider the following code fragment:

```
PriorityQueue pq = new ListPriorityQueue();
            // ListPriorityQueue implements Queue
for (int i=0; i<N; i++)
{
  String s = readString();
            // readString gets a String from the keyboard
  pq.insert(s);
}
for(int j=5; j>0; j- -)
{
  System.out.println(pq.removeMin());
}
```

What will be the asymptotic growth rate of time to execute this code fragment? Express your answer in big-oh notation.

48. A trucking company loads its trucks as follows: When packages arrive to be shipped, they are placed on the loading dock. When loading a truck, the workers examine the packages on the dock, select one, and place it in the truck. They select the package that will be the "best fit" in the truck, i.e., the largest one that will fit in the available capacity of the truck. Which of the following structures would be best to implement the collection of packages on the loading dock?

A. A stack
B. A queue
C. A priority queue using the negative of the size as the priority
D. A HashSet where packages are compared based upon their size
E. A binary search tree of TreeNodes containing packages compared based upon their size

49. Which of the following trees does not represent a min-heap? (You may choose more than one answer.)

A.

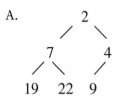

D.

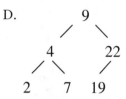

B.

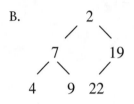

E.

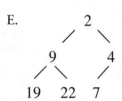

C.

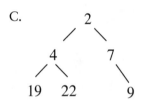

SCORING THE DIAGNOSTIC TEST

As noted earlier, this diagnostic test is not designed to be scored in a traditional sense. The purpose of this test is to help you identify areas that you would benefit from more concentrated study. The solutions indicate which questions are drawn from which chapters. Many questions, however, draw upon material from more than one chapter. For each question that you got wrong, try to identify the cause of your error. (If you understood the `Fish` aspects of a Marine Biology question but miscoded a loop, that is different from not knowing about the behavior of a `Fish`.)

You should look for patterns in both your errors and your confidence level. If you find certain questions difficult (either because you got them wrong or because you lacked confidence in arriving at your answers), use that as a guide for what to study. Remember that no one but you is going to see the results of this test. The more honest you are, the better you will perform on the real exam.

SOLUTIONS TO THE DIAGNOSTIC TEST

Note: The solutions involving code are not unique. Many variations would be equally correct. Before considering yours correct, however, make sure that you have all the same elements in your solution that exist in the given solution.

1. The correct answer is A. This code raises `val` to the 4th power. `pow` is a static method in the `Math` class that takes a base and exponent as its parameters.

2. The correct answer is D. You can get data out of a `Word` object only by using the accessor method.

3. Alex is using the following principles of good design: abstraction, encapsulation, problem decomposition, and reusability.

4.

```
int count = 1;
PairOfDice dice = new PairOfDice(6);
while (dice.roll() != 9)
{
  count++;
}
System.out.println("It took "+count+" rolls to get a 9.");
```

5. The correct answers are B and D. A constant value may be used in a conditional expression, as part of a mathematical expression or in an output statement. It may not be read in or reassigned a new value during program execution.

6. The correct answer is D. If the precondition is met, the postcondition will be met. The precondition says the product of parameters x and y must be positive. The product of two negative numbers is positive.

7. As a client of the class, you should have no knowledge of how Owen is storing the data. As long as the methods work as advertised, it is none of your business how he stores the data. This is what it means for the data to be private.

8.

```
// precondition: 1 <= position <= 3
// postcondition: returns the positionth number of the combination
public int getNumber(int position) {...}
```

9. All the methods in a given class must have signatures that differ in at least the method name or the number and types of the parameters; it is not sufficient to differ only in the return type or visibility.

Questions 1–9 require that you understand the basic structure of a class, including the difference between public and private data and methods as well as how to create and manipulate objects of a given class. If you have not done well on these questions, you should pay particular attention to the material in Chapters 1 and 2. Note that Chapter 2 also contains a sample "design" question that illustrates how questions on these concepts may appear on the actual exam.

10. The correct answer is B. The question is testing string concatenation and order of operations. Since / has higher precedence than +, the first operation is c/3. After the division is performed, the additions are performed in left-to-right order, so string concatenation occurs, not addition.

11. There are (at least) six errors:

   - sum and count are not initialized. The place to initialize is between loops; inside the for loop but before entering the while loop.
   - The while loop won't end because no new grade is ever read.
   - Before finding the student average, there should be a guard (an if) that checks to be sure count > 0.
   - The student average should be found by dividing sum, not grade, by count.
   - There should be an additional variable to keep a running total of the student averages in order to calculate the class average.
   - A return statement is missing.

12. The correct answer is C. The inner loop adds n to x every time it executes to completion. The outer loop ensures that this happens n times, so x will hold the value of n*n.

Questions 10–12 are representative of the types of material covered in Chapter 3, but they only begin to scratch the surface of Java programming. You will need to be able to use all the standard programming constructs in Java. If Java issues are causing you difficulty with coding problems on this diagnostic test (in any of the problems that ask for code), then Chapter 3 should be a focus of your study.

13.

```
public Derived(String s, int n)
{
  super(s);
  secret = n;
}
```

14.
   (a) Because there are two parameters, the method in the Derived class will be invoked.
   (b) Because there is only one parameter and because the Derived class has no such method, the (inherited) method from the Base class will be invoked.
   (c) There is no version of the method that is parameterless, so this line will cause a compilation error.
   (d) (Note: the cast on the line before this is unnecessary, but harmless.) As in (b), there is only one parameter, and there is such a method in the Base class, so that method will be invoked.
   (e) The only two-parameter method is in the Derived class. Although the object being referenced is indeed of type Derived, this particular reference (foo) is not sufficient to cause that method to be invoked. A compilation error will result.

15A. False. The Comparable interface requires that the compareTo method be implemented, and the class Base does so, but it never indicates that by stating, "implements Comparable" in the class header.

15B. False. The Derived class inherits the compareTo method, but it has the same flaw as 15A.

16. There are, of course, many differences between abstract classes and interfaces. The most important are:

   • Abstract classes may contain instance data; interfaces cannot.
   • Abstract classes may define some (or all) of their methods; interfaces contain no code.
   • Other classes may implement many interfaces; they may extend only one class (abstract or concrete).

Questions 13–16 test your knowledge of some aspects of inheritance in Java. If your mistakes on these questions (or on question 30) relate to these concepts, then you need to study Chapter 4.

17. The correct answer is E. All three code fragments will return the correct answer. There is an extra conditional test in the third fragment, but the code produces the correct answer.

18. The correct answer is C. You can't invoke the add method on a cell of an array (unless the array contains Collections), so choices A and B are wrong. Choice D is an improper invocation of add, and choice E reverses the order. In the third choice, as the loop counter traverses array a, since no index for b is specified, each value is copied to the end of b.

19.

```
int count = 0;
for (int i=0; i< stuff.length-1; i++)
{
  if (stuff[i].equals(stuff [i+1])
    count++;
}
```

[Note that it is incorrect to use = = instead of .equals.]

20. The correct answer is D. Tracing the code in the case where n is 2 should be sufficient to verify this.

Questions 17–20 represent some of the types of questions that will be asked concerning arrays, ArrayLists, recursive algorithms, and exceptions. This material is covered in Chapter 5.

21. The correct answer is E. It is equally easy to "invert" any sorting algorithm based upon comparisons. All one needs to do is to reverse the Boolean test in the appropriate conditional statement.

22. The correct answer is D. When the data are unsorted, binary search will almost always fail to find the sought-after item. In each of the other cases, it might or might not be more efficient to use binary search.

23A.

```
if (items.size() == 0)
{
  return null;
}
else
{
  Comparable c = (Comparable) items.get(0);
  for (int i=1; i<items.size(); i++)
  {
    if (c.compareTo(items.get(i)) < 0)
    {
      c = (Comparable) items.get(i);
    }
  }
  return c;
}
```

23B.

```
if (items.size() == 0)
{
  return null;
}
else
{
  return items.get(items.size()-1);
}
```

(Of course, the answer to A is an acceptable answer to B as well. Note also that the problem didn't specify what to do with an empty list, but returning null is certainly a safe option.)

24.

```
ArrayList has = new ArrayList();
ArrayList hasNot = new ArrayList();
for (int i=0; i<list.size(); i++)
{
  Magic m = (Magic) list.get(i);
  if (m.hasProperty())
  {
    has.add(m);
  }
  else
  {
    hasNot.add(m);
  }
}
list = null;
```

The problem was ambiguous about whether or not list was to contain its original data after the two smaller lists had been created. The solution presented does not, but only because of the assignment of null to list in the last line. (Removing that line would cause list to be unchanged.)

An alternative solution that leaves list empty, but not null, can be constructed by removing each item from list just prior to inserting it into its appropriate sublist. This causes list to shrink as the loop progresses, so the initial item should always be the one removed. A common error is to use get(i) in such a circumstance rather than get(0).

Questions 21–24 cover the material from Chapter 6. Note that there is a mix of skills (questions that ask you to code things) and facts (discuss the efficiency of an operation). If you are uncomfortable with either, you should review Chapter 6 with that in mind.

25A. DarterFish attempt to move two spots forward. If they can do so, they do. Failing that, they try to move one spot forward. If they can do so, they do. If both of these attempts fail, they do not change location, but they do reverse their direction.

Eighty percent (four out of five) of the time, SlowFish do not move at all. At other times, they will move to a random location adjacent to them with the exception that they will never move backwards nor will they move to an occupied location.

25B. Both classes illustrate inheritance, but each demonstrates a unique feature. DarterFish simply call the Fish constructor but redefine the move and nextLocation methods. SlowFish call the Fish constructor but also have to initialize a private instance variable of their own. A SlowFish moves in the same way as a Fish but redefines nextLocation. Moreover, the redefined nextLocation calls nextLocation from the Fish class. Both classes need their own generateChild methods.

26. The list of objects to be acted upon (including moving) is generated before the first Fish acts. Thus, it is impossible for that list to include any Fish that were born during this step. Therefore, such Fish will not move during this step.

27.

```java
public class LeftFish extends Fish
{
  private boolean justMovedForward;
  public LeftFish(Environment env, Location loc)
  {
    // Construct/initialize the inherited attributes
    super(env, loc, env.randomDirection(), Color.green);
    justMovedForward = false;
  }
  protected void generateChild(Location loc)
  {
    // Create new fish, which adds itself to the environment.
      LeftFish child = new LeftFish(environment(), loc,
              environment().randomDirection(), color());
    Debug.println(" New LeftFish created: " + child.toString());
  }
  protected void move()
  {
    // Find a location to move to.
    Debug.print("LeftFish " + toString() + " attempting to move. ");
    Location nextLoc = nextLocation();

    // If the next location is different, move there.
    if ( ! nextLoc.equals(location()) )
    {
      changeLocation(nextLoc);
      Debug.println(" Moves to " + location());
    }
    else
    {
      // Otherwise, reverse direction.
      changeDirection(direction().toLeft());
      Debug.println(" Now facing " + direction());
    }
  }
  protected Location nextLocation()
  {
    Environment env = environment();
    Location oneInFront = env.getNeighbor(location(), direction());
    if ( env.isEmpty(oneInFront) && ! justMovedForward )
    {
      justMovedForward = true;
      return oneInFront;
    }
    else
    {
      justMovedForward = false;
      return location();
    }
  }
}
```

There are two other constructors that must be added, but the code is so similar to the code here that they are omitted. Note the great similarities between this code and the code for the DarterFish. During an exam, knowing where to find code exemplars can result in great time savings.

Questions 25–27 show the types of material that an A (and AB) student should expect to have mastered concerning the Java Marine Biology Simulation (MBS.) If you are not at all familiar with the MBS, then you should follow the instructions at the beginning of Chapter 7 regarding familiarizing yourself with the case study. If you have worked with the MBS, but are simply rusty, then you should review Chapter 7 carefully.

28. The UnboundedEnv class simply maintains an ArrayList of Fish, but it does not keep that list in row-major order, nor does it sort the list in any way when executing the allObjects method. Thus, Fish in an UnboundedEnv act in the order in which they were added to the environment which is not (usually) row-major order.

29. Only those methods whose bodies have changed are shown below. (If the only change is in the name of the instance variable, the method is omitted.)

```
private HashMap objectMap;
  // map of Locatable objects in environment
public HashUnboundedEnv()
{
  objectMap = new HashMap();
}
public Locatable[] allObjects()
{
  Locatable[] objectArray = new Locatable[objectMap.size()];
  Set s = objectMap.keySet();
  Iterator it = s.iterator();
  int index=0;
  // Put all the environment objects in the list.
  while (it.hasNext())
  {
    objectArray[index] = (Locatable) objectMap.get(it.next());
    index++;
  }
  return objectArray;
}
public Locatable objectAt(Location loc)
{
  return (Locatable) objectMap.get(loc);
}
public void add(Locatable obj)
{
  // Check precondition. Location should be empty.
  Location loc = obj.location();
  if ( ! isEmpty(loc) )
    throw new IllegalArgumentException("Location " + loc
              +" is not a valid empty location");
  // Add object to the environment.
  objectMap.put(loc,obj);
}
public void remove(Locatable obj)
{
  // Remove the object.
  objectMap.remove(obj.location());
}
public void recordMove(Locatable obj, Location oldLoc)
{
  if (oldLoc.equals(obj.location()))
  {
    return;
  }
  if (isEmpty(oldLoc) || ! isEmpty(obj.location()))
  {
    throw new IllegalArgumentException("Recording illegal move of "
              + obj + " from " + oldLoc);
  }
  objectMap.remove(oldLoc);
  add(obj);
}
```

In addition to these changes, the private method indexOf is no longer part of the class.

Questions 28 and 29 illustrate some further topics that an AB student would be expected to have mastered concerning the MBS. Once again, the pertinent discussion is in Chapter 7.

30. The correct answer is C. Although the subscripts may appear to be reversed from "normal," the loops set each cell equal to its distance from the upper left corner.

31A.

```
double averageScore(int quizNo)
{
  double total = 0.0;
  for (int stud=0; stud < quizScores.length; stud++)
    total += quizScores[stud][quizNo];
  if(quizScores.length > 0)
    return total/quizScores.length;
  else
    return 0.0;
}
```

31B.

```
int aboveAverage(int studentNo)
{
  int count = 0;
  for (int quiz=0; quiz<quizScores[0].length; quiz++)
  {
    if (quizScores[studentNo][quiz] >= averageScore(quiz))
    {
      count++;
    }
  }
  return count;
}
```

Questions 30 and 31 are typical AP questions concerning matrices. AB students who are uncomfortable with these questions should review Chapter 5 in general and the section "Two-Dimensional Arrays" in particular.

32. Quicksort runs least efficiently when the data are ordered (in either direction). In such cases, Quicksort behaves in a quadratic manner, so the appropriate bound is $O(N^2)$.

Question 32 covers material from Chapter 6.

33. Asymptotically, the outer loop runs $O(N)$ times (actually N/4) and the inner loop could run as many as N times, so the overall bound on the number of times "Wow" is printed by the inner loop is $O(N^2)$. The outer loop will add $O(N)$ to this, but that does not affect the (asymptotic) total. The bound is $O(N^2)$.

34. The outer loop runs $O(\log N)$ (actually $\log_2 N$) times. The inner loop runs $O(N)$ (actually N/2) times. The final bound is $O(N*\log N)$.

35. In an asymptotic sense, both the array and the `ArrayList` will use $O(N)$ storage, so they are equivalent.

Questions 33–35 exercise the skills of code analysis that you will be expected to display on the exam. If you aren't confident of your skills in this area, you should review Chapter 9.

36. The two most fundamental differences between `Lists` and `Sets` are:

   • Items can appear more than once in a `List` and cannot appear more than once in a `Set`.
   • Items in a `List` can be accessed via an index ("get me the 13th element"); items in a `Set` have no associated index.

37. Both a `TreeSet` and a `HashSet` support the same basic operations, but they do so in different ways. A `TreeSet` uses a balanced binary search tree to store items, while a `HashSet` uses a hash table. Because of the nature of the search tree, it is required that elements in a `TreeSet` be `Comparable`.

38. In both cases, the loop executes N times at a cost of O(1) per iteration for the loop itself. Excepting the `get` operation, the body of the loop takes O(1) time. Thus, the cost of the loop is O(N*<cost of get>). If a `TreeMap` is used, `get` takes O(logN) time, so the total cost is O(N*logN). If a `HashMap` is used, `get` takes O(1) time on average and O(N) time worst case, so the average cost is O(N), but the worst-case cost is O(N²).

39.

```
if (s.size() == 0)
{ return null; }
else
{
  Iterator it = s.iterator();
  Comparable best = (Comparable) it.next();
  while (it.hasNext())
  {
    Comparable current = (Comparable) it.next();
    if (current.compareTo(best) > 0)
    { best = current; }
  }
  return best;
}
```

An alternate algorithm is to copy everything from s into a `TreeSet` and then take the last item returned by the iterator. This is less efficient, but it would be acceptable on the exam.

Questions 36–39 show the types of knowledge that you will be expected to have concerning the Java `Collections` classes. If you are unfamiliar with those classes and how they apply to the AP Computer Science curricula, then you should review Chapter 10.

40. The first line creates a single `ListNode`. The second line gets its "next" value which is `null` and then tries to get the value of that node. Since that node is `null`, a `NullPointerException` is raised.

41. The figure below has been "untangled" in that the node that was drawn in the middle before has swapped positions with the node on the left.

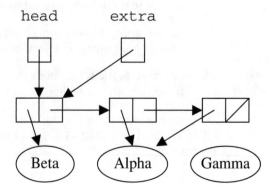

The object containing Gamma may or may not be reclaimed by the Java garbage collector at a later time.

42.

```
if (head != null)
{
  ListNode current = null;
  ListNode oneDown = head;
  while (oneDown.getNext() != null)
  {
    ListNode twoDown = oneDown.getNext();
    oneDown.setNext(current); // Links node to predecessor
    current = oneDown;
    oneDown = twoDown;
  }
  oneDown.setNext(current);
  head = oneDown;
}
```

Note the concern for the empty list. Note also that there are *many* ways to solve this problem, including recursively. This problem was actually presented as a free-response question many years ago (when the language of the exam was Pascal), and there was a great diversity of solutions.

43. The first item inserted into a binary search tree will be at the root. If it is the first item printed by an in-order traversal, then the left subtree must be empty, i.e., the root is the minimal element. Then the right child of the root must have been the second item inserted, and it must be minimal (other than the root.) In fact, all the left subtrees in this "tree" must be empty, and it is essentially a linked list of right children.

44.

```
if (root == null)
{
  return 0;
}
else
{
  Task rootTask = (Task) root.getData();
  int rootValue = rootTask.getValue();
  int leftValue = maxValue(root.getLeft());
  int rightValue = maxValue(root.getRight());
  if (leftValue>rightValue)
    rootValue += leftValue;
  else
    rootValue += rightValue;
  return rootValue;
}
```

Even though the precondition implies that the tree is not `null`, some guard must be placed in the code to ensure that the recursion terminates. It could be placed on the recursive calls, but the logic is more cumbersome.

Questions 40–44 are typical of the types of questions that are often asked about linked lists and binary search trees. The exam will make specific use of both the `ListNode` and `TreeNode` classes that are discussed in these questions. For more information about both the class and the structures more generally, review Chapter 11.

45. The correct answer is A. A stack is a LIFO (last in, first out) structure. A queue is a (first in, first out) structure. A priority queue is an any in, lowest priority out structure. Sets and maps have no protocol about which items go in or out.

46. The output is:

```
5
empty
21
not empty at end
```

(Bonus question: could you solve the problem if a queue—or a priority queue—were used, with the attendant changes in method names?)

47. The first loop executes N times taking O(logN) per execution—assuming that readString is O(1). Thus, the first loop takes O(N*logN) time. The second loop executes five times regardless of the value of N. Since we are discussing asymptotic behavior, it can be assumed that N>5 and that no exception results because of missing items. The body of the second loop takes O(logN) time per execution, so the cost of the second loop is only O(logN). Putting the two loops together, we get that the bound for the entire fragment is O(N*logN).

48. The correct answer is E. Stacks and queues are inappropriate because the workers choose neither the most recent nor the least recent package. A priority queue might appear to be best, but if the package does not fit, it will still be removed from the structure. A HashSet could work, but it would iterate to find the appropriate package and would thus take O(N) time per package. The binary search tree will be able to find the appropriate package in O(logN) time and to remove it just as quickly (on average).

49. The correct answers are B, C, and D. B is not a heap because the heap property is violated at the left child of the root, when 7 is not less than 4. C is not a heap because the tree has not been filled from left to right on the bottom level. (Note: this is a very picky concern, and by some people's definitions this would be a heap. This tree would not, however, support the standard array-based implementation of a heap that AP students are expected to study.) D is not a heap because the heap condition is violated at every nonleaf; this is because D is really a binary search tree.

Questions 45–49 test some of the material covered in Chapter 12. AP students are expected to know about behavior and efficiency of elementary data structures and should also be familiar with the particular AP interfaces that will be used in exam questions.

PART III

COMPREHENSIVE REVIEW

Chapter 1

Talking about Programs

SPECIFYING PROGRAMS AND PROGRAMMING UNITS

A *program* is a set of instructions within a computer. The purpose of the instructions is to make it possible for a task to be completed. The approach to completing a task using a computer has evolved in recent years to an approach that is parallel to the way we solve everyday problems using available tools to simplify and enhance our solution process.

Perhaps you have an assignment to develop a presentation for your public speaking class. You might research your topic on the Internet, interview resource people using a video camera or tape recorder, prepare a PowerPoint presentation, and bring in specific items to demonstrate your point. Did you build the camera, the tape recorder, or the Internet from the ground up? No, you used available tools, without necessarily knowing how any of them work on the inside. They were black boxes to you, yet you were able to use them to build your presentation.

Writing a program is like building your presentation. There are tools on the shelf. We take down the appropriate tools and use them to complete a task. We do have to know how to plug into the tools, but we don't have to know how the tools themselves work, nor do we need to be able to build them ourselves. The tools are **objects, instances** of **classes,** and we plug in through the **interface,** the public methods that give us access to the services the classes provide. Inside the classes are private instance variables (data) and **implementation** of the methods (code). The **client** (user) has no need to know how a method performs its task, only that it does the job.

Of course, if a new tool is needed, someone has to design that tool, determine the tasks it will perform and how the client will operate the tool, and then build it. The programmer makes use of available classes, combining them to build new classes (tools) to solve problems.

In this chapter we examine the building blocks of classes as well as how to make use of these tools. Design of classes themselves is reserved for Chapter 2.

! MAKING THINGS HAPPEN

Without worrying about any Java code, consider the following statements:

```
Calculator c = new Calculator();
System.out.print( c.add(3, 4) );
System.out.print( c.multiply(5, -7) );
System.out.print( c.average(75, 85, 90) );
```

What do we suppose is happening here? Each of the last three lines causes a value to be computed and then printed to the console. The request comes in several parts. In the first part, before the period, we name the object ("c"). Immediately following the period, we specify the task that we wish to have the object perform ("add," "multiply," "average"). Following that name, we specify any data that we wish to provide to the object to aid it in performing the task (the numbers in parentheses). These three components make up a request of an object. Upon receiving such a request, the object will execute the program unit associated with the given name and perform the task for us. If the object's name is well chosen and the task name is also well chosen, then the Java code can be almost as easy to read as English. Even nonprogrammers can usually tell you that the code above will cause 7, −35, and 83.333333 to be printed. Consider another code snippet:

```
Cadet giJoe = new Cadet();
giJoe.pushUp(20);
Cadet giJane = new Cadet();
giJane.run(15);
```

We have apparently created a Cadet named giJoe who will perform 20 push-ups for us. We have also created a Cadet named giJane. It is not clear whether giJane will run 15 feet, 15 miles, or for 15 minutes; we would need to read more carefully about Cadets to know for sure. Notice that we have two instances (objects) of Cadets even though there is only one Cadet class. Some people say that the class is the mold and the instances are the actual objects that are made out of that mold.

The key lesson here is that a request consists of three parts. Each of the parts must be present to complete the request, but we do not need to know how a class is built to make good use of it. (Note: the third component of the request—the data to be used—may be empty, but the parentheses will still be present.)

! PROGRAMMING UNITS

Class

A **class** is a programming unit that captures an abstraction, the *state* and *behavior* of an abstract object (idea) it defines. A class may represent a tangible object such as a book or a car, but it can also capture a concept. For example, time and distance, while not things one can hold in one's hand, do have attributes (state) and perform services (behavior).

The first line of code in a class is called the **class heading** or **signature**. Consider a Game class.

```
public class Game
```

The modifier public is optional but is usually included. Everything in Java is, by default, public, but this can be overridden with the **private** modifier. **Public** means that a client program has access to the unit. All classes tested by the AP exam are public. It is standard practice to capitalize the first letter of the name of a class.

In our earlier example, Calculator and Cadet were the names of the classes. c, giJoe, and giJane were the names referring to actual objects (instances of the classes) that exist in our program.

State

When you think about the state of an object, think about the attributes associated with it. A game has rules and some type of score keeping. It is also possible to maintain control over the progress of the game, determine who the current player is, and establish whether or not there is a winner.

Instance Variables

The variables that represent the state of an object are called **instance variables** or **fields.** These variables are declared private and hold the data about each individual instance of the class. It is standard practice for variables to have names starting with a lowercase letter.

Constants

A class may have **constant** values. Constants are identified with the keyword final. The value of a constant is defined when it is declared and cannot be changed during execution of a program. Constants are usually declared public and static. public allows the constant to be used by any client method. static means there is one constant value that is used for all objects of the class rather than a separate constant for each instance. It is standard practice for the name of a constant to have all uppercase letters.

Class Variables

Sometimes all the objects of a given class may share a single object (or value). For instance, all the players in a game might share the same clock. Variables used for this purpose are called **class variables.** Class variables are different from instance variables and are declared private static. static means there is one variable shared by all objects of the class. private means the variable can only be accessed by instances of the class. It is, however, still a variable. If changed by an instance of the class, it is changed for all current and future instances of the class during execution of the program. In the Marine Biology Simulation case study a Fish's id is a class variable (see Chapter 7). The following constant and variables might be added to the Game class example:

```
public class Game
{
   public static final int MAXGAMES = 100; // constant
   private static int gameNum = 1;         // class variable

   // instance variables
   private String    rules;
   private int       score;
   private Player     currentPlayer;
   private boolean   winner;

   // other private data and methods not shown
}
```

Behavior

The **methods** of a class define what tasks an object of a given class can perform for the programmer. In the previous examples, the names of the methods included add, multiply, average, pushUp, and run.

Method Categories

Methods generally fall into the following categories:

1. **Constructors** initialize the private instance variables of a class.
2. **Modifiers** alter the state of the object.

3. **Accessors** return information about the current state of the object.
4. **Helpers** are private methods used internally by the class. For example, the `initialize` method in the `Fish` class of the Marine Biology Simulation is called by each constructor to avoid redundant code.

Commenting Methods

While the name of a method may give the programmer a clue as to its behavior, the true nature of a method should always be explained in the associated documentation. When reading this documentation, one should pay attention to **precondition** and **postcondition** comments. *Preconditions* assert what must be true in order for a method or block of code to perform as intended. They are often written in terms of a method's parameters. *Postconditions* assert what is true when the method or block of code completes execution, often in terms of the return value. (See Chapter 2 for a more complete discussion.)

The Method Signature (Header)

The first line of a method is known as the *method signature*. There are four significant parts in a method signature, detailed below. As an example, let's consider the method signature

```
public boolean hasWinner(Player player1, Player player2)
```

in which the parts are

```
<visibility> <return type> <method name> (<parameter list>)
```

1. `public` or `private` modifier
   a. This determines the **visibility** of the method, that is, who has access to the method.
   b. Ask yourself if this method is to be called from another class or whether it is intended for use only by the class in which it is defined. Public methods can be called from outside the class; private methods cannot.
2. return type
   a. If the return type is `void`, there should be no return statement (although there can be an empty return).
   b. If the return type is nonvoid, the method must return a value of the correct type. For example, if the return type is `int`, an integer must be returned; if the return type is `Cadet`, a `Cadet` must be returned.
   c. The exception is a constructor, which has no return type.
3. method name
   a. This descriptive identifier should clearly indicate the method's task.
4. parameter list
   a. If empty, the method is about the **implicit parameter** (see section on parameters below) and additional information is unnecessary.
   b. If nonempty, notice the type and name of each parameter. These are the values being sent in. If the method call is shown, check to see that the number and types of values being sent to the method match the number and types expected in the parameter list.

Look again at the example shown above.

```
public boolean hasWinner(Player player1, Player player2)
```

The method is public, so it is visible to clients; its return type is `boolean`, so it returns true or false; its name indicates that this method determines if the game has a winner at this time; and there are two parameters named `player1` and `player2`—both are `Players`.

Constructors

Constructors are methods whose job is to build an instance of a class. A constructor's signature is distinguished by the fact that there is no specified return type. The name of the constructor must match the name of the class exactly.

```
public class Game
{
  // constructor
  public Game(String gameRules)
  {...}
  // private data and other methods not shown
}
```

The purpose of a constructor is to initialize the instance variables. Values for those instance variables may be sent in through the parameter list. Any values not sent as parameters should be initialized to **default** values chosen by the programmer. A class may have more than one constructor; each signature must have a distinct parameter list, differing either in the number of parameters or in parameter type(s). Distinctions in the parameter list determine which version is invoked when a new object is constructed. Having more than one method with the same name and return type but different parameter lists is known as method **overloading**. A class may also contain a default (parameterless) constructor in which all instance variables are initialized to default values.

Consider the following line from an earlier example:

```
Calculator c = new Calculator();
```

The expression `new Calculator()` causes the Java environment to invoke the constructor for the `Calculator` class. Once the `Calculator` object is constructed, `c` is assigned a reference to it. The first instance of the word `Calculator` simply indicates that the name `c` will be associated with a `Calculator` object.

Accessors

Users of a class cannot directly access private instance variables. The client isn't supposed to know anything about the implementation of private data or methods. The client simply uses a method. A programmer can change the implementation without the client's knowledge or concern; the method still performs the task and still returns the appropriate type. *Accessor methods* allow the client to retrieve information about the state of an object. The information may be stored in an instance variable. For example, a client could access the current player in the Game class using the following method. *Note:* this should be the only way a client has access to private data.

```
public Player getPlayer()
{
  return currentPlayer;
}
```

An accessor method may also return the result of doing something with private data. For example

```
public int totalScore()
```

may calculate and return the sum of individual scores.
Note: Accessor methods often do not have parameters, but there are many exceptions to this rule.

Modifiers (Sometimes Referred to as Mutators)

Modifier methods allow the client to change the state of an object. These methods are usually void and generally have one or more parameters. For example, the Game class might include the following modifier:

```
public void setPlayer(Player newPlayer)
{
  currentPlayer = newPlayer;
}
```

Modifiers are likely to do much more than the example above. A change in state may be based on a conditional statement (decision) or the result of repeated actions (loop). (These statements are discussed in Chapter 3.) A modifier method may invoke other methods in the same or in different classes.

Helpers

Helper methods are private methods that help with the implementation of other methods in the same class. A constructor might invoke a private helper method to initialize variables in order to avoid repetitious code. A modifier may call on helper methods to simplify code, isolate tasks, or separate out reusable code. Helper methods are more common when classes become complex. The Marine Biology Simulation (Chapter 7) provides many examples of helper methods. You may notice that the visibility modifier for many of these methods is "protected," which means they are visible to subclasses of the class in which they are declared. The **protected** modifier is not tested on the AP exam but is used in the case study.

Parameters

Parameters are values required by a method in order to execute its task. **Formal parameters** are listed in the method signature. **Actual parameters** are the specific values sent to the method in the method call.

In Java, parameters are passed by *value*. If a parameter is a primitive type, the method receives a copy of the stored value. If the parameter is an object, the method receives a copy of the reference to the object, that is, a copy of the memory location (address) of the object. In the case of primitives, any change made to the parameter has no effect on the original value in the client code. But in the case of objects, changes can be made to the object because it can be referenced by the parameter as well as its original reference. The original reference can't be changed, but the object referred to can be modified within the method.

A method's parameter list provides data required by the method. These are the **explicit parameters,** parameters that are specified by the method. The instance of the class—the current object in other words—upon which a method is called is the implicit parameter. Private data belong to the implicit parameter, and methods called within the class apply to the implicit parameter. If a method inside the class needs to refer to the implicit parameter, it uses the term **this.** Recall the earlier examples invoking pushUp and run from the Cadet class. The explicit parameters were the various integers supplied. giJoe and giJane were the implicit parameters.

Note that objects can refer to other objects through parameter lists. It shouldn't be hard to imagine the effect of the following code:

```
giJane.command( giJoe, "charge" );
```

A common mistake is to initialize parameters inside the method implementation, as if the parameters were sent in as names only. Trust that parameters do have a value. Don't create **local variables** with the same names as parameters and don't reassign values to the parameters at the beginning of a method.

Classes can be designed in many ways. Some provide nothing more than a way to group related pieces of data such as a Time that groups hours, minutes, and seconds. Others provide ways to collect large numbers of similar items into one unit. Still others specify behavior without storing any data. Each type has its purpose and is discussed in turn in later chapters. What each of them has in common, however, is that it can perform various tasks if asked to do so and if supplied with the appropriate data.

> **Tip**
>
> The Marine Biology Simulation includes many examples of the various types of classes described above.

EDIT-COMPILE-TEST-DEBUG CYCLE

Grady Booch, a well-known author and programmer, once said, "Programming is incremental and iterative."

Writing bug-free software is not an easy task. A systematic approach to testing software is essential. The basic idea is that the programmer writes code, compiles it, tests it, and then verifies that the test turned out properly. If it did, the programmer moves on to the next task. If not, then the programmer examines the code, attempts to fix the bug, and repeats the cycle.

Two habits substantially aid in this process. The first is to always test after making any modification. That way, if the test fails, you can be certain where the incorrect modification was made. Classes and methods facilitate this habit through their very nature. They break code down into small units (single tasks) that can be examined individually. Experienced programmers know that it is much easier to find a bug in a single block of code than to have to search through pages of code.

The second habit is to design tests before writing code. If you code first, then the tendency is to test only what you wrote, resulting in incomplete testing. On the other hand, if you write a complete set of tests first—while you are thinking about the problem as a whole and not about programming—then you are likely to test more completely. Furthermore, the tests will give you insight into how to write the code.

On the AP exam, you may be asked about test data. It is often best to consider test data while considering the problem statement rather than while reading the code.

> **Tip**
>
> There are certain types of errors that students seem to make on the AP Computer Science exam, particularly in the free-response section. Some of those related to classes are shown in the list below:
>
> - Declaring a local variable with the same name as a parameter already passed to the method (basically not understanding that the parameter *has* a value)
> - Reassigning a parameter at the beginning of a method (not understanding the parameter *has* a value when it is passed in)
> - Missing return statement in a nonvoid method
> - Not matching the return value to the return type

✓ RAPID REVIEW

This chapter is about the basic building blocks of a program. Concepts and vocabulary fundamental to the AP exam are reviewed.

Class: A programming unit that captures abstraction. We talk about the **state** or attributes (nouns that describe) of an **object** (the abstraction) and its **behavior,** the services or tasks it can perform (think of verbs), encapsulated in its methods.

Class heading: The line of code that names the class and defines its relationship, if any, to another class or to interfaces.

Instance: An object of a specified class type. More than one object may be instantiated at any given time.

Instance variable: A variable that must be referenced through an instance of the class. These variables define the attributes of a particular instance and are private.

Field: Another name for *instance variable*.

Constant: A value that cannot be changed during program execution. The purpose of constants is to make programs more readable and to make it easier for the programmer to change a value that is used repeatedly throughout the program, for example, a tax rate, specified with the keyword final.

Class variable: A variable that is shared by all instances of a class. The keyword static is used to define a class variable. It may be referenced using the class name, but, more importantly, if changed by one instance of the class, its value is changed for all instances.

Method: A task that an instance of a class can perform.

Signature: The method heading. This defines the method as public, private, or protected; specifies its return type; lists the method name; and specifies its parameters. The name is not important to the definition of signature but, if the method is well named, it tells you what the method does.

Overloading: The idea that two methods may have the same name as long as they have different signatures. (A consequence of this is that the system can distinguish which method is to be used based upon the parameter sequence.)

Visibility modifier: Defines how a construct can be accessed; for our purposes, usually applied to a variable or a method.

Public: Visible to all users of the class.

Private: Invisible to users of the class; visible only within the class itself.

Protected (not covered on the AP exam, except in the context of the case study): Visible only to the class and subclasses of the class.

Constructor: A method whose task is to instantiate (create or build) an object, accomplished by initializing the instance variables. You can pick out a constructor easily because its name must be the same name as the class name and there is no return type. There may be more than one constructor (this is called **overloading**), distinguished by a difference in number or types of arguments in the parameter list.

Default: A value that will be used instead of a programmer-specified parameter, often for a constructor. A constructor that uses no parameters at all, instead substituting predefined values, is often called a *default constructor*.

Accessor method: A method that returns the value stored in an instance variable. This is the way a client program or another class gains access to information about the state of an object.

Modifier or **mutator method:** A method that changes the state of an object. These methods are usually, but not always, void, meaning they do not return a value.

Helper method: Private method used within a class. A helper method may avoid repetition of code or may aid in breaking down a complicated method into simpler tasks.

Parameter: Required information passed to a method so that it may accomplish its task.

Formal parameters: The parameters listed in a method signature. For example, in the method signature

```
public int sumUp(int first, int last)
```

the formal parameters are `first` and `last`.

Actual parameters: The values supplied by the client in the parameter list of a method call. In the method call,

```
int sum = nums.sumUp(start, end)
```

the actual parameters are `start` and `end`.

Explicit parameter: Information passed in the parameter list, `start` and `end` in the previous example.

Implicit parameter: The object upon which a method is called, `nums` in the previous example.

Local variable: Variable declared within a method.

Client: User of a class; may be the main method or the method of another class.

Main method: The method in an application where execution begins.

Implementation: Code that defines a construct.

Precondition: An assertion (precisely worded comment) that specifies what must be true for a method to succeed in its task; usually written in terms of the parameters

Postcondition: An assertion that specifies what will be true when a method terminates; usually written in terms of the return value or change of state.

`this`: A reserved word for the implicit parameter; used within a class when a reference to the implicit parameter is needed.

◖2 PRACTICE PROBLEMS

1. Consider the following incomplete class declaration.

```
public class Student
{
  public static final int numTests= 3;
  private String name; //student's name
  private int test1, test2, test3;

  public double average()
  { /* implementation not shown */ }

  // other variables and methods not shown
}
```

Assume `s1` is a properly defined `Student` and `t1`, `t2`, and `t3` are properly defined test scores. Which of the following is a correct call to `average`?

A. `System.out.println(average.s1(t1, t2, t3));`
B. `double avg = s1.average(t1, t2, t3);`
C. `double avg = average(s1);`
D. `double avg = average();`
E. `double avg = s1.average();`

2. Which of the following best describes the term *method overloading*?

A. A method that attempts to do too many tasks is overloaded. It should be decomposed into two or more separate methods.
B. A method with more than three parameters is overloaded.
C. Two methods with the same signature but different return types are overloaded.
D. Two or more methods with the same signature except for the number or types of parameters are overloaded
E. A method that appears in more than one class is overloaded.

3. Consider the following incomplete class declaration:

```
public class Sample
{
  private int myVal;
  // constructor not shown
  public void setVal(int value)
  {
    myVal = value;
  }
  public int getVal()
  {
    return myVal;
  }
}
```

If, in a client program, a `Sample` object s is properly declared, which of the following is a valid statement?

A. `Sample s = 123;`
B. `System.out.println(myVal);`
C. `System.out.println(s.setVal());`
D. `int val = 0; val += (s.getVal());`
E. `return myVal.getVal();`

4. Which of the following is not typically accessible to a client program?

   A. Public constants
   B. Instance variables
   C. Class constructors
   D. Modifier methods
   E. Accessor methods

5. Consider method `calculate` shown below:

```
static double calculate(double z)
{
  for(int count = 4; count > 1; count--)
    z *= z;
}
```

`calculate` does not work as intended. Which of the following best describes the problem?

   A. The keyword *public* is missing.
   B. The direction of the loop is backward.
   C. There are missing braces.
   D. The loop has no body.
   E. The proper value is not returned.

6. Which of the following statements is true about classes or objects?

   A. All classes contain at least one private variable.
   B. All classes are subclasses of some other class.
   C. A class is an instantiation of an object.
   D. An object has state and behavior.
   E. An object is an address in memory.

7. Which of the following statements is true about methods?

   A. The purpose of a void method is to modify an instance variable.
   B. A method cannot modify the original copy of its parameters.
   C. A method cannot declare a variable.
   D. A method cannot declare a constant.
   E. A nonvoid method may contain an empty return.

8. Consider the following incomplete class definition:

```
public class Sample
{
  private int num;
  private String word;

  public Sample() {<code not shown>}
  public Sample(int n) {<code not shown>}
  public Sample(int n, String s){<code not shown>}

  // other methods not shown
}
```

Which of the following is a true statement?

A. The code will not compile because all three methods have the same name.
B. The code will not compile because none of the methods specifies a return type.
C. The first method will not compile because it has an empty parameter list.
D. The first and second methods will not compile because their parameter lists are incomplete.
E. The code will compile provided the body of each method is error free.

9. Which of the following is a true statement about parameters?

A. Object parameters are passed by reference.
B. Actual parameters are those named in a method signature.
C. Implicit parameters are those named in a method call.
D. The type of a parameter is an important part of a method signature.
E. An empty parameter list means that no information is sent to the method.

10. Consider the following method:

```
static String doSomething(String wd, int j)
{
  wd = "";
  int j = 0;
  wd += j;
  return j;
}
```

The method illustrates programmer misconceptions. Misconceptions may or may not cause compiler errors but are likely to interfere with the intended result of executing the code. How many programmer misconceptions are there in this code?

A. 1
B. 2
C. 3
D. 4
E. 5

SOLUTIONS TO THE PRACTICE PROBLEMS

1. **E.** Answers A and B are incorrect because they call the method with parameters. Answer C tries to pass the student as a parameter. D fails to call the method on an instance of the class.

2. **D.** This is the definition of overloaded methods. A is incorrect. While a method that attempts to do too many tasks should be decomposed, it is not characterized as overloaded. B is wrong because, while it is not good practice, a method can have virtually any number of parameters. C is incorrect because overloading means that you can call methods of the same name with different parameters and have the

same type of information returned by the method. E is incorrect because more than one class can have the same method. In that case, the type of object on which the method is invoked determines the class whose method will be called.

3. **D.** Answer A is an incorrect way to construct or assign a sample object. B and E attempt to access private data. C invokes a modifier method where an accessor is needed.

4. **B.** Instance variables are private. All the other answers are public.

5. **E.** A is incorrect because Java methods are `public` by default. The loop will work in either direction, so B is incorrect (see Chapter 3 for more on loops). C is wrong because braces are unnecessary when the body of the loop contains only one line of code, and therefore D is wrong because the body consists of a single statement. The method signature indicates a `double` will be returned but there is no `return` statement.

6. **D.** A is incorrect; a class may contain a group of related methods, such as the `Math` class. B is incorrect; `Object` is the one class that is not a subclass of any other. The reverse of C is true. E is incorrect; a reference to an object is a memory address; the object itself takes up space in memory.

7. **B.** Modifier methods are usually void, but a void method may have another purpose such as outputting, rather than returning, a message. Methods can, and often do, have local variables. A local constant is unusual but would not cause an error. The return statement in a nonvoid method must match the return type.

8. **E.** The class contains three constructors. This is clear because the name of each method matches the name of the class. Constructors do not have a specified return type. The first constructor is a default constructor. The variables will be initialized to default values. The constructors differ in their parameter lists, which is just what is needed when we overload methods. If the body of each constructor contains correct code, this part of the class will compile without error.

9. **D.** All parameters are passed by value; object variables contain a reference to the object, but this reference is itself still passed by value. Formal parameters are those in the signature; actual parameters are those in the method call and are explicit parameters. Even when the parameter list is empty, the implicit parameter provides information (specifically which instance of the class, along with its private data, is being invoked) to the method.

10. **C.** This question is far too open-ended for an AP exam, but it illustrates common errors made by students in writing answers to free-response questions. Three misconceptions are illustrated: The first is reassigning the `String` parameter a different value (any value, not necessarily an empty string). The second is declaring a local variable of the same name as one of the parameters. This overrides the parameter; it might as well never have been sent in. The third is returning the wrong type. This one will cause a compile time error. It is not a mistake to leave public out of the method header, but we generally include it; static was used here because the method was not declared in the context of a class. It is also not a mistake to add an integer to a `String`. Java invokes the `toString` method on the integer and concatenates it to the `String`. This does not change the integer to a `String`.

Chapter 2

Object-Oriented Design

PROGRAMMING BY CONTRACT

Object-oriented design is a complex and evolving methodology. While the history of the methodology may be told from many perspectives, many of the key ideas follow simply from the desire to encourage reuse of program code. The AP Computer Science curriculum emphasizes many of the principles of object-oriented design, and a thorough understanding of these principles will help you do well on the exam as a whole.

Object-oriented design is a language-independent design paradigm. As a programming language, Java itself was designed to support object-oriented programming. Given that AP Computer Science uses Java as its language of instruction, it is therefore not surprising that the curriculum is built upon the object-oriented paradigm. This chapter is designed to review the paradigm in general but, in keeping with the AP curriculum, when code is shown, it will be Java code.

An Illustrative Example

To illustrate portions of the paradigm, we consider the story of two programmers, Mark and Sarah, who wish to work together to write a program. They can get together only every now and then, so they must be able to work independently as much as possible. Each of them will work on different parts of the program. Let us imagine that Sarah is writing some code involving complex collections of data, and Mark is writing code that makes use of these collections. One solution to the problem is to have Sarah complete all her programming before Mark begins his. This will work, but it isn't an efficient use of either programmer's time. It would be much better if Mark could begin his work before Sarah completed hers.

To accomplish this, Sarah will **encapsulate** her code into a **class** that Mark can make use of. To enable Mark to begin work immediately, Sarah must provide Mark with an **interface** to her code. In other words, Sarah and Mark must agree on what services, or **methods,** her code will provide to him. They must agree on the names of these methods as well as on the data that are to be communicated back and forth between their two pieces of code. Once they have this agreement, each can begin to work independently.

(In the case of Java, these interfaces are often expressed in javadoc format that results in beautiful documentation in the form of Web pages. The AP exam, however, uses traditional commenting style to explain its interfaces.)

Mark and Sarah may agree in principle on their interface, but if their collective program is to work, that agreement must be much more precise. Object-oriented programmers often refer to the idea of **programming by contract**; by this they mean that interfaces are expressed as one or more contracts between the programmers. In our case, Sarah might agree to compute a certain value for Mark if—and only if—he provides her with the necessary data. For example, she might say, "If you give me the name of a student currently enrolled in AP Computer Science, then I will give you that student's current term average." Note that there are two parts to this statement. The first clause specifies what Mark must give to Sarah (the name of a student currently enrolled in AP Computer Science.) This is the **precondition**—it is what must be true *before* she begins her work. The second clause specifies what Sarah will do for Mark (give him the student's current term average.) This is the **postcondition**—it states what will be true *after* Sarah has completed her task. The contract is binding upon Sarah *only* if Mark has met the precondition. If Mark does not meet the precondition, then the contract does not apply and anything might happen. For example, suppose that Mark misspells a student's name; what should Sarah do? She might return the value of 0 or −1 (since the student doesn't exist); she might return 283.92 (a random value); she might return the average of the student whose name was closest to the name Mark provided; she might return the average of the last student on the list; or she might cause the computer to crash. Any of these actions are "correct" since Mark did not meet the precondition of the contract. A key concept here is that it is Mark's job, not Sarah's, to ensure that the name he provides is valid.

> **Tip**
>
> Unless it is part of the contract, do not bother to verify that the preconditions of a method have been met within that method. It is the job of the client to have done so. You will receive no credit on the exam for any code whose sole job is to verify the preconditions. (If you verify correctly, you won't lose any credit, but why waste the time? If you verify incorrectly, you may lose credit.)

Writing Contracts

Writing legal contracts is not easy. In fact, law students take at least one course simply to learn the basics of doing so. Writing Java contracts, with their pre- and postconditions, is not easy either. Let us consider an example method that is meant to help a teacher with grading.

Precondition: A list of student grades is provided.
Postcondition: The average student grade is returned.

On the surface, this looks like a reasonable contract, but it is not. The precondition is deficient because it fails to state the format of the list. Too many questions remain: Are these letter grades or grades in number form? If numeric, are they all based on the same standard, or do different grades represent assignments with different "maximum possible points"? The postcondition is also deficient. In particular, the notion of "average" is ambiguous. Is it the intent that the median (middle) grade be returned, or is it expected that the arithmetic mean will be computed? If the grades are letter grades, how is the arithmetic mean of a C− and a B determined? Or what if the list of student grades is empty?

It is almost certainly the case that the author of these conditions knew exactly what was desired when the conditions were written. But, as with matters of law, contracts are written to be interpreted by outside parties, and an outside party would find this contract to be ambiguous. Careful writing of pre- and postconditions can avoid ambiguities such as these.

> **Tip**
>
> The authors of the exam will provide many sets of pre- and postconditions. Especially on the free-response section, these are meant to clarify the problem. If it seems that one of these conditions is making the problem suspiciously easy, incredibly difficult, or even just different from what you expected, then you should reread both the question and the conditions. It is a big mistake to write an overly trivial solution that exploits a "loophole" in the conditions. You might hope for a good score, but your solution will not receive much credit.

CLASS DESIGN

In addition to good writing skills, systems analysts make use of a guiding principle when designing classes. In a nutshell, the idea is to emulate Albert Einstein and make each class "as simple as [possible], but not simpler."

Consider for a moment the hypothetical class that Sarah wrote in our earlier scenario. Perhaps the class is very useful, and a third programmer, John, wishes to use it. If Sarah's class is too general, then John may need to use only a portion of her work. This suggests that perhaps Sarah should have broken her code into two pieces. Mark could have continued to use both, but John would only need the one. Each of the two pieces would be simpler than the combination, so it would seem to achieve the goal of simplicity.

Well-designed classes implement a single concept. That concept may exhibit many behaviors, but the entirety should have a simple expression—preferably without the use of the word *and* to create a compound sentence. For instance, a car can do many things, but it is fundamentally "a vehicle for transporting objects (people and[1] other goods) along a network of roads." To the degree that a class achieves this goal, it is highly **cohesive.** A class that does two distinct things—"It's great! It processes your food and does your laundry!"—is not very cohesive.

Returning to Sarah, perhaps she should simplify everything by splitting her class into many smaller classes with one method each. These classes would clearly be cohesive, but another problem would emerge. Many of these "miniclasses" would need to depend upon the specific behaviors of other classes. Then a change to how one class did its job would result in changes in many other classes. This interdependency of classes is called **coupling** and results in programs that are difficult to maintain. Basically, this difficulty results from ignoring the "as simple as possible" portion of Einstein's dictum.

Programming by contract makes it quite possible to reduce coupling. If all Mark knows about Sarah's work is what has been expressed in the contract, then it is very unlikely that his code is highly coupled with hers. How could he rely upon details of which he is unaware? Mark knows what services Sarah's code will provide, but not how those goals will be achieved. Mark's ignorance of the details of Sarah's code is an example of **information hiding.** All object-oriented languages (and many others) provide some mechanism for information hiding. In Java, the keywords `public` and `private` are the primary vehicles for achieving this goal.

---

[1]Note that the use of the word *and* in this description is to build a list of nouns, *not* to create a compound sentence.

To see information hiding in action, let us imagine that Sarah is programming some form of rectangle class. Rectangles have lengths and widths and will provide the service of returning their areas. Sarah has at least two ways to provide this service. She could keep track of the length and width of a given rectangle and then multiply those two numbers whenever she is asked for the area. Alternatively, she could compute (and store) the area in advance and then simply give back the precomputed quantity whenever asked. Mark (or any other client) will never know which she is doing—nor should he care as long as he gets the correct answer whenever he asks! If, in the future, Sarah wishes to change how she manages this task, she can do so without affecting Mark's code. The figure below illustrates this concept.

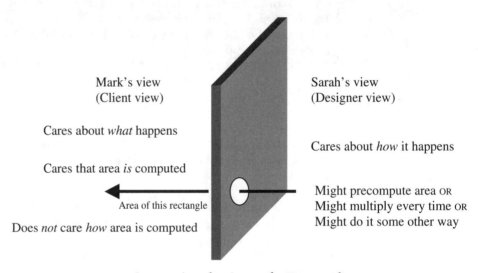

Computing the Area of a Rectangle

Notice that Sarah's view of (this portion of) the world is very cohesive. She is worried only about rectangles. She is implementing "a software version of a rectangle." If she is later asked to compute perimeters as well as areas, the basic description of her class does not change, even though its capabilities are enhanced. Notice also how the fact that Sarah is preserving the privacy of her data prevents Mark from making any assumptions that would increase the degree of coupling of their code. This is a classic example of the interaction of the concepts of programming by contract, information hiding, cohesion, and coupling.

! INHERITANCE

Object-oriented design is often said to arise from three concepts: encapsulation, **inheritance,** and **runtime polymorphism.** We have already discussed encapsulation. Simply put, *inheritance* is a mechanism that allows one class to extend the capabilities of another by adding new attributes and behaviors, while runtime polymorphism is the idea that we can delay decisions about which behaviors to use until the program is actually running. From a design point of view, these three provide a mechanism that allows programmers to work as a team—dividing up work among team members (through the use of encapsulation via classes) while still sharing as much code as possible (through inheritance and runtime polymorphism.) If this is done well, the result is an easy-to-understand and easy-to-maintain program.

! PUTTING ALL INTO A CLASS

Different programming languages support object-oriented design to different degrees. Within most object-oriented programming languages, the most obvious support for encapsulation is through the use of classes. By their very nature, classes provide encapsulation of both data and **algorithms**. Proper design of the programmer's interface can then achieve the goal of information hiding. Two "rules" tend to dominate the design process:

- Methods that provide services (or exhibit behaviors) to clients are to be made **public.** (If this isn't so, then the client cannot invoke the given method.)
- Data that are used to store state information (or help implement algorithms) should be made **private.** (In this way, client programmers cannot have their code rely upon such data, even if they are somehow otherwise aware of its existence.)

Note that it is *not* the case that all methods are public nor are all data private. Methods written for the convenience of the (class) programmer but not intended for the client should be private. And sometimes the class will wish to share particular data—usually constant data—with the client without a method; that data may be public. And, when inheritance is used (see Chapter 4), some private items may be indicated as **protected.**

DESIGNING A CLASS FOR THE EXAM

The free-response section of the exam is very likely to have a question that will ask you to design a class. This question will generally feature a narrative describing a "real world" problem for which a class is being developed. In one part of the question, you will be asked to design the interface for the class. (Although not part of the interface, you will usually also be asked to show the private data types for the class as well.) The purpose of this question is to let you show that you can analyze an English description of a problem and produce a class interface that supports information hiding. In the remainder of the question, you will generally be asked to implement a specific method and/or to use the class that you have defined in some way. Do not write code for the methods of the class unless you are specifically asked to do so!

When writing your solution, examine the narrative closely and determine the list of behaviors that is being requested. Some students like to underline the relevant verbs in the description; this is a fine thing to do. Sometimes the exam will contain a list of behaviors; that is a good start, but be sure to read carefully—additional behaviors may be necessary!

Once you have identified the entire list, create one *public* method for each behavior. You will need to give only the **signature** for the method; skip the code for now.

Then examine your list and determine what data must be stored to facilitate these behaviors. Create appropriate *private* instance variables as necessary to store these data. (*Exception:* constants for use outside of the class can be indicated as `public static final`.)

In both cases, choose appropriate, descriptive identifiers. Remember that there is no single best name for most methods, but there are some names that are clearly incorrect. You will never be penalized for using the second or third best name available, but single letter names, names of your teacher or friends, or inappropriate language will result in some credit being deducted from your score.

In Parts b and c, it is vital that you use the same names (and return types) that you chose as part of your design. For all the free-response questions, but especially any that refer to design, you should read all parts of the question before beginning work on any part. In the case of a question on design, you may get good hints about what to include in the class from the uses that a client will make of that class.

✓ RAPID REVIEW

Object-oriented design was developed to help increase the quality of software by reducing bugs and increasing maintainability. The basic terms involved are:

Encapsulation: The process by which one portion of a program is isolated from other portions with access limited to a (generally small) number of methods. (In the scenario in the text, it is Sarah's work that is being put into a capsule.)

Class: A mechanism used in object-oriented programming to encapsulate a block of code and/or data.

Method: The general term used to describe a single service provided by (or behavior shown by) a class.

Interface: The collection of all methods provided by a class. (*Warning:* interface is also a keyword in Java that has a similar, but slightly different meaning. That meaning is explained in Chapter 4.)

To make classes (or indeed any encapsulated unit) easier to develop and use, various techniques have been adopted by the programming community. Within the AP Computer Science curriculum, the most commonly used are:

Programming by contract: The idea that interfaces are specified in terms of contracts wherein a class that provides a service (or more precisely, the programmer of such a class) agrees to provide particular services for clients provided that the client first provides certain data (often expressed as preconditions.)

Preconditions: The stipulations put on the data provided to a method. Unless these stipulations are met, the programmer of the method is under no obligation to do anything!

Postconditions: A description of the results of a method invocation. It is the job of the programmer of the method to ensure that these results occur whenever the associated preconditions have been met.

Even assuming that all the contracts are well written, the concept of information hiding is used to increase the overall quality of the design.

Information hiding: The idea that someone who uses a block of code needs to know what the code does but does not need to know how it does it. Information hiding promotes reusable code and is therefore a desirable feature in a software system.

Algorithm: A step-by-step process for solving a problem.

Inheritance: A component of object-oriented design that permits data, methods, and/or algorithms to be shared among different data types that are related. (A more complete explanation of inheritance is given in Chapter 4.)

Runtime polymorphism: A component of object-oriented design that causes each object in a system to behave in a specialized manner even when its properties are otherwise known only in a general way. (A more complete explanation of runtime polymorphism is given in Chapter 4.)

Public: A description of data and/or methods that a class provides for use by software from outside of the class.

Private: A description of data and/or methods that a class provides only for use within that class.

Protected: A description of data and/or methods that a class provides only for use within itself and any inherited classes.

To help evaluate the quality of a design, one considers various measures. Two that are important are:

Cohesion: The degree to which a portion of a program (i.e., a class) can be viewed as an independent entity that performs a single task. Cohesion in program units is highly desirable.

> **Coupling:** The degree to which one portion of a program depends upon how another portion of the program does its job. Since high degrees of coupling make it difficult to maintain large programs, high degrees of coupling are to be avoided if possible.

2 PRACTICE PROBLEMS

1. Which of the following statements strongly justifies the use of the object-oriented design methodology?

    I.   Encapsulation and clear interfaces make it easier for different programmers to work on the same program.
    II. The use of classes increases the security of data by preventing unauthorized users from accessing private information.
    III. Methods within classes are easier to write than other types of code.

    A. I only
    B. II only
    C. III only
    D. I and II only
    E. I and III only

For questions 2 and 3, refer to the method below.

```
public int mystery(int a, int b)
{
  while (a%b != 0)
  {
    int temp = a;
    a = b;
    b = temp%b;
  }
  return b;
}
```

2. Which of the following is the best precondition for this code?

    A. b > 0
    B. a > 0
    C. a > 0 and b > 0
    D. a >= 0 and b >= 0
    E. No precondition is necessary.

3. Which of the following is the best postcondition for this code?

    A. Returns the larger of a and b
    B. Returns the larger of a and b divided by the smaller of a and b
    C. Returns the remainder when the larger of a and b is divided by the smaller of a and b
    D. Returns the largest number that divides evenly into both a and b
    E. Always returns 0

Questions 4 and 5 refer to method `alphabetize` for which pre- and postconditions are given below:

```
//precondition: nameList contains at least two distinct names
//postcondition: returns a new alphabetized list of names
public ArrayList alphabetize(ArrayList nameList)
{...}
```

Suppose that `alphabetize` does not work as intended. No matter what `ArrayList` of names is sent to the method, `alphabetize` returns an `ArrayList` containing the names "Alice," "Barbara," and "Carol."

4. Which of the following best characterizes the situation?

   A. The method works as intended only on lists of size 3.
   B. While the method does satisfy the postcondition as written, that condition has been worded inappropriately.
   C. The precondition never specified the number of names to be given; therefore, the postcondition is irrelevant.
   D. The postcondition fails to account for the possibility of nondistinct names.
   E. The method never works as intended.

5. In the code above, the postcondition is not well specified. Which of the following would have been a better postcondition for `alphabetize`?

   A. Returns an `ArrayList` containing the names "Alice," "Barbara," and "Carol."
   B. The original list is returned with the names in a new order.
   C. The names in `nameList` have been alphabetized.
   D. An `ArrayList` containing the original names is returned such that each name in the list, other than the first, is alphabetically later than its predecessor.
   E. No postcondition is necessary; the name of the method makes the intent clear.

6. Suppose we wish to design a thermometer class. A thermometer needs to give readings using both Celsius and Fahrenheit scales. Three implementations have been proposed for this:

   I.   Store the temperature only in Fahrenheit, and compute the Celsius temperature when asked.
   II. Store the temperature only in Celsius, and compute the Fahrenheit temperature when asked.
   III. Store both the Celsius and Fahrenheit temperatures.

   From the point of view of a client program, which of these is the best implementation?

   A. Implementation I is superior to the other two implementations.
   B. Implementation II is superior to the other two implementations.
   C. Implementation III is superior to the other two implementations.
   D. Implementations I and II are equally good and superior to Implementation III.
   E. Implementations I, II, and III are equally good.

SOLUTIONS TO THE PRACTICE PROBLEMS

1. **A.** Statement I is true; statement II addresses an issue (hackers stealing data) that is irrelevant to the discussion; and statement III is false—the code is equally easy (or difficult) to write. The correct answer is A.

2. **A.** If b is zero, a divide-by-zero error will occur when computing a%b. On the other hand, there are no restrictions on a. Therefore the answer is A.

3. **D.** `mystery` implements Euclid's algorithm to compute the greatest common divisor of a and b. While recognizing the algorithm might enable a student to answer this question quickly, it is expected that the student would trace one or two quick examples. Based upon the options, choosing a=15, b=9 should distinguish all cases.

4. **B.** The problem states that the answer is always the same; therefore, while the list "Tom," "Dick," "Harry" would give the wrong answer, the list "Carol," "Alice," "Barbara" would yield the correct answer. Thus, choices A and E are both incorrect. The method should work for lists of all sizes, so the precondition should not have to specify anything about the list size; it is fine. Thus, choice C is incorrect. And, since the precondition has guaranteed that all of the names are distinct, the postcondition does not need to refer to such data; therefore choice D is incorrect. The given output does indeed satisfy the postcondition as written, but the method does not do what is intended. Therefore the correct answer is B.

5. **D.** All nonempty methods should have postconditions; therefore, choice E is incorrect. Choice C does not address the issue of the return value, so it cannot be correct. The specification did not state that the original list should change; therefore, choice B is also incorrect; equally problematic, B does not specify what the new order should be! Choice A is an accurate description of the current situation, but is not what was intended. The correct choice is D.

6. **E.** The principle of information hiding states that a client program should never care how the class is implemented.

◖◗2 SAMPLE FREE-RESPONSE QUESTION

The following question represents one part of a typical free-response question concerning design. The parts involving the use of the class have been omitted.

A recipe consists of a name, a list of ingredients needed to make the dish, a number of servings produced, and assembly instructions (in English.) Part of the interface for the `Ingredient` class is shown below:

```
public class Ingredient
{
  public String getName() {...}
  public int getQuantityNeeded() {...}
  /* Other methods/constructors not shown */
}
```

The kitchen staff at a restaurant wishes to use recipes to help customize menus. At a minimum, workers wish to be able to scale a recipe to produce a given number of servings; to know if a given ingredient is used in a recipe; and to know the preparation time for the dish. `Recipe` objects are to be created by having the program analyze a long block of text.

Write a class definition for the `Recipe` class, putting only "{...}" in for the bodies of the constructor(s) and method(s). In writing this definition you must:

- Choose appropriate names for all identifiers.
- Provide (at least) the functionality specified above.
- Make data representation decisions consistent with the specification above.
- Make design decisions that are consistent with the principles of object-oriented design.

Comments are not required, but may be included to explain your intent.

Do not write the implementations of the constructors or the methods of the `Recipe` class.

SOLUTION TO AND COMMENT FOR SAMPLE FREE-RESPONSE QUESTION

The following is but one of many possible answers to the question. The essential elements are discussed in the commentary following the answer.

```
public class Recipe
{
  private String name;
  private ArrayList ingredients;
  private int numServings;
  private ArrayList instructions;
  private int preparationTime;
  public Recipe(String aRecipe) {...}
  public Recipe scale(String aRecipe, int size) {...}
  public boolean isInRecipe(String aRecipe, Ingredient item) {...}
  public int getPrepTime(String aRecipe) {...}
}
```

✓ Comments on the Answer

The key factors in determining the grade for a question concerning design would be the proper use of information hiding (public/private), the completeness of the list of methods, and the inclusion of instance variables to hold the necessary state information. In this case, the specifications directly imply the existence of a constructor that is passed a single String; they also imply the existence of the three methods: scale, isinRecipe, and getPrepTime; finally, they also suggest the existence of each of the five instance variables: name, ingredients, numServings, instructions, and preparationTime. There is great latitude granted in some of the details. With the exception of the constructor, none of the names must match exactly. It is also reasonable to have chosen other types for some of the instance variables. For example, the preparation time might have been stored as a double, the ingredients might have been stored in an array, and the instructions might have been stored as a single String (remember, Strings can have embedded newlines!). The return types of the methods are more fixed, but there is some room for variation there as well. getPrepTime should always return the type of the associated instance variable, and isInRecipe must return a boolean, but scale might return a String. (Such a String would be helpful for immediate display and/or printing and easily converted to a Recipe if need be.) In short, the question is about "big" concepts, and what matters most is that your answer shows that you have mastered those concepts. You are likely to be asked to implement one or more of the methods of your class in a subsequent part of the problem.

Chapter 3

Statement-Level Java Programming

Programming involves looking at the big picture, analyzing the problem, designing an algorithm for a solution, deciding which classes are needed, and determining dependencies between the classes. There comes a point, however, when the programmer must write the individual statements in the body of the methods. Errors in these statements may cause compile-time and runtime exceptions or (worse still) may go undetected and produce intent errors, i.e., incorrect output that the programmer may not realize is faulty. This chapter examines programming at the level of individual statements.

DATA TYPES

! Recall that in Java there are two distinct types of data, **primitives** and **objects.** You will be tested on only three primitive types: `int`, `double`, and `boolean`. Arrays are also tested. Data that aren't primitive are objects. Objects are **instances** of classes. Standard classes tested on both the A and AB exams are `Object`, `String`, and `ArrayList` and the `Comparable` interface. Several additional classes and interfaces are tested only on the AB exam. (See Chapters 9, 10, and 11.)

Primitive (or Simple) Types

A **primitive** is a simple data type, the simplest building block for representing data. Primitives do not have methods, constructors, or private instance data. Therefore, a primitive is not defined using the `new` operator, but is instead assigned a value directly via the **assignment** operator, "`=`". Of the primitive types you are responsible for on the AP exam, two are numeric (`int` and `double`), and one is logical (**boolean**).

Numeric Types

Remember that variables of type `int` represent integers and therefore have no fractional part. A `double`, on the other hand, approximates a real number, such as 3.14. Since all integers are real numbers, an `int` may be assigned directly to a `double`, but

71

a `double` must be explicitly converted to an `int` before any assignment can be made. The way to accomplish this is through **casting.** When a `double` is cast to an `int`, the `double` will be truncated rather than rounded. In effect this means the `double` is rounded "down" as illustrated by the code below:

```
int i = 5;
double d = 1.4;
d = i;          // This is legal; d now contains 5.0
d = 8.7;
i = d;          // This is NOT legal; you can't
                // assign a double to an int;
                // throws a possible loss of precision
                // exception (not tested)
i = (int) d;    // This is legal; i now contains 8
```

There are three types of operators in Java programming: **arithmetic operators, relational operators,** and **logical operators.** We'll discuss arithmetic operators now and visit the others later in this chapter.

Java's basic five arithmetic operations are: addition (+), subtraction (−), multiplication (*), division (/), and remainder or modulus (%). All the arithmetic operators work on both `int`s and `double`s. Since any `int` can be a `double`, the rule for performing the arithmetic is, "If either argument is a `double`, then the result is a `double`; if both arguments are `int`s, then the result is an `int`." Division can be tricky, however. Consider the expression 7/3. Since 3 does not divide into 7 evenly, how could an `int` hold such a value? To resolve this, integer division is handled as in elementary school. Seven divided by three is said to be, "two, with a remainder of one." The quotient of two `int`s is the integer part of the quotient. Java also provides a remainder operator, %, to compute the remainder directly. The remainder operator is particularly useful when checking for odd or even numbers (odd numbers have a remainder of 1 when divided by 2; the remainder for even numbers is 0), the number left over when a collection is divided into groups of a given size, determining the greatest common factor of two or more numbers, and so forth. In the heat of the exam try not to forget that this tool is available. (Note that remainder can be used with `double`s in Java, but this will not be tested as part of the exam.) Here are a few examples. (Assume all variables have been correctly declared and initialized.)

Test for an even number

```
if(num % 2 == 0) //remainder when divided by 2 is 0
```

Test to see if one number is a factor of another

```
if(num1 % num2 == 0) //num2 is a factor of num1
```

Store the remainder in a variable

```
int extra = num1 % num2; //extra contains the remainder
```

One algorithm for finding the greatest common factor of two positive integers

```
int gcf = 1;          //looking for greatest common factor
if(num2 == num1)      //same value in each
{
  gcf = num2;         //num2 is gcf for both num1 and num2
}
else if(num2 < num1) //gcf must be num2 or less
{
  int temp = num2;
  while(num1 % temp != 0 || num2 % temp != 0)
    temp -= 1;        //could go all the way down to 1
  gcf = temp;
}
else <imagine parallel code for (num1 < num2) >
```

As demonstrated in the above code, Java also provides shortcuts for each of the operators. The exam may use the +=, -=, *=, /=, and %= operators as a shortcut for adding, subtracting, etc., a value to the current variable.

```
val += <some number>;      // These two statements
                           // accomplish the same
val = val + <some number>; // thing
```

Java also provides increment (++) and decrement operators (--) which can be used to add (or subtract) 1 from a given integer variable. Within the context of an exam, these will not be used in combination with other operators. Even System.out.println(x++) is not used. Java will permit you to do so, but it is generally a poor idea because it often leads to unclear code.

Concerns about `doubles`

There are two main cautions to keep in mind when working with doubles. First, if you need to turn a double into an int, remember to cast the double to an int rather than merely assign it without a cast. Second, remember that doubles are stored with limited precision and that they are stored in binary as opposed to decimal form. As a result, two doubles that are arithmetically equal but have been computed through different steps may not be stored in exactly the same manner. A **conditional statement** testing doubles for equality is best written as follows:

```
if(abs(x - y) < 0.0001) // or some other tolerance
{...}
```

In other words, test to see if the absolute value of the difference between the two double values is arbitrarily small. If the difference is small enough, the variables may be considered essentially equal. The problem of comparing doubles for equality may come up in a multiple-choice question.

Comparing Primitives

The values of primitive types int and double are compared directly for inequality using the relational operators <, <=, >, and >=. Since a single equal sign is used for assignment, two consecutive equal signs (==) is the symbol used to compare primitives for equality. An exclamation point represents "not," so we write x != y or !(x == y).

Primitives as Parameters

Information required by a method is known as parameters or arguments. There are two types of parameters, implicit and explicit (discussed in Chapter 1). An implicit parameter is the object upon which a method is invoked, so an implicit parameter will never be a primitive type. Explicit parameters are the public information specified in parentheses in the method signature. When an explicit parameter is a primitive type, what is passed to the method is a copy of the stored value, not the value itself. Any change made to the parameter by the method affects the copy but has no effect upon the value of the original variable.

Type `boolean`

A `boolean` variable takes on the value `true` or `false`. Here `true` and `false` are values; don't enclose them in quotes, since doing so would mean you are treating them as strings. We sometimes use a `boolean` variable as a switch to control program flow in a conditional statement or a **loop statement.**

```
boolean done = false;
while(!done)            // continue the process
{...}
```

A `boolean` variable may improve the readability of a complicated conditional expression (see compound conditions later in this chapter in the section about conditional statements). We sometimes use `boolean` as the type for the elements stored in an array, indicating whether or not an element, represented by the index of the array, is available or has already been used. For example, a deck of cards might be represented as an array of fifty-two `boolean` values where `false` means `card[index]` has already been dealt and `true` means it is still "in the deck."

Constants

Constants are used to improve the readability of code and to make it easier to change a value that is used several times throughout a program. As we saw in Chapter 1, the `final` modifier is used to declare a constant. Here is a sample declaration:

```
public static final double TAXRATE = 0.075;
```

Because the value of a constant can't be changed, constants are often declared `public static`. `public static final` variables (i.e., constants) are included in the AP subset. Other static variables are not included, except in the context of the case study.

Scope of Variables

A variable can be referenced only within the opening and closing braces in which it is declared, unless it is declared public. Outside of those braces the variable is undefined and has no meaning. For example, declaring a loop control variable within a `for` statement means that the variable can be used only within the loop. If you want to use the loop control variable outside the **scope** of the loop, you must declare it outside the loop. Notice the difference in the following two code segments. In this case, the variable k is undefined outside the loop:

```
for(int k = 0; k <= max; k++) {...}
```

By contrast, in this case, the variable k is still defined and may be used by code after the loop terminates:

```
int k;
for(k = 0; k <= max; k++) {...}
```

Objects and Standard Classes

In addition to the primitive types, there are some specific data types supplied in the Java library that may appear on the exam. You will be provided a **Quick Reference Guide** with your AP exam for the standard classes that are tested. You will be expected to be able to use these classes to solve problems in both the multiple-choice and free-response sections of the exam. As with the simple examples in Chapter 1, you need only understand how to invoke the appropriate methods of the classes; you need not understand how a class actually accomplishes the task. The Quick Reference contains the method signatures but none of the implementation code. Pay careful attention to the number and type of parameters and to the return type of each method, both in selecting your answers to multiple-choice questions and in writing free-response answers. We discuss some of the most basic AP Java subset classes and their methods here. Other classes are discussed in detail in later chapters that focus on those classes. You are not expected to memorize the classes and methods in the AP Java subset, but it helps to be familiar with them and to have written code using them prior to taking the exam, since you simply won't have time to look everything up while the exam is in progress.

The *Object* Class

In Java, the `Object` class is the parent of all other classes. In other words, all other classes are subclasses of `Object` and, therefore, extend `Object`, even if the class declaration doesn't say so. This is particularly significant when we look at parameter and return types of some of the standard classes in the AP Java subset. While the `Object` class contains many methods, you are expected to know only three. They are

```
boolean equals(Object other)   // compares equality of this
                               // object to other
String toString()              // returns a Stringized version
                               // of this object
int hashCode()                 // AB only topic; see discussion
                               // in Chapter 10
```

Notice that the `Object` class has a `toString` method that returns a "stringized" version of an instance of `Object`. All classes either have their own `toString` methods or default to the `Object toString`. If you don't want to take your chances on how `Object` might "stringize" an instance of a subclass, your subclass should include its own `toString` method. See "Escape Sequences" (below) for additional information.

The *equals* Method

While primitives can be compared for equality directly using the relational operator ==, this is not true of objects. If we have two objects, `obj1` and `obj2`, of some class and we test if `obj1 == obj2`, what will be compared are the references (the memory addresses) of the two objects, not the contents. If both `obj1` and `obj2` refer to the same place in memory, the expression will evaluate to `true`. Otherwise, it will evaluate to `false`. To compare the contents of two objects, you must test if `obj1.equals(obj2)`. The `Object` class provides a default implementation for **equals**. However, equality of two objects generally depends upon what the objects represent. Testing if two books are equal is not the same as testing if two bank accounts are equal. If we expect to compare specialized objects for equality, we usually override the `equals` method provided by the `Object` class and write an appropriate `equals` for our class.

The *Comparable* Interface

The **Comparable** interface contains a single method, `compareTo`, that must be implemented by any class that implements `Comparable`. The purpose of `compareTo` is to compare two objects for inequality (or equality). Implementing `Comparable` makes sense only if the objects can logically have a "less than, greater than" relationship. Any implementation of `compareTo` must return an integer: a negative integer if the first object (the implicit parameter) is less than the second object (the explicit parameter), 0 if the objects are equal, and a positive integer if the first object is greater than the second. (See Chapter 4 for additional explanation of the `compareTo` method.)

Wrapper Classes

Sometimes we need to treat a primitive value as an object. This often occurs when we wish to add such a value to a collection of data. (A **collection** is a way of grouping data together into a single object and thus being able to process it using methods of the collection type.) To facilitate this, Java provides **wrapper classes**. These classes "wrap" a primitive value into an object, giving it a constructor and methods and allowing it to be stored in container classes that require the contents to be objects. Wrapper classes implement the `Comparable` interface. You are responsible for recognizing and using the following methods of the `Integer` and `Double` wrapper classes. Note that the methods in these classes are parallel, which helps make them easier for you to remember.

The `Integer` Class

```
Integer(int value)              // constructor
int intValue()                  // returns the Integer as an int
boolean equals(Object other)    // returns true if this
                                // Integer = other;
                                // otherwise, returns false
String toString()               // returns a Stringized version of
                                // this Integer
int compareTo(Object other)     // specified by
                                // Comparable, see above
```

The `Double` Class

```
Double(double value)            // constructor
double doubleValue()            // returns the Double as a
                                // double
boolean equals(Object other)    // returns true if this
                                // Double = other;
                                // otherwise, returns false
String toString()               // returns a Stringized version of
                                // this Double
int compareTo(Object other)     // specified by
                                // Comparable, see above
```

The `String` Class

A **String** object is a sequence of characters. `String` constants are enclosed within double quotes. The `String` class differs from most other Java classes in several ways. One difference is that a `String` may be constructed without the use of the `new` operator. A second is that objects of the class are immutable—that is, once constructed, they cannot be changed (though they can be reassigned).

A `String` can be constructed in two different ways:

```
String s = "Hello, World!";                 // constructed as you
                                            // would a primitive
String s = new String ("Hello, World!");    // using the
                                            // class constructor
```

There is also a default constructor.

```
String s = new String(); // sets s to "" (empty)
```

A `String` may be reassigned.

```
s = "Goodbye, World";
```

`Strings` may be concatenated. **Concatenation** means that we can add two or more `Strings` together. We can also add a nonstring to a `String`. The nonstring is converted to a `String` and is concatenated to the `String`.

```
String s = "This sentence has ";
int numWords = 4;
String newstr = s + numWords + " words.";
newstr += " (not counting the number 4)";
```

`newstr` will contain *This sentence has 4 words. (not counting the number 4).*

The `String` class has many methods, but only a few will be tested. The testable methods are listed below. (Note: `String` implements `Comparable`.)

```
int compareTo(Object other)        // specified by the
                                    // Comparable class
boolean equals(Object other)       // compares equality of
                                    // this and other
int length()                       // returns the number of characters in
                                    // the string
String substring(int from, int to) // returns the
                                    // substring beginning at from
                                    // and ending at (to - 1)
String substring(int from)         // returns
                                    // substring(from, length())
int indexOf(String s)              // returns the index of the
                                    // first occurrence of s;
                                    // returns -1 if not found
```

Escape Sequences

Certain characters or combinations of characters cannot be printed within a `String`. For example, a double quotation mark can't be printed because quotation marks are themselves `String` delimiters. Preceding the quotation mark with a backslash character, however, signals the computer to print the quotation mark rather than interpreting it as the end of the `String`. Within a `String` a backslash indicates a directive to give the next character some special meaning. These special codes are known as **escape sequences.** Three escape sequences are included in the **AP subset:**

\"   print the quotation mark
\n   carriage return, line feed combination (go to a new line)
\t   tab to the next print field

Why is this important? Suppose you want a `toString` method for an `Address` class. You want an `Address` object to be printed on three lines for name, street, and city, state, and zip code. Your code might look like the following:

```
public String toString()
{
   return name + "\n" + street + "\n" + cityStateZip;
}
```

Java includes several additional escape sequences, but only these three will appear on the AP exam.

The Math Class

The **Math class** consists of a library of useful methods. We never construct a Math object. Instead, the methods of the Math class are static methods. That means that we invoke them using the class name. We do not need and cannot build a Math object. For example, to invoke the square root method we write the following:

```
double root = Math.sqrt(<some variable or value>);
```

The following methods of the Math class are included in the AP subset:

```
static int abs(int x)          // absolute value of x
static double abs(double x)    // absolute value x
static double pow(double base, double exponent)
                               // base to the exponent power
static double sqrt(double x)   // square root of x
```

The Random Class

The **Random class** is a utility class. It consists of useful methods for generating random numbers. To use the Random class, you must import `java.util.Random`. We construct Random objects, but the constructor is not among the methods that will be tested. You may be told you already have a Random object whose name is, for example, r or generator. The testable methods are the following:

```
int nextInt(int n)    // returns an integer in the range
                      // 0..(n - 1)
double nextDouble()   // returns a double in the range
                      // 0.0..0.99999 (not including 1.0)
```

An exam question may involve generating a random number within a specified range of values. For example, generate a number to represent a common die object (one of a pair of dice) in the range 1 to 6. To do this you would write the following:

```
int die = r.nextInt(6) + 1;
```

The nextInt method will return a value between 0 and 5, inclusive. Adding 1 bumps any integer generated up 1, so you will have integers in the range of 1 to 6.

```
int num = r.nextInt(25) + 25;
        // returns an integer in the range 25..49
```

To generate double values in the range 5 <= val < 15, use

```
double val = r.nextDouble() * 10 + 5;
```

`r.nextDouble()` returns a value from 0.0 to 0.99999. Multiplying by 10 (the difference between 5 and 15) yields values between 0.0 and 9.999. Adding 5 (the lower bound) bumps these up to 5.0 to 14.9999.

If a question gives the probability of an event and you are asked to generate a random number representing that the event occurs, you will need to generate a random double. If the number generated is less than the given probability, the event occurs. If it is greater than or equal to the probability of the event, the event does not occur.

```
if(r.nextDouble() < 0.25) // win 1/4 of the time
{
  System.out.println("You win!");
}
```

In addition to these classes, you are expected to be able to use some of Java's "container classes," discussed in later chapters.

STATEMENTS

Statement level programming includes declaration and initialization statements, assignment statements, input (not tested) and output (`System.out.print` and `System.out.println`), conditional statements, and iteration. We will concentrate on statements that control the flow of a program, i.e., conditional statements and iteration (loops).

Conditional Statements

The flow of a program is not always sequential. The `if` statement allows a decision to be made based on a condition, to follow one path or another through the code. The basic conditional statement is

```
if (<some test condition is true>)
{
  <do something>;
}
```

When the test condition is true, the "if clause" is executed once; otherwise, the "if clause" is skipped. In either case flow continues to the next statement in the program following the `if` statement (provided the `if` clause doesn't contain a `return` statement).

The `if . . . else` statement decides which of two branches to execute. When the test condition is true, the "if clause" is executed; otherwise, the "else clause" is executed.

An important point for you to remember is that a conditional statement (`if` or `if . . . else`) is executed only once, as opposed to code that is executed repeatedly, covered below in the section on iteration.

`if` statements may be nested. Here is an example:

```
if(dayNum == 7)
{
  if(hour == 12)
  {
    <do something>;
  }
  else <do something else>;
}
else
{
  <do something else>;
}
```

When nesting becomes too deep, it may be difficult for us humans to keep track of what is true. We can become lost in the logic. In place of the nested `if`, sometimes we call a method that contains the inner `if . . . else` statement.

```
if(dayNum == 7)
{
  checkHour(hour);
}
else
{
  <do something else>;
}
```

`checkHour` would contain the nested code.

Nested ifs can also lead to the problem of a "dangling else." Consider the following code segment. Assume x is a properly initialized integer.

```
if(x >= 0)
  if(Math.sqrt(x) == (int)Math.pow(Math.sqrt(x), 2))
    System.out.println("perfect square");
else // misleading indentation
  System.out.println("negative number");
```

The problem most often occurs when there are two or more ifs but a lone else. Often the programmer will line up the else with the intended if. Even though the code may be out-dented so that it *appears* to be correct, it isn't. As far as the compiler is concerned, the else belongs with the nested if statement. An else will be paired with the most recent if unless separated by curly brace delimiters.

For any positive integer that is not a perfect square, the above code will output the message "negative number." (No message is output if the variable actually is negative.) To correct the problem, either include braces around the if clause or reverse the condition being tested. Here is corrected code:

```
if(x >= 0)
{
  if(Math.sqrt(x) == (int)Math.pow(Math.sqrt(x), 2))
    System.out.println("perfect square");
}
else
  System.out.println("negative number");
```

Still nothing is printed if the variable is nonnegative and not a perfect square, but now the else clause is clearly associated with the outer if. When in doubt, include curly braces.

Alternatively, reversing the order of the tests produces the following code:

```
if(x < 0)
  System.out.println("negative number");
else if(Math.sqrt(x) == (int)Math.pow(Math.sqrt(x), 2))
  System.out.println("perfect square");
```

A third alternative is to combine the two if tests into a single, compound condition. See the section on logical operators later in this chapter.

Test reversal, as illustrated by the above example, is one technique for simplifying a decision. This tool is also useful when you can't think of any code to write for an if clause and everything you want to write belongs in the else.

```
if(x < 0)
  <do nothing>;
else
  <do something>;
```

With test reversal the code becomes

```
if(x >= 0)
  <do something>;   //there is no else
```

We sometimes write a series of if . . . else ifs, known as an "else if ladder," when we have a variable that might be classified in one of several categories. In this case, the final else does not need an if. All other categories have been tested, and there is only one remaining possibility. For example, assume that grade is a valid integer such that 0 <= grade <= 100 and letterGrade is a valid String.

```
if(grade >= 90)
  letterGrade = "A";
else if(grade >= 80)
  letterGrade = "B";
```

```
    else if(grade >= 70)
      letterGrade = "C";
    else if(grade >= 60)
      letterGrade = "D";
    else letterGrade = "F";
```

Notice that a trace of the above code using various values for `grade` separates each grade category by its lower bound. Any grade that does not fall into one of the bounded categories must be less than 60 and, therefore, is an F.

When using laddering, one must often be careful with the order of the tests. Consider what happens if the first test in the ladder above were:

```
    if (grade >= 60)
      letterGrade = "D";
```

Iteration (Looping)

Iteration, or looping, controls the flow of a program by *repeating* a block of code as long as the condition being tested remains true.

This is the major difference between a conditional statement and a loop. A conditional statement is executed exactly once; a loop repeats as long as the test condition is true. Under different conditions, a loop may execute zero, one, or multiple times. If a loop does repeat, there must be progress within each iteration toward the loop condition becoming false. A fundamental property of a loop is that when the loop ends, the condition being tested *is* false. In fact, when designing a loop, you should think, "What do I want to be true when the loop terminates?" and use the opposite of that condition to determine the conditional expression tested by the loop.

The AP exam tests two kinds of loops, **while** loops and **for** loops. The following demonstrates the general form of these loops in the context of a simple routine to find the sum of the numbers from 1 to 10.

Don't forget you need to initialize a separate variable to zero to accumulate the sum.

`int sum = 0;`
`for(int num = 1; num <= 10; num++)`
`{`
`  sum += num;`
`}`
	`int sum = 0;`
	`int num = 1;`
	`while(num <= 10)`
	`{`
	`  sum += num;`
	`  num++;`
	`}`

There are four parts in any loop:

1. Initialization of the loop control variable
2. Testing the condition to see if the loop should continue
3. The body of the loop, i.e., whatever the processing entails
4. Updating the control variable, i.e., making progress toward termination

Notice that the `for` loop wraps three of the four parts into a single line of code, whereas in the `while` loop each part has an individual line. (In truth, some more sophisticated loops may be controlled by a "computed condition" rather than an explicit loop control variable. In such a case the four parts still exist, but it is the condition that is initialized and updated rather than the explicit variable.)

One other point to keep in mind with respect to the example above is that we often count from 0 to (n – 1), where n is the number of times we want the loop to execute. The loop actually executes the correct number of times because we started our count at zero. This helps us transition into array processing, which is covered in Chapter 5. In the example above, it made sense to count from 1 to 10 because those were the values being summed.

In general, a `for` loop is considered a counting loop, and a `while` loop is considered an "all purpose" loop. A counting loop is used when we know in advance the number of times the loop is to be executed. A `while` loop is most often used when we are waiting for the test condition to change due to some occurrence or when there is a compound condition (an "and" or "or" situation). This distinction is not as cut and dried in Java as it has been with other languages, but it is still a good rule of thumb for you, as a beginning programmer, to follow.

Just as decisions may be nested, the same is true of loops. However, when loops are nested, you must keep in mind the flow of control. The outer loop is not executed a second time until execution of the inner loop is completely finished. When the outer loop begins its next iteration, the inner loop starts all over again. Trace the variables carefully. Here is an example:

```
for(int row = 0; row < 3; row++)
{
  for(int stars = 0; stars < 5; stars++);
    System.out.print("*");
  System.out.println();
}
```

When the above code is executed, the output is the following:

```
*****
*****
*****
```

A slight change in this code, controlling the inner loop with the value of `row`, rather than a constant value, is shown here. (The change is indicated in boldface type.)

```
for(int row = 0; row <= 3; row++)
{
  for(int stars = 0; stars <= row; stars++);
    System.out.print("*");
  System.out.println();
}
```

This is how the output changes.

```
*
**
***
```

> **Tip**
>
> Read code in multiple-choice questions carefully to understand how loops are controlled.
> A loop must make progress toward the test condition becoming false; otherwise, it is an **infinite loop**. Another problem is the "obob," off-by-one-bug, that occurs when a loop executes one too many or one too few times. Watch out for <= versus < and >= versus > in loop conditions.

ITERATORS (AB TOPIC)

Iterators are classes in the Java language that provide a way to loop through collections of objects. More is said about iterators in later chapters.

LOOP INVARIANTS (AB TOPIC)

A **loop invariant** is a statement that is true before a loop executes, at the beginning of each iteration, and after the loop terminates. A carefully chosen loop invariant can be used to prove the correctness of an algorithm. Here is an example using code that finds the sum of the integers 1 to n, where n >= 1:

```
// loop invariant: sum = the sum of integers 1 through num-1
int sum = 0;
int num = 1;
while(num < n)
{
  sum += num;
  num++;
}
```

In truth, loop invariants are not often used for simple loops, such as this one, to sum numbers. In practice, they are more often used to prove the correctness of loops within more complex algorithms such as those that are used to sort or search through collections of data.

LOGICAL OPERATORS

We already discussed arithmetic and relational operators. The logical operators are && (and), || (or), and ! (not). With the exception of not, logical operators have a lower **precedence** than either arithmetic or relational operators.

PRECEDENCE RULES

Grouping Operators (take precedence over all others) { }, ( ), . (dot operator for method calls)		
Arithmetic Operators	**Logical Operators**	**Relational Operators**
Increment and Decrement ++, −−	Negation !	
Multiplication and Division *, /, %		
Addition and Subtraction +, − String Concatenation +		
		Inequalities <, <=, >, >=
		Equalities ==, !=
	And &&	
	Or ||	
Arithmetic and Assign +=, −=, *=, /=, %=		Assign =

COMPOUND TEST CONDITIONS

!

Logical operators allow us to write compound conditions, which may be used in place of nested decision statements. Earlier in this chapter we looked at the code segment below:

```
if(x >= 0)
{
  if(Math.sqrt(x) == (int)Math.pow(Math.sqrt(x), 2))
    System.out.println("perfect square");
}
else
  System.out.println("negative number");
```

The nested if statements may be combined into a single compound if, but now the second message should be changed.

```
if(x >= 0 && Math.sqrt(x) == (int)Math.pow(Math.sqrt(x), 2))
  System.out.println("perfect square");
else
  System.out.println("negative number or not a perfect square");
```

Be careful when using && and ||. It's easy to become confused and choose the wrong operator. Here are the truth tables for "and" and "or." p and q represent expressions that can be assigned the value true (T) or false (F).

p	q	p && q
T	T	T
T	F	F
F	T	F
F	F	F

p	q	p || q
T	T	T
T	F	T
F	T	T
F	F	F

Keep in mind that the only time "and" is true is when both expressions are true. The only time "or" is false is when both expressions are false.

This leads to an understanding of **"short-circuit" evaluation**. In a compound condition using "and," if the first part is false, the entire condition evaluates to false without it being necessary to test the second part. If the first part of a compound condition testing "or" is true, the entire condition evaluates to true without the second part being tested. This can be particularly helpful if testing the second part of the condition depends upon the truth of the first part. For example, consider the following code in which x and y are numeric values:

```
if(x != 0 && y/x > <some value>)
  <do something>;
```

The above code prevents a division by zero exception. If x = 0, the first part of the condition is false, making the entire condition false, and the second part of the condition is not tested.

!

In terms of writing compound conditions, most student errors occur in the logic of while loops. Students often mistakenly use "or" when they want a loop to continue as long as both conditions are true. For example, suppose one is tabulating test scores and wants to continue as long as the score entered is in the range 0 to 100. An incorrect test would be the following.

```
while(score >= 0 || score <= 100 )
{. . .}
```

What score could possibly cause the loop to terminate? It should have been written this way:

```
while(score >= 0 && score <= 100)
{...}
```

To apply test reversal to a compound condition, use **DeMorgan's Laws,** the negation of an "and" or the negation of an "or" statement. You can check the logic of these two laws by constructing truth tables. Here is the equivalent code where p and q represent Boolean expressions.

The negation of an "and" is   `!(p && q) = !p || !q`

If one expression or the other is false, the entire condition is false.

The negation of an "or" is   `!(p || q) = !p && !q`

If both expressions are false, the entire condition is false.

A final note about Booleans—an elegant way to return a Boolean value is simply to return the result of evaluating a Boolean expression. The two code segments below have the same effect.

```
if(x > 0)                return x > 0;
  return true;
else return false;
```

Tip

There are certain types of errors that students tend to make on the AP Computer Science exam, particularly in the free-response section. Some of the errors relating to classes are listed below:

- == for equals
- the dangling "else"
- an uninitialized loop control variable
- infinite loop (not updating the loop control variable)
- confusion with "and" and "or" in a compound condition (you have to think through the logic—"and" means both parts must be true to continue iteration; "or" means only one must be true to continue)

Tip

It is a virtual certainty that the exam will contain questions involving evaluation of Boolean expressions, directly or indirectly, including DeMorgan's Laws. Be sure to be comfortable with Boolean logic.

RECURSION

A process that calls itself is a **recursive** process. When recursive, rather than iterative, methods are used, two very important criteria must be met.

- There must be a *base case,* or simplest case. That is, there must be a condition that stops the recursion.

- There must be a *general case,* or recursive case, in which a simpler, but similar call is made to the method itself. Something in the parameters to the method must change so that the recursive calls eventually result in a call to the base case.

A recursive algorithm consists of one or more conditional (`if . . . else`) statements that take the place of the loop in an iterative algorithm. (See also recursion and stacks in a later chapter.) A-level students should be able to write and trace simple recursive methods such as method `power` that returns a to the b power. (Often these simple methods are more efficient when written nonrecursively.)

```
public int power(int a, int b)
{
  if(b == 0)
    return 1;
  else
    return a * power(a, b - 1);
}
```

While you probably would not write `power` recursively, there are times when recursion is by far the simplest way to solve a problem. You may need to trace a recursive method to determine its return value, but sometimes, by studying the algorithm, a pattern is apparent and a complete trace can be avoided. We revisit recursion several times in subsequent chapters.

TEST DATA

It is important to design appropriate test data for methods you write. In fact, the test cases should be determined before the code is written. **Test data** includes the general case, boundary cases, different paths through the code, and any rarely occurring cases you can think of. The goal of testing is to anticipate errors and program defensively against them before they occur. When code is modified, test cases should be retested to be sure the modification doesn't cause a test that previously ran without error to suddenly fail. This is called **regression testing**. Among other things, the Marine Biology Simulation focuses on developing test cases. (See Chapter 7.)

EXCEPTIONS

Programs are generally written under the assumption that the computation will proceed in an expected manner. This is not always the case, however; data may be inappropriate (e.g., division by zero) or missing entirely (when a file is not found.) An **Exception** is an object that describes a problem or error that occurs at runtime. The Exceptions below will be tested on both the A and AB exams.

- `ArithmeticException` is thrown when an illegal arithmetic operation is attempted, such as division by zero.
- `ClassCastException` is thrown when there is an attempt to cast an object to a class of which it is not an object.
- `NullPointerException` is thrown when there is an attempt to use `null` where an object is expected.
- `ArrayIndexOutOfBoundsException` (explained in Chapter 5).
- `IllegalArgumentException` (explained in Chapter 5).

Students taking the AB exam are expected to be able to throw the `IllegalArgumentException` and the `NoSuchElementException`. See Chapter 5 for more information.

RAPID REVIEW

This chapter reviews many of the lower-level details and basic constructs tested on the AP exam.

Data types can be categorized as **primitive,** of which `int`, `double`, and `boolean` are the only three tested, and **objects,** which are instances of classes. Keep in mind that the primitive types are not objects and do not have methods associated with them. There are three types of **operators: arithmetic** (+, −, *, /, %), **relational** (<, <=, >, >=, ==, !=), and **Boolean** (&&, ||, !). You should be able to use all these operators in program statements.

Sometimes two or more expressions are combined into a compound expression connected by "and" (&&) or "or" (||). **DeMorgan's Laws** are used to write the negation of a compound expression. The statement ! (a && b), where a and b are expressions, is !a || !b (the negation of a or the negation of b). The statement ! (a || b) is !a && !b (neither a nor b is true). Java uses **short-circuit evaluation.** If the first part in the compound expression a && b is false, there is no need to even bother evaluating the second part, b, because "and" is false if either part is false. If the first part of the compound expression a || b is true, there is no need to evaluate the second part because "or" is true if either part is true.

Boolean variable: Assigned one of two values, `true` or `false`. These variables are often used to simplify an expression that controls the flow of a program or to indicate that a value does or does not exist.

Primitive data type: An `int`, `double`, `boolean`, or `char`. The first three are tested as part of the AP curriculum; `char` is not tested.

`Object` class: The parent of all other classes. All other classes **extend** (inherit from) this class, even though the class declaration may not explicitly say so. Methods include `equals` and `toString`.

`Equals` method: Compares instances of a class for equality.

Wrapper classes, Integer, and **Double:** Provide a way to treat integers and doubles as objects, particularly when we wish to add such a value to a **collection** of data.

`Collection`: A way of grouping data together into a single object so that it is possible to compute using methods of the collection type.

`String`: A class that represents a sequence of characters. String constants are enclosed in double quotation marks. Be able to construct a `String` and use the methods listed in the AP Computer Science Quick Reference. Refer to testable methods listed earlier in this chapter.

Escape sequences: Characters beginning with a backslash character, \, used in `String` literals to format output. You are responsible for "\n" (new line), "\t" (tab), and "\"" (printed double quotation mark) for the AP exam.

`Math` class: Consists of a library of math methods. These are **static methods,** methods that are invoked using the class name rather than with an instance of the class (`Math.sqrt(5)`). Refer to the testable methods listed earlier in this chapter.

`Random` class: Generates random numbers. Testable methods are `int nextInt(int n)` and `double nextDouble()`

Assignment: The = operator gives a value to a variable; assignment is always a right-to-left operation.

Cast: Cause a data item to be treated as a different type; often used when an `Object` must be treated as a particular type in order to invoke a method on that type.

Precedence rules: The order in which the components of an expression are evaluated.

Conditional statement: A decision statement that controls program flow based upon a **condition** (an expression that can be evaluated to true or false). The form of this statement is `if(< test condition >)` . . . and may include an `else` . . . . A conditional statement is executed exactly once. Conditional statements may be nested. Compound conditional expressions combine simple conditions using "and" and "or."

Loop statement: A statement that causes a block of code (possibly a single statement) to be executed some number of times, repeating the entire block each time. Both `for` and `while` statements are examples of loop statements. Loop statements may be nested and/or combined with conditional statements.

Iteration: Looping; a statement that controls the flow of a program through repetition.

Infinite loop: An iterative process that fails to make progress toward ending.

`for` loop: Counting loop; generally used when there is a definite number of iterations; for example, `for(int k = 0; k < 10; k++)`.

`while` loop: Iterative process based on a condition, while the condition is true; must make progress toward the condition becoming false. Sometimes the condition is compound ("and" or "or" situation), so an understanding of logic is required.

Iterators (AB topic): Classes provided by the Java language for looping through a collection (see Chapters 4 and 5).

Loop invariant (AB topic): A statement about the loop that is true before a loop executes, at the beginning of each iteration, and at the end of each iteration.

Scope of a variable: Determines the block of code in which a variable is defined.

Recursion: Name given to an algorithmic process (in Java, usually a method) that invokes itself.

Test data: Set of values used to test a method; the purpose is to try to expose and correct errors; should include a general case, boundary cases, and each path through the code.

Concatenate: Attach the beginning of one `String` to the end of another to form a new `String`.

`Comparable` interface: A Java construct similar to a class but containing only method signatures, not code. The `Comparable` interface contains a single method, `compareTo`, which must be implemented by any class that implements the interface.

Exception: An error or unusual situation arising in a program. In Java, this situation is represented by an Exception object of a specific type, such as `ArithmeticErrorException`.

PRACTICE PROBLEMS

1. Consider the following code segment that is intended to count the number of values read from the keyboard until a negative value is entered. You may assume `readDouble` allows the user to enter a `double` from the keyboard.

```
int count = 0;
double num = readDouble();
while(num >= 0)
{
  count++;
}
```

The code segment does not work as intended. Which of the following best describes the problem?

A. There is an uninitialized variable.
B. The loop may never be executed.
C. The loop may never terminate.
D. The loop does not test the right condition.
E. The counter is incorrectly initialized.

2. Consider the following method. You may assume that `readInt` reads integer values input at the keyboard.

```
public int mystery()
{
  int j = readInt();
  int k = j;
  int m = 1;
  while(!(j < 0))
  {
    j = readInt();
    if(j == k)
      m++;
  }
  return m;
}
```

Which statement below best describes the value that is returned by mystery?

A. The total number of values entered
B. One more than the number of negative values entered
C. The number of nonnegative values entered
D. The number of duplicates of the first number entered
E. The total number of occurrences of the first number

3. Consider the incomplete Point class as started below:

```
public class Point
{
  private int myX;
  private int myY;

  public boolean inAQuadrant()
  {
    return < missing code >;
  }
  // Other code not shown
}
```

Which of the following conditional expressions returns true if a point is neither on the x-axis nor the y-axis?

A. myX == 0 && myY == 0
B. myX == 0 || myY == 0
C. !(myX == 0 && myY == 0)
D. !(myX == 0 || myY == 0)
E. !(myX != 0 && myY != 0)

4. Consider the following method:

```
public double confuse(double a)
{
  a = a*a;
  a = a*a;
  a = a*a;
  return a;
}
```

Which of the following could replace the first three lines of the body of confuse so that an equivalent result is returned?

A. a = Math.pow(a, 2);
B. a = Math.pow(a, 4);
C. a = Math.pow(a, 6);
D. a = Math.pow(a, 8);
E. a = Math.pow(a, a);

5. Consider the following code segment:

```
String s = "APCS";
String temp = "";
for(int j = 0; j < s.length(); j++)
  for(int k = 0; k < j; k++)
    temp += s.substring(k, j);
System.out.println(temp);
```

What is the output when the code segment is executed?

A. APCS
B. AAPAPCAPCS
C. AAPPAPCPCC
D. AAPAPCAPCS
E. An IndexOutOfBoundsException is thrown.

6. Consider the following method:

```
public static int scramble(int a, int b)
{
  while(b != 0 && a % b > 0)
  {
    a += b;
    b = b - 1;
  }
  return a;
}
```

When the while loop terminates, which of the following is true?

A. The value of b is 0.
B. The remainder when a is divided by b is 0.
C. The value of b is 0, or the remainder when a is divided by b is 0.
D. The value of b is 0, and the remainder when a is divided by b is 0.
E. There is not enough information to make a statement about the value of a or b.

7. Which of the following expressions evaluates to false?

A. (true) && (!false)
B. (!true) && (!false)
C. (true) || (false)
D. (true) || (!false)
E. (!true) || (!false)

8. Consider the following code segment that is intended to print the greatest of three different int values, x, y, and z. The code does not work as intended.

```
if(x > y)
{
  if(y > z)
    System.out.println(x);
  else
    System.out.println(z);
}
else if(y > z)
{
  System.out.println(y);
}
```

Which of the following best describes the problem?

I. The printing of z and y should be interchanged.
II. The else in the nested if is missing a test involving x and z and matching output.
III. The else in the outer if is missing an else and an output line when the test fails.

A. I only
B. II only
C. III only
D. II and III only
E. I, II, and III

9. Consider the code segment below:

```
if((a < b) || (c && d))
{...}
```

Which values of a, b, c, or d will cause this code to short-circuit?

A. a = 2, b = 2
B. a = 3 b = 2
C. a = 1, b = 2, c = true, d = false
D. c = true, d = true
E. c = false, d = false

10. Consider the problem of determining the value of an investment (amt) that has a given interest rate (rate), compounded annually, after a given period of years (yrs). Each of the following methods correctly computes the value. You may assume all variables have been properly initialized.

```
public static double method1(double amt, int yrs, double rate)
{
  if(yrs >= 1)
    for(int y = 1; y <= yrs; y++)
      amt += rate * amt;
  return amt;
}
public static double method2(double amt, int yrs, double rate)
{
  if(yrs < 1)
    return amt;
  else
    return method2(amt, yrs-1, rate)
                    + method2(amt, yrs-1, rate)*rate;
}

public static double method3(double amt, int yrs, double rate)
{
  amt = amt * Math.pow((1 + rate), yrs);
}
```

For a large number of years, which statement below best characterizes the execution efficiency of the three code segments?

A. Method 1 is more efficient than 2 or 3 because it is the most straightforward and understandable method.
B. Method 2 is more efficient than 1 or 3 because recursion is always the most efficient solution.
C. Method 3 is more efficient than 1 or 2 because it requires fewer operations.

D. Methods 1 and 2 are more efficient than 3 because they do not call a method from another class.

E. Methods 1, 2, and 3 execute equally efficiently.

SOLUTIONS TO THE PRACTICE PROBLEMS

1. **C.** Both variables are initialized. The loop may never be executed, but that will not cause an error condition because in that event count does contain the correct value. The loop does make the right test, and count is correctly initialized to 0. Since no new values of num are read within the body of the loop, if the first value of num is >= 0, the code will produce an infinite loop.

2. **E.** m is initialized to 1, so the first occurrence of j is counted. If j is negative, m returns the correct value. Otherwise, m is incremented every time the new number matches the first value read.

3. **D.** This is an example of DeMorgan's Law. Neither myX nor myY equals 0. Answer A tests for a point at the origin; B tests that at least one of myX or myY is on an axis; C tests that one of myX or myY is not on an axis (the other could be); and E tests the same thing as B.

4. **D.** The first line stores a-squared in a; then a to the fourth; then a to the eighth.

5. **C.** Upon each iteration of the j-loop, the k-loop starts at 0 and marches toward j, so the successive concatenated substrings start at length j − 1 and shrink by one letter until the length is 1. On the last iteration of the j-loop, the strings that are concatenated are "APC," "PC," and "C."

6. **C.** When a loop based on a compound condition terminates, at least one of the conditions must be false.

7. **B.** A Boolean expression cannot be both not true and not false at the same time. In an "and" expression, if either part is false, the whole expression is false. In answer A, both parts of the expression evaluate to true. In the "or" expressions, answers C, D, and E, at least one part is true. Therefore, the entire expression is true.

8. **D.** There are two errors. If x is greater than y and y is not greater than z, we don't know the relationship between x and z. If x is not greater than y, x is certainly not the greatest value, but we do not know the relationship between y and z. Both of these must be tested and appropriate output statements written. (This is not the only or necessarily the optimal code for this problem.)

9. **C.** If the first half of the condition is true, there is no need to test the second half of an "or" compound condition; the entire condition is already true. Short-circuit evaluation doesn't need to examine the second part of the condition, so the values of c and d are of no consequence in this problem.

10. **C.** Although all three methods execute quickly, the third segment, which uses a formula, is more efficient for large numbers of years because the calculation is done with one line of code. The iterative method is less efficient because it requires calculating a partial answer for each year. The recursive method is less efficient still because it not only requires repeated calculations but also requires additional memory each time it is invoked.

Chapter 4

Inheritance

SOLVING SIMILAR PROBLEMS

 Much of computer science is about problem solving, and much of problem solving involves recognizing similarities among problems and solutions. In the world of software design, similar problems can often be solved by similar programs, or even by programs that share much of their code. This idea of reusing code has been around since the advent of programming. It led to the idea of subroutines in programs before modern programming languages even existed! Through the use of classes, we may have distinct blocks of data that share the algorithms (methods) which may be performed (invoked) upon that data. Each block of data is then encapsulated in its own object. Any two objects of the same class will each use the same code to perform the given operations. This level of abstraction is achieved through the encapsulation properties of objects and classes.

Code reuse can be taken one step further, however. When the data associated with them are appropriately similar, entire classes can share the code to perform given methods. Within object-oriented languages in general, and Java in particular, this is achieved through the mechanism of inheritance. *Inheritance* is the term used to describe a relationship between two classes where one of them is a generalization of the other. For instance, we might have the idea of a Car class; we might also conceive of a Ford Mustang class. Clearly a Car is a generalization of a Mustang; alternatively, we could say that a Mustang is a specialization of a Car. Notice that all Mustangs are Cars, but not all Cars are Mustangs. Any task that a Car can perform, a Mustang can perform as well, but there are some tasks that a Mustang can perform that a general Car either cannot perform or can only perform in some other manner. Mustangs and Cars share many attributes, but are distinct. It is this type of relationship that inheritance is designed to capture. If this example were implemented in Java, the Car class would be called the **superclass,** and the Mustang class would be called the **subclass.**

IS-A AND HAS-A

 When one is presented with a new tool, there is a tendency to use it for all applications; therefore, there must be a test that can be applied to determine if two classes should share an inheritance relationship. This test is quite simple: one simply considers the two objects and asks if the first **IS-A** second. To see how simple this is, state whether each of the following is true:

- A Car   IS-A   TransportationVehicle
- A Bicycle   IS-A   TransportationVehicle
- A Car   IS-A   Banana
- A Bicycle   IS-A   Car
- A MountainBike   IS-A   Bicycle

(Hopefully, you answered, "yes," "yes," "no," "no," and "yes.")

Any time you answered "yes," there is an inheritance relationship between the classes. The class on the left is the subclass, and the class on the right is the superclass. Notice that a class can play both roles, albeit at different times. Notice also that you were able to answer the question about inheritance without worrying about Java programming; this is as it should be—the objects that you are modeling should dictate the organization of the program, not the other way around.

To further understand the inheritance relationship, try the following more abstract questions:

- An X IS-A X
- Suppose that you knew that X and Y were different and that an X IS-A Y. Is the following true: A Y IS-A X
- Suppose that you knew that an X IS-A Y, and a Y IS-A Z. Is the following true? An X IS-A Z.

Hopefully, you answered "yes," "no," and "yes" to these.

> **Tip**
>
> When abstract questions such as these appear on an exam, try substituting real examples. Thinking about the third one there, we already agreed that a MountainBike IS-A Bicycle, and that a Bicycle IS-A TransportationVehicle. And isn't a MountainBike IS-A TransportationVehicle? How could it not be?

There is a similar relationship that can occur between two classes, the **HAS-A** relationship. Two classes share the HAS-A relationship if the first includes at least one object as a component. In real life, people rarely confuse IS-A and HAS-A, but sometimes programmers make that error. If one lets the data describe the program instead of the other way around, there is no difficulty here. To see how simple it is, try the following quiz:

- A Car   HAS-A   Horn
- A TransportationVehicle HAS-A   Horn
- A Car   IS-A   Horn
- A Horn   IS-A   TransportationVehicle

Hopefully, you answered: "yes," "no" (consider A StageCoach), "no," and "no."

Within a Java program, if an object HAS-A something, then there should be an instance variable of that type within the class definition for the object. Inheritance is neither needed nor desired.

IMPLEMENTING SUBCLASSES

As with all programming tasks, the first order of business is to recognize what it is that is being modeled. After that, it is necessary to determine how to implement that in a given programming language. In Java, inheritance is implemented through the keyword **extends.** When the implementation of one class is inherited from another, we say that that class *extends* the other. For example, the first relationship from the earlier quiz would be expressed as:

```
public class Car extends TransportationVehicle {...}
```

Looking backwards, this Java code tells us that a `Car` IS-A `TransportationVehicle`. It is a Java restriction that a class may extend only one other class.

Because a `Car` IS-A `TransportationVehicle`, it must be intrinsically able to perform all the tasks of a `TransportationVehicle`. To help us understand how this happens, we will concentrate on only two methods of its class: `move` and `describe`. The former causes the vehicle in question to move forward, while the latter provides a textual description of the vehicle. The appropriate Java code is shown below:

```
public class TransportationVehicle
{
  public void move()
  {
    /* implementation not shown */
  }
  public String describe()
  {
    return "generic transportation vehicle";
  }
  // Other methods and instance variables not shown
}
```

Now, a `Car` can do anything that a `TransportationVehicle` can, so it must be able to both `move` and `describe`. (It must also be able to perform any methods that weren't shown.) In addition, since we know that a `Car` HAS-A `Horn`, it must presumably be able to `honk`. One possible `Car` implementation is shown below:

```
public class Car extends TransportationVehicle
{
  public String describe()
  {
    return "internal combustion automobile";
  }
  public void honk()
  {
    /* Implementation not shown */
  }
  private Horn myHorn;
  /* Other methods and instance variables not shown */
}
```

Notice that the `Car` class contains its own `describe` method, but does not include a `move` method. This means that a `Car` and a `TransportationVehicle` will `move` using the same Java code, but that they will `describe` themselves differently since they each implement that method. Suppose that we have a `TransportationVehicle` named `tv` and a `Car` named `c` already constructed. Then the following code has the following effects:

```
tv.move();        // moves the TransportationVehicle
c.move();         // moves the Car
tv.describe();    // returns "generic transportation vehicle"
c.describe();     // returns "internal combustion automobile"
tv.honk();        // ERROR: no such method for TransportationVehicles
c.honk();         // presumably causes some noise
```

The first statement is a simple method call; this is the same as in Chapter 1.

The second statement is an example of inheritance. Since c is a Car and therefore a TransportationVehicle, it can respond to the move message. When a Car object receives this message, the Java environment determines that the Car class did not define this method, so it uses the code from the parent class (TransportationVehicle). If there was no such code there, then the code from the next parent class would be used, and so on. If there were no such code ever, then the invocation would have generated a compiler error.

The third statement is a simple method call; the fact that the Car class redefined the method is irrelevant to this line of code—in fact, the Car class is irrelevant to all lines of code involving the variable tv.

The fourth statement invokes c's describe method. Since c is a Car and since the Car class defined the describe method, that code is executed.

The fifth statement reiterates the previous point. Since there is no honk method in the TransportationVehicle class, this is an error.

The sixth statement is once again a simple method invocation, as in Chapter 1.

When a subclass defines a method that already exists in a superclass, it is said to **override** that method. If the subclass fails to define a method that exists in a superclass, it is said to inherit that method. Note that any redefinitions are in terms of the entire signature. If the same name is used but the parameter sequence is different, then the signature is different and no overriding takes place.

Similarly to how we can invoke methods across class boundaries, we can also perform variable assignments between classes when the IS-A relationship guarantees that the assignment makes sense.

```
TransportationVehicle tv2;
Car d;
tv2 = c;    // Legal since a Car IS-A TransportationVehicle
d = tv;     // ERROR: tv might not be a Car. (It could be a Bicycle.)
```

Suppose that we have executed the first assignment so that the variable tv2 now contains a reference to a Car; in fact it references the same Car that variable c does. The picture below illustrates the current state of memory:

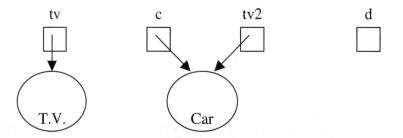

What would be returned if we executed the expression:

```
tv2.describe();
```

The answer is that "internal combustion automobile" would be returned. Some students believe that since tv2 is a TransportationVehicle, the code executed in response to the describe message would be the code in that class. This arises from a misunderstanding. The variable tv2 refers to a TransportationVehicle; that is true. However, the particular TransportationVehicle it refers to is, in fact, a Car. Thus, the implementation of describe that is used is the one for the Car class. Looked at a different way, since c and tv2 refer to the same object, they are synonyms. Thus, c.anyMethod() and tv2.anyMethod() should have the same effect. In Java, *it is the type of the actual object, not the type of the reference variable, that determines which block of code gets executed.*

> **Tip**
>
> When questions start to mix types, particularly among classes sharing inheritance relationships, draw a figure in the exam book such as the one above. You will not earn any points for the figure, but it may very well help you get the right answer to the question.

Suppose that we are still in the situation described by the memory diagram in the previous figure. We would like to execute the line:

```
d = tv2;    // ERROR: TransportationVehicles are not Cars
```

but the compiler will not permit it. The error message states that we cannot assign a `TransportationVehicle` to a `Car`. While this would seem to make sense in general, it would appear that the compiler got it wrong this time. After all, `tv2` does indeed refer to a `Car`. The problem here is one of perspective. Because we are aware of how the reference was established in the variable `tv2`, we know that the variable does refer to a `Car`. Unfortunately, there is no guarantee that the reference was established this way, so the compiler will not let the assignment take place. We can get around this through the use of **casting**. Casting is, in essence, a promise from the programmer to the compiler that a variable is indeed of the correct type. The compiler will then permit the appropriate operation to take place. Casting is indicated by placing the name of the type in parentheses in front of the expression to be cast:

```
d = (Car) tv2;        // Legal, due to the cast
```

What happens if the promise is not fulfilled, as in the following example:

```
c = (Car) tv;          // Will compile, but will raise
                       // a ClassCastException at runtime
```

Note that while `tv` *might* have been a `Car`, it was not. This will cause a **ClassCastException** to be generated at runtime. Such an exception is thrown whenever the promise indicated by a cast is shown to be incorrect at runtime.

Java provides a keyword, `instanceof`, that can be used to detect when a `ClassCastException` might arise. `instanceof` is used to determine if an object does indeed have a given type. Imagine that we had lost track of the type to which the variable `tv2` was pointing. The following code would prevent a `ClassCastException` from arising:

```
if (tv2 instanceof Car)
{
  d = (Car) tv2;
}
```

In the event that `tv2` was referring to a `Bicycle`, the Boolean test would return false and thus the assignment would not be attempted and the `ClassCastException` would not arise. While it is a handy tool, you should be aware that `instanceof` is not part of the Java subset and thus will not be tested.

Public, Private, and Protected

Java permits the programmer to specify how variables and methods of a class may be used by other classes. The three modifiers that apply are public, private, and protected. These are described in Chapter 2, but the definitions have consequences vis-à-vis inheritance hierarchies as well. As stated in Chapter 2, anything that is declared as public may be used anywhere; data may be referenced or modified and methods may be invoked. And, as stated in Chapter 2, anything that is declared as private may be used only *within that class*. This means that such data or methods may not be referenced within a subclass, even though the inheritance hierarchy exists. It is a common error to violate this rule, and the rule itself may be tested on the exam. The protected modifier is used to describe data and/or methods that are not public but that may be used in subclasses as well as in the class in which it is defined. If one believes that a class may later be extended, it is sometimes better to declare methods or variables as protected instead of private. The protected modifier is not part of the AP Computer Science Java subset per se, but it does arise in the context of the Marine Biology Simulation, so it is expected that students will be familiar with it. As a general rule, any method that is overridden in a subclass should retain its appropriate public/private/protected modifier.

As a result of these levels of information hiding, subclasses often reference or modify data in the parent class through `getData` or `setData` methods.

super and this

Earlier we explained how the Java environment chooses which block of code to execute for a given method. The programmer has some choice in this matter, however. This can be handy if you wish to use the superclass's code as part of an implementation of an overridden method. Suppose that we wished to include the description of the superclass along with the description of the car. We can reference the `describe` method in the superclass by using the reserved word **super** to refer to method definitions in the superclass. Thus, we could have written the `describe` method in the `Car` class as follows:

```
public String describe()
{
  return super.describe() +
    "-internal combustion automobile";
}
```

With this implementation, invoking the `describe` method on a `Car` object would cause the `String` "generic transportation vehicle—internal combustion automobile" to be returned. The use of the keyword `super` is very important in this example. If it were not there, then the runtime environment would start `Car`'s `describe` method by invoking the `describe` method in `Car` which would in turn invoke the `describe` method in `Car` and so on. The result would be an infinite recursion that would eventually generate a runtime error.

It is also possible to use the keyword **this** in a similar manner, but there is no difference between saying "`this.anyMethod`" and "`anyMethod`." It is similar to saying `1*x` rather than `x` with a numeric variable. The first is longer to type and a bit more confusing, but it is really no different from the second. The keyword `this` will not appear on the exam as a prefix to a method call. (It is, however, used to refer to the entire object itself in parts of the Marine Biology Simulation—see Chapter 7.)

Constructors

Given the prevalence of private data, it can be difficult for an object to initialize all its data properly. Initial values for instance variables are often passed to the constructor, but the constructor for a subclass can't always access the instance variables in the superclass. The solution to the dilemma is effectively described in the preceding section: one simply uses the superclass constructor. An example follows:

```
public class Parent
{
  private int parentData;
  public Parent( int pd ) { parentData = pd; }
  /* Other methods and data not shown */
}
public class Child extends Parent
{
  private double childData;
  public Child( int parentInfo, double kid )
  {
    super(parentInfo);
    childData = kid;
  }
  /* Other methods and data not shown */
}
```

In this case, the Child class could not assign the parentData field directly because that integer is private. The solution is to use the constructor from the superclass to make the assignment. (Note: had there been a public setParentData method, that could have been used as well.) In general, a constructor for a subclass should invoke a constructor for the superclass to ensure that all appropriate initialization is done. This must be the first thing done in such a constructor.

The Object Class

The Java environment supplies an entire library of classes for the programmer to use and/or extend. The most special class, in one sense, in this library is the Object class. Object is a superclass of all other classes. Earlier when we said,

```
public class TransportationVehicle
```

it was, in fact, equivalent to saying

```
public class TransportationVehicle extends Object
```

Thus, every class in Java can perform all the tasks that an Object can. From an AP Computer Science perspective, there are two (three for AB) methods of concern: equals and toString. The former is used to determine whether two objects are the same; the latter is used to convert the Object to a String, often for display purposes. (AB students are also expected to be familiar with the hashCode method; this is discussed in Chapter 10.) In general, every class that inherits from Object, i.e., all classes, should override these methods.

INTERFACES

Sometimes it is convenient to know that a class can perform a given task even though that class does not have an IS-A relationship to some other class. Consider the class Student which is a subclass of the class Person. Some students have "extra" abilities that are not universal. For instance, some students might be certified as life guards for the school pool. Since Student already extends Person, it could not also extend a hypothetical LifeGuard class to establish this capability. Stated one way, a LifeGuardingStudent IS-A Student with the capability of LifeGuarding. Java provides a way for a class to assert that it has a set of capabilities without having to extend another class. It does so through **interfaces**.

In one sense, an interface is nothing more than one or more method signatures that a class must *implement*. Any class that does implement the methods can announce this fact in its class definition, and the compiler will then permit the class to be used appropriately. In the example above, we would say:

```
public class LifeGuardingStudent extends Student implements LifeGuarding
```

This states that a `LifeGuardingStudent` IS-A `Student` (and, by transitivity, IS-A `Person`) who can also perform all the tasks listed in the `LifeGuarding` interface. If the definition for the `LifeGuardingStudent` does not implement (or inherit) all the methods described in the `LifeGuarding` interface, then the compiler will generate an appropriate error message when the class is compiled.

The interface is declared simply by listing the signatures of the methods involved:

```
public interface LifeGuarding
{
  public void openPool();
  public void rescue(Person p);
  // other methods declared similarly
}
```

The benefit to interfaces is perhaps best seen when several different classes implement the interface. Consider two more such classes:

```
public class LifeGuardingTeacher extends Teacher implements LifeGuarding
```

and

```
public class SuperStudent extends Student implements LifeGuarding implements
SafetyPatrol implements Tutor
```

In this situation, any object of type `LifeGuardingStudent`, `LifeGuardingTeacher`, or `SuperStudent` could be asked to perform an `openPool` or a `rescue` operation. These three classes share this capability without having to share an inheritance relationship. Notice that it would be impossible for any of these classes to inherit the actual code definition from the `LifeGuarding` interface because there was no code there. This is one of the characteristics of an interface: it contains no code, only a list of methods—no code and no instance variables. Note that the `SuperStudent` class above shows another aspect of interfaces: while a class can only extend one other class, it can implement any number of interfaces.

The Comparable Interface

There is one interface in the Java library on which both A and AB students will be tested on the AP Computer Science exam, the `Comparable` interface. It is so short that a version is shown below:

```
public interface Comparable
{
  public int compareTo( Object other );
}
```

To implement the `Comparable` interface, a class need only include this one `compareTo` method. The purpose of the method is to compare two items using their "natural" order. As examples, the natural order of type `Integer` is simply the "greater than" relationship, and the natural order for type `String` is lexicographical (dictionary) order, albeit where the case of the letters is *not* ignored. The postconditions for `compareTo` state that `x.compareTo(y)` should return:

- A positive number if x is naturally larger than y
- A negative number if x is naturally smaller than y
- Zero if x and y are equal

Note that y can be any type of Object, but not a primitive. When asked to implement compareTo for some class, you have to ask yourself how to define less than, greater than, and equal to for objects of that type. Ultimately, it must come down to some attribute of the object (or of an object that is an attribute, such as Date or Address) that we compare in a natural way. (In the context of a problem on the exam, you will be told how to define these concepts.) If the type of y prevents it from being compared to x in a natural way, then a ClassCastException will be raised.

Suppose that we have a class Event that includes (among other data) a Date on which the event is to be held. Assume further that this Date can be accessed through a getDate method. If Events are to be compared via these Dates, then the compareTo method of the Event class would be as shown below:

```java
public int compareTo( Object other )
{
  return this.getDate().compareTo( other.getDate() );
}
```

! Be careful when comparing objects stored in an array, ArrayList, or other data structure that contains Object. If you want to use a compareTo written for a specific class, you must cast the stored object to its class type before calling compareTo. No cast was necessary in the example above because the getDate method was returning a Date, not an Object.

ABSTRACT CLASSES

! Java programmers use the extends keyword when they wish to share data and methods between two classes. They use the implements keyword when they wish to share only the capabilities, but not the code. There is, however, a middle ground, wherein two classes might wish to share a set of capabilities and some amount of code. Consider the case of a drawing program. Such a program might provide the user with a variety of shapes that could be drawn, such as Oval, Rectangle, Polygon, etc. These shapes might share some code—for instance, a getColor method, but would require completely distinct sets of code to implement other methods such as draw. One way to organize such a class hierarchy would be to pick one shape as the parent, say Oval, and have all the other shapes extend that class. These shapes could then inherit the code for getColor and override the code for draw. This would work, but is a poor design decision. The reason is that it suggests that a Polygon IS-An Oval, and a Rectangle IS-An Oval. This is clearly not how we think about such shapes. A better solution is to create a whole new class that will serve as the parent class, perhaps named Shape, and have the other classes extend this one. All Shapes will have a color, so the instance variable for this information will be defined in the Shape class, and the code for getColor will reside there as well. Each of the subclasses will override the draw method as before. The hierarchy now looks like this:

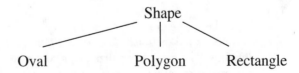

The problem is with the Shape class. If it does not define a draw method, then that method cannot be invoked upon the various Shapes (Oval, Polygon, and Rectangle) without the benefit of a cast operation. But, there is no sensible way to define such a method. (It could be left blank, if draw is a void method, but if there is a return type, then things become problematic.) What is needed is a way to tell the compiler that all subclasses have a given capability without having to write the code here. Such a class is called an **abstract class** and is indicated through the use of the `abstract` keyword. Placing this keyword in front of a declaration says, in essence, that the declaration is incomplete and that it will be filled in by the subclasses. If this modifier is placed in front of any method, then the entire class is also considered to be abstract. The (partial) code for this example is below:

```
abstract public class Shape
{
  private Color myColor;
  public Color getColor() { return myColor; }
  abstract public void draw();
  /* Constructor and other items not shown */
}
public class Oval extends Shape
{
  public void draw()
  {
    /* Implementation not shown */
  }
  /* Constructor and other items not shown */
}
```

Note that the subclass overrides an abstract method in exactly the same manner that it overrides any other method. In fact, if the subclass is a **concrete class** (the opposite of an abstract class), then there is no explicit indication that its parent was abstract.

Basically, a class is abstract if one or more of its (promised) methods is not yet defined. The Java environment will not let you construct an object from an abstract class using the new operator for that class. This is because if it did so, there would be no way to respond to an invocation of an abstract method.

Finally, note that it is not required for a subclass of an abstract class to implement all the missing methods. It may implement some, all, or none of them. If, however, it omits any, then the subclass must also be declared to be abstract—as it is also missing methods.

One can imagine a "pure" abstract class—i.e., one which has no code or data at all. Such a class would look (and behave) a lot like an interface. From a design point of view the distinction between these two concepts is subtle (and unlikely to be tested on an AP exam), but remember that in Java one can extend only a single class.

The design of (good) class hierarchies is a challenging task. Some scholars have developed so-called *design recipes* to help with this. The interested student should certainly learn more about this, but the scoring of the exam will never hinge on such a fine distinction. It is much more important to understand how the system works than to get involved in subtle debates about certain issues.

RAPID REVIEW

 Inheritance captures a relationship between two classes, one of which is a generalization of another.

Superclass: The more general of two classes in an inheritance relationship. Also sometimes called the *base class,* or the *parent class.*
Subclass: The more specialized of two classes in an inheritance relationship. Also sometimes called the *derived class,* or the *child class.*

Some people feel that these two concepts are misnamed. Given that the subclass can do more than the superclass, things would seem to be backwards. The names are correct, however, when one regards the data. All objects in the *sub*class are also objects of the *super*class. Thus, the set of objects in the *sub*class is a *sub*set of the set of objects in the *super*class. It is from this relationship that the names derive.

extends: The Java keyword that is used to express the inheritance (IS-A) relationship between classes.

When deciding whether or not the relationship between two classes is an inheritance relationship, two expressions are often used to help one make the decision:

IS-A: We say that X IS-A Y if the objects that X models are *always* also considered to be objects of type Y. This means that it must be the case that any method that can be invoked on an object of type Y can also be invoked on an object of type X.
HAS-A: We say that X HAS-A Y if any object of type X would necessarily contain an object of type Y. Note that with a HAS-A relationship, X could "handle" an invocation of a method on Y by simply having its instance of Y "handle" the invocation. (In essence, X just passes on the message like a courier.)

Classes that share the IS-A relationship are best organized through inheritance. The HAS-A relationship is best handled through the inclusion of an instance variable.
A subclass can choose to redefine, or not to redefine, any method in the parent class. If the subclass redefines the method, then the redefined method will be used in response to any invocation on an object of the subclass's type. If the subclass does not redefine the method, then an invocation of that method will have the same effect as it would in the parent class. In all cases, redefinition is said to occur only if the signature is the same in both the subclass and the superclass.

Override: We say that a subclass overrides a method from a superclass if it (re)defines a method with the same signature as one in the superclass. In such a case, the redefined method will be invoked on any object of the subclass's type.
Inherit: We say that a subclass inherits a method from a superclass when it fails to (re)define that method in its own class definition. In such a case the code from the superclass is used when the method is invoked on any object of the subclass's type.

Assignments can be made between types within an inheritance hierarchy. The IS-A relationship determines when such assignments are legal. If the programmer has additional knowledge about the types of variables, then a cast operation can be used to allow the compiler to accept assignments that might otherwise appear to be illegal.

Casting: Casting is a declaration from the programmer to the compiler that a variable is actually of the correct type to permit an assignment to be made. It is indicated by placing the type name within parentheses immediately preceding the expression to be cast.
ClassCastException: An exception raised by the Java environment when a line is executed involving a cast operation involving an object whose type is *not* as promised by the cast operation.

Interfaces are another way that Java provides for the programmer to share capabilities between classes. While a class can extend only one other class, it may implement any number of interfaces.

interface: A Java construct that consists of a list of method signatures that are required of classes that implement the interface of this name.
implements: The Java keyword that indicates that a class will provide all the capabilities specified by the given interface.

Java provides two keywords to refer to objects within an inheritance hierarchy: super and this.

super: The Java keyword used to indicate that the method or data being referred to should come from the superclass rather than from the class that is making the reference.

`this:` The Java keyword used to indicate that the method or data being referred to should come from the class making the reference. The use of `this` is often redundant unless it is the entire object itself which is being referred to.

It is not required to define all the methods in a class, provided that they are defined by the subclasses that will actually be used to construct objects. Any class that is to be constructed must have defined all such methods.

Abstract class: A class is considered *abstract* if some of its methods, either named locally or inherited, have not been defined. Such methods, and indeed the class itself, are labeled with the keyword `abstract`.

Concrete class: A class is considered concrete if it has definitions for all its methods, including those that were inherited. Only concrete classes can be instantiated to create objects.

PRACTICE PROBLEMS

1. A programmer has noticed that the curve that a teacher uses to convert raw test scores to "curved test scores" uses the same formula as the conversion from Fahrenheit to Celsius. He proposes to use inheritance so that the code used when curving test scores may be reused when converting temperatures. Which of the following represents the best reason why he should *not* use inheritance to model this scenario?

A. If the teacher changes her mind about the curve, the code would no longer work.
B. The Fahrenheit to Celsius conversion uses doubles, but test scores are always integers.
C. Test scores and thermometers do not share an IS-A relationship.
D. There are likely to be many students taking the test, but there is generally only one thermometer at a given location.
E. Actually, the programmer should do this. Reusing code is generally a good idea.

Questions 2–6 refer to a software system used by a library to check out various items. The library stores all the items in an array of `LoanItems`. A given `LoanItem` may be "on loan" to a `Customer` at any time. If not on loan, a `LoanItem` is considered to be "checked in." This particular library loans out books, videos, and CDs of music.

```java
public class LoanItem
{
    private String      itemName;
    private String      itemID;
    private Customer     loanedTo;
        // loanedTo is null if item is "checked in"
    private Date        dueDate
    public LoanItem(String name, String ID)
    {
        // Implementation not shown
    }
    public boolean isCheckedIn()
    {
        <code omitted>
    }
    public String getName()  { return itemName;    }
    public String getID()    { return itemID;      }
    /* Other constructors, methods, and data not shown */
}
```

```
public class Book extends LoanItem
{
  private String    author;
  public Book(String name, String ID, String authorName)
  {
     <code omitted>
  }
  public String getAuthor()
  { return author; }
}
public class Video extends LoanItem
{
  private ArrayList cast;
  public Video(String name, String ID, ArrayList stars)
  {
     // Implementation not shown
  }
}
```

2. Which of the following represents code that could be used to correctly implement the `isCheckedIn` method in the `LoanItem` class?

A. `return loanedTo.getName().equals("checked in");`
B. `return loanedTo.isNull();`
C. `return itemName.length()==0;`
D. `return loanedTo == null;`
E. `return loanedTo.checkedIn();`

3. Which of the following blocks of code could be used to fill in the constructor for the `Book` class?

I. `super.itemName = name;`
    `super.itemID = ID;`
    `this.author = authorName;`
II. `super(name, ID);`
    `author = authorName;`
III. `LoanItem(name, ID);`
     `author = authorName;`

A. II only.
B. III only.
C. I and II.
D. II and III.
E. Any of the three may be used.

4. The library has decided that it wishes to keep its items sorted by ID number within the `ArrayList` that holds the collection. Based only upon the given information, which of the following would be the most appropriate modification of the code?

A. Have the `LoanItem` class declare that it implements the `Comparable` interface, but leave the implementation of the `compareTo` method to each of the subclasses.
B. Have the `LoanItem` class declare that it implements the `Comparable` interface and define the `compareTo` method itself.
C. Have each subclass, e.g., `Book`, `Video`, implement the `Comparable` interface on its own.
D. Instead of using the `Comparable` interface, simply compare the ID fields directly using the `getID` method.
E. The task can't be done because you can't compare `Books` to `Videos`.

5. The CD class was not shown in the listing above. In the absence of other information, what is the *simplest* way to integrate that class into this hierarchy without violating any standard principles of design?

   A. Since CDs and Videos both have performers, CD should extend Video.
   B. Since CDs and Videos both have performers, a new class PerformanceItem should be added. PerformanceItem should extend LoanItem, and CD and Video should extend PerformanceItem.
   C. The LoanItem class should be made an interface, and all three classes (Book, Video, and CD) should implement that interface.
   D. The instance variable "cast" should be moved from the Video class to the LoanItem class, and CD should extend LoanItem.
   E. CD should extend LoanItem with no other changes necessary.

6. (AB only) Which of the following statements about the classes in this problem is false?

   A. The isCheckedIn method will need to be redefined in each subclass.
   B. There is no requirement for a constructor in LoanItem since the all objects will be either Books, Videos, or CDs.
   C. The Library class could be an abstract class.
   D. The Video class must be a concrete class.
   E. It is possible, though not wise, for the Book class to override the getID method.

For questions 7–8 consider the code below:

```
public class Pet
{
  public Pet()
  {}
  public void animal()
  {
    System.out.print("some animals ");
  }
  public void story()
  {
    System.out.println("are good pets.");
  }
  public void sentence()
  {
    animal();
    story();
  }
}
public class Feline extends Pet
{
  public Feline()
  {}
  public void animal()
  {
    System.out.print("cats ");
  }
}
```

7. What is printed as a result of executing the following code:

```
Feline s = new Feline();
s.sentence();
```

A. some animals are good pets.
B. cats are good pets.
C. cats.
D. cats some animals are good pets.
E. nothing is printed; a `ClassCastException` is raised.

8. What is printed as a result of executing the following code:

```
Pet a = new Pet();
Feline b = new Feline();
Pet c = b;
a.animal();
b.animal();
c.animal();
```

A. some animals are good pets.
B. some animals cats some animals are good pets.
C. some animals cats some animals.
D. some animals cats cats.
E. nothing is printed; a `ClassCastException` is raised.

9. Consider the following partial definition of a `Date` class

```
public class Date implements Comparable
{
    private int myDay;      // 1...31
    private int myMonth;    // 1...12
    private int myYear;     // 0...10, for 2000 to 2010

    public int compareTo(Object d)
    { // missing code }

    public int getDay() { return myDay; }
    public int getMonth() { return myMonth; }
    public int getYear() { return myYear; }

    // other public methods not shown
}
```

Which of the following correctly replaces < `missing code` > in `compareTo` for the `Date` class, if we live on a planet where all years are 360 days long and all months are 30 days long?

I. `return (myDay - d.getDay()) + (myMonth - d.getMonth()) + myYear - d.getYear());`
II. `if(myYear != d.getYear()) return myYear - d.getYear(); if(myMonth != d.getMonth()) return myMonth - d.getMonth(); return myDay - d.getDay();`
III. `return 360*(myYear - d.getYear()) + 30*(myMonth - d.getMonth()) + (myDay - d.getDay());`

A. I only.
B. II only.
C. III only.
D. I and II only.
E. II and III only.

10. Consider interface `Something` below.

```
public interface Something
{
  public void describe(String s);
}
```

Which of the following statements about a class that implements the `Something` interface is true?

A. If an abstract class implements `Something`, `describe` must be declared abstract.
B. If a nonabstract class implements `Something`, `describe` must be implemented but there may be other methods with the same name as long as they have different parameter lists.
C. If a nonabstract class implements `Something`, it must implement `describe` but may not define another method with a single `String` parameter and void return type.
D. If a nonabstract class implements `Something`, `describe` may be declared abstract.
0An abstract class may not implement the `Something` interface.

SOLUTIONS TO THE PRACTICE PROBLEMS

1. **C.** The IS-A relationship indicates when inheritance should be used, and there is no such relationship between these classes. Option B suggests that the two formulas are not the same, contradicting the statement in the problem. Options A and D are true, but they are simply facts of life; they do not represent reasons to avoid using inheritance. And while code reuse is generally a good idea, it should be avoided when the reason for reuse is coincidental rather than due to the nature of the problem, so option E is also incorrect.

2. **D.** The comment on the `loanedTo` instance variable indicates that this is the correct option. Even if we assume that the named methods exist for the `Customer` class, option A refers to a constant `String` that was never discussed and option E asks if the `Customer` is checked in, not if the item is. Option B appears to ask an object if it is null itself, but if `loanedTo` is null, then that code would generate a `NullPointerException`. Option C refers only to the name of the item, which presumably does not change when the item is checked out.

3. **A.** Option I refers to private data in the superclass and is incorrect. Option III calls a constructor by name, which is also incorrect. Option II represents the proper way to write the code. Thus, the answer is A.

4. **B.** When a class states that it implements an interface, it must have code for that interface; thus Option A would not compile. Option C would work, but would require putting the same code in every class, thereby losing all the advantages of inheritance. Option D might work, but would be much less general than implementing the interface. Option E is a red herring. The code compares `LoanItems` to `LoanItems`. `Books` and `Videos` are both `LoanItems`, so there is no problem. The correct answer is B.

5. **E.** Option A is wrong because `CD` and `Video` do not share an IS-A relationship. Option C won't work because the `LoanItem` class has code and data. Option D

might work, but it is inappropriate because Books have no need for the new instance variable. Options B and E both work, but E is much simpler. The correct answer is E.

6. **A.** The whole idea of inheritance is that code need only be written once unless the behavior of the method is to change. There is no reason to rewrite isCheckedIn. The other statements are true. The correct answer is A.

7. **B.** Although s inherits the implementation of sentence from Pet, it uses its own (Feline's) implementation of animal. It then uses the inherited implementation of kind to generate the latter portion of the output.

8. **D.** The variables b and c refer to the same object, which happens to be of type Feline. Therefore the last two statements have the same effect. Note that the kind method is never invoked in this code fragment.

9. **E.** Both II and III are correct. Option II checks against equality at each level, year, month, day. If the values are unequal, their difference is returned, positive if the first date is greater than the second (meaning later); otherwise, negative. If both the year and the month are the same, the third statement simply returns the difference in the days, positive, negative, or zero. Option III converts the dates to total days and sums their differences. Option I is incorrect. It sums differences in years plus months plus days but fails to convert to a common unit, days.

10. **B.** Abstract classes can implement interfaces, and may include the code to implement the associated methods, so options A and E are incorrect. Nonabstract classes may not have abstract methods, so option D is wrong. Methods with different names intrinsically have different signatures, so there is no restriction such as that proposed by option C. By contrast, option B describes a typical example of method name overloading.

Chapter 5

Lots of Data

Data, for better or worse, have been collected on each one of us almost from the moment of conception and certainly from the moment of our birth. Height, weight, Social Security number, grades in school, paychecks earned, tuition paid, driving record, inoculations, bank account, purchases made with a credit card, subscriptions, and who knows what else has been entered into databases to be accessed by interested parties. That is lots of data.

How do computers process all that data? Surely there isn't a separate variable for each item. In fact, there are many ways to store and retrieve large amounts of data. Data structures, collections of simple data types, group data together under one name. All students taking the AP Computer Science exam are tested on two structured data types, array and `ArrayList`. The AB exam tests several additional data structures covered in Chapters 9 through 11.

THE ARRAY TYPE

Think of an **array** as a one-dimensional row of mailboxes in an apartment building. The mailboxes all have the same street address (the array name), but each has its individual box number (the array index). The mailboxes (array elements) can hold any type, primitives or objects, but the elements must all be the same type. For example, there can be an array of `int`s, `double`s, `boolean`s, `String`s, or any class type.

The size of an array is fixed at the time the array is defined and cannot easily be changed during program execution. If the programmer hasn't defined the array with enough room for all the data, a second, larger, temporary array must be defined and the contents of the original array copied into the second. The original array can then be reassigned to refer to the temporary one. This is an inefficient procedure, and to avoid having to go through it very often, the array size is usually doubled.

This leads to another consideration. Because the size of the array is fixed, a programmer may choose to overestimate the actual number of cells needed. In such a case, a separate variable usually keeps track of the actual number of items stored in the array.

Until an array of `int`s or `double`s is initialized, its elements are zero by default; for objects, the default assignment is `null`.

Since an array is an `Object`, it inherits the methods of the `Object` class, listed in Chapter 3. Arrays can be declared in two ways: general form using the `new` operator and a form that lists each element explicitly.

```
int[] vals1 = new int[50];           //50 elements; 0 by default
int[] vals2 = {2, 4, 6, 8, 10};      // initializer list
String[] words1 = new String[50];    //null by default
String[] words2 = {"good," "better," "best"};
```

Arrays are built into the Java language and include a public field, `length`, which holds the size of the array. The length is determined when the array is declared. An array **element** is accessed through its index. Indices are integers, starting with zero and ending with one less than the array's length. Individual elements can be accessed, but you can also traverse the entire array using a loop variable. The code segments below show how this might be done in two cases: first when the array is known to be full, and then when the array might have unused cells.

```
// precondition:  words1 is full; use words1.length
// postcondition: all words1 elements have been output
for(int index = 0; index < words1.length; index++)
{
  System.out.print(words1[index] + " ");
}

// precondition:  words2 may not be full; use numEls
//                words2 contains numEls elements
// postcondition: all words2 elements have been output
for(int index = 0; index < numEls; index++)
{
  System.out.print(words2[index] + " ");
}
```

Array Processing Tasks

What kinds of things might you be asked to do with an array? The tasks fall into two categories: those that can be done directly with a single line of code and those that are processed in a loop (either a `for` loop or a `while` loop)

- Single operation
  - Get or set the value of an element when the index is provided.
  - Add a new last element provided the array is not full.
  - Remove the last element.
- Loop traversal required (may be partial traversal or may require nested loops)
  - Print all the elements, forward or backward.
  - Search for a particular element (if sorted, a more efficient algorithm may be used).
  - Reverse the elements.
  - Insert an element in an arbitrary position.
  - Remove an element from an arbitrary position.
  - Process all the elements in some way (i.e., summing, sorting).
  - Copy the elements to another array.
  - Remove all duplicate values.
  - Rotate the elements.

Arrays as Parameters

Arrays can be passed as parameters. In fact, we have an example in the signature for `main`.

```
public static void main(String[] args)
```

When an entire array is passed, the method receives a copy of the reference to the array (remember, an array is an object), so individual elements can be changed.

Single elements can also be passed. Suppose a method doSomething requires a String parameter from an array that contains strings. The invoking statement might look like this.

```
doSomething(words1[index]); // sends one String item
```

Copying One Array to Another

Be careful about copying one array to another. If all you do is copy the array name, words2 = words1, you have simply copied the reference so that now both variables reference the same array as in the figure below:

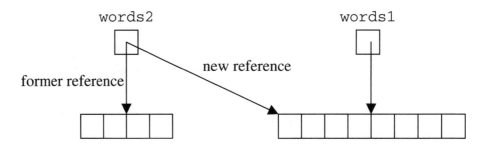

If the intent was to copy all the elements into a second array, significantly more work needs to be done. Let's say you want to double the size of an array named words and you are using an auxiliary array temp to help in the process. Here is the code segment:

```
String[] temp = new String[words.length * 2];
int numEls = words.length;
for(int index = 0; index < numEls; index++)
{
  temp[index] = words[index]; //copy each element
}
words = temp;
// reference to the old words no longer exists;
// memory used for old words will be freed up in
// Java's automatic garbage collection (not tested)
```

ArrayList

Java provides a second way to store large amounts of data in a one-dimensional data structure, the ArrayList class in the java.util package. You can visualize an ArrayList in much the same way you picture an array. The major differences are the fact that while everything stored in an ArrayList must be an Object, the Objects can be different types and that ArrayList, being a class, provides methods for processing the data. These methods mimic the capabilities of an array, but their implementations are invisible to the programmer. Here are the methods included in the AP subset that are tested on the AP exam:

Method Signature	Method Description
`boolean add(Object x)`	Adds x to the end of the list; adjusts the size of the list; returns true
`void add(int index, Object x)`	Inserts x at position index, sliding elements at position index and higher to the right (adds 1 to their indices) and adjusts size
`Object get(int index)`	Returns the element at index
`Object set(int index, Object x)`	Replaces the element at index with x and returns the element formerly at the specified position
`Object remove (int index)`	Removes element from position index, sliding elements at position index + 1 and higher to the left (subtracts 1 from their indices) and adjusts size
`int size()`	Returns the number of elements in the list

We think of the size of an `ArrayList` as dynamic, rather than fixed. An `ArrayList` can grow and shrink during program execution. Of course, unseen by the client, the `ArrayList` methods, `add` and `remove`, are creating temporary arrays, copying values, and renaming back to the original array just as we described the process for arrays. The efficiency level is the same. The advantage is that the methods are provided for you.

The `size` method returns the current number of elements. There is no need for a second variable to keep track of the number of elements actually in the list (`numEls` in the previous example) because the list is always exactly that size.

The fact that an `ArrayList` must contain objects has the following implications:

- Stored elements may be of different types. For example, objects of type `Animal`, `Vegetable`, and `Mineral` could all be stored in the same `ArrayList`. (In truth, since `Object` is a superclass of `Animal`, `Vegetable`, and `Mineral`, in some sense everything in an `ArrayList` does have the same type, namely `Object`.)
- You do need to be concerned about the type returned by an `ArrayList` method. Notice that the return type for `get`, `set`, and `remove` is `Object`. If the returned object is to be used with a particular class, it needs to be cast to that class type.
- Primitives cannot be stored in an `ArrayList`. This is the reason we need the wrapper classes `Integer` and `Double` (see Chapter 3). Notice the methods that allow you to compare two instances of these classes and convert their values to `int` or `double`. You may find it easier to use an array than an `ArrayList` when storing numbers, especially if the task involves computation.

Consider the problem of storing a set of test scores in an `ArrayList`. Assume `readInt` is a method that reads integers.

```
public static ArrayList setScores(int numTests)
{
  ArrayList scores = new ArrayList();
  for(int k = 0; k < numTests; k++)
  {
    int aScore = readInt();
    scores.add(new Integer(aScore));
  }
}
```

Notice in the above code, the loop control variable was not needed in the body of the loop.

Suppose now we want to print the scores.

```
public static void printScores(ArrayList scores)
{
  for(int k = 0; k < scores.size(); k++)
  {
    System.out.println(scores.get(k));
  }
}
```

Finally, we want to print the highest score. This code uses the `Integer` class implementation of `compareTo`, so the scores are downcast to `Integer`.

```
public static Integer getMaxScore(ArrayList scores)
{
  // assume first element is maximum score
  Integer max = (Integer)scores.get(0);
  for(int k = 1; k < scores.size(); k++)
  {
    Integer temp = (Integer)scores.get(k);
    if(temp.compareTo(max) > 0)
    {
      max = temp;
    }
  }
  return max;
}
```

You should be able to code the array processing tasks listed earlier using `ArrayList` as well as an array.

TWO-DIMENSIONAL ARRAYS (AB TOPIC)

Sometimes data are accessed with more than one index, referred to as a multidimensional array. For purposes of the AP exam, we will limit our discussion to the two-dimensional array, or **matrix**. Think of a table with rows and columns, a calendar, a chart showing distances between cities, board games, or a graph of two interacting variables.

To construct a two-dimensional (2-D) array, the number of rows and number of columns must be specified. For example, a table showing the amount of rainfall each hour of the day for a 31-day month might be declared as follows.

```
double[][] table = new double[31][24];
```

You may instantiate a 2-D array (matrix) with an initializer list.

```
int[][] simpleNums = {{0, 1, 2}, {1, 2, 0}};
```

The index operators are always in row, column order, so `table` has 31 rows and 24 columns, and `simpleNums` has 2 rows and 3 columns. Like a one-dimensional (1-D) array, the elements of a 2-D array can be primitives or objects, but all elements must be the same type.

Whereas one-dimensional arrays are traversed with a single loop, two-dimensional arrays use nested loops. Usually the traversal is row-major order (outer loop controls the row; inner, the column), meaning we stay on one row and go through all the columns, then go to the next row and start the columns over. By switching the order of the loops, we can process a matrix in column-major order.

There is no length or size method for a 2-D array, but if you think of the data structure as an array of arrays, you can see how the 1-D array `length` variable is used to determine loop bounds for a 2-D array. Rows may be of different lengths (ragged arrays), but that is not part of the AP subset. For matrices that will be tested, all rows are the same length. We are guaranteed that there is at least one row, so the length of row[0] tells us the number of columns in that, and indeed all, the rows. The following code segment demonstrates printing a matrix:

```
public static void printMatrix(int[][] table)
{
  for(int row = 0; row < table.length; row++)
  {
    for(int col = 0; col < table[0].length; col++)
    {
      System.out.print(table[row][col] + " ");
    }
    System.out.println(); // go to the next line
  }
}
```

Notice how the length of the rows and columns is determined.

Common Tasks for Two-Dimensional Arrays

- Single operation
  - ○ Process a single element whose row and column are given: (`table[r][c]`)
- Single loop
  - ○ Process a single row whose row number is given.
  - ○ Process a single column whose column number is given.
  - ○ For a square matrix, process the **main** or **secondary diagonal**.
  - ○ Find the sum or average of a row or column.
  - ○ Reverse a row or column.
- Nested loops
  - ○ Process the entire matrix in row-major or column-major order.
  - ○ Find the sum or average of the entire matrix.
  - ○ Reverse the entire matrix.
  - ○ Enlarge a matrix by some factor.
  - ○ Search for some value or adjacent values.

The **main diagonal** of a square matrix goes from the upper left-hand corner to the lower right; the **secondary diagonal** goes from the lower left-hand corner to the upper right.

Tip

Here are some common errors:

- Attempting to access an array element outside the array bounds, i.e., index < 0 or index >= the length of the array; throws an `ArrayIndexOutOfBoundsException`
- Off-by-one errors (also called off-by-one-bugs or obob) occur when the loop processes one too many or one too few elements; check loop bounds, problem usually associated with <= or >=
- Sending an entire array as a parameter when all that is called for is a single element

RECURSIVE ALGORITHMS

Recursion may be tested in the context of processing one- or two-dimensional data structures. Common routines for one-dimensional arrays are sorting and searching algorithms, covered in Chapter 6.

Below is an example of a recursive method for printing the elements of an array beginning at position index and continuing to the end of the array. This example illustrates three points:

- Recursion need not process an array in reverse order, as long as there is a stopping mechanism (base case).
- The recursive process may be applied to a portion of an array, again, as long as there are bounds.
- The body of the recursion (the process being performed) may be done before the recursive call, after the recursive call, or both. In the case of printing, this means that the output will be in forward, backward, or forward followed by backward order. (The last option creates a palindrome.)

(Assume someType has a toString method.)

```
//Precondition: 0 <= index < a.length
public static void process(someType[] a, int index)
{
  System.out.print(a[index] + " ");
  if(index == a.length)
    return;
  else process(a, index + 1);
}
```

If the print statement follows the conditional statement, the elements of the array will be printed in reverse order. If both print statements are included, the elements will be printed both in order and in reverse order. The following variation processes the array from index down to 0, rather than going from index to the end of the array.

```
//Precondition: 0 <= index < a.length
public static void process(someType[] a, int index)
{
  System.out.print(a[index] + " ");
  if(index == 0)
    return;
  else process(a, index - 1);
}
```

Many other processes could be substituted for the print statement in the above code.

Solving a maze or erasing objects that take up several continuous cells in a two-dimensional array (AB topic) are examples where recursion can significantly simplify the code. Here is an example in which we are interested in the four primary directions, up, down, left, and right, of a given cell. Assume a method isValid tests to see if a cell is located within the array bounds. Further assume erase is called from the body of nested loops that traverse all or part of a two-dimensional array.

```
public static void erase(boolean[] pic, int row, int col)
{
  if(isValid(row, col))
  {
    if(pic[row][col] == true)       //is part of object
    {
      pic[row][col] = false;        //erase this cell
      erase(pic, row - 1, col);     //check above
      erase(pic, row + 1, col);     //check below
```

```
        erase(pic, row, col - 1);    //check left
        erase(pic, row, col + 1);    //check right
      }
    }
  }
```

The code above is an example of recursion with an empty else. There are two base cases, `row` and `col` represent an invalid location, or `pic[row][col]` is not part of an object to be erased. In either base case there is nothing to be done, and the call to `erase` ends by default.

EXCEPTIONS

In addition to exceptions discussed earlier, these exceptions apply to one- and two-dimensional arrays in particular.

- `IndexOutOfBoundsException` is thrown when there is an attempt to access an element with either a negative index or an index greater than or equal to the size of the array.
- `ArrayIndexOutOfBoundsException` is a subclass of the `IndexOutOfBoundsException` and is simply more specific.
- `NoSuchElementException` may be thrown when attempting to access an out of bounds index for an `ArrayList`; it means there is an attempt to access a nonexistent element.

RAPID REVIEW

The topics in this chapter are one-dimensional and two-dimensional arrays and the `ArrayList` class. These are container classes.

Arrays can hold either primitive types or objects but all **elements,** the data in the array, must be of the same type. The size of an array is set when the array is declared and cannot easily be changed. If an array is not full, a separate variable is needed to hold the current number of valid elements.

An `ArrayList` can grow and shrink dynamically without concern to the programmer. Elements of an `ArrayList` must be objects. Numeric data must be converted into objects through wrapper classes, `Integer` and `Double`, to be stored in an `ArrayList`, and converted back into `int`s and `double`s through the `Integer` and `Double` methods, `parseInt` and `parseDouble`, to perform arithmetic operations.

Arrays and `ArrayLists` can be passed as parameters and return types of methods. `ArrayList` methods are listed in the chapter.

The elements of arrays and `ArrayLists` are usually processed by traversing a single loop (although AB students may wish to use an `Iterator`). Two-dimensional arrays are traversed using nested loops to process each row and column location. These data structures may also be traversed using recursive algorithms. Examples of these techniques are given in the chapter.

Common tasks that might be tested are the following.

One-dimensional data structures processed in a loop (either a `for` loop or a `while` loop)

- Single operation
  - Get or set the value of an element when the index is provided.
  - Add a new last element provided the array is not full.
  - Remove the last element.

- Loop traversal required (may be partial traversal or may require nested loops)
  - ○ Print all the elements, forward or backward.
  - ○ Search for a particular element (if sorted, a more efficient algorithm may be used).
  - ○ Reverse the elements.
  - ○ Insert an element in an arbitrary position.
  - ○ Remove an element from an arbitrary position.
  - ○ Process all the elements in some way (i.e., summing, sorting).
  - ○ Copy the elements to another array.
  - ○ Remove all duplicate values.
  - ○ Rotate the elements.

Two-dimensional arrays:

- Single operation
  - ○ Process a single element whose row and column are given. (`table[r][c]`).
- Single loop
  - ○ Process a single row whose row number is given (single loop).
  - ○ Process a single column whose column number is given (single loop).
  - ○ For a square matrix, process the **main** or **secondary diagonal.**
  - ○ Find the sum or average of a row or column.
  - ○ Reverse a row or column.
- Nested loops
  - ○ Process the entire matrix in row-major or column-major order (nested loops).
  - ○ Find the sum or average of the entire matrix.
  - ○ Reverse the entire matrix.
  - ○ Enlarge a matrix by some factor.
  - ○ Search for some value or adjacent values.

The **main diagonal** of a square matrix goes from the upper left-hand corner to the lower right; the **secondary diagonal** goes from the lower left-hand corner to the upper right.

PRACTICE PROBLEMS

1. Consider the following code segment.

```
ArrayList names = new ArrayList();
names.add("Alex");
names.add("Sam");
names.add(0, "Tasha");
names.add(2, "Randy");
names.add(2, "Sandy")
names.set(2, "Mandy");
names.remove(0);
names.remove(2);
```

What is the content of `names` after this code segment is executed?

A. Tasha, Alex, Mandy
B. Sam, Mandy, Randy
C. Mandy, Sandy, Randy, Sam
D. Alex, Mandy, Randy, Sam
E. `NoSuchElementException` is thrown

2. Consider the incomplete method `rotate` started below. `rotate` is intended to rotate the elements of array, `elems`, one position toward the end. The last element should become the first. You may assume the elements are of type `Object`.

```
public static void rotate(Object[] elems)
{
  Object temp = elems[elems.length - 1];
  < missing code >
  elems[0] = temp;
}
```

Which of the following is the best replacement for < *missing code* >?

A.
```
for(int k = elems.length - 1; k > 0; k--)
{
  elems[k] = elems[k - 1];
}
```

B.
```
for(int k = elems.length - 1; k >= 0; k--)
{
  elems[k - 1] = elems[k];
}
```

C.
```
for(int k = elems.length - 2; k >= 0; k--)
{
  elems[k] = elems[k + 1];
}
```

D.
```
for(int k = 0; k < elems.length - 1; k++)
{
  elems[k] = elems[k + 1];
}
```

E.
```
for(int k = 1; k <= elems.length; k++)
{
  elems[k] = elems[k - 1];
}
```

Questions 3 and 4 refer to the following method:

```
public static int doSomething(int[] a)
{
  int p = 0;
  for(int k = 1; k < a.length; k++)
  {
    if(a[k] < a[p])
      return a[k];
  }
  return a[p];
}
```

3. Which of the following best describes the intended purpose of doSomething?

   A. Return the position of the smallest value.
   B. Return the smallest value in the array.
   C. Return the position of the first value less than the value in the first position.
   D. Return the first value less than the value in the first position.
   E. Return the second smallest value in the array.

4. What conclusion can be drawn if the second return statement in the above code is executed?

   A. The value in the first position is the smallest in the array.
   B. The array is empty.
   C. The last position contains the smallest value.
   D. All elements in the array have the same value.
   E. The length of the array is one.

5. In which situation would an array be preferable to an `ArrayList`?

   A. Different types of objects will be stored.
   B. Frequent access to individual elements is required.
   C. The number of items stored will change frequently.
   D. Data will be frequently added to the end of the list.
   E. Numeric data requiring frequent calculations will be stored.

6. Consider the following method. Assume mat is a nonempty, square array of ints.

```
public static boolean check(int[][] mat)
{
  for(int c = 0; c < mat[0].length; c++)
  {
    for(int r = 0; r < mat.length; r++)
      if(mat[r][c] != mat[c][r])
        return false;
  }
  return true;
}
```

Under what circumstances will `check` return true?

   A. Only the elements on the two diagonals are equal.
   B. The main diagonal splits the array into two halves that are mirror images of each other.
   C. The secondary diagonal splits the array into two halves that are mirror images of each other.
   D. The left half of the array is a mirror image of the right half of the array.
   E. The top half of the array is a mirror image of the bottom half of the array.

7. Assume that `ArrayList container` contains objects of type `Package`, and `Package` has instance variable `weight` with an appropriate accessor. Consider the following method that is intended to return the average weight of all the `Package` objects in `container`.

```
public double weightPerUnit()
{
  double total = 0.0;
  int index = 0;
  while(index < container.size())
  {
    total += (Package)container.get(index).parseDouble();
    index++;
  }
  if(container.size() > 0)
    return total/container.size();
  return 0.0;
}
```

Which of the following is a true statement about method `weightPerUnit`?

   A. The code fails because `container` should have been cast to a `Double`.
   B. The code fails because `total` should be of type `Double`.
   C. The code fails because `parseDouble` is invoked incorrectly.
   D. The code fails whenever `container` is empty.
   E. The code works as intended.

8. Consider a class that contains the following instance variables and method `makeList`:

```
private int[][] table = {{1, 2, 3},
                         {4, 5, 6},
                         {7, 8, 9}};
private int[] list = new int[6];
```

Suppose the following method is executed.

```
public void makeList()
{
  int j = 0;
  for(int k = 0; k < table.length; k++)
  {
    list[j] = table[table[k].length - 1 - j][k];
    list[j + 1] = table[k][table[k].length - 1 - j];
    j += 2;
  }
}
```

Which of the following represents the contents of list after the above code is executed?

A. 1, 1, 5, 5, 9, 9
B. 1, 3, 5, 5, 9, 7
C. 7, 3, 2, 4, 6, 8
D. 9, 3, 5, 5, 1, 7
E. An Exception is thrown before the method completes.

9. Ordering from the Internet often involves adding items to a virtual "shopping cart." As the user looks at items in the catalog, the computer asks, "Do you want to add the item to your shopping cart?" and "Are you ready to check out?" The user can add and remove items until the final steps of the check-out process.

   Suppose we wish to write a program that tests this type of "shopping cart." The following capabilities are to be implemented:

   • For each item the shopping cart must keep track of its catalog number, the quantity ordered, and the price.
   • Items may be added to the cart.
   • Items may be removed from the cart.
   • The total price, along with tax and shipping charges, must be calculated.

   Which of the following is the best representation of the shopping cart?

   A. Create a ShoppingCartItem class with state variables for catalog number, quantity, and price. In the test driver (main) class have a ShoppingCartItem object for each item ordered.
   B. Create a ShoppingCartItem class with state variables for catalog number, quantity, and price. Create a ShoppingCart class with a ShoppingCartItem[] instance variable.
   C. Create a ShoppingCartItem class with state variables for catalog number, quantity, and price. Create a ShoppingCart class with an ArrayList instance variable that contains ShoppingCartItem objects.
   D. Create a ShoppingCart class with an instance variable String[][] shoppingCartItems in which each row contains three columns of String objects, a column for the catalog number, one for quantity, and one for price.
   E. Create a ShoppingCart class with an instance variable double[][] shoppingCartItems in which each row contains three columns of type double, one for the catalog number, one for quantity, and one for price.

10. Consider a program that manages an electronic directory of type `Info` by keeping the entries in `ArrayList directory`. Given the precondition `directory.size() >= n`, which code segment below correctly removes the first n `Info` items from `directory`?

    I. ```
        for(int k = 0; k < n; k++)
        {
          Info item = (Info)directory.get(k);
          item.remove();
        }
        ```
    II. ```
        for(int k = 0; k < n; k++)
          directory.remove(0);
        ```
    III. ```
        int k = 0;
        while(k < n)
        {
          directory.remove(k);
          k++;
        }
        ```

    A. I only
    B. II only
    C. III only
    D. I and III only
    E. None of the segments is correct.

## SOLUTIONS TO THE PRACTICE PROBLEMS

1. **D.** The size of an `ArrayList` changes as items are added or removed. When an element is removed, the next element moves down to take its place. Unless the same position is reexamined, the element that filled in that position is left unexamined. In either case, the size of the array is reduced by one. It is possible to add or remove using the same index in consecutive lines of code.

2. **A.** This answer processes the array in the right direction and has the correct loop bounds. Answers B, C, and E fill the array with the first or last value. Answer D rotates in the wrong direction.

3. **D.** A value, not a position is returned, so answers A and C are incorrect. Answers B and E are incorrect because the entire array may not even be examined.

4. **A.** If the array is traversed from the second element to the last and no value is returned, the test condition failed and there is no element with a value less than the element in position 0.

5. **E.** To avoid involving wrapper classes and calling methods that complicate calculations, it is better to store numbers in an array. Answers A and C are better paired with an `ArrayList`; B and D could work equally well in either data structure.

6. **B.** Drawing a little diagram will show you that elements are being compared across the main diagonal, rather than horizontally or vertically. The fact that the array is being traversed in column-major order makes no difference in this code.

7. **C.** Casting `container.get(index)` to a `Package` object is appropriate, but then `container[index]` should invoke a `Package` accessor method to get the
        ```

weight. It is reasonable to assume that `weight` will be a `double`, not a `Double`. There is no need to use `Double` at all in this scenario. Clearly there are errors in the code, so the method does not work as intended.

8. **E.** By the third iteration, j is four, and thus one of the indices of the `table` matrix will be negative and either an `IndexOutOfBoundsException` or an `ArrayOutOfBoundsException` will be thrown.

9. **C.** The best choice is an `ArrayList` because it allows for easy addition, removal, and processing of all items. Keeping a separate variable for each item, as in answer A, is unreasonable because we don't know how many there will be and all the requirements would involve much repetitious code. The array, answer B, is not a good choice because the number of items is not known in advance. Answers D and E, using a two-dimensional array, are also not good choices because of the same size problem, and they also fail to properly encapsulate the concept of one item.

10. **B.** Each time an element is removed from the front of the list, the rest of the items are moved down one position, so item 1 becomes item 0. Therefore, when removing from the front of the list, the loop must count n times, but the item being removed is always the 0th element. Code segment III removes the kth item, which means it would actually remove every other item, beginning with the first and ending with the item originally in position $2n - 1$. In fact, it is possible since the size of the `ArrayList` keeps shrinking, if n is large, that eventually there may be fewer than n elements remaining in the list and an `ArrayIndexOutOfBounds` exception will be thrown. Code segment I attempts to call remove on an `Info` object, rather than on the `ArrayList`.

Algorithmic Techniques: Searching, Sorting, and Other Common Algorithms

In Chapter 5 we talk about storing "lots of data." What do we want to do with all that data? We may want to process all the items (printing, examining, or modifying each one, summing, averaging). We may want to add or remove a single item at the beginning or end of the collection. We may want to find an individual item, perhaps to examine or change its state, and we don't know where it is, or even if it occurs in the collection. The term for finding an item is *searching*. If data are organized in some way, chances are we can reduce the search time. The term for organizing data is *sorting*. In this chapter we review searching and sorting algorithms, as well as other common algorithms tested on the AP exam.

SEARCHING ALGORITHMS

Sequential search and binary search are the two searching algorithms you must recognize and understand. Sometimes data are stored in a hash table, where in an ideal world they can be found in a single try, but this is a topic that only AB students need to study. Hashing is discussed in Chapter 10.

Sequential Search

Sequential search is the easiest searching algorithm to understand, but it is less efficient than other algorithms. The idea is to loop through the data (not necessarily sorted) comparing each element to the target value until the target is found or the entire list has been searched and it is thus determined the target isn't there. Usually the index of the target within the list (array or `ArrayList`) is returned, although a method could return a copy of the item, if it is a primitive type, or a reference to the object itself. If the target is not present, then a predetermined value such as −1 is typically returned for an index. If the method was returning the item itself, a `null` value is often used. Here is an array implementation of a sequential search:

```
public static int sequentialSearch(int[] a, int target)
{
  for(int k = 0; k < a.length; k++)
  {
    if(a[k] == target)
      return k;
  }
  return -1;
}
```

Here is an implementation using an `ArrayList`. Note that since an `ArrayList` stores `Objects`, we use the `equals` method to check for the target.

```
public static int seqSearch(ArrayList arr, Integer target)
{
  for(int k = 0; k < arr.size(); k++)
  {
    if(arr.get(k).equals(target))
      return k;
  }
  return -1;
}
```

A search might be made on only a segment of an array. In that case, the indices of the endpoints of the search must be passed as parameters along with the array and target value.

In the best case, `target` is the first item in the array; in the worst case, the last; on average, somewhere in the middle. This means that if there are n items in the array, on average half (n/2) of them are examined to find the target. Students taking the A exam should be able to identify the best, worst, and average case efficiency of this algorithm, and others discussed in this chapter. Students taking the AB exam must be able to express these efficiencies mathematically in terms of big-oh (order of magnitude) notation. In the case of sequential search, the average case is n/2 comparisons. When discussing the order of magnitude, however, we ignore constants that appear (in this case the ½) and consider only the part of the expression that has the biggest impact on efficiency—the number of elements, n. We can do this because if n is 5,000 or 50,000, it is the size of n, not the dividing by 2 that causes the biggest difference in efficiency. Notationally, we say that sequential search is O(n) or simply that it is linear. Chapter 9 provides a more complete discussion of order of magnitude, including the use of big-oh notation (an AB-only topic.)

Binary Search

If data are already in sorted (we will assume in ascending) order one can *usually* find a target value faster using a **binary search** algorithm than a sequential search. Binary search is a "divide and conquer" algorithm. That is, the segment of data to be searched is continually reduced by a factor of one-half until either the target is found or the size of the remaining segment is zero, and, therefore, it is determined that the target is not in the collection.

The best case for a binary search occurs when the target is the middle element; the worst case occurs when the target is first, last, or in any of a number of other positions (including adjacent to the middle) because it will require a maximum number of comparisons. Even when that happens, binary search usually beats sequential search. In a rare case the position of the target occurs so early in the array that finding it with a sequential search takes fewer than $\log_2 n$ comparisons; only then is sequential search better.

An array-based version of binary search is shown below:

```
public static int binarySearch(int[] a, int target)
{
  int first = 0;
  int last = a.length - 1;
  int mid;
  while(first <= last)          // segment size > 0
  {
    mid = (first + last)/2;     // locate middle position
    if(a[mid] == target)        // target index found
      return mid;               // return the index
    else if(target < a[mid])    // look in first half
      last = mid - 1;           // move last down
    else                        // look in last half
      first = mid + 1;          // move first up
  }                             // first and last crossed over
  return -1;                    // target not found
}
```

The iterative (loop) approach shown above is one way to code binary search. In this example, the entire array is being searched. If only a segment of the array is to be searched, first and last would be parameters representing the indices where the segment begins and ends.

Binary search may be coded as a recursive algorithm, as shown in the following example. Notice the need for the two additional parameters, first and last. If we are searching the entire array, the initial actual values will be 0 and a.length−1. Notice, also, that a conditional statement replaces the loop (a trademark of recursion).

```
public static int recurBinSearch(int[] a, int target, int first, int last)
{
  if(first > last)
    return -1;                //target not in a
  else
  {
    int mid = (first + last)/2;
    if(a[mid] == target)
      return mid;
    else if(target < a[mid])
        return recurBinSearch(a, target, first, mid-1);
    else return recurBinSearch(a, target, mid+1, last);
  }
}
```

Because the binary search algorithm is based on repeatedly reducing the remaining segment of the array by half, the order of magnitude is $\log_2 n$. Once again, because the term with the biggest impact is n, we ignore the base and simply write log n.

ITERATIVE SORTING ALGORITHMS

Binary search requires that elements by sorted. Sorting means arranging a set of data in ascending (or sometimes descending) order. Selection sort and Insertion sort are members of a category of sorts that uses nested loops. These sorts are less efficient than other sorting algorithms but are a good starting point for students because they are easy to understand.

Selection Sort

The **Selection sort** algorithm works by scanning the entire array, selecting the smallest value, and swapping that value with the first element (the one in position 0). It then scans the array starting at position 1, looking for the second smallest value, and swaps that one with the element in position 1. The process continues in this manner, always scanning a segment that is one element closer to the end of the array. The last element doesn't need to be checked. It will be the only value left, the largest value in the array (or the smallest if the array is sorted in descending, rather than ascending, order).

```java
public static void selectionSort(int[] a)
{
  for(int j = 0; j < a.length - 1; j++)
  {
    int minPos = j;
    for(int k = j + 1; k < a.length; k++)
    {
      if(a[k] < a[minPos])
        minPos = k;              // save the position
    }
    int temp = a[j];             // Swap the starting element
    a[j] = a[minPos];            // with the smallest one
    a[minPos] = temp;
  }
}
```

How easy is it to modify the code to sort objects? The objects to be sorted must be objects of a class that implements the `Comparable` interface; otherwise they can't be ordered because we have no notion of when one object comes before another. (Note that this applies to *any* sorting algorithm, not just Selection sort.)

```java
public static void selectionSort(Comparable[] a)
{
  for(int j = 0; j < a.length - 1; j++)
  {
    int minPos = j;
    for(int k = j + 1; k < a.length; k++)
    {
      if(a[k].compareTo(a[minPos]) < 0)
        minPos = k;
    }
    Object temp = a[j];          // Swap the starting element
    a[j] = a[minPos];            // with the smallest one
    a[minPos] = temp;
  }
}
```

Selection sort performs the same amount of work regardless of the order of the data. Even if the data are already in order, the algorithm will still blindly go through all the steps. In terms of efficiency, Selection sort is known as a quadratic sort. As the elements are scanned in the nested loops, the number of comparisons is $n - 1$, then $n - 2, n - 3$, and so on down to 1. The total number of comparisons is $(n - 1) + (n - 2) + (n - 3) \ldots + 2 + 1 = (n^2 - n)/2$. The term that most strongly influences the result of evaluation of this expression is n^2, categorizing the algorithm as "n-squared," or "quadratic."

Most sorting algorithms can be understood in terms of a fairly simple invariant, a statement about the algorithm that is always true. In this case, the invariant is that elements 0 through $k - 1$ are the k smallest elements in the array and are in the correct order. Elements k through $n - 1$ are in no particular order.

Insertion Sort

Insertion sort is also a quadratic sort. The algorithm works by making a single pass through the array (the outer loop). As each new element is examined, an inner loop traverses backward from the current position through the elements already examined to insert the current item into its correct position with respect to all items already considered. The item in position 0 is trivially in order with respect to itself, so the outer loop starts at index 1.

```
public static void insertionSort(int[] a)
{
  for(int j = 1; j < a.length; j++)
  {
    int k = j;
    int temp = a[j];
    while(k > 0 && temp < a[k - 1])
    {
      a[k] = a[k - 1];
      k--;
    }
    a[k] = temp;
  }
}
```

The algorithm uses nested loops, but the outer loop moves forward and the inner loop moves backward only as far as necessary to insert the current item. This explains why the inner loop is a while loop. (A for loop can be used, but you would have to include a break statement or a compound test in the for statement.) The inner loop must test two conditions: Will the index continue to be in range? And are we still looking for the location where the item should be inserted? The body of the loop shifts each element over to make room for the current item and finally, when the while loop terminates, places that item into the correct location.

The best case for Insertion sort occurs if the data are already in ascending order. In that event, the body of the inner loop is never executed. In this case n - 1 comparisons will be made by the algorithm. The worst case happens if the data are in exactly opposite order. On average, about n² comparisons will be made.

The invariant for Insertion sort is that elements 0 through j - 1 are in ascending order with respect to each other and elements j through n - 1 are unexamined.

RECURSIVE SORTING ALGORITHMS

Merge sort and Quicksort (AB only) are recursive algorithms. Both use the "divide and conquer" concept discussed in the context of binary search. As is the case with searching algorithms, a divide and conquer strategy tends to lead to a more efficient algorithm.

Merge Sort

Merge sort works by dividing the array in half, sorting the left side into a second array, sorting the right side into the second array, and then merging the two sorted halves back into the original array. The process is repeated recursively when the array is split until a subarray contains a single value. Merging works its way back up to the original.

0	1	2	3	4	5	6	7
8	5	7	3	0	1	9	4

8	5	7	3	0	1	9	4

8	5	7	3	0	1	9	4

8	5	7	3	0	1	9	4

5	8		3	7		0	1		4	9

3	5	7	8		0	1	4	9

0	1	3	4	5	7	8	9

The code for Merge sort is in two parts, recursively splitting the array in half and then merging the halves. Because of the recursion, parameters must include the endpoints of the segment to be sorted. The initial call will send 0 and a.length.

```java
// split the array into two halves until the size <= 1
public static void mergeSort(int[] a, int first, int last)
{
  int mid = (first + last)/2;
  mergeSort(a, first, mid);
  mergeSort(a, mid + 1, last);
  merge(a, first, mid, last);
}

// merge two halves of an array
public static void merge(int[] a, int first, int mid, int last)
{
  int[] temp = new int(last - first + 1); //auxiliary
  int index1 = first;          //traverse first half
  int index2 = mid + 1;        //traverse second half
  int index3 = 0;              //traverse auxiliary array

  // loop as long as both arrays have values to merge
  while(index1 <= mid && index2 <= last)
  {
    if(a[index1] < a[index2])
    {
      temp[index3] = a[index1];
      index1++;
    }
    else
    {
      temp[index3] = a[index2];
      index2++;
    }
    index3++;
  }

  // empty the values from the remaining array into temp
  while(index1 <= mid)
  {
    temp[index3] = a[index1];
    index1++;
    index3++;
  }
  while(index2 <= last)
  {
    temp[index3] = a[index2];
    index2++;
    index3++;
  }

  // copy the merged segment into a
  for(index3 = 0; index3 < temp.length; index3++)
  {
    a[start + index3] = temp[index3];
  }
}
```

As with Selection sort, Merge sort performs the same operations regardless of the original order of the data. Thus, there is no specific best or worst case for this version of Merge sort. The average case is n items subdivided $\log_2 n$ times, yielding (for AB students) $O(n \log n)$.

A disadvantage of Merge sort is the need for a second, temporary array that doubles the amount of memory used. For a very large set of data, this could be significant, especially if the individual data items are complex.

Invariants are generally associated with loops, and thus it is difficult to phrase an invariant for Merge sort. Instead, we will simply say that with each recursive call the segment to be examined is half the size of the previous level; at the end of each recursive call a sorted segment is returned.

Quicksort (AB topic)

Quicksort works by partitioning the array into two parts based on a splitting or "pivot" value. With each recursive partitioning, all elements less than the pivot value end up to the pivot's left, and all elements greater than or equal to the pivot value are to its right. There are two parts to the Quicksort algorithm: a call to a partition routine and recursive calls to the sort itself on the left and right segments of the array. Here is one implementation of Quicksort:

```
public static void quickSort(int[] a, int first, int last)
{
  if(first >= last)
    return;
  int pivot = partition(a, first, last);
  quickSort(a, first, pivot);
  quickSort(a, pivot + 1, last);
}

public static int partition(int[] a, int first, int last)
{
  int pivotVal = a[first];      //element in left-most position
  int left = first - 1;         //artificial starting values;
                                //while loop adjusts

  int right = last + 1;
  while(left < right)
  {
    left++;
    while(a[left] < pivotVal)
      left++;                   //move left toward right

    right--;
    while(a[right] > pivotVal)
      right--;                  //move right toward left

    if(left < right)            //swap values to opposite side
    {
      int temp = a[left];
      a[left] = a[right];
      a[right] = temp;
    }
  }
  //left and right crossed over
  return right;                 //pivot value is in position right
}
```

The element chosen as the *pivot value* could be anywhere in the array. Common choices for the pivot value include the first, last, or middle element of the array; the code above uses the first element. In a different implementation of Quicksort, after the values are swapped to the correct side, the splitting value is swapped into its correct location in the array and never moves again.

The best case for this version of Quicksort occurs when the data are arranged randomly; in such a case, Quicksort makes about $n*\log_2 n$ comparisons. The worst case is when the array is already in order or in reverse order. In that case, the array is repeatedly partitioned into two segments, a segment of size 1 and a segment containing all the rest of the array, rendering the recursive calls no better than a quadratic algorithm. (In fact, in such a circumstance, Quicksort behaves almost exactly like Selection sort.) Alternative versions of Quicksort will have slightly different best and worst cases.

The invariant observation for Quicksort is: elements 0 through k are less than the splitting (pivot) value; elements k + 1 through the n - 1 are greater than or equal to the splitting value.

Heapsort (AB topic)

The Heapsort algorithm is based on trees and the "heap property." This sorting algorithm is discussed in Chapter 12.

> **Tip**
>
> Keep in mind, sorting is *always* less efficient than searching. If your program doesn't need to search very often, it may be better to just use a sequential search.

OTHER COMMONLY TESTED ALGORITHMS

There are other algorithms with which it is expected that an AP student is familiar. Experience has shown that students familiar with the following algorithms will be better prepared for the examination.

Maximum or Minimum of Three Numbers

This simple little problem can be solved multiple ways. One possible solution is shown below. (Assume all variables have been properly defined.)

```
if(a < b)
  min = a;
else
  min = b;
if(c < min)
  min = c;
```

Traversing, Inserting, Removing, Processing

Algorithms specific to arrays are listed in Chapter 5. Those specific to other data structures are discussed in later chapters. In general, you should be able to do the following:

- Traverse a data structure in whatever manner is most appropriate for that structure.
- Add an element, in any appropriate location.
- Find an element or determine it isn't there.
- Exchange (or swap) two elements.
- Remove an element (possibly based upon its location; possibly after a search).
- Process all elements or a subgroup of the elements.

Recursive Algorithms

Students taking the A exam are not expected to write recursive code but must be able to trace recursive routines (in multiple-choice questions). During an exam, tracing may be time-consuming. Try to look for the overall picture. You may be able to "see" what is happening without doing a complete trace by examining how the parameters change and analyzing the body of the method in general terms. For example, what is returned by the following recursive method?

```
// precondition: num >= 0
public static int mystery(int num)
{
  if(num < 10)
    return 1;
  else
    return 1 + mystery(num/10);
}
```

This is a very short method, so you might find tracing it with some integer value an easy way to discover what it does. But if you take a minute to analyze the code, you may not need to trace. It seems to make repeated calls on the result of dividing the number by 10 until the parameter is a single digit number. The base case returns 1, and at each level, as we return, another 1 is added. This algorithm is counting something. What it is counting is the number of digits in the original integer parameter. It takes practice to be able to understand an algorithm by analyzing the code, but if you can do that, it may save some time for you during the exam and it will probably help you write your own recursive methods.

Some of the data structures that an AB student might find on the exam are expressed recursively. In such cases, it may be appropriate to use recursive algorithms to search or update such structures. For binary trees (AB students only), it may be almost impossible to code a solution nonrecursively; by contrast, the recursive solution is elegantly simple. In all cases, it is important to remember that recursive algorithms require two cases:

- A test that separates a base case from the general (recursive) case.
- A recursive call that diminishes the size of the problem in some manner.

In the case of binary search, the test was the comparison of the value to the middle element, and the recursive call reduced the number of remaining elements to be searched by a factor of 2. For Merge sort, the test was based upon the size of the remaining list, and the recursive call again reduced the number of elements to sort by a factor of 2. (In the case of binary trees—AB students only—the recursive call is typically made on one, or both, of the subtrees of a given node.)

Organizing Data, Choosing a Data Structure

It is common for AP students to be asked to select the best choice of algorithm or data structure to meet specific criteria. Typical criteria include:

- Being able to output all the data
- Being able to search quickly for a specific item
- Being able to add or remove items frequently

In all cases, the first question that should be asked is whether or not the given solution will return the correct answer. If it will, then the efficiency of the solution is the next item to consider. If two solutions are equally good at this point, then the simpler (if the difference is obvious) is preferred.

RAPID REVIEW

This chapter is about *algorithms,* step-by-step processes for solving problems. These processes may be classified into categories. Two such categories are *searching,* finding an item in a collection, and *sorting,* organizing data in such a way that it will be easier to search the data for a desired item.

Students taking the A exam are expected to know the two searching and three of the four sorting algorithms described below.

Sequential search: An algorithm that loops through the data from beginning to end, or until the target item is found. Data need not be in any particular order. Sequential search looks at each item, one by one. AB students need to know that it is an O(n) algorithm, where n is the number of items to be searched.

Binary search: An algorithm that works by successively eliminating half the data to be searched. The precondition for binary search is that the data are ordered (ascending or descending). Note that this implies that the items to be searched are comparable. Binary search can be coded iteratively or recursively. AB students should know that binary search is an O(log n) algorithm.

In order to implement binary search (and other more specialized algorithms), data must be sorted. All students are expected to be familiar with the following three sorting algorithms:

Selection sort: A sorting algorithm that works by repeatedly selecting the next smallest (or largest) value and swapping it with the item in the first, then the second, then the third, and so on position in the data list. The algorithm is iterative and uses nested loops. There is no best or worst case; Selection sort does the same amount of work regardless of the original arrangement of the data. AB students must be able to express the efficiency of algorithms in big-oh (order of magnitude) notation. For example, Selection sort runs in O(n^2) time. This is discussed in Chapter 9.

Insertion sort: A sorting algorithm that works by traversing the array from left to right; with each new element, a second loop traverses backward until it inserts this element in its correct order with respect to the data already examined. AB students should know that the best, worst, and average running times are O(n), O(n^2), and O(n^2), respectively.

Merge sort: A recursive sorting algorithm that works by repeatedly dividing the array in half, then in half again, etc., until the subarrays are of size 1; then the subarrays are merged in ascending (or descending) order until all are merged back together. Merge sort typically uses an auxiliary array, thus doubling the amount of memory required. AB students should know that the running time of this algorithm is O(n*log n).

In addition to the three sorts listed above, AB students are also responsible for knowing Quicksort and Heapsort. The latter is discussed in Chapter 12.

Quicksort: A recursive sorting algorithm that works by selecting a splitting value, often called a pivot point, and separating the array into two sides. The left side contains all values less than the splitting value; the right side, all values greater than or equal to the splitting value. The process is applied recursively to each side and continues until the two sides, or segments, are of size one, at which time the array is sorted. The arrangement of the data and the choice of the pivot are critical factors. The more random the distribution and the closer the pivot is to the mean data value, the better Quicksort will work. AB students should know that the best, worst, and average running times are O(n log n), O(n^2), and O(n log n), respectively.

Searching and sorting algorithms are commonly tested on the AP Computer Science exam, but other algorithms are tested as well. You will find information about other categories of algorithms in this chapter and algorithms specific to different data structures in chapters devoted to those data structures.

PRACTICE PROBLEMS

1. For which set of data will a sequential search perform more efficiently than a binary search, if the value being searched for is 5?

   A. {4, 5, 6, 8, 9, 11}
   B. {1, 2, 4, 5, 7, 10}
   C. {2, 4, 6, 8, 10, 12}
   D. {1, 2, 3, 4, 5, 6}
   E. {0, 1, 2, 3, 4, 5}

2. For which set of data will Selection sort require the fewest comparisons?

   A. {1, 2, 3, 4, 5}
   B. {5, 4, 3, 2, 1}
   C. {5, 1, 2, 3, 4}
   D. {1, 3, 5, 4, 2}
   E. Data sets A through D require the same number of comparisons.

3. An array containing the following integers is to be processed using a searching or sorting algorithm: {12, 6, −5, 23, 15, −1, 7}

   After two iterations of the process, the array looks like this:
   {−5, 6, 12, 23, 15, −1, 7}

   Which of the following algorithms is being applied?

   A. Insertion sort
   B. Selection sort
   C. Merge sort
   D. Sequential search
   E. Binary search

Questions 4 and 5 refer to the following recursive method:

```
public static int mystery(int n, int r)
{
  int val = r;
  if(n != 0)
  {
    r = (r*10) + (n%10);
    val = mystery(n/10, r);
  }
  return val;
}
```

4. What value is returned by the call mystery(1234, 0)?

   A. 1234
   B. 4321
   C. 8642
   D. 12340
   E. 4

5. How many recursive calls, including the first, are made to `mystery` by the call `mystery(1234, 0)`?

    A. 1
    B. 2
    C. 4
    D. 5
    E. 6

Questions 6 and 7 refer to the incomplete binary search algorithm given below:

```
// postcondition:   returns index where keyVal is found
//                  returns -1 if keyVal not found
public static int binSearch(Comparable[] elems, Comparable keyVal)
{
  if(elems.length == 0)
    return -1;
  int low = 0;
  int high = elems.length - 1;
  int mid;
  while(<missing code 1>)
  {
    mid = (low + high)/2;
    if(<missing code 2>)
      low = mid + 1;
    else
      high = mid;
  }
  if(elems[low].compareTo(keyVal) == 0)
    return low;
  return -1;
}
```

6. Which of the following should replace *<missing code 1>* and *<missing code 2>* in the code above so that `binSearch` works as intended?

<missing code 1>	*<missing code 2>*
A. `low < high`	`elems[mid].compareTo(keyVal) < 0`
B. `low > high`	`elems[mid].compareTo(keyVal) != 0`
C. `low < mid`	`elems[low].compareTo(keyVal) < 0`
D. `high > mid`	`elems[high].compareTo(keyVal) > 0`
E. `(high - low) > 0`	`elems[high - low].compareTo(keyVal) != 0`

7. In the binary search code above, what would be the consequences of modifying the line

```
    low = mid + 1;
```
    to
```
    low = mid; ?
```

    A. The correct index is returned only if the key value is located in the middle of the list.
    B. The correct index is returned only if the key value is the first or last element.
    C. An infinite loop is generated.
    D. The loop is executed exactly once.
    E. The code continues to return the correct value in all cases.

8. Consider the following method that is intended to return the maximum value in an array of integers:

```
public static int findMax(int[] nums)
{
  int max = 0;
  int index = 1;
  while(index < nums.length)
  {
    if(nums[index] > nums[max]);
      return nums[index];
    else
      index++;
  }
  return nums[0];
}
```

If nums contains more than two elements, findMax does not always work as intended. Which of the following best describes a condition under which findMax fails to return the correct value?

A. All elements of the array are the same value.
B. The second value is the maximum.
C. The first value is the second largest in the array.
D. The values in the array are in ascending order.
E. The values in the array are in descending order.

9. If sum is initialized to 0 and n is the same value for all five code fragments, which code fragment results in the greatest value in sum?

A.
```
for(int j = 0; j < n; j++)
    sum++;
for(int k = 0; k < n; k++)
    sum++;
```

B.
```
for(int j = 0; j < n; j++)
    for(int k = 0, k < n; k++)
        sum++;
```

C.
```
for(int j = 0; j < n; j += 2)
    sum++;
```

D.
```
for(int j = 0; j < n; j *= 2)
    sum++;
```

E.
```
for(int j = 0; j < n; j++)
    for(int k = 0; k < j; k++)
        sum++;
```

10. (AB only) Of the following, which best describes the case in which Quicksort is least efficient?

A. The data are already in the correct order.
B. The data are in exactly reverse order.
C. The data are in random order.
D. The data are either in the correct order or in exactly reverse order.
E. Quicksort is equally efficient, regardless of the arrangement of the data.

SOLUTIONS TO THE PRACTICE PROBLEMS

1. **A.** With binary search on six items, the total number of comparisons will be at most three. Sequential search will take at least that many comparisons to find the value 5 in all of the lists except the first. In that case, sequential search will find the item in two steps while binary search will take three steps.

2. **E.** Selection sort has no best or worst case. Even if the data are already in order, the algorithm will still make the same number of comparisons.

3. **A.** After two passes with Insertion sort, the first three values are in order with respect to each other. The rest of the data are unexamined. If this had been Selection sort, –1 and 12 would have been swapped and –5 and 6 would have been swapped. For Merge sort you can't really refer to "two iterations" but, after two recursive calls, the data would have been broken down into groups of two. After one more call, merging would begin to occur and you would see the data rearranged by pairs, then in groups of four, and then the entire set of data. Answers D and E are incorrect because searching algorithms do not rearrange data.

4. **B.** Method `mystery` reverses the digits of its integer parameter. The old result of the remainder when the number is divided by 10 is next multiplied by 10, moving it over one place in terms of place value; the next remainder is added; then the integer result of dividing by 10 is processed.

5. **D.** There is the initial call and a recursive call each time the number is divided by 10 (or once for each digit).

6. **A.** This version of binary search uses a two-way comparison rather than the more common three-way comparison demonstrated in this chapter. The two-way algorithm does not directly compare the key (or target) value to the value in the middle location. When `high` is reassigned it changes to `mid`, not `mid - 1`. The loop terminates when `low` and `high` point to the same location (the value is found) or when `low` and `high` cross over (the key value is not in the list).

7. **C.** A trace of this code reveals that when the key value is finally located, `low` doesn't have the opportunity to become equal to `high`. The `while` loop is never exited, and `mid` is repeatedly assigned the same value, thus, generating an infinite loop.

8. **D.** As soon as the algorithm finds one element whose value is greater than the value stored in location 0, that value is returned. It does not continue to search the array for a larger value. If the elements are in ascending order and there are at least three different integers, an incorrect value will be returned.

9. **B.** `sum` is actually counting the number of passes through the loop(s). You might expect that nested loops will generate the largest count, and in this case that is correct, although it may take a little tracing to determine that the count for B is greater than for E. Fragment D fails to terminate; `sum` remains 0, and `j` is never incremented so it is always less than `n`.

10. **D.** Quicksort works best when the original data are randomly distributed. If the data are in order, either ascending or descending, the two segments that Quicksort partitions the data into are inefficient—one segment is of size one, and the other has all the rest of the elements.

Chapter 7

Marine Biology Simulation Case Study

GENERAL OBSERVATIONS

! If you were enrolled in a Computer Science I course in college, you might be expected to write a very large program as a culminating project. An alternative to that requirement is to provide a large body of code and to be expected to be able to use, modify, and add to that code. Along with the code there is a narrative, a story that provides a background for developing the code, as well as analysis questions and lab exercises. That is the basic idea of a case study in computer science.

The Marine Biology Simulation (MBS) case study, however, is much more than text and code. First, there is the overall design picture. Your textbook or teacher has probably taught you about the **design cycle:** analysis, design, implementation, and testing. A key concept here is *cycle*. The process is iterative. In reviewing the case study, notice the broad picture, how the design cycle is illustrated throughout the case study.

Next consider the case study as a **code model.** Questions on the AP exam are likely to be written in a similar style, and you should imitate that style when writing your answers to free-response questions. If you practice this, you will be better prepared to write straightforward, readable answers to exam questions.

Between five and ten of the forty multiple-choice and one of the four free-response questions will be based upon the case study. You must acquire a thorough understanding of the classes and interfaces and how they work together prior to exam day. Be attentive to the methods in the classes, how to invoke a method of a particular class, the return types, and inheritance and polymorphism with respect to the case study.

Be sure to make use of the case study **object diagrams.** You can download the full set of object diagrams by going to http://max.cs.kzoo.edu/~abrady/[1] and following the AP Computer Science Teaching Resources link. These diagrams will not be provided with the exam, nor will you be permitted to bring copies to the exam, but they provide

---

[1]Alyce Brady of the Department of Computer Science at Kalamazoo College, Kalamazoo, Michigan, author of the Marine Biology Simulation case study, and developer of the object diagrams, maintains this Web site. In addition to the object diagrams, Dr. Brady's site provides a wide range of helpful information.

a very helpful visual reference as you prepare. The diagrams show instance variables; public, private, and protected methods; and the interactions within and between classes.

Each object, or class, is represented by a rectangle. Public methods are shown as smaller rectangles that extend across the outside boundary of the object; private methods are shown as rectangles entirely within the object boundary. Arrows indicate that one method invokes another, which in turn may invoke another, and so on. These arrows illustrate the interaction between classes, class responsibilities, and the use of helper methods within a class. (For more information about these diagrams and their uses, as well as an abundance of other material related to the case study, visit the site itself.)

All students are tested on the first four chapters of the case study. Only students taking the AB exam are tested on Chapter 5. The dynamic Fish class from Chapter 3, fish that breed and die, is the version of the Fish class tested on both the A and AB exams.

An appendix booklet containing the following is provided with the examination:

- A Java Quick Reference
- Source code for the visible classes
- Summary class documentation for the Environment interface and black box classes
- Source code for the Environment implementations (AB only)
- A Java MBS Quick Reference specific to the A or AB exam
- An index for quickly locating specific methods

You can download this booklet from http://www.collegeboard.com/student/testing/ap/compsci_a/case.html. Follow the links to the AP Computer Science Home Page, Examination Information, Reference Materials for the Computer Science A Examination (pdf/391KB). Print a copy and use it as a reference whenever you are working on the case study or taking a quiz or exam. You should not be seeing this booklet for the first time on the day you actually take the test. Know where to find frequently used methods, the interface or class each one belongs to, what type of parameters are expected, and the type being returned.

Questions about the Marine Biology Simulation may involve but are not limited to the following types:

- Add new functionality (a new method) to a class.
- Design a new class (possibly more than one class).
  - ○ Determine appropriate instance variables.
  - ○ Implement a constructor.
  - ○ Implement one or more methods for the new class.
  - ○ Design test cases or a test driver.
- Reimplement a method using a new design.
- Determine a set of test data to test code modifications or new code.
- Determine the efficiency (big-oh for AB students) of an implementation.

As with the rest of this book, the material in this chapter is not enough, on its own, to teach you the case study. Rather, it will draw your attention to many of the important aspects of the code and the narrative. It is assumed that you have already read the narrative and executed the program.

VISIBLE CLASSES (A AND AB EXAMS)

The visible classes are Simulation, Fish, DarterFish, and SlowFish.

DarterFish and SlowFish illustrate properties of inheritance and polymorphism. These classes also provide a model for designing new subclasses. Be careful, though, not to blindly copy code but to think about how you can adapt code to represent the distinct properties of the subclass or method in question.

The `Simulation` Class

The `Simulation` class is straightforward. It contains only two instance variables, `theEnv` and `theDisplay`, a single constructor, and a single method, `step`, which processes each fish in the environment through one step of the simulation.

`step` invokes the `Environment`'s `allObjects` method from which it receives an array of `Locatable` objects. The array is named `theFishes`, but don't be fooled by the name. It contains not fish, but generic `Locatable` objects. Inside the loop each `Locatable` object is cast to a `Fish`. This is necessary because only a `Fish` knows how to act. A `Fish` is a `Locatable`, but a `Locatable` is not necessarily a `Fish`. Remember, we're talking about an inheritance hierarchy, and superclasses don't know about subclasses.

Simulation.java

```
private Environment theEnv;
private EnvDisplay theDisplay;
```

```
// constructs an object for a particular environment
// the constructor shows the initial display of the Environment
public Simulation(Environment env, EnvDisplay display)
```

```
// asks the Environment for a list of all the Fish and takes each fish through
// a single time step in the simulation
public void step()
{
  // local variable for the array of Locatable objects returned by allObjects
  Locatable[] theFishes = theEnv.allObjects();
  // inside for loop each Locatable object is cast to a Fish and told to act
      . . . ((Fish) theFishes[index]).act();
}
```

The `Fish` Class

`Fish` objects, of course, are central to the Marine Biology Simulation. A fish knows its identification number, location, direction, and color. It also has a probability of breeding and a probability of dying although these last two pieces of data are not shared with other objects.

Constructors

The `Fish` class contains three constructors. Each constructor is passed a reference to the environment and a location for the `Fish` that is about to be constructed. In addition the constructor may be passed the fish's initial direction and color. If the direction or color is not specified, the `Fish` constructor selects random `Direction` and `Color` values by anonymously constructing them within the parameter list of a call to the private helper method `initialize`. The purpose of the `initialize` method is to avoid duplication of code needed to initialize the instance variables.

Accessors

Accessor methods are provided for most of the instance variables. For example, the `id` method returns `myId`, and the `location` method returns `myLoc`. Be careful when you read or write these variables. In several cases the name of the class and the name of the accessor method are the same except for the first letter. For example,

```
public Environment environment()
```

returns a reference to the Environment where the Fish is located. Pay attention to capitalization so that you are aware of whether the text is talking about the class or the method that accesses the class. Pay even closer attention when writing code in the free-response section. Don't let sloppy thinking or poor handwriting cause you to receive a deduction!

Modifiers

There is one modifier (or mutator) method, act, in the Fish class. In the body of act a fish may attempt to breed or move. Whether successful or not at breeding or moving, there is a chance the fish may die, but it always tries to breed or move first.

Protected Methods

All other methods of the Fish class are internal helper methods, necessary to act, and are declared protected. That means these methods are accessible to Fish and sub-classes of Fish, but not to other classes.

The act method is broken down into three lower-level helper methods—breed, move, and die. These methods are examined below.

breed Method

A fish has a one in seven probability of breeding (initialized in the constructor). breed generates a random double. If the value of this double is less than probOfBreeding, the fish will breed into each valid (in the grid and empty) location around it (north, south, east, west), regardless of the direction the fish is facing.

A fish breeds by

1. Calling helper method emptyNeighbors that returns an ArrayList (size not known in advance), emptyNbrs, of valid, empty locations
2. Checking the size of emptyNbrs
   a. if 0, there are no empty neighboring locations so the fish does not breed
   b. if greater than 0, the fish can breed into each location in emptyNbrs
3. Calling helper method generateChild that constructs a new fish in each location in emptyNbrs

If a fish breeds, it fills all empty locations around it and, therefore, cannot move.

move Method

If a fish fails to breed, then it may move. To accomplish a move, the fish

1. Calls a helper method nextLocation
   a. nextLocation asks emptyNeighbors (reuse of code) for a list of all valid, empty, neighboring locations
      i. If the list is not empty

(1) Removes the location directly behind the fish (if in the list)

(2) Randomly selects one of the remaining locations

  b. Returns

    i. An adjacent location, other than the current one, if the fish is able to move

    ii. The fish's current location if there is no adjacent location to which the fish can move

2. If the fish moves, it updates itself and the environment (maintains consistency)

  a. Saves the old location in variable `oldLoc`

  b. Calls helper method `changeLocation`

    i. Adjusts `myLoc` to the new location

    ii. Tells the environment to `recordMove`

  c. Calls helper method `changeDirection`

    i. Adjusts `myDir` to the direction taken to make the move

Note: You may wonder why the `Fish` methods often invoke accessor methods rather than use instance variables directly (`environment` for `theEnv`, `location` for `myLoc`). This allows subclasses (`DarterFish`, `SlowFish`, and others you create) to inherit and use these methods. Subclasses cannot access instance variables of a superclass directly.

`die` Method

After a fish breeds, moves, or, perhaps, does neither, it still may die. `act` generates a random `double` and tests to see if it is less than the one in five chance of dying that `probOfDying` is initialized to in the `Fish` constructor. The `die` method works by simply telling the environment to `remove(this)`, the current fish.

Class Variable

Class variables are specified by the keyword `static`. There is one occurrence of a class variable, shared by all instances of a class. `nextAvailableID` is a class variable. `nextAvailableID` is initialized to 1 when the first fish is constructed, each new fish is assigned its ID, and then `nextAvailableID` is incremented by one in the constructor, ready to be assigned to the next new fish. Other than in the context of the case study, class variables will not be tested.

Here is an overview of the `Fish` class.

Fish.java

```
// class variable shared by all Fish objects so that each has a unique ID.
private static int nextAvailableID = 1;
// instance variables
private Environment theEnv;        // each fish has a unique reference to the
                                   // environment.
private int myId;                  // each of the following is unique to this Fish.
private Location myLoc;
private Direction myDir;
private Color myColor;
private double probOfBreeding;
private double probOfDying;
```

```
// There are three constructors with the following headings.
public Fish(Environment env, Location loc) {...}
public Fish(Environment env, Location loc, Direction dir) {...}
public Fish(Environment env, Location loc, Direction dir, Color col) {...}
```

```
// Helper method called from all three constructors to initialize instance
// variables.
// The direction is randomly generated if not specified from data by calling
// initialize with parameter env.randomDirection().
```

```
// The color is randomly generated if not specified from data by calling the
// protected method randomColor in the Fish class.
private void initialize(Environment env, Location loc, Direction dir, Color col)
```

```
// This method to generate a random color is protected, meaning it can be used by
// subclasses of Fish. It creates a local Random object randNumGen and calls the
// method getInstance three times to generate red, green, and blue values.
protected Color randomColor() {...}
```

```
// Accessor methods
// Each returns the unique instance value stored for this Fish.
// Be careful about these identifiers. While the names are logical, you must
// be alert when reading and writing code to note whether the identifier
// begins with a capital letter and therefore names a class or a lowercase
// letter and names a method.
public int id()
public Environment environment()
public Color color()
public Location location()
public Direction direction()
public boolean isInEnv()
public String toString()
```

```
// Modifier method
// act calls helper methods breed and move, which, in turn, call other helpers;
// whether a fish breeds or moves, it may then die.
public void act()
```

```
// All other methods are internal helper methods and are protected.
protected boolean breed()
protected void generateChild(Location loc)
protected void move()
protected Location nextLocation()
protected ArrayList emptyNeighbors()
protected void changeLocation(Location newLoc)
protected void changeDirection(Direction newDir)
protected void die()
```

Note: Keep in mind that the Fish class implements Locatable. Therefore, it *must* include a location method, the accessor method mentioned above. By contrast, there is no location method in the Location class, so we know Location does *not* implement Locatable. It may be difficult to keep these distinctions straight. Just remember, a Fish IS-A Locatable object and HAS-A Location.

VISIBLE SUBCLASSES

 Two subclasses of Fish, DarterFish and SlowFish, are included in the case study. Each implements a variation of fish movement and each demonstrates different features of inheritance and polymorphism. One class inherits from another by using the keyword extends. Again recall the IS-A relationship. A DarterFish IS-A Fish. A SlowFish IS-A Fish.

DarterFish

A DarterFish moves two spaces straight ahead if this is feasible; otherwise, it moves one space ahead. When neither of these is possible, it reverses direction without moving. A darter never turns left or right but always travels the horizontal or vertical path determined by its original location and direction.

Constructors

Subclasses do not inherit constructors. `DarterFish` has three constructors whose parameters vary in the same way as its parent class, `Fish`. The `DarterFish` class has no private instance variables peculiar to the class, so the body of its three constructors consists only of a call to `super`, sending the appropriate parameters (including `Color.yellow` for darters). The call to `super` invokes the matching `Fish` constructor, which, in turn, invokes `initialize`. Subclasses cannot invoke `initialize` directly because `initialize` is a private method of the `Fish` class.

Redefined (Reimplemented) Methods

`DarterFish` redefines the "inherited" methods `move` and `nextLocation` to reflect its movement pattern:

1. Move forward two positions, if possible.
2. Move forward one position if two doesn't work but one is possible.
3. Remain in the same position but reverse direction.

Redefined methods can give rise to some confusion. You might have declared

```
Fish charlie;
charlie = new Fish(env, loc);
```

Suppose instead, that you declared the following.

```
charlie = new DarterFish(env, loc);
```

Now when `charlie.move()` is invoked, is it the `move` for `Fish` or the `move` for `DarterFish`? Being able to store different types in the same variable is an example of polymorphism. As a result of this polymorphism, it is often not possible to determine which block of code will be executed at compile time; the decision of which `move` to execute is made at run time. This is quite similar to the examples covered in Chapter 4.

`DarterFish` must redefine the `generateChild` method because it must generate its own species. If the class failed to redefine the method, the simulation would still run, but the children of that species of fish would be of the `Fish` class rather than `DarterFish`.

SlowFish

A `SlowFish` moves in the same way as a `Fish`, but it's slow because it does so, on average, only one time in five. The rest of the time it stays still.

Constructors

An additional private instance variable, `probOfMoving`, initialized in the `SlowFish` constructors to `1.0/5.0` controls whether or not a `SlowFish` moves. These constructors illustrate that a call to `super` must come before any other code in the body of a constructor.

Redefined (Reimplemented) Methods

It isn't necessary to override `move` because a `SlowFish` moves in the same way as a `Fish`. Determining the `nextLocation`, however, is not the same for a `SlowFish` as for a `Fish` because a `SlowFish` doesn't always move. `nextLocation` is redefined, but notice that it calls upon `nextLocation` from the `Fish` class to accomplish most of the work.

1. A random `double` is generated.
2. If the random `number` is less than `1.0/5.0`, the `SlowFish` will attempt to move on this time step.
   a. Returns `super.nextLocation()` (code reuse from within the `SlowFish` `nextLocation` method, because a `SlowFish` ultimately finds its next location in the same way a `Fish` does).
3. Otherwise, returns the current location; the net effect is that the `SlowFish` doesn't move.

Note: In redefining methods, remember that subclasses cannot access private instance variables of the parent class directly. The accessor methods of the parent class must be used. Also remember, if you redefine a method and then want to invoke the method with the same name from the parent class, you will need to write `super.<method name>`. These points are demonstrated by the `DarterFish` and `SlowFish` classes.

As with `DarterFish`, `SlowFish` must also redefine `generateChild` to generate fish of its own species.

> **Tip**
>
> If asked to design a new subclass, you may look to `DarterFish` and `SlowFish` as models. However, don't lock yourself into copying code without thinking carefully about the similarities and differences between the new subclass, `DarterFish`, and `SlowFish`. Remember the inheritance and polymorphism features illustrated by these classes and consider how they apply to the class you are creating.

BLACK BOX CLASSES

You do not know the implementation of the black box classes. All you see is their method signatures. You cannot make any inferences about how the data are represented or how the methods are implemented. The methods are tools. Think about how to use the tools to solve a problem, not about how the tools are built.

The `Debug` Class

The purpose of the `Debug` class is to allow you to watch execution of a program through statements that are printed when `Debug` is turned on. All methods are `static`, meaning they are called using the name of the class. You do not need to instantiate a `Debug` object. For example, suppose you have added an instance variable `myAge` to the `Fish` class and want to see if `myAge` is behaving as expected in some method. The following lines could be added to the method:

```
Debug.turnOn();
Debug.println(toString() + " is now age " + myAge);
Debug.restore();
```

turnOn activates the Debug methods. toString prints the fish's ID, location, and direction (calling toString methods for Location and Direction objects). restore returns Debug to its former state, prior to the call to turnOn.

The Direction Class

Three Direction class constructors are provided: the default (sets direction to north); a second constructor accepts degrees; a third accepts a String parameter. The methods of this class return

- This direction in degrees
- A direction left, right, or reverse of this direction
- A random direction
- A boolean indicating if two Direction objects are equal
- A String indicating the direction (toString)

(There are other methods, but these are the most likely tasks to be tested.)

The Location Class

A Location object is constructed with a row and a column. Methods exist to access the row and column, to check for equality, and to compare locations for order (less than, greater than) of two locations. Location also overrides the toString method.

The RandNumGenerator Class

There is only one method in the RandNumGenerator class, getInstance, which always returns the same Random object. Having just one, rather than several, Random objects provides the programmer with greater control; the random numbers are being drawn from the same sequence.

THE INTERFACES

An interface differs from a class in that it specifies all the method signatures but contains none of the implementations. Because there are no instance variables and no method bodies, one can't construct an instance of an interface.

The Environment Interface

The Environment interface simulates a rectangular grid that contains Locatable (see the next section) objects. There are 16 public methods, described below. Even though the Environment implementation is black box to students taking the A exam, it is very important to understand what these 16 methods do, because most of the code you write will require using one or more of them. In writing code that invokes these methods, be careful to be consistent in terms of parameters and return types. More is said about the Environment interface in "Implementing the Environment" later in this chapter.

Environment.java

Accessor Methods for Retrieving Environment Dimensions

```
// Returns the number of columns if the environment is bounded; otherwise,
// returns -1.
public int numCols()
```

```
// Returns true if loc is valid in this environment; otherwise, returns
// false. Valid depends upon the environment implementation.
public boolean isValid(Location loc)
```

Accessor Methods for Navigating within This Environment

```
// Returns the number of sides around each cell.
public int numCellSides()
```

```
// Returns the number of adjacent neighbors around each cell.
public int numAdjacentNeighbors()
```

```
// Returns a random direction, reflecting the direction from a cell in the
// environment to an adjacent cell.
public Direction randomDirection()
```

```
// Returns the direction from one location to another.
public Direction getDirection(Location fromLoc, Location toLoc)
```

```
// Returns the adjacent neighboring location of a specified location in a
// specified direction (whether valid or invalid).
public Location getNeighbor(Location fromLoc, Direction compassDir)
```

```
// Returns an ArrayList of all valid, adjacent neighboring locations of a
// specified location, empty or not.
public java.util.ArrayList neighborsOf(Location ofLoc)
```

Accessor Methods about Objects in This Environment

```
// Returns the number of objects in this environment.
public int numObjects()
```

```
// Returns an array of all objects in this environment.
public Locatable[] allObjects()
```

```
// Returns true if loc is a valid location in the context of this environment
// and is empty; otherwise returns false.
public boolean isEmpty(Location loc)
```

```
// Returns the object at location loc; null if loc is not in the environment
// or is empty.
public Locatable objectAt(Location loc)
```

Modifier Methods

```
// Adds a new object to this environment at the location specified by obj.
// Precondition: obj.location() is a valid empty location.
public void add(Locatable obj)
```

```
// Removes the object from this environment.
// Precondition: obj is in this environment.
public void remove(Locatable obj)
```

```
// Updates this environment to reflect the fact that an object moved.
// Precondition: obj.location() is valid and there is no other object there.
// Postcondition: obj is at the appropriate location (obj.location()), and
// either oldLoc is equal to obj.location() (no movement) or oldLoc is empty.
public void recordMove(Locatable obj, Location oldLoc)
```

The EnvDisplay Interface

EnvDisplay specifies a single method, showEnv, intended to display the current state of the environment. EnvDisplay is written as an interface to allow for various implementations of showEnv (text or graphical user interface).

The `Locatable` Interface

`Locatable` specifies a single method, `location`, that returns the location of this object. The `Environment` contains `Locatable` objects, so any objects (such as `Fish`) in the environment must implement `Locatable`.

IMPLEMENTING THE ENVIRONMENT (AB TOPIC)

 For the A exam you need only *use* the `Environment` methods listed above. If you are taking the AB exam, you will need to know the following *implementations* of the `Environment` interface as well.

The `SquareEnvironment` Abstract Class (`Implements Environment`)

The `SquareEnvironment` class is an abstract class, implementing only the methods specified by the `Environment` interface that are needed to define an environment composed of square cells. (**Note:** This does not mean that the environment itself is square.) It does not fully implement the `Environment` interface but it does implement methods that can be used by either a bounded or an unbounded environment class. As with an interface, one cannot create an instance of an abstract class because not all the methods are implemented.

Although you can't create an instance of the `SquareEnvironment` class, it does specify two constructors: The default constructor creates an environment with four adjacent neighbors around each cell. The second constructor provides a way (through a `boolean` parameter) to create an environment in which cells have either four or eight adjacent neighbors, where eight means including neighboring cells diagonally adjacent to each cell as well as those sharing a side.

The complete list of `SquareEnvironment` methods is as follows:

SquareEnvironment.java

```
// Construct a square environment where cells have four adjacent neighbors.
public SquareEnvironment()
```

```
// Construct a square environment where cells have either eight adjacent
// neighbors if includeDiagonalNeighbors is true; otherwise, cells have four
// adjacent neighbors.
public SquareEnvironment(boolean includeDiagonalNeighbors)
```

```
// Returns the number of sides around each cell (defines the shape).
public int numCellSides()
```

```
// Returns the number of adjacent neighbors around each cell (generally the
// same as the number of cell sides).
public int numAdjacentNeighbors()
```

```
// Returns a random direction in the range of [0, 360) degrees (the interval
// notation shown means 0 <= degrees < 360).
public Direction randomDirection()
```

```
// Returns the direction from fromLoc to toLoc.
public Direction getDirection(Location fromLoc, Direction toLoc)
```

```
// Returns the adjacent neighbor (whether valid or invalid) of a specified
// location in the specified direction.
public Location getNeighbor(Location fromLoc, Direction compassDir)
```

```
// Returns the valid adjacent neighbors of a specified location.
public java.util.ArrayList neighborsOf(Location ofLoc)
```

The **BoundedEnv** Class

The BoundedEnv class extends SquareEnvironment and has two instance variables.

- theGrid, a two-dimensional array of Locatable objects, that represents the environment
- objectCount, an integer that keeps track of the number of objects in the environment

The constructor invokes super on the parent class, SquareEnvironment, to initialize inherited attributes, if there are any. SquareEnvironment is a black box class so we don't know if there are any inherited attributes. Calling super, while unnecessary (because the default constructor would be invoked anyway), is playing it safe.

Below is a list of the BoundedEnv methods.

BoundedEnv.java

Accessor Methods

```
// Returns theGrid.length, the number of rows in the grid.
public int numRows()
```

```
// Returns theGrid[0].length, the number of columns in the first row of the
// grid (it is assumed that all rows have the same number of columns).
public int numCols()
```

```
// Returns objectCount, the number of objects in the bounded environment.
public int numObjects()
```

```
// Returns true if loc is not null and is located within the grid.
public boolean isValid(Location loc)
```

```
// If loc is not valid, returns null; otherwise returns the object at
// loc.row(), loc.col().
public Object objectAt(Location loc)
```

```
// Returns true if loc is a valid location and objectAt(loc) is null; otherwise,
// returns false.
public boolean isEmpty(Location loc)
```

```
// Returns an array containing all the Locatable objects in the grid.
public Object[] allObjects()
```

```
// Returns a String consisting of all the objects in the environment.
public String toString()
```

Modifying Methods

```
// If obj.location() is not empty, throws IllegalArgumentException; otherwise,
// adds obj to the grid at the location specified by obj and increments
// objectCount.
public void add(Locatable obj)
```

```
// Consistency check, if obj.location() does not agree with the object at the
// same location, throws IllegalArgumentException; otherwise, sets the
// location specified by obj to null and decrements objectCount.
public void remove(Locatable obj)
```

```
// If obj.location() equals oldLoc, the object did not move and an empty
// return is issued; consistency check for obj equal to the object at the old
// location and the new location is empty; if both are true, obj is placed in
// the new location and the old location is set to null; otherwise, throws
// IllegalArgumentException.
public void recordMove(Locatable obj, Location oldLoc)
```

 Note: One lesson learned from the 2004 exam is this: while isEmpty checks that a location is both valid and null, the reverse, ! isEmpty could be false for either reason, not valid or not null. If you are looking for a nonempty cell in the grid, you must test isValid and ! isEmpty.

A second lesson learned from the 2004 exam (and the C++ version of this case study as well) is the need for a consistency test. An object that has been removed during execution of the `Simulation step` method may still remain in the list of objects `step` is traversing. That list was sent to `step` before any of the fish acted, and the simulation does not know if an action has caused a fish to be removed.

The `UnboundedEnv` Class

The `UnboundedEnv` class also extends `SquareEnvironment` but requires only one instance variable, an `ArrayList` of `Locatable` objects called `objectList`. It isn't necessary to maintain a separate variable such as `objectCount` in the `BoundedEnv`; `objectList.size()` serves that purpose. While the concept of a grid remains, there is no grid object. Each `Locatable` object (fish) knows its location, and that is sufficient.

As with the `BoundedEnv`, the `UnboundedEnv` constructor invokes `super` on the parent class and then declares `objectList = new ArrayList()`.

Here are the other methods.

UnboundedEnv.java

Accessor Methods

```
// Returns -1, indicating the environment is unbounded.
public int numRows()
```

```
// Returns -1, indicating the environment is unbounded.
public int numCols()
```

```
// Returns objectList.size(), the length of the ArrayList.
public int numObjects()
```

```
// Returns loc != null (all locations are valid, if they exist).
public boolean isValid(Location loc)
```

```
// If loc is not valid, returns null; otherwise uses helper method indexOf to
// find the object in objectList, casts the object to a Locatable and returns
// the Locatable.
public Object objectAt(Location loc)
```

```
// Returns true if objectAt(loc) is null (meaning empty); otherwise, returns
// false.
public boolean isEmpty(Location loc)
```

```
// Creates an array, copies objectList into the array, and returns the array.
public Object[] allObjects()
```

```
// Returns a String consisting of all the objects in the environment.
public String toString()
```

Modifying Methods

```
// If obj.location() is not empty, throws IllegalArgumentException;
// otherwise, adds obj to the end of objectList.
public void add(Locatable obj)
```

```
// Uses helper method indexOf to locate the object in objectList; if index = -1,
// throws IllegalArgumentException; otherwise, calls the ArrayList remove
// method (not part of the Java subset except for use in the case study).
public void remove(Locatable obj)
```

```
// Counts the number of objects at the old location and the new location; there
// should be one at the new location and one at the old (if object didn't move)
// or zero at old (if object moved); otherwise, throws
// IllegalArgumentException.
public void recordMove(Locatable obj, Location oldLoc)
```

Helper Method

```
protected int indexOf(Location loc)
// Returns the index of the object at loc; if not found, returns -1.
```

Note: AB students may be asked to reimplement the `Environment` or some other aspect of the case study using advanced data structures.

AB students are expected to be able to determine the big-oh efficiency for the `BoundedEnv` and `UnboundedEnv` methods as well as for other implementations of the Environment that may be proposed in a question. Practice questions related to advanced (AB) topics can be found at the end of chapters on those topics and on the AB practice examinations.

TEST CASES

Throughout the case study there is a strong emphasis on developing **test cases** and testing code as it is written. Test cases fall into two categories.

- Black box test cases test the code against the preconditions and postconditions.
- Code-based test cases test each path through the code.

It is important to select appropriate data to thoroughly test both of these categories. Sometimes a set of test data can serve to test several conditions at once.

Testing should be done following each modification or addition to a program. If several changes are made before tests are run, it is more difficult to pinpoint the source of errors. **Regression testing** means revisiting cases previously tested when modifying code to be sure the modification hasn't created errors in code that worked before the changes were introduced.

RAPID REVIEW

Design cycle: An iterative process consisting of analysis, design, implementation, and testing; illustrated throughout the case study.

Code model: A set of code provided as a good model to follow when writing code; illustrated by the case study.

Object diagrams: Visualization of the classes, helpful in understanding individual classes and coupling; not tested but a good study aid.

Quick Reference: Appendix provided with the exam; download from Internet address provided earlier in this chapter.

Visible classes: `Simulation`, `Fish`, `DarterFish`, and `SlowFish`; the code that is tested on the A exam (provided with the exam in the Quick Reference appendix). In addition, `Bounded` and `UnBounded` environments are tested on the AB exam, for which a separate Quick Reference is provided.

`Simulation`: Represents fish behavior and display in every timestep of the simulation; collaborates with the `Environment` and `EnvDisplay` interfaces.

`Fish`: Encapsulates state and behavior of fish objects; breeds or moves and may die.

Protected: Method modifier that means the method is accessible only by this class and subclasses of this class.

Class variable: Identified by the keyword `static`; a single instance variable shared by all instances of a class, in this case the fish's ID.

`DarterFish` class: Subclass of `Fish` with the following characteristics:

1. Moves according to the following rules
   a. Move forward two positions, if possible
   b. Move forward one position if two don't work but one is possible
   c. Remain in the same position but reverse direction
2. Illustrates call to the super constructor
3. Reimplements `move`, `nextLocation`, and `generateChild` methods

SlowFish class: Subclass of **Fish** with the following characteristics:

1. Moves according the following rules
   a. A random `double` is generated.
   b. If the random `number` is less than `1.0/5.0`, the `SlowFish` will attempt to move on this time step. Returns `super.nextLocation()` (code reuse from within the `SlowFish` `nextLocation` method, because a `SlowFish` ultimately finds its next location in the same way a `Fish` does).
   c. Otherwise, returns the current location; the `SlowFish` doesn't move.
2. Illustrates a subclass that has its own private data
3. Reimplements `nextLocation` and `generateChild`
4. Uses `super` to call a method, other than the constructor, from the super class

Black box class: Class for which only the method signatures are visible; it would be a mistake to make any inferences about how the data are represented or how the methods are implemented.

Debug class: Black box class that allows one to watch execution of a program through statements that are printed when `Debug` is turned on.

Direction class: The methods of this class can return:

- this direction in degrees
- a direction left, right, or reverse of this direction
- a random direction
- a Boolean indicating if two `Direction` objects are equal
- a `String` representing the direction (via the `toString` method)

Location class: Represents a row and a column; methods allow access to the row and column, check for equality, and comparison for order (less than, greater than) of two locations.

RandNumGenerator class: Contains one method, `getInstance`, which always returns the same `Random` object.

Environment interface: Simulates a rectangular grid that contains `Locatable` objects; declares 16 public methods (described in this chapter).

SquareEnvironment class (AB topic): An abstract class, implements only the methods specified by the `Environment` interface that are needed to define an environment composed of square cells; does not fully implement the `Environment` interface but does implement methods that can be used by either a bounded or unbounded environment class.

BoundedEnv class (AB topic): Extends `SquareEnvironment` and implements the `Environment` interface as a two-dimensional array, `theGrid`, with `objectCount` number of `Locatable` objects.

UnboundedEnv class (AB topic): Extends `SquareEnvironment` and implements the `Environment` interface as an `ArrayList`, `objectList`, of `Locatable` objects.

Test cases: Categories for which data are designed to see if the code works as intended; *regression testing* retests data when code has been modified.

- **black box:** tests according to preconditions and postconditions
- **code based:** tests paths through the code

PRACTICE PROBLEMS

1. Which of the following instantiates a `Locatable` object?

   A. `Location loc = new Location();`
   B. `Fish f1 = new Fish(env, loc);`
   C. `Locatable loc = new Location(row, col);`
   D. `Environment env;`
   E. `Neighbor n;`

2. What must be true of any class that implements `Locatable`?

   A. Must have a default constructor
   B. Must have a `locatable` method
   C. Must have a `location` method
   D. Must instantiate a `Locatable` object
   E. Must extend `Locatable`

3. Which of the following processes in the MBS illustrates a principle of good design?

   A. The case study determines a set of methods for a new type of object.
   B. The case study determines code-based test cases.
   C. The case study analyzes the movement pattern for a new species of fish.
   D. The case study modifies code to produce a new movement pattern.
   E. All the above illustrate principles of good design.

4. If the loop in the `Simulation step` method is modified as follows and no other changes are made anywhere in the code, in what order will `Fish act`?

   ```
   for(int index = theFishes.length - 1; index >= 0; index--)
   ```

   A. top-down, left to right
   B. top-down, right to left
   C. bottom-up, left to right
   D. bottom-up, right to left
   E. diagonally up, left to right

5. Suppose the biologists wish to add a new method `changeOrder` that will change the order in which fish act. Of the following, which is the best design choice and justification? (Since this question is about design, you may assume changes can be made to the black box classes.)

   A. Make `changeOrder` private to the `Fish` class because each `Fish` tells the `Environment` its location.
   B. Make `changeOrder` private to the `Simulation` class because the simulation models how fish behave.
   C. Make `changeOrder` public to the `EnvDisplay` class because `showEnv` determines the order in which `Fish` are displayed.
   D. Make `changeOrder` public to the `Fish` class so it can be called from the `step` method.
   E. Make `changeOrder` private to the `Environment` class because the environment prohibits two fish from being in the same location at the same time.

6. What is required of objects in an `Environment`?

   A. The objects must be able to report a location.
   B. The objects must be able to change location and direction.
   C. The environment must be able to add and remove objects.
   D. The objects must be displayable.
   E. All the above must be true.

7. Suppose in the Fish act method, the statement

```
if ( ! isInEnv() )
  return;
```

is removed. Which of the following best describes the consequences?

A. The method will continue to work as intended.
B. The method will fail to work as intended in some cases when fish breed.
C. The method will fail to work as intended in some cases when fish move.
D. The method will fail to work as intended in some cases when fish die.
E. The method will fail to work as intended in all cases.

8. (AB only) Consider the isEmpty method in the BoundedEnv class. Which of the following actions is not guarded by a call to isEmpty?

A. A fish moving backward
B. A fish moving to an occupied location
C. A fish moving outside the boundary of the environment
D. A fish breeding into adjacent locations
E. A fish being added to the environment

SOLUTIONS TO THE PRACTICE PROBLEMS

1. **B.** Fish implements Locatable, so when a Fish is instantiated, a Locatable object is instantiated. While the environment contains only Locatable objects, it and the other classes and interfaces do not implement Locatable.

2. **C.** Any class that implements Locatable must implement a location method. Every class has, by default, a default constructor. Locatable is a class name; the method is location. One cannot instantiate an object of an interface type, and we implement an interface; we extend a class.

3. **E.** Good design includes analysis, design, implementation, and testing.

4. **D.** Fish will be processed in the reverse order from the way in which the environment puts them into the array returned by allObjects.

5. **B.** The fact that Simulation models fish movement makes it a good choice for the new method. A fish has individual behavior but should not control the overall movement pattern. The fact that the environment checks to see if a location is empty is a poor reason for including the new method there.

6. **A.** The environment contains Locatable objects. The only thing Locatable objects must be able to do is return their location.

7. **D.** If a fish is removed from the environment, there may be a consistency problem. This could happen if the fish and the environment are not in agreement (the environment was not updated). It could also happen if a fish sent to step through allObjects dies before its turn to act.

8. **A.** isEmpty is called from the BoundedEnv add method, so it is called when a fish is being added to the environment, whether initially or by breeding. isEmpty is called when the fish is seeking a next location through the emptyNeighbors method. However, the SquareEnvironment's getNeigbor method returns the Location behind the fish, valid or invalid.

Chapter 8

Nonprogramming Issues

GENERAL OBSERVATIONS

The AP Computer Science course of study includes "computing in context" among the testable topics. Knowledge of nonprogramming issues is acquired through day-to-day use of computers and programming. This information is often found in the first chapter of a computer science textbook, although some authors insert special notes about these issues at appropriate points throughout the text.

HARDWARE

 Hardware refers to the physical parts of a computer. You do not need to know details, but there are some terms with which you should be familiar.

Primary and Secondary Memory

Primary memory is the active part of memory where you enter and edit your code. Known as **random access memory (RAM),** or main memory, a program can both read from and write to this part of memory. It is volatile, meaning when you turn the computer off, this part of memory is lost.

    Secondary memory is used to store information on a nonvolatile, long-term (or permanent) basis. Storage devices for secondary memory include the hard drive, floppy disks, compact disks (CD), digital versatile disks (DVD), and memory sticks (USB).

    The **central processing unit (CPU)** is the hardware that controls primary memory. It reads and executes instructions one at a time. The CPU is actually made up of three components: the control unit for processing, registers that store a small amount of general purpose and special purpose memory, and the arithmetic-logic unit (ALU) that can perform arithmetic operations.

    Computer registers are simply sets of on-off switches. The switches are chemical, rather than physical, in nature, which allows them to be minute in size. Because everything a computer does must ultimately be reduced to on-off switches representing coded instructions, computers are based on binary code and binary (base two) arithmetic. See the section "Computer Number Systems" later in this chapter for an explanation of binary code.

The arithmetic-logic unit (ALU) can operate on only two numbers at a time. Evaluating complex arithmetic expressions involves determining which part of the expression should be evaluated first (order of operations), performing either a unary (raising to a power, taking absolute value, etc.) or binary (addition, subtraction, etc.) operation on that one or those two values, and putting the result on hold (saving the result) while another part of the expression is evaluated. Values that are "put on hold" are pushed onto a **stack** in memory until they are needed to combine with some other part of the evaluation. This may seem like a long process, but it is actually very fast. AB students should be aware of this practical application of stacks. Prefix, infix, and postfix notation, used in the conversion of mathematical expressions to forms that can be evaluated without the need for parentheses to specify order of operations, are employed in the underlying code of the ALU. (See Chapter 12 for details about these AB topics.)

Peripheral Devices

Almost any device other than the CPU and main memory is a **peripheral device,** including disk drives within the same box as the CPU (secondary memory). The keyboard, monitor, printer, scanner, speakers, and external drives are examples of peripheral devices. These provide a way for the user to communicate with the computer, or vice versa.

SOFTWARE

 Software encompasses programs and data. System software, or the **operating system,** is an umbrella term for a collection of programs (instructions) that combine to oversee a computer system. The operating system is responsible for managing and prioritizing computer resources such as the user interface, loading and saving files, program execution, printing, memory allocation, and the CPU. (Windows, Linux, and MacOS are examples of popular operating systems.) The operating system makes use of an internal stack to save data and return-addresses when program execution shifts to a method call or a recursive call within a method. It makes use of a **queue,** and possibly a **priority queue** (AB topics), when determining which task should be executed first, second, third, etc. (See Chapter 12.)

Compilers and Interpreters

Code that is high level, written in a form that is relatively easy for humans to read and understand, is known as **source code.** This code must be translated into instructions that a computer can recognize and execute, low-level code known as **object code.**

A **compiler** is a program that translates source code written in a high-level language into object, or machine code. A compiler *translates* the code as a whole entity; execution cannot begin until all the code is translated, or compiled, into an executable file. Compiled software offers the advantage of being able to write and compile program components into separate executable files. These files can then be utilized by individual applications or combined into precompiled libraries and reused in many programs.

An **interpreter** is a program that reads and executes code on a particular machine (such as the Java virtual machine, or JVM). An interpreter *translates and executes* code in small segments, one statement at a time.

Java was developed to allow the same code to be run on different types of computers. Java byte code, which is machine-independent, provides an intermediate step between source and machine code. To run Java byte code, we need a Java virtual machine. Each JVM is specific to a particular operating system. A JVM takes byte code, which is non-specific, and executes it on the specific operating system it is designed for.

Networks

A computer system may be single-user (stand-alone) or a part of a **network,** where two or more computers are linked (with or without wires) in order to share resources. A network may be a LAN (local area network), within a room or a building, or a WAN (wide area network), connecting two or more LANs. Of course, the Internet provides a vast network for the exchange of information.

Integrated Development Environment

You may be using an integrated development environment (IDE) when you develop your Java programs. An IDE provides a way to organize, enter and edit, compile, and execute your programs. This is an alternative to writing your programs in an editor and using command line instructions to compile and run them. The IDE insulates some programmers from the direct commands preferred by other programmers.

COMPUTER NUMBER SYSTEMS

All information in a computer is stored as on-off switches, represented by the numbers 0 and 1. A single switch is known as a bit. A set of eight bits is a byte.

A system that uses only two digits, 0 and 1, is known as a **binary** system (or base 2, when we think in terms of arithmetic). As with our decimal system, the individual digits in other number systems receive their value from their placement, or place value, in the numbers. Each digit as we go from right to left represents that digit times the next higher power of the base. While place values in the decimal system are 1, 10, 100, 1000, . . . , (powers of 10), in base 2 the place values are 1, 2, 4, 8, 16, . . . (powers of 2).

Given that base 2 numbers rapidly become long strings of ones and zeros, they are often rewritten in base 8 (**octal**) or base 16 (**hexadecimal**). Base 8 uses the digits 0 through 7, and the place values are powers of 8, namely 1, 8, 64, 512, ... Base 16 needs 16 digits to represent the values 0 through 15. 0 . . . 9 represent their decimal equivalents; the letters A . . . F represent values 10 through 15. Place values for base 16 are powers of 16, namely 1, 16, 256, 4096, ...

Representation of numbers in these bases may be tested, either as a multiple-choice or free-response question. It is very easy to convert back and forth between base 10 and other bases and also between bases 2, 8, and 16, but you are not expected to have learned those algorithms. A multiple-choice question on this topic would provide you with enough information to determine the answer. A free-response question would lead you through the algorithm and have you implement appropriate methods.

RESPONSIBLE COMPUTER USE

Considering the powerful impact of computers in daily life and the programmer's role in design and development of ever-expanding computer capabilities, developing a responsible attitude toward computer use is imperative. Common sense and basic honesty are the foundation of responsible computer use. Questions on this topic usually have common sense answers. Here are a few issues that might be tested:

- Copyright protection and intellectual property
- Privacy issues, databases
- Life-critical applications; ensuring that they are as reliable and error-free as possible
- Viruses; economic and legal concerns
- Illegal, unethical, and/or immoral Web sites

RAPID REVIEW

Hardware: The physical parts of a computer.

Primary memory: The active part of memory where you enter and edit your program.

Random access memory (RAM): Main memory; read and write; volatile, cleared when the computer is turned off.

Secondary memory: Nonvolatile, long-term memory; includes hard drive, floppy drive, CD, DVD, memory stick, external drive, tape.

Central processing unit (CPU): The control unit reads and processes program instructions; registers are a small amount of memory space needed to keep track of instructions and some data; arithmetic-logic unit performs arithmetic.

Stack (AB topic): A data structure used in computer memory to hold values temporarily.

Queue or **priority queue** (AB topic): A data structure used by the CPU to determine the order in which tasks will be performed.

Peripheral device: Internal drives, external drives, keyboard, monitor, printer, etc.

Software: Instructions and data.

System software or **operating system:** A collection of programs that manages and prioritizes computer resources such as the user interface, loading and saving files, program execution, printing, memory allocation, and the CPU.

Compiler: A program that translates a program written in a **high-level language** (human readable) into **machine code** (**low-level,** machine readable); Java's machine code is known as **byte code.**

Interpreter: A program that reads and executes code on a particular machine.

Source code: Code written in a high-level, human-readable form.

Object code: Low-level code, machine executable.

Network: Two or more connected computers, sharing resources.

Binary, octal, hexadecimal: Base 2, base 8, base 16 number systems; base 2, 0 and 1, used to represent all data and code as groups of on-off switches; base 8 and base 16 condense the writing of base 2 numbers.

PRACTICE PROBLEMS

1. Which of the following turns Java source code into object code?

   A. Integrated development environment
   B. Arithmetic logic unit
   C. Central processing unit
   D. Compiler/interpreter
   E. Linker/translator

2. Consider the following storage devices:

   floppy disk
   compact disk (CD)
   disk drive

   Which statement about these storage devices is true?

   A. Ordered from least storage to most, the list should be: floppy disk, disk drive, CD.
   B. Among the three, only the floppy disk stores volatile data.
   C. Disk drives are built into the computer and hence not considered peripheral devices as are floppy disks and CDs.
   D. The central processing unit for the computer is typically located somewhere on the disk drive.
   E. Files stored on any one of these media can typically be copied to any of the other media.

3. Which of the following is *not* typically a social concern for programmers?

   A. Security
   B. Safety
   C. Privacy
   D. Reliability
   E. Internal data formats

4. Consider the following table that lists decimal values and their corresponding binary representation:

Decimal	Binary
1	1
2	10
3	11
4	100
5	101
6	110

   Following this pattern, what is the binary representation of decimal 10?

   A. 10
   B. 11
   C. 111
   D. 1000
   E. 1010

5. Three programming students are given an assignment. They divide the problem into three parts, each taking one part to code, planning eventually to combine the parts.

I. Student 1 codes Part 1, then uses the Internet to verify the solution by searching for similar work.

II. To make life easier for Students 1 and 3, Student 2 removes the password protection from his account so that the code may more easily be shared.

III. Student 3, in writing Part 3, discovers a way to leave an image of a smiley face on the desktop of anyone running the program and adds this capability to the project.

Which of these students exhibits an irresponsible attitude toward computer use?

A. I only
B. II and III only
C. III only
D. I, II, and III
E. The students are all behaving responsibly.

SOLUTIONS TO THE PRACTICE PROBLEMS

1. **D.** Both the compiler and the interpreter translate a high-level language into machine code. The purposes of the IDE, the ALU, and the CPU are explained in the chapter.

2. **E.** Each of the others is a false statement.

3. **E.** While there are social issues surrounding data formats, e.g., which alphabets will be included in a character set, they are typically decided by professional societies, not by individual programmers.

4. **E.** There is one group of 2^3 and one group of 2^1.

5. **B.** Student 1's behavior is somewhat questionable, but it is not necessarily irresponsible to verify one's work by checking it against other, published solutions. Although the intentions may be honorable, Student 2 is inviting trouble by making it easy for others to access data (and presumably cheat) on the network; passwords are generally in place for a good reason. Student 3 is the most irresponsible. No program should be written so as to engage in unexpected behavior, even as a joke.

Chapter 9

Asymptotic Analysis of Programs (Big-Oh)

ANALYZING RUNNING TIME

!

No scientist is content to design a solution to a problem. After it is created, a solution must be examined and analyzed so that its quality can be ascertained. Within the field of computer science, one primary measurement of the quality of a program is its **asymptotic behavior**, most typically its **asymptotic running time**, commonly called *big-oh*.

Asymptotic running times give us a measure of how much more (or less!) time a program will take to execute when the amount of data is changed by a fixed factor. The techniques involved would appear to give only a rough estimate, but these rough estimates can often predict running times of programs to within a few percent.

The most general approach to measuring asymptotic running times is to group programs into categories (what mathematicians call *equivalence classes*) such that all the programs in a given category behave similarly. For instance, all programs with a quadratic asymptotic running time have the property that if you double the size of the input, the program will take about four times $(4 = 2^2)$ as long to run. Furthermore, if you triple the size of the input, these programs will take about nine times $(9 = 3^2)$ as long to run.

Within the context of AP Computer Science, it is expected that you will be able to use asymptotic analysis in two distinct ways:

- That you will be able to determine the asymptotic behavior (the big-oh) of a program, or more likely a fragment of a program.
- That you will know the asymptotic behaviors of methods within the standard Java classes covered in the syllabus (in particular that you will be able to specify big-oh estimates for standard algorithms, including searching and sorting algorithms)—and that you will be able to use this knowledge to choose between two or more classes that can perform the same task.

The former of these skills is discussed in this chapter. The latter skill set is discussed on an ongoing basis as the various classes are introduced. (Some are introduced in Chapter 4; others are introduced in later chapters.)

Chapters 9–12 contain material that falls only within the AB curriculum. Students studying for the A examination may safely skip these four chapters.

Counting How Many Statements Are Executed

At its most basic level, analysis of asymptotic running time consists simply of counting the number of statements that a program executes. Such counting might seem to imply that all statements take the same amount of time to execute—yet clearly some statements are more complex than others. In fact, the analysis relies only upon the fact that any single statement takes only a finite (usually a very small) amount of time to execute. This simplifies the analysis but still enables computer scientists to make accurate predictions.

Consider the following fragment of code:

```
for (int x=0; x<N; x++)
{
  System.out.println("Wow");
}
```

How many times will the word *Wow* be printed? Clearly this depends upon the value of N. If N = 100, then the word will be printed one hundred times. If N = 2500, then the word will be printed two thousand five hundred times. In general, if the value of N doubles, the number of times that the word will be printed will also double. This is an example of **linear behavior** and is expressed as O(N).

Next we consider a more complex example:

```
for (int y=0; y<N; y++)
{
  for (int x=0; x<N; x++)
  {
    System.out.println("Wow");
  }
}
```

If N = 100, then as noted above, the inner loop causes the word to be printed one hundred times. This inner loop, however, is itself executed one hundred times; therefore, there will be one hundred instances of the word being printed one hundred times. In all there will be ten thousand (10,000 = 100*100) occurrences of the word. If N = 300, there would be ninety thousand (90,000 = 300*300) occurrences of the word. In general, if the value of N doubles, the number of times that the word will be printed will increase by a factor of four. This is an example of **quadratic behavior,** expressed O(N²).

Estimating How Many Statements Are Executed

Unfortunately, not all loops run from 0 to N − 1, and thus not all loops are so easy to count. Consider the following small modification of the second code fragment from above:

```
for (int y=0; y<N; y++)
{
  for (int x=y; x<N; x++) // new initialization!
  {
    System.out.println("Wow");
  }
}
```

The inner loop no longer executes exactly N times. Now each pass through the inner loop will cause the word to be printed N − y times. Since y varies, it is not clear how to compute the total number of times the word is printed. We could try counting carefully: The first time through the outer loop, y = 0, so the word does print N times. The next time through the outer loop, $y = 1$, so the word does print $N - 1$ times. Continuing in this manner, we can observe that the word is printed $N + (N - 1) + (N - 2) + \cdots + 3 + 2 + 1$ times. It turns out that this series sums to $(N^2 + N)/2$. Thus, if $N = 100$, the word will print 5,050 times. If $N = 200$, the word will print 20,100 times. In this case, if N doubles, the word is printed *approximately* four times as many times. Because the N^2 term is the largest in the expression above, the behavior is still described as quadratic.

Suppose that instead of trying to get an exact count, we merely tried to estimate the number of times that the word would be printed. Furthermore, suppose that we wished to be sure that our estimate was, if anything, too high. (This makes sense; few people complain when a program runs too fast!) In that case, we could have simply said that the inner loop prints the word no more than N times. The first time through, this is accurate; the second time, it is a pretty good estimate. By the end of the execution, it is a valid overestimate, although not a very precise estimate. If we made this approximation, however, we would then believe that the word would be printed N^2 times. This is off by (nearly) a factor of 2 from the actual number, but the behavior is still quadratic. Since the purpose of this analysis is to predict the general pattern of behavior, it turns out that applying this simplification will have no effect on our final answer!

Mathematicians (and computer scientists) have developed a notation to describe these categories of behavior. A program is said to run in $O(N)$ time (pronounced "big-oh of N") if it executes some number of statements that is at most a constant times N. (In such a case, N is usually the size of the input, but might be some other parameter of the program.) The notation is general. A program is said to run in $O(N^2)$ time if it executes some number of statements that is at most a constant times N^2. In fact, any function can be placed between the parentheses, although it is common practice to use a simple function of N. In terms of **big-oh notation,** the first example runs in $O(N)$ time, while the second and third examples run in $O(N^2)$ time.

Combining Estimates

Even the second and third fragments above represent only the simplest forms of loops. Therefore, we need to know how to analyze general programs. The procedure is similar to that used to evaluate long arithmetic expressions: we start with the innermost block of code and work our way out. We use a few simple rules to create our estimates:

1. The cost of a single statement (such as an assignment) is 1.
2. The cost of sequential statements is the sum of their individual costs.
3. The cost of a loop is the number of times it executes times the cost of its body.

We used the first and third of these rules to derive the exact counts in the first two examples earlier and to derive the estimate in the third example. Two more rules will enable us to analyze even more programs:

4. The cost of a conditional statement is the cost of the highest branch the code might take. (Technically, we need to add the costs, but if the cost of one branch is greater than the cost of the other, its cost will dominate the sum and we may safely ignore the lower cost.)
5. The cost of a method call is the cost of the statements in the method call.

It should be obvious that both these rules will lead to an overestimate of the overall cost as well. A more complex example follows:

```java
for (int y = 0; y<N; y++)
{
  if (y%3 == 0)
  {
    for (int x=y; x<N; x++)
    {
      System.out.println("Wow");
    }
  }
  else
  {
    for (int z=0; z<N*N; z++)
    {
      System.out.println("Wow");
    }
  }
}
```

To analyze this fragment, we start with the innermost blocks. Using the simplified estimations, the loop indexed by x has a cost of N. The loop indexed by z has a cost of N^2. (Note the termination condition!) Thus, the *if* statement has a cost of the larger of N and N^2, namely N^2. The loop indexed by y executes N times, and its body has a cost of N^2, thus we say that this fragment runs in $N*N^2$, or $O(N^3)$ time. (This is an example of **cubic behavior**.)

Multiplicative Loops

Many loops add one to the loop control variable each time they iterate. Some loops, however, control the loop in a more complex manner. Consider the following loop:

```java
for (int x = 1; x<N; x *= 2)
```

This loop doubles x repeatedly until it reaches the value of N. Such a loop executes approximately $\log_2 N$ times (pronounced "log base 2 of N" or "log of N to the base 2.") For large values of N, $\log_2 N$ is much smaller than N. For instance, $\log_2 1,000$ is about 10, and $\log_2 1,000,000$ is approximately 20. Simply put, the loop above does not execute that many times!

The value of the multiplicative factor (two in the example above) is unimportant. If the loop control variable increases by a multiplicative, as opposed to an additive, factor, then the number of times that the loop will execute is approximately $\log N$. (Since we are not concerned about exact values, the base of the logarithm can be dropped.) Fragments that behave in this manner are said to exhibit **logarithmic behavior**.

Consider the following example:

```java
for (int y=0; y<N; y += 3)
{
  for (int x=1; x<N; x *= 4)
  {
    System.out.println("Wow");
  }
}
```

The inner loop has a cost of about $\log N$. The outer loop executes N times (really N/3, but the factor of $\frac{1}{3}$ is not relevant). Thus, this fragment will print the word **O(NlogN)** times.

Worst Case versus Average Case

The code below is intended to search an array, A, of Objects for a given value:

```
int pos = 0;
while ((pos < A.length) && ! (key.equals(A[pos]))
{
  pos++;
}
```

The body of this loop clearly has cost 1, but the question remains as to how many times it executes. If we are very lucky, the loop body never executes because we find the item in A[0]. If we are very unlucky, the loop will go N times, where N is assumed to be the length of the array. If we wish to overestimate the number of statements, we must assume the worst, namely that the item is in the last position—or not there at all! In this case, our overestimate would state that this fragment executes in O(N) time. This is an example of worst-case analysis. It is also possible to do an average-case analysis. Assuming that the item *is* in the list, how many times would the loop go on average? Well, on average, the item will be halfway through the list, so the loop would execute N/2 times. Since the factor of ½ doesn't matter, we would say that this fragment also exhibits an average case behavior of O(N). (It is possible to do a best-case analysis—which would turn out to be O(1) in this example—but such analysis is rarely used in practice and is not part of the AP Computer Science curriculum.)

In general, if an operation, such as a comparison in the above example, is to be performed on every item in the collection, then the cost will be the cost of a single operation times the number of items in the collection. Be aware that matrices are sometimes described as N×N and in such cases actually have N^2 items in the collection.

Although the average case and the worst case turned out to have the same complexity in this example, they often differ. In particular, they differ for most algorithms that use unbalanced binary trees and for those that use hash tables. They also differ when the Quicksort algorithm is used.

Dangers of Overestimation

Big-oh notation guarantees an overestimation. What is not guaranteed is how much of an overestimate is being provided. In each of the examples we have studied, the overestimation has been minimal. It is important to realize that there is no guarantee that the overestimate will be a good estimate. Big-oh notation only promises that it is an overestimate. To see the difference, consider being cited for a speeding ticket when you were doing only 45 miles per hour in a 65 miles per hour zone. (You are clearly innocent of the charge of speeding, but how can you prove it?) The statement, "Your honor, I was doing less than 2000 miles per hour" is both true and an overestimate, but is not likely to be helpful to your cause. On the other hand, the statement, "Your honor, I was doing less than 50 miles per hour" is also true and an overestimate, and is likely to be of more use if you can back it up. What this means in terms of our examples is that our first example, which we said was O(N), *can also be said to be* O(N^2) since N^2 is an overestimate for N.

To handle this situation, questions about asymptotic analysis will likely ask you either for "the best possible big-oh bound" or "the most accurate description of the runtime behavior" or some such. Do not try to "outsmart" the test by going for the largest bound simply because it will include all the others; the question will be worded so that such a strategy will work only in rare instances.

ANALYZING MEMORY USAGE

Thus far, all our analyses have focused on running time, but computer scientists also evaluate programs in terms of the amount of memory that they use; this is called **asymptotic space analysis**. The rules for determining the memory usage are simple:

1. Primitive types use one unit of memory.
2. The memory usage of a simple object is the sum of the memory usages of its instance variables.
3. The memory usage of a collection of objects (such as a list or an array) is the usage of a single object in the collection times the number of objects in the collection.

Although it is not strictly true, for purposes of space analysis on the exam, you may consider Strings as if they were primitive types. Also, as when analyzing runtimes, when analyzing the memory usage of a matrix, be sure to account for the dimensions properly.

HOW GOOD ARE THE ESTIMATES?

Students frequently wonder about the usefulness of estimates that are as rough as the ones in this chapter. It may seem that such rough estimating techniques could not possibly yield any information of real value. In a world where computing speeds seem to double every 18 months (Moore's law), how can it make sense to ignore factors of 2 or 3? The value of the estimations, though, arises from the ability to place programs into broad categories, and the differences between these categories dwarf any improvement in hardware. Consider the following "race": one computer will run a program that takes $O(N\log N)$ time; this computer will be an original Macintosh, a home computer from 1984. The other computer will run a program that takes $O(N^2)$ time; this computer will be a 2004 supercomputer. If the data set is of size 10,000,000 (perhaps we are working with income tax returns for the government), the Macintosh will probably win by a huge margin, perhaps finishing in minutes as opposed to days. The difference between the algorithms is that much greater than the difference in hardware speeds. The estimates are more than accurate enough to measure such differences, and such differences do matter!

EXAM QUESTIONS

It is a pretty good bet that the exam will feature questions that ask you to consider using several different data structures to solve a problem and then ask you to choose the best one. To make this choice, you will need to know the cost of the various operations (discussed in this book whenever the relevant data structures are introduced) as well as the frequency with which those operations will be invoked. Once you have figured out these values, it is usually a simple matter to choose the one with the lowest cost. The key thing to remember is to compute the total cost quite carefully. Sometimes performing a single "expensive" operation is cheaper than performing many "cheaper" operations.

If an exam question asks about the memory usage of a piece of code, it is necessary that you read the question carefully. There are two types of questions: those that ask about the total amount of memory used and those that ask about "additional" memory used. The answers may be different depending upon which version of the question is being asked.

RAPID REVIEW

Computer scientists use a variety of methods to evaluate the quality of a piece of software:

Asymptotic behavior: A description of the performance of a system as its size increases. In the context of AP Computer Science, the behavior of a program as the amount of data it processes increases.

Asymptotic running time: A description of the amount of time that a program (or program fragment) will need to complete execution as the amount of data increases.

Asymptotic space analysis: A description of the amount of memory that a program (or program fragment) will need to complete execution as the amount of data increases. Sometimes this analysis includes the memory used to hold the original data; sometimes only "additional" memory is counted. This should always be clear from the context of the question.

Big-oh notation: A way of expressing an overestimate for an asymptotic behavior of a system, usually either the running time or the memory usage of a program (or program fragment.) For example, traversing an array or `ArrayList` is linear, so it is usually O(N), where N is the number of elements. Traversing a two-dimensional array, which requires nested loops, is usually O(N^2).

There are several adjectives that are applied to particular categories of behavior. They are presented here in increasing order of size:

Constant: Also described as O(1). The behavior is independent of the amount of data.

Logarithmic: Also described as O(logN). The behavior is proportional to the number of digits in the parameter. As a running time, this means that the program will run *very* quickly.

Linear: Also described as O(N). The behavior is proportional to the parameter. In terms of running time, this means that doubling the amount of data will double the running time.

O(NlogN): The behavior is proportional to a function slightly larger than the parameter itself. Although clumsy to pronounce, this behavior is seen fairly often, particularly in sorting algorithms.

Quadratic: Also described as O(N^2). The behavior is proportional to square of the parameter. In terms of running time, this means that doubling the amount of data will quadruple the running time.

Cubic: Also described as O(N^3). The behavior is proportional to cube of the parameter. In terms of running time, this means that doubling the amount of data will cause the running time to increase by a factor of eight.

PRACTICE PROBLEMS

1. Which of the following statements about big-oh notation is true?

   I. Any valid big-oh bound for the running time of a program fragment will let us approximate the behavior of the running time if the size of the input doubles.

   II. A big-oh bound for the running time of a program fragment serves as an accurate estimate for the number of statements that will be executed by that block of code.

   III. Well-measured big-oh bounds for the running time of two program fragments may serve as a good basis for comparing the efficiencies of those two program fragments.

   A. I only
   B. II only
   C. III only
   D. I and II only
   E. I and III only

2. What is the best possible big-oh bound for the number of times the word Wow is printed by the code below?

```
for (int y=N; y>0; y--)
{
  for (int x=0; x<3*N; x++)
  {
    System.out.println("Wow");
  }
}
```

A. O(logN)
B. O(N)
C. O(NlogN)
D. O(N^2)
E. Cannot be determined

3. What is the best possible big-oh bound for the number of times the word Wow is printed by the code below?

```
for (int y=0; y<N; y++)
{
  for (int x=1; x<3*N; x *= 3)
  {
    System.out.println("Wow");
  }
}
```

A. O(logN)
B. O(N)
C. O(NlogN)
D. O(N^2)
E. Cannot be determined

4. What is the best possible big-oh bound for the number of times the word Wow is printed by the code below?

```
for (int y=0; y<N; y++)
{
  System.out.println("Wow");
  for (int x=0; x<N; x += 4)
  {
    System.out.println("Wow");
  }
}
```

A. O(logN)
B. O(N)
C. O(NlogN)
D. O(N^2)
E. Cannot be determined

5. What is the best possible big-oh bound for the number of times the word Wow is printed by the code below?

```java
for (int y=0; y<2*N; y++)
{
  if (y<N)
  {
    for (int x=0; x<N; x++)
    {
      for (int z=5; z<N; z++)
      {
        System.out.println("Wow");
      }
    }
  }
  else
  {
    for (int w=0; w<y/2; w++)
    {
      System.out.println("Wow");
    }
  }
}
```

A. O(NlogN)
B. O(N^2)
C. O(N^2logN)
D. O(N^3)
E. Cannot be determined

6. What is the best possible big-oh bound for the number of times the word Wow is printed by the code below?

```java
for (int y=0; y<N*N; y++)
{
  if (y%N == 0)
  {
    for (int x=0; x<N; x++)
    {
      for (int z=0; z<N; z++)
      {
        System.out.println("Wow");
      }
    }
  }
  else
  {
    for (int w=y; w>0; w--)
    {
      System.out.println("Wow");
    }
  }
}
```

A. O(NlogN)
B. O(N^2)
C. O(N^3)
D. O(N^4)
E. Cannot be determined

7. Consider the class StudentScores below. Suppose that an ArrayList of N StudentScores is maintained. Which of the following expressions best describes the amount of storage needed?

```
public class StudentScores
{
  int ID;
  int quizScores[8];
  int finalExamScore;
  double courseAverage;
  // Methods not shown, but these are all
  // of the instance variables
}
```

A. 10N + N
B. O(N)
C. O(N²)
D. We cannot determine the expression because it depends upon the maximum score values; if the maximum score values were known, then we could determine the answer.
E. There is no expression that best describes the amount of storage needed.

8. The following code is meant to return the position at which the String key is found within an ArrayList, a, (of Strings) whose items are sorted in order. The String key is known to exist somewhere within the list. Which of the following is true about this code?

```
int pos = a.size()/2;
if (key.compareTo(a.get(pos)) == 0)
{
  return pos;
}
if (key.compareTo(a.get(pos)) > 0)
{
  while (true)
  {
    pos++;
    if (key.compareTo(a.get(pos)) == 0)
    {
      return pos;
    }
  }
}
else
{
  while (true)
  {
    pos--;
    if (key.compareTo(a.get(pos)) == 0)
    {
      return pos;
    }
  }
}
```

A. The average number of words examined from the ArrayList is O(1).
B. The average number of words examined from the ArrayList is O(N).
C. The code will raise an exception when looking for certain words in the list.
D. The code will go into an infinite loop under some circumstances.
E. The code will always return a value, but it will give an incorrect answer for some words.

SOLUTIONS TO THE PRACTICE PROBLEMS

1. **C.** Statements I and II are true only if the estimate is fairly precise. Statement III is always true when the big-oh estimate is a good one. The correct answer is C.

2. **D.** The inner loop executes approximately N times. The outer loop does the same—even though the loop control variable is counting down. Hence the approximate count is N^2. The answer is D.

3. **C.** The inner loop executes approximately $\log N$ times (actually it is $1 + \log_3 N$). The outer loop executes N times. Thus the estimate is $N\log N$. The answer is C.

4. **D.** The inner loop executes approximately N times (actually it is $N/4$). The first printing statement adds only one to the cost of the body and can thus be ignored. The outer loop executes N times. Hence the approximate count is N^2. The answer is D.

5. **D.** The x and z loops combine to print the word N^2 times when they are executed. The w loop can be approximated as printing N times. Since each branch of the conditional is used half the time, the body of the loop can thus be approximated as printing N^2 times. The outer loop executes N times (actually $2N$, but again we approximate), so the final estimate is N^3. The answer is D.

6. **C.** The x and z loops combine to print the word N^2 times when they are executed. They are, however, executed only N times (as there are N multiples of N that are less than N^2!) Thus, they contribute only N^3 total printings. The w loop can be approximated as printing N times. The challenge is to determine how many times this loop is executed. It will be executed whenever the *if* test is false. The *if* test is made N^2 times; it is true N times. Therefore, this loop will be executed $N^2 - N$ times, so it also contributes N^3 total printings. The final estimate is thus $2N^3$, which is $O(N^3)$. The answer is C. (Note: This is a trickier analysis than you would typically be expected to perform on the exam. If you understand this problem, you are well prepared for this type of question.)

7. **B.** Each StudentScores object contains 10 integers and one double. That means that each StudentScores object takes O(1) storage. [Note that summing 11 items that are each constant will result only in a larger constant, so O(1) is the correct bound for a single StudentScores object.] There are N such objects, so the total amount of memory needed is O(N). The answer is B.

8. **B.** The code looks at the middle item and then searches either forward or backward from that point. There are N/2 items to be searched on each side, and each will be examined if key is either the first or last item in the list. On average, half those items will be examined, meaning about N/4 words. Since the fraction does not matter, this is O(N). The answer is B.

Chapter 10

Collections of Data

FEW OBJECTS VERSUS MANY OBJECTS

! When a problem involves only a few objects or other pieces of data, the solution usually involves a program with a named variable for each data item. Problems such as these are relatively easy to comprehend and do not require the programmer to structure the data. Unfortunately, most computer applications require the manipulation of so many data items that one cannot give each of them an individual name. In such circumstances, the solution is to use a programming construct designed to gather large amounts of data into a single collection. Much of the material in the AB curriculum concerns the various ways in which this can be done and the trade-offs that arise as one chooses which of them to implement.

SOME WAYS TO STRUCTURE DATA

! There are, of course, an essentially infinite number of ways that one can organize data, but fortunately, only a few of them are relevant within the context of AP Computer Science. The three most important are **Lists**, **Sets**, and **Maps**. Each of these is capitalized because each is implemented in Java through the use of an interface; in fact, each of these interfaces has two implementations with which an AP student must be familiar. The basic differences between these collections are summarized in the table below:

Lists	Hold individual items and have an intrinsic order (that is, they are indexed); the index order may or may not be related to the comparability of the items; may also contain the same item more than once.
Sets	Hold individual items and have no intrinsic order (are not indexed); they may *not* contain multiple instances of (or references to) the same item.
Maps	Hold pairs of data organized as (key, value); keys may not be duplicated, although the same value may appear more than one time in a given Map.

Chapters 9–12 contain material that falls only within the AB curriculum. Students studying for the A examination may safely skip these four chapters.

Any large collection of data may potentially require that data be added to it, data be removed from it, or that there be some way to go through it, e.g., to search for an item or to print out the collection. Therefore, when confronted with a problem involving large amounts of data, the first question that should be asked is: "In what way should the data be organized?" The answer to this question will usually be one of the three ways described above. Once that question has been answered, other coding options open up, but we concentrate first on the distinctions between these three main options.

LISTS

!

Lists are a concept with which you are already familiar. Lists can be found everywhere in our lives, from "to do" lists to grocery lists to "top ten" lists to lists of high school graduates in a given year. As with most properly designed objects, Lists in Java mimic lists in the real world. As a mental model for the list, it may be most fitting to consider a grocery list as it is kept on the door of a refrigerator. Such a list may require that data be added to it (we're out of milk, so we add "milk" to the list), or removed (I picked up milk on my way home from school, so we remove "milk" from the list.) Similarly, we may wish to process the entire list when we go grocery shopping.

AP students must be familiar with the following operations that can be performed on all `List`s:

boolean add(Object x)	Adds x to the end of the List; always returns true.
int size()	Returns the size of the List.
Object get(int index)	Returns the item at position index in the List.
Object set(int index, Object x)	Places x at position index in the List and returns the item that was previously in that location.
Iterator iterator()	Returns an Iterator for the List (Iterators are explained later).
ListIterator listIterator()	Returns a ListIterator for the List.

AP students must be familiar with the two most common forms of `List`s in Java: **ArrayList**s and **LinkedLists**. These classes are similar in that they both implement the same basic set of operations, but they do so in very different ways. As a result, each is more efficient at some operations than the other, and each supplies a few "specialized" operations that the other does not. Throughout our discussion of `List`s, we use the variable N to indicate the number of items in a `List` at any given time.

ArrayLists

Internally, the `ArrayList` class uses a Java-style array to hold the data in a `List`. This means that getting or setting an item is an O(1) operation, because the index is a parameter. Adding an item at the end of the `List` requires no movement of data so that, too, is usually an O(1) operation. Unfortunately, if the array is full, more complex work must be done (essentially asking the operating system for a larger array and copying the current data into that new array.) While the client does not need to worry about this, the cost of this work is O(N). Fortunately, it is guaranteed to happen rarely so that the average time for an add operation is only O(1).

In addition to the standard `List` operations, `ArrayLists` support adding an item to the middle of a `List` and removing an item (based upon its position) from the `List` (see Chapter 5). Adding an item in the middle of the `List` will require that all the items after that one to be shifted one position right to "make room" for the new item. A similar situation results when an item is removed from the middle of the `List`, but in this case the items shift to the left to "fill in the gap." As a result, both these operations take O(N) time.

LinkedLists

From the point of view of the class designer, the `LinkedList` class uses a doubly linked structure to hold the data in a list as in the figure below.

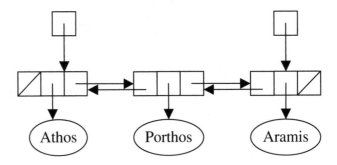

The `List` maintains references to the first and last items, but it has no mechanism to access items in the middle of the list in a direct manner. As a result, adding an item at the end of the list is O(1), but getting or setting an item takes O(N) time.

In addition to the standard `List` operations, `LinkedLists` support adding, getting, or removing the item at either end of the `List`. Since references to each end of the `List` are maintained by the class, these operations can be performed in O(1) time.

ArrayLists versus LinkedLists

Optimizing the choice of a `List` implementation requires that you have some knowledge concerning how often each of the various operations is likely to be performed. Such knowledge is usually the result of understanding the properties of the application using the `List`. The table below summarizes the running times of various operations for the two classes. The notation "by hand" means that the class does not directly support the operation, but that one could accomplish the same task through some additional coding. In the case of `ArrayLists`, the coding is actually quite easy and is shown in the table, but in the case of `LinkedLists` that coding is relatively complex and is thus omitted.

List type	ArrayList	LinkedList
add(x)	O(1) on average, but will sometimes be O(N)	O(1)
size()	O(1)	O(1)
get(index)	O(1)	O(N)
set(index, x)	O(1)	O(N)
add(index, x)	O(N)	by hand O(N)
remove(index)	O(N)	by hand O(N)
addFirst(x)	by hand O(N) [add(0,x)]	O(1)
addLast(x)	by hand, see add(x) above [add(x)]	O(1)
getFirst()	by hand O(1) [get(0)]	O(1)
getLast()	by hand O(1) [get(size()–1)]	O(1)
removeFirst()	by hand O(N) [remove(0)]	O(1)
removeLast()	by hand O(1) [remove(size()–1)]	O(1)

The most common reason to choose an ArrayList over a LinkedList is that the problem requires the ability to get (frequently) the item at a particular location. Since ArrayLists are much more efficient at this operation, they would be preferred in such a situation.

The most common reason to choose a LinkedList over an ArrayList is that the problem requires that data be removed from the list at the opposite end from which it is inserted. LinkedLists are much better for this type of operation. (Note that this is precisely what happens when one is using the List to process data in a first in, first out fashion, as with a queue. See Chapter 12 for queues.) LinkedLists are also better than ArrayLists at removing an item from the middle of a List when using an Iterator (see the section "Iterators" later in this chapter).

Lists and Comparability

There is no requirement that the items in a List be Comparable. Even if the items are Comparable, there is no requirement that the List maintain them in such an order. In fact, these List classes do not test items against each other in any sense. On the other hand, if the client code wishes, List methods can be invoked in such a manner that the resulting List is indeed kept in comparability order. This requires extra code in the client class, but such extra code may be justified by other concerns, especially overall efficiency. Note that if the data are stored in order, it is possible to use the binary search algorithm on a List. Note also that such an algorithm is regularly getting the item at an arbitrary location; therefore ArrayLists are most frequently used in such a situation.

Sets

Unlike lists, sets do not occur as obviously in our everyday lives. Sets differ from lists in two important ways: they have no intrinsic order, and they do not permit duplicate entries. A real-world example of a set might be the collection of people in a given room. If you are asked simply to list the people in a room at a given time (and notice the unfortunate use of the word "list" in this case), the order in which you name the people does not matter, and it is the case that the same person cannot be thought of as being "in the room" more than once. For most of us, however, sets arise most often in a mathematical context; fortunately the `Set` interface in Java is designed to mimic the behavior of mathematical sets, so the intuition is carried over.

AP students must be familiar with the following operations on `Set`s:

`boolean add(Object x)`	Adds x to the `Set`; returns false if the item was not added because it was already in the `Set`.
`boolean contains(Object x)`	Returns `true` if the `Set` contains x.
`boolean remove(Object x)`	Removes x from the `Set` if it is there; returns `false` if x was not present and therefore not removed.
`int size()`	Returns the size of the `Set`.
`Iterator iterator()`	Returns an `Iterator` for the `Set` (`Iterator`s are explained later).

AP students must be familiar with the two most common forms of `Set`s in Java: **TreeSet**s and **HashSet**s. These classes are similar in that they both implement the same basic set of operations, but they do so in very different ways. As a result, each is more efficient at some operations than the other. As with our discussion of `Lists`, we use the variable N to indicate the number of items in a `Set` at any given time.

TreeSets

From the view of the class designer, the `TreeSet` class uses a balanced binary search tree array to hold the data in the set. Search trees (of any type) require that data items be compared to each other; therefore, any data placed into a `TreeSet` must have such a capability. This constraint is enforced by requiring that elements of a `TreeSet` implement the `Comparable` interface. As a result of the difficulties of correctly implementing the `compareTo` method when the objects are of vastly different types, `TreeSet`s are generally used only for homogeneous collections, i.e., those in which all the objects are of the same type (or inherit from the same type.)

Because the search tree is balanced, `TreeSet`s can guarantee that no addition, removal, or search operation will take more than O(log N) time.

HashSets

From the view of the class designer, the `HashSet` class uses a hash table to hold the data in the set. Hash tables require that all data items be reducible to an integer through the use of a hash function. In Java, this means that they must implement the **hashCode** method. All objects have such a method (inherited from the `Object` class), so any object may be placed in a `HashSet`, even if it simply inherits the implementation of `hashCode`. `HashSet`s will work correctly but if the elements merely inherit the method rather than redefine it, a `HashSet` will not perform its methods efficiently.

Under optimal conditions, `HashSets` can expect that addition, removal, and search operations complete in O(1) time. Under poor conditions, however, these operations may take O(N) time. The most common cause of such conditions is a poorly written hash function. A hash function must:

- Convert the object into an integer (much the same as the `toString` method converts an object into a `String`), but it must do so in a manner that does not change over time—even if the data in the object change.
- To the greatest degree possible, it must convert different objects to different integers.

The first condition is mandatory for the hash table to work at all; the second is required for the hash table to work efficiently. Thus, if a programmer simply converts all objects to the same integer, say 7, then a `HashSet` could be used, but it would run very inefficiently. In this case, all the elements would be placed in the same hash location in memory. The `HashSet` methods are coded so that the correct results would be attained, but it could take O(N) time to access an item rather than O(1). [Warning: if all elements of a `Set` hash to the same value (i.e., if the hash value is based upon the `Set` and not the elements themselves) exactly this situation will occur.] If the same programmer used a random number generator in an effort to get lots of different values, then the same object would not always be converted to the same integer, and therefore the `HashSet` would not work correctly at all. Writing good hash functions is quite difficult, although the ones incorporated into the Java library classes are indeed well written.

Even when perfect hash functions are used, it is possible that an add operation may take O(N) time. From an efficiency point of view, this situation is the same as with the `add` method on `ArrayLists`; it occurs very rarely, so that while the worst-case cost of an `add` operation is O(N), the average case is O(1).

`TreeSets` versus `HashSets`

Optimizing the choice of a `Set` implementation necessitates that you keep in mind the requirements of the problem and of the classes you wish to use. The performance characteristics of the candidate `Set`s are summarized in the table below:

`Set` type	`TreeSet`	`HashSet`
add(x) contains(x) remove(x)	O(log N)	O(1) on average with a good hash function; O(N) in worst case
size()	O(1)	O(1)

Sometimes the choice between a `TreeSet` and a `HashSet` is more or less forced upon the programmer; at other times, it requires judgment.

- If the data to be placed in the `Set` are not `Comparable`, then there are no options; a `HashSet` *must* be used.
- If the data to be placed in the set are `Comparable`, then other factors come into play:
  - If the occasional O(N) behavior is unacceptable for some reason (e.g., safety), then a `TreeSet` must be used.
  - If a good hash function cannot be written for some reason, then a `TreeSet` must be used.
  - Otherwise, a `HashSet` is the best choice.

Constructing a Set

Within Java, Set is an interface, not a class. TreeSet and HashSet are classes that implement that interface. Therefore, it is not possible to apply the new operator to a Set; one must construct either a TreeSet or a HashSet as indicated below:

```
Set s = new Set();           // ERROR: Cannot instantiate the Set s,
                             // since it is not a concrete class
TreeSet ts = new TreeSet();  // Legal
HashSet hs = new HashSet();  // Legal
```

Iterators

For the most part, the operations discussed so far concerning collections of data focus on adding to or removing from the collection. It is also the case, however, that one might wish to perform some operation on the entire data set such as print each item. If printing is all that is desired, then the toString method will take care of the problem. Suppose, however, that more sophisticated processing is desired. For instance, a teacher wishes to add 10 points to the grade of each student in a course, or a sales manager wants a list of only those salespeople who have sold fewer items than their quota. In such cases, it is necessary to go through the entire collection, processing each item as we go.

With Lists, we could easily accomplish this using a loop such as:

```
for (int pos = 0; pos < myList.size(); pos++)
{
  Item x = (Item) myList.get(pos);
  // process x
}
```

This would work, but it has some drawbacks. The loop will execute N times. If the list in question happens to be an ArrayList, the get method will take O(1) time and thus the total time will be O(N), assuming that processing is also O(1). If, however, the list in question happens to be a LinkedList, the get method will take O(N) time itself, and the total time will be O(N²). [One teacher we know had students processing a large list and was surprised when one group's program seemed to be in an infinite loop while everyone else's ran almost instantly. Upon closer examination, the "infinite" loop was not infinite at all, but the code was using the get method with a LinkedList. The difference between O(N) and O(N²) in this case was the difference between "instant" and "infinite"!]

The problem is even worse if we are working with a Set. Since Sets are unordered, there is no get method available. [In fact, given that Sets are unordered, the idea of a "fifth" (or any other) element, makes no sense.] On the other hand, the idea of performing an operation on every element of a Set is one that Java does support; this is achieved through the use of an **Iterator**.

Iterators are objects whose entire function is to go through a Collection (List or Set) and return each of the items in that Collection one at a time. Iterators have three methods of interest to AP students: next, hasNext, and remove. Any Collection can provide an Iterator through a method designed for that purpose. To process a Collection in the same manner as above, one uses code such as:

```
Iterator it = myCollection.iterator();
while (it.hasNext())
{
  Item x = (Item) it.next();
  // process x
}
```

The first line of this code constructs the Iterator named it. Thereafter this Iterator will give us items one at a time from the Collection. As long as there are more items to be given to us, the method hasNext will return true. Once the last item has been given (or initially, if the Collection was empty), hasNext will return false. The method next gives us back some item from the Collection that has not yet been returned by this iterator. An important consequence of this is that *it is almost always an error to have two invocations of next in the same loop!* This is a fundamental difference between next and get. Multiple invocations of get may be inefficient but will not usually result in an incorrect program. Multiple invocations of next will almost always result in incorrect code. Both the hasNext and next methods will run in O(1) time.[1] Thus, had the students in the earlier example used an Iterator, their program would have run quickly even with a LinkedList.

The remove method removes the most recently iterated item from the Collection. To purge graduates from a list of students, one could use the following code:

```
Iterator it = pupils.iterator();
while (it.hasNext())
{
  Student s = (Student) it.next();
  if (s.hasGraduated())
  {
    it.remove();
  }
}
```

The running time of the remove method depends on the specifics of the Collection used: in the case of ArrayLists, it is O(N); in the case of LinkedLists, it is O(1); in the case of TreeSets, it is O(logN); and in the case of HashSets, it is O(1) on average, but O(N) in the worst case.

In general, using Iterators instead of the get method will not lengthen your code, will make it easier to use the code with other Collections, and may improve the efficiency. Once you have mastered them, there is no downside to using them, and when you are using Sets, they are the only way to perform an operation on each element.

ListIterators

Java supplies a "fancier" type of Iterator, called a **ListIterator**, that can work only on Lists. As the ListIterators are subinterfaces of the Iterator interface, they support the three methods discussed above. They actually support about six other methods, but only two are of interest to the AP student, add and set.

| set(Object x) | Replace the Object most recently returned by the Iterator with the parameter, x. |
| add(Object x) | Place the Object x into the List immediately following the Object most recently returned by the Iterator. |

[1]With tree implementations the first invocation of the next method will take O(logN) time although all subsequent invocations will take O(1) time.

Sets, Iterators, and Ordering

Students are often confused by the following question: "If a Set has no order but an Iterator returns the items in a specific order, then doesn't the Set have an order after all—namely the one returned by the Iterator?" It might seem that this is the case, but consider having a set of friends. If you were asked to name them all, you would, of necessity, name them in some order. This order does not, however, mean that you have a ranking that distinguishes a fine order so that you can state that Chris is your 23rd best friend and Barbara is your 24th. The Iterator will indeed give "an order," but it is not "the Set's order" since the Set, by its very definition, does not have an order.

Having said all this, we can sometimes predict the order that an Iterator will use. For a List, it is—as one might expect—the order of the List. For a TreeSet, it is the order used by the compareTo method that stores the items in the tree. For a HashSet, it is the hashCode order. Of course, in this case, it is usually difficult or impossible to understand that order; it just appears to be random.

Maps

Sometimes when one is building collections of objects, one piece of data is "key" in the sense that it is unique and is used to "index" the other items. For instance, student records are often organized by student identification number. (Names are not used for this purpose in case two students have the same name; one of the authors went to school with two students named Jonathan Robert Miller III.) In such a case, the student ID number is used as the key to extract all the data from the Collection. One can imagine a loosely structured Collection such as in the figure.

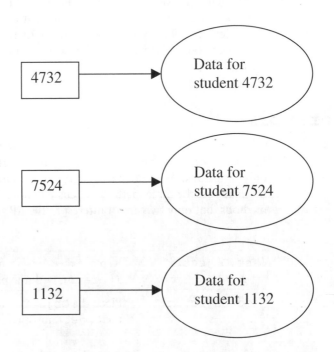

The data in the boxes represent the student ID numbers. None of these is ever duplicated. The data in the ovals represent all the stored data for the student, e.g., name, address, grades, class rank. Some of these data may be duplicated; two students might very well have the same grade—or even the same name.

A **Map** is a construct that stores (key, value) pairs. The keys must form a Set, that is each one must be unique, and each key must be associated with a value. There is no restriction on the values; although it is not common, two keys may have the same value.

Java supports Maps in the same way that it supports Sets. There are six methods that one can perform on Maps. The first four of these are similar to the methods invoked upon Sets. The last two are unique to Maps. These six methods are described in the table below:

put(Object key, Object value)	If key is not already in the Map, then the pair (key, value) is added to the Map. If key was present in the Map, then the value associated with key is updated to be the one specified in the parameter and the old value is returned. (If there was no pair there, then null is returned.)
get(Object key)	Returns the value that is associated with key in the Map. If key is not present in the Map, null is returned.
remove(Object key)	Removes the pair associated with key from the Map. Returns the value associated with key in the Map or null if key was not present within the Map.
size()	Returns the number of pairs in the Map.
keySet()	Returns a Set of all keys currently in the Map.
containsKey (Object key)	Returns a boolean indicating whether or not the Object key is present (as a key) in the Map.

As is the case with Set, Map is an interface, and one cannot construct a Map in Java. There are two classes that implement the Map interface: **TreeMap** and **HashMap**. From an AP perspective, each of these classes implements only the six methods described above.

TreeMaps

TreeMaps store their keys in a balanced binary search tree. Thus, as with TreeSets, the items (in this case the keys) must be Comparable. The fact that the items are in TreeSets will affect the running time of the various methods.

HashMaps

HashMaps store their keys in a hash table. Thus, as with HashSets, the items (in this case the keys) must support the hashCode method. Again, as with HashSets, since the keys are Objects, they support the hashCode method via inheritance, but the hashCode method from the Object class is not likely to lead to very good performance. It will probably be necessary to override the hashCode method in the key's class. Note, however, that if the keys are Strings (or really any other library class), then this has already been done.

TreeMaps versus HashMaps

Optimizing the choice of a `Map` implementation requires that you keep in mind the requirements of the problem and of the classes you wish to use. The performance characteristics of the candidate `Map`s are summarized in the table below:

Set implementation	TreeMap	HashMap
put(key, value) get(key) remove(key) containsKey(key)	O(log N)	O(1) on average with a good hash function; O(N) in worst case
keySet()	O(N)	O(N)
size()	O(1)	O(1)

Sometimes the choice between a `TreeMap` and a `HashMap` is more or less forced upon the programmer; at other times, it requires judgment. The criteria for making the decision are the same as with `TreeSet`s and `HashSet`s although the restrictions apply only to the keys.

- If the data to be used as keys are not `Comparable`, then there are no options; a `HashMap` *must* be used.
- If the data to be used as keys are `Comparable`, then other factors come into play:
  - If the occasional O(N) behavior is unacceptable for some reason (e.g., safety), then a `TreeMap` must be used.
  - If a good hash function cannot be written for some reason, then a `TreeMap` must be used.
  - Otherwise, a `HashMap` is the best choice.

When Is a Collection Not a `Collection`?

`Maps` are clearly collections of data, and one will often hear them referred to as such. On the other hand, many Java programmers will correctly state that `Maps` are not `Collections`. This problem is caused because we cannot tell from pronunciation alone whether or not the first letter of the word "collection" has been capitalized. When we refer to `Collections` (capital C), we are referring to the Java class library. `Lists` and `Sets` support a common set of operations (found in the `Collections` interface). As `Maps` do not support the same operations as `Lists` and `Sets`, the `Map` interface is *not* a subinterface of the `Collections` interface. Thus, in Java terms, a `Map` is not a `Collection`. In the English sense of the word, however, a `Map` is a collection. If you are ever in any doubt as to which sense is meant, check the capitalization.

Iterating over a Map

Given that `Maps` are not `Collections`, one cannot use an `Iterator` to perform some task on each pair. Instead one gathers the `keySet` and then iterates over that, using the `get` method. The code below gives a grade boost to each student in the `Map`:

```
Set idSet = pupilMap.keySet();
Iterator it = idSet.iterator();
while (it.hasNext())
{
  Object key = it.next();
  Student s = (Student) pupilMap.get(key);
  s.giveGradeBoost();
}
```

Note that since we never invoke any method on `key`, we don't need to perform a casting operation. Note also that some of the above lines can be combined to make the code more compact, but this will not affect the efficiency at all.

RAPID REVIEW

Data can be gathered together in many ways. The Java library provides a variety of interfaces and classes that can be used to arrange data in programs. Some of these are fundamental parts of the AP Computer Science curriculum.

`Collection`: A Java interface that defines a common set of operations on large amounts of data that are gathered into one object. Since `Collection` is an interface, a `Collection` is never constructed, but several specific classes, including `ArrayList` and `TreeSet`, implement this interface.

`List`: A Java interface that extends the `Collection` interface. The interface defines additional methods that take advantage of the fact that items in a list are inherently ordered by position, even if the list is not kept in sorted order.

`ArrayList`: A Java class that implements the `List` interface using an array-based implementation. This permits random access, i.e., O(1) access to all elements, but it may be inefficient to update the list on the fly.

`LinkedList`: A Java class that implements the `List` interface using a doubly linked list of objects. This permits relatively easy modification of the class, but randomly accessing elements of the `List` using the `get` method may be inefficient.

`Set`: A Java interface that extends the `Collection` interface. This interface defines additional methods that are appropriate for an unordered collection of distinct elements.

`TreeSet`: A Java class that implements the `Set` interface using a balanced binary tree to hold the objects. Most operations run in O(logN) time, but the objects inserted into the set must be `Comparable`.

`HashSet`: A Java class that implements the `Set` interface using a hash table to hold the objects. When the `hashCode` method is well implemented, most operations run in O(1) time, but the worst-case behavior will be O(N).

`Map`: A Java interface for large numbers of objects that does *not* extend the `Collection` interface. Rather `Map`s store key-value pairs of objects. The key values are used to "look up" the value portions of the pairs. The keys in a `Map` are distinct by definition, but values may be duplicated.

`TreeMap`: A Java class that implements the `Map` interface using a balanced binary tree to hold the keys. Most operations run in O(logN) time, but the objects used as keys must be `Comparable`.

`HashMap`: A Java class that implements the `Map` interface using a hash table to hold the keys. When the `hashCode` method (on the keys) is well implemented, most operations run in O(1) time, but the worst-case behavior will be O(N).

`hashCode`: A method in the `Object` class (and hence in all classes) that converts the object to an integer. It must always convert the same object to the same integer (to work at all) and should convert different objects to different integers as often as possible to attain the best possible performance of hash tables.

In addition to the classes that actually store the data, there are two utility classes with which AP students should be familiar:

Iterator: A Java class whose objects can be used to range through a Collection in such a way that each item that has been inserted into that Collection is visited once and only once. The order of visits is not controllable by the programmer, but it is known for certain of the Collection classes.

ListIterator: A Java class that extends Iterator to include additional methods to set and add elements during a traversal of a List. (It also contains methods to reverse the traversal process although these are not tested on the AP exam.)

PRACTICE PROBLEMS

1. Which of the following best describes how items are stored in a java.util.TreeMap?

   A. The keys are stored in an ArrayList; the values are stored in a balanced binary search tree.
   B. The keys are stored in a balanced binary search tree; the values are stored in an ArrayList.
   C. The keys are stored in an unspecified Collection; the values are stored in a balanced binary search tree.
   D. The keys are stored in a balanced binary search tree; the values are stored in an unspecified Collection.
   E. The keys and values are stored together in a balanced binary search tree, in which the keys are used as the basis for comparisons.

2. Consider the code below. What are the best possible time estimates for the running time of this fragment if the List is an ArrayList or a LinkedList, respectively?

```
final int N = <some value>;
List data = new _____( ); // Some type of List
for (int i=0; i<N; i++)
{
  data.add( new Integer(i*N) );
}
```

   A. O(N); O(N)
   B. O(N); O(N²)
   C. O(N²); O(N)
   D. O(N²); O(N²)
   E. None of the above

3. A bag (sometimes called a *multiset*) is an unordered collection of data that *does* permit duplicated elements. Which of the following data structures is likely to yield the best average-case behavior when a large number of items of unknown type are to be added to and removed from the bag?

   A. An ArrayList of all the items.
   B. A TreeMap in which the item is the key, and an Integer holds its frequency in the list.
   C. A TreeSet of all the items.
   D. A HashSet of all the items.
   E. A HashMap in which the keys are the types of the items, and the values are the items themselves.

Questions 4–6 relate to the following scenario: At a certain school, a teacher will serve as an advisor to many students, but a student will have only a single teacher as an advisor. We wish to support two operations: given the name of a student, return the name of the advisor—this method is named findAdvisor; and given the name of a teacher, return a set of students for whom that teacher is the advisor—this method is named findStudents. There are N teachers and K students. Two methods of storing this data are proposed:

I.   Store the data in a HashMap with the teacher names as the key and TreeSets of student names (for whom that teacher is the advisor) as the values.
II. Store the data in a TreeMap with the student names as the keys and the name of that student's teacher as the associated value.

4. If Method I is used, what will likely be the best estimate of the average running time of the findAdvisor method?

   A. O(1)
   B. O(logN)
   C. O(N)
   D. O(N*logK)
   E. O(N*K)

5. If Method II is used, what will likely be the best estimate of the average running time of the findAdvisor method?

   A. O(1)
   B. O(logN)
   C. O(logK)
   D. O(N)
   E. O(K)

6. Which of the following statements about the findStudents method is true?

   A. It will be easier to write with Method I than with Method II and will run faster, on average.
   B. It will be easier to write with Method II than with Method I and will run faster, on average.
   C. It will be easier to write with Method I than with Method II, but the code for Method II will run faster, on average.
   D. It will be easier to write with Method II than with Method I, but the code for Method I will run faster, on average.
   E. There will be no significant difference in either code complexity or running time no matter which method is used.

7. What is the effect of running the code below on LinkedList named data?

```
for (int k=0; k<data.size(); k++)
{
  Object temp = data.removeFirst();
  data.addLast( temp );
}
```

   A. The code will loop forever.
   B. The items in the List will be unchanged.
   C. The items in the List will be the same, but the order will be reversed.
   D. The items in the first half of the List will be moved to the end.
   E. If the List has an odd number of elements, an exception will be thrown; if it has an even number of elements, every other one will have been moved to the end of the List.

8. The code below is intended to determine if the elements in a nonempty `ArrayList` named data are in increasing order. (All the items in the `List` are known to be `Animal` objects, and `Animal` objects are known to be `Comparable`.) Which of the following statements describes the effectiveness of the code?

```
public static boolean isIncreasing( List data)
{
  Iterator it = data.iterator();
  Animal first = (Animal) data.get(0);
  while (it.hasNext())
  {
    Animal other = (Animal) it.next();
    if (first.compareTo(other) <= 0)
    {
      return false;
    }
    first = other;
  }
  return true;
}
```

A. The method works as intended.
B. The method gives the wrong answer on all `Lists`, i.e., returns `true` when it should return `false` and vice versa.
C. The method returns `true` only when the items are in decreasing, not increasing, order.
D. The method always returns `false`.
E. The method always returns `true`.

9. Which of the following is the best reason to use `Iterators` instead of the `get` method when trying to list all the elements of a `List`?

A. The `get` method is not implemented for all `Lists` and so cannot be used.
B. `Iterators` will run faster than using the `get` method no matter what kind of `List` is being used.
C. `Iterators` will run at least as fast as the `get` method no matter what kind of `List` is being used, and they will run faster for some types of `Lists`.
D. The code using `Iterators` will be significantly shorter than the code using the `get` method.
E. The statement is not true; it is better to use the `get` method when listing all the elements of a `List`.

SOLUTIONS TO THE PRACTICE PROBLEMS

1. **E.** Values are paired with and stored with their keys, not in some other `Collection`. Each of the first four answers separates the keys and the values. The answer is E.

2. **A.** Adding at the end of either an `ArrayList` or a `LinkedList` is an $O(1)$ operation. Since this happens N times, the running times will be $O(N)$ in each case. The answer is A.

3. **A.** Since the items are of unknown type, they cannot be assumed to be `Comparable`, so trees cannot be used to store them. Since there may be duplicates, `Sets` cannot be used to store them. Since there is no need to store the type of the item, the answer is A.

4. **D.** It will be necessary to iterate over all the keys (teacher names) in the `Map`. Each associated `Set` must then be checked to see if it contains the desired student. There are N teachers, and each lookup takes O(1) time on average; for each teacher, we must ask if the desired student is contained in the associated `Set`. The `contains` operation on a `TreeSet` with (up to) K items takes O(logK) time, so the expected time is O(N*logK). The answer is D.

5. **C.** It takes O(logK) time to find the student in the tree of keys. One step more will give us the name of the advisor. The answer is C.

6. **A.** Using Method I, all that is needed is to perform a `get` operation on the map. Using Method II, we must traverse the entire tree which will require an `Iterator` and will also take at least O(N) time. Thus, Method I will be both simpler and faster. The answer is A.

7. **B.** Each pass through the loop moves the front element to the back of the `List`. Since this is done once for each element, there will be no net effect on the `List`. The answer is B.

8. **D.** The first time through the loop, the initial item is compared to itself. This will yield a return value of 0, so the method will always return false. The answer is D. [Note that this flaw could be fixed by using `it.next()` rather than `data.get(0)` in the statement immediately preceding the `while` loop. If such a fix were made, the code would still be flawed because the test on the comparison is backwards.]

9. **C.** `Iterators` will be just as fast as the `get` method for an `ArrayList` and much faster than the `get` method for a `LinkedList`. The code is essentially the same in length. The answer is C.

Chapter 11

Dynamically Linked Structures

WHEN THE LIBRARY ISN'T ENOUGH

The Java Collection classes are particularly well written and are reasonably efficient, but they do not represent the definitive solution to all programming problems. The AP Computer Science (AB) curriculum expects that students will be able to work directly with "customized" data structures as well as being able to use the ones provided by the library. There are at least three reasons why this is a good idea: (1) such ability indicates an understanding of the way data are organized in the Java environment, (2) it promotes a deeper understanding of the library classes, and (3) in specific situations, it may be possible to achieve greater efficiency than the class library options provide.

CLASSES FOR DYNAMICALLY LINKED STRUCTURES

The data structures in this chapter all share the property that they are frequently changing (hence they are called dynamic) and that the various pieces of data within them refer to other pieces of data within them (hence they are called linked). There are many ways to build dynamically linked structures, but the AP exam will make use of two particular classes when asking questions about them. These two classes will be provided with the exam, but they are simple and you will save time if you become familiar with them prior to taking the exam. The first class, **ListNode** combines data and one reference to another object; the second class, **TreeNode** combines data and two references to other objects. These two classes are shown in their entirety below:

```
public class ListNode
{
  private Object value;
  private ListNode next;

  public ListNode( Object initValue, ListNode initNext)
    { value = initValue; next = initNext; }
```

Chapters 9–12 contain material that falls only within the AB curriculum. Students studying for the A examination may safely skip these four chapters.

```
      public Object getValue() { return value; }
      public ListNode getNext() { return next; }

      public void setValue(Object theNewValue)
        { value = theNewValue; }

      public void setNext(ListNode theNewNext)
        { next = theNewNext; }
  }

  public class TreeNode
  {
    private Object value;
    private TreeNode left;
    private TreeNode right;

    public TreeNode( Object initValue)
      { value = initValue; left = null;
          right = null; }

    public TreeNode( Object initValue, TreeNode initLeft,
        TreeNode initRight)
      { value = initValue; left = initLeft;
          right = initRight; }

    public Object getValue() { return value; }
    public TreeNode getLeft() { return left; }
    public TreeNode getRight() { return right; }

    public void setValue(Object theNewValue)
      { value = theNewValue; }

    public void setLeft(TreeNode theNewLeft)
      { left = theNewLeft; }

    public void setRight(TreeNode theNewRight)
      { right = theNewRight; }
  }
```

Objects of these two classes are like Lego blocks: they are each simple, but if you know how to connect them properly, they can be used to make very complex structures.

SINGLY LINKED LISTS

The simplest structure that is typically made out of `ListNodes` is a **singly linked list.** One such list, featuring the names of the original three musketeers, is shown below:

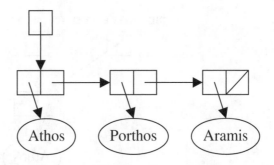

The "double square" objects represent `ListNodes`, while the ellipses represent `Strings`. It is important to recognize that a `ListNode` does not contain other objects; rather it contains a reference to a data object (in the left-hand box) and a reference to another `ListNode` (in the right-hand box). In the case of the rightmost `ListNode`, the diagonal slash indicates that the reference is `null`, i.e., there is no additional `ListNode` referenced. The variable `musketeers` contains a reference to the first `ListNode`. The first node of a list is sometimes referred to as the **head** of the list.

There are many ways in which this list might be built. The simplest is to create three `ListNodes` and then link them together. This is done via the code below:

```
ListNode a = new ListNode( new String("Athos"), null);
ListNode b = new ListNode( new String("Porthos"), null);
ListNode c = new ListNode( new String("Aramis"), null);
```

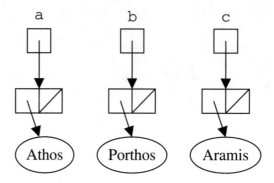

```
a.setNext(b);
b.setNext(c);
```

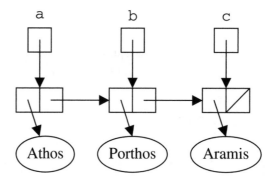

```
ListNode musketeers = a;
```

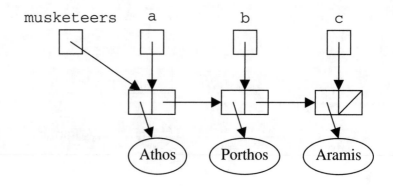

 Several aspects of the code above merit comment. First is that the use of the phrase "`new String`" is not truly necessary in the first segment. However, this is because the

String objects can be constructed without the use of the keyword new. If one is building a list of objects other than Strings, then the code would be as above. The second point of note is that the setNext method causes the next field to refer to the same object as its parameter does. Thus, the next field of b refers to the same object as c; it does not refer to c itself! This is a common student error. The third point is that there is no use of the keyword new when assigning to the musketeers object. This is because we never did create a new object in this case. In fact, the figure clearly has only three ListNodes; therefore the code should only say "new ListNode" three times, as in fact it does.

> **Tip**
>
> Diagrams such as the ones shown above are a great tool in writing code involving linked structures. Most experienced programmers use them on a regular basis. In fact, the graders of any linked structure problem given on the AP Computer Science exam will have many sheets of paper with such diagrams on them to help them trace the code that students have written. Furthermore, a study done years ago showed that students who drew such diagrams on the exam tended to score higher on such problems even though they did not earn credit for the diagrams themselves; rather it appears that this is just a habit of good students and good programmers.

ALGORITHMS ON SINGLY LINKED LISTS

The exam will test your ability to manipulate singly linked lists. Three of the most common tasks would be to add an item to such a list, to remove an item from such a list, or to scan the list for some purpose. Brief examples of each of these are shown below.

Adding to the Front of a List

The following code is an especially compact way of adding to the front of a linked list:

```
musketeers = new ListNode( new String("D'Artagnan"),
                           musketeers );
```

This creates a new ListNode which references the first item in the list. It then reassigns the reference to the front of the list to be this new node. The previous list would now appear as below:

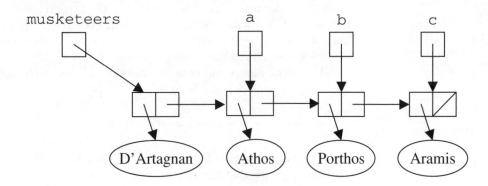

To print all the items in the list, one simply uses a loop and an extra `ListNode` reference, as with the code below:

```
for (ListNode m = musketeers; m != null; m = m.getNext())
{
  System.out.println( m.getValue() );
}
```

For this code to work, it is vital for the last node to have a `null` reference in its next field. This is, in fact, a condition upon which a large number of algorithms rely and should be maintained by all code that works on linked structures (except circularly linked lists; see the section Circularly Linked Lists later in the chapter).

Removing an Item from the List

To remove an item from a list, we simply assign the next field of its predecessor to its successor. Thus, to remove the node for Porthos from the list, we assign the next field of the node for Athos to refer to the node for Aramis. The code below accomplishes this:

```
a.setNext(c);
```

The picture is now:

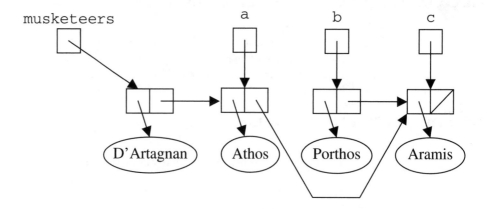

Note that we have not actually destroyed the node that refers to Porthos, but if we run the loop to print the list, we will never print his name. (Some programmers would also wish to set that node's next field to `null`. There is no harm in doing so, but it is not necessary.) It is worthwhile noting that if the node referring to Porthos is not otherwise used, the garbage collection facility of the Java environment will automatically reclaim this use of memory at some point.

The astute reader will note that deleting the first node of the list might be tricky. Actually, the code below will do so:

```
musketeers = musketeers.getNext();
```

As with many aspects of linked structures, the code itself is not difficult; the challenge is in remembering that a separate block of code is needed.

One difficulty that arises with deletion is that it is not always easy to find the predecessor of a given node. In the case above, we were fortunate that the variable a was already known to refer to the predecessor of our target. We could have found such a node via a search of the list. The following code would remove the node referring to Porthos, assuming that such a node existed:

```
if (musketeers.getValue().equals("Porthos"))   // Porthos was first
{                                               // just skip it
  musketeers = musketeers.getNext();
}
else
{
  ListNode pred = musketeers;
  ListNode target = pred.getNext();
  while (! target.getValue().equals("Porthos"))
  {
    pred = target;
    target = pred.getNext();
  }                                             // predecessor is 'pred'
  pred.getNext (target.getNext());              // remove node
}
```

TREES

While one uses the `ListNode` class to create singly linked lists, one uses the `TreeNode` class to create binary trees. A typical **binary tree** might look like this:

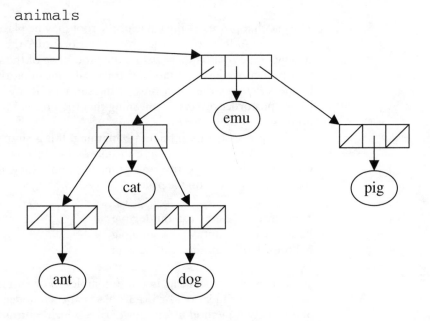

This tree contains the names of various animals. The name of the tree is in fact "animals" as indicated by the reference in the top left corner. Each of the three-box items is a `TreeNode`. The left box represents the `left` field; the middle box represents the `value` field; and the right box represents the `right` field of the `TreeNode`. The "original" `TreeNode` (in this case the one referring to "emu") is called the **root** of the tree. The nodes referred to by the left and right fields of a given node are called the **left child** and **right child** of that node. The nodes with no non-null children are called **leaves.**

All the logic that applies to manipulating singly linked lists also applies to binary trees.

Tree Traversals

One of the differences between binary trees and singly linked lists is that while there is really only one way to move through a singly linked list, there are a variety of ways to process the data in a tree. The most common are three algorithms which perform recursive traversals of the tree. By *traversal,* we mean that the algorithm visits each node of the tree. By *recursive,* we mean that the same algorithm is used independently on the left and right subtrees.

As with any recursive algorithm, traversals need a base case. The simplest tree to traverse is the empty tree; if there are no nodes, we do not need to do anything. Otherwise, there are three steps to the traversal; we must traverse the left and right subtrees, and we must process the data at the root. There are six possible traversals that result from performing these three tasks in all possible orders, but since we usually process from left to right, there are three that occur frequently. The code below shows all three:

```
public void traverse (TreeNode root)
{
  if (root != null)
  {
                          <--A--+
    traverse(root.getLeft());  |
                          <--B--+-process(root.getValue());
    traverse(root.getRight()); |
                          <--C--+
  }
}
```

The line that processes the value of the root may be placed in any of three locations. If it is placed in location A, then we have a **preorder** traversal—meaning that the processing of the root happens *before* the processing of the subtrees. If it is placed in location B, then we have an **in-order** traversal—meaning that the processing of the root happens *between* the processing of the subtrees. If it is placed in location C, then we have a **postorder** traversal—meaning that the processing of the root happens *after* the processing of the subtrees.

The processing itself might be anything. If it is simply, `System.out.println(root.getValue());` then the following output would result from the various traversals of the tree above (new lines have been changed to spaces to save space on the page):

- Preorder: emu cat ant dog pig
- In-order: ant cat dog emu pig
- Postorder: ant dog cat pig emu

Sometimes the processing is more complex. For instance, imagine that instead of `Strings`, we had stored `Animal` objects at each node. Suppose further that `Animal` objects have a method `averageWeight` which returns the average weight of an animal of that type. The following code would return the `Animal` with the highest average weight:

```
public Animal heaviest( TreeNode root )
{
  if (root == null)
     return null;
  Animal bigLeft = traverse( root.getLeft() );
  Animal bigRight = traverse( root.getRight() );

  Animal answer = root.averageWeight();
```

```
    if ( (bigLeft != null) &&
         (bigLeft.averageWeight() > answer.averageWeight() )
      answer = bigLeft;
    if ( (bigRight != null) &&
         (bigRight.averageWeight() > answer.averageWeight() )
      answer = bigRight;

    return answer;
}
```

Note that in this case we traversed the tree before we processed the data. The processing itself was simply comparing three weights to find the largest. In this case, we could have processed the data in any order; the heaviest animal is not dependent upon when we look at its node! Another interesting aspect of this code is how we handled the case when the tree (or subtree) was empty; we simply returned a null `Animal`. This also explains why we check to see if `bigLeft` and `bigRight` are not equal to `null`. On the one hand, they may be null references if that subtree is empty. On the other hand, if they are `null`, we can't do the comparison because you cannot ask a null object to perform the `averageWeight` method; if you do, a **NullPointerException** will be thrown. So, in the end, there are two lessons from this code fragment: process your data when it is easiest to do so, and always be careful about the case when the tree is empty.

BINARY SEARCH TREES

If the values that are associated with the `TreeNodes` have an underlying order (in Java, if they implement the `Comparable` interface), then a slightly more sophisticated structure can be built. If all the values associated with nodes in the left subtree are less than or equal to the value of the item associated with the root *and* if all the values associated with nodes in the right subtree are greater than or equal to the value of the item associated with the root *and* if this condition applies to every subtree, then the tree is a **binary search tree**. The tree shown earlier is, in fact, a binary search tree.

Binary search trees are excellent structures in which to store data. They permit easy access to the data as well as efficient additions to and deletions from the data set. As a result, binary search trees are a popular way to implement some of the standard data types in the Java library.

For any given item that you might wish to find in a binary search tree, there is only one place where it can be found. For instance, suppose that you wished to find dog in our original tree. You would look first at the value of the root, which is emu. This, alas, is not the node we want, but since this is a binary search tree and since emu is greater than dog, the node for dog must be in the left subtree. The node at the root of the left subtree has value cat. Again, this is not the node that we want, but this time cat is less than dog, so the node for dog must be in the right subtree. Finally, when we look at the root of that subtree, we find dog.

This algorithm can be expressed either iteratively or recursively. In either case, only one side of the tree needs to be searched at any given time.

Adding to a binary search tree is also easy. One simply searches for the item, stopping when one finds a null subtree. The new `TreeNode` is then inserted in place of the null subtree.

From a programming point of view, there are a few tricky circumstances that arise with respect to empty trees, so code to add an item to a binary search tree is shown below:

```
public TreeNode add( Object item, TreeNode root )
{
  if (root == null)
  {
    return new TreeNode(item);
  }

  Comparable rootItem = (Comparable) root.getValue();
```

```
if (rootItem.compareTo( item ) > 0)
{
  root.setRight( add(item, root.getRight() ) );
}
else
{
  root.setLeft( add(item, root.getLeft() ) );
}
return root;
}
```

The main subtlety in this code is that we are returning a `TreeNode` rather than modifying the parameter root directly. This is because all parameters in Java are passed by value, and any changes made to them would not be reflected in the code that invoked the `add` method. To understand the return values, we need consider only two cases: (1) if the tree is originally empty, then the entire tree (and hence the new root) should now be the new node created; (2) if the tree is not originally empty, then the new root should be the same as the initial root, since adding an element to a nonempty tree does not change the root. This idea of returning the tree, even as you modify it, is an important one. It applies to any structure that you modify—even singly linked lists; we just didn't mention it then to keep things simple.

Efficiency of Binary Search Trees

The efficiency of binary search trees is notoriously sensitive to the order in which operations are performed. If the simplest algorithms are used and data arrive in increasing order, then no node of the binary search tree will ever have a non-`null` left child. This effectively turns the binary search tree into a singly linked list. Fortunately, if the data arrive in random order, then the behavior is better, even with the simplest algorithms. Even more fortunately, more sophisticated, so-called *balancing algorithms* can be used to adjust the tree as new data arrive so as to ensure good behavior. Rough big-oh estimates for the various operations are summarized in the table below:

Operation	Simple Algorithm Worst Case	Balancing Algorithm
Add	O(N)	O(logN)
Find	O(N)	O(logN)
Remove	O(N)	O(logN)

HEAPS

A slightly different organizational property can be applied to binary trees. If a tree has no gaps in its structure and if the root's value is smaller than any other value in the tree and if the same is true for all subtrees, then the binary tree is said to be a **heap**. (Technically, the tree just described is a *min-heap*. An alternative definition of a heap substitutes the criterion that the root's value must be the largest. In such a case, the tree would be a *max-heap*. Most heaps in AP Computer Science are min-heaps. In any event, it should be clear from context.) While heaps are often thought of as trees, they are rarely implemented as dynamically linked structures. AP Computer Science students are expected to know about heaps, but only as they are implemented using arrays. Such an implementation is discussed in Chapter 12.

DOUBLY LINKED LISTS

The TreeNode class can be used in a slightly different manner as well. If the nodes are organized as below, a structure known as a **doubly linked list** results:

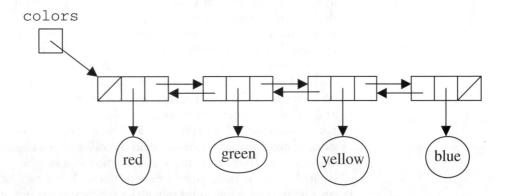

While similar to a singly linked list, this list uses the left and right fields to refer to the previous and next items in the list. Although this increases the complexity of adding something to the list—since four fields need to be updated instead of two—it makes other operations easier. In particular, it is now trivial to find the predecessor of a given node. The LinkedList class uses a doubly linked list to store its data.

CIRCULARLY LINKED LISTS

One other linked list variation is to have the last item point back to the first item. This variation, known as a **circularly linked list,** has the benefit of there being no null references in the list (and hence no NullPointerExceptions), but it has the disadvantage of it being more difficult to detect the end of the list. The end of the list is now detected when the next field is equal to the head of the list. Very little else changes about the list.

RAPID REVIEW

The classes provided by the Java library are very efficient, but they are also very general. The AP curriculum requires that students be able to manipulate data structures directly so that other, presumably more efficient, classes can be used. There are two classes that will be used on the exam for this purpose:

ListNode: A simple class that contains a reference to an Object as well as a reference to one ListNode. This class is used to create singly linked lists.

TreeNode: A simple class that contains a reference to an Object as well as two references to TreeNodes. This class is primarily used to create binary trees, although it may also be used to create doubly linked lists.

These two classes can be used to create a variety of data structures, including:

Singly linked list: Sometimes simply referred to as "linked list," this data structure consists of a series of objects, each of which can reference the next item in the series. A null, or missing, object terminates the list.

Head (of a list): A reference to the initial object in a linked list.

Binary tree: A group of objects arranged such that each object can reference up to two additional objects with no object being referenced more than once. Null, or missing, references indicate the end of a particular path.

Root: A reference to the initial object in a binary tree.

Left (right) child: The name of one (or the other) of the two references from an object in a binary tree. The adjective usually applies to the relative position on the page if the data structure is drawn out.

Leaf: An object in a binary tree that references no other objects.

Binary search tree: A specialized type of binary tree that stores objects that are comparable to each other in some way. In a binary search tree, all the objects referenceable via the left child of a given node are no greater than the object at that node, and all the objects referenceable via the right child of that node are at least as large as the object at that node.

Heap: A binary tree whose leaves are as close to the root as possible and where the value of any object is no greater than the value of any object reachable from that object's node. (Note that this is a description of a min-heap. If the word *less* is substituted for the word *greater* in the definition, then a max-heap results.)

Doubly linked list: A linked list in which each item refers not only to its successor, but also to its predecessor.

Circularly linked list: A linked list whose last node refers to the first node in the list. Note that this means that the list is not terminated via a null reference.

With all dynamic structures there is a danger that a programming error could cause an attempt to invoke a method on a null reference. Such an occurrence will result in a:

NullPointerException: A particular Exception thrown by the Java Virtual Machine when a method is invoked upon a null Object. Since the Object does not exist, the method cannot be invoked.

Algorithms that visit each node in one of these structures are called:

Traversals: An algorithm that visits each element of a linked structure. If the structure is a tree, the algorithm is often called a *tree traversal.*

There are three special tree traversals that have their own names:

Preorder traversal: A traversal of a tree in which the data in the root are traversed first, followed by the data to the left of the root, and finally by the data to the right of the root, where left and right are determined by the linking structure.

In-order traversal: A traversal of a tree in which the data to the left of the root are traversed first, followed by the data in the root itself, and finally by the data to the right of the root, where left and right are determined by the linking structure.

Postorder traversal: A traversal of a tree in which the data to the left of the root are traversed first, followed by the data to the right of the root, and finally by the data in the root itself, where left and right are determined by the linking structure.

PRACTICE PROBLEMS

1. Which of the following statements about linked lists is true?

   A. A linked list must end with a null reference.
   B. The same object may not be placed in more than one linked list at a time.
   C. One cannot put both Strings and Integers into the same linked list.

D. It takes O(N) time to traverse a linked list (not counting any time spent on processing the data in the list).

E. The first node in a linked list must be named `head`.

2. Suppose that a linked list named `heroes` holds the values [Hamlet, MacBeth, Caesar, Othello, Lear]. What values will it hold after executing the following code?

```
ListNode p = heroes.getNext();
ListNode q = p.getNext();
heroes.setNext(null);
p.setNext(heroes);
q.setNext(p);
heroes = q;
```

A. [Caesar, Othello, Lear]
B. [Caesar, MacBeth, Hamlet]
C. [Caesar, MacBeth, Hamlet, Othello, Lear]
D. [Hamlet]
E. The list is empty.

Questions 3 and 4 refer to the tree below:

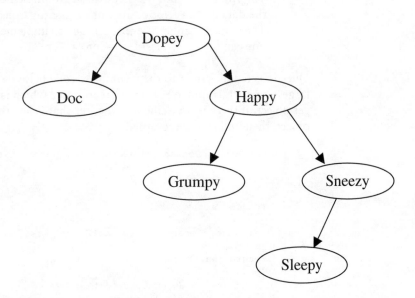

3. Which of the following represents an order in which the strings might have been inserted to create this tree?

I.   [Doc, Dopey, Grumpy, Happy, Sleepy, Sneezy]
II. [Dopey, Happy, Sneezy, Grumpy, Sleepy, Doc]
III. [Dopey, Happy, Doc, Sleepy, Sneezy, Grumpy]

A. I only
B. II only
C. III only
D. II and III only
E. None of the orders would produce that tree.

4. In what order would the names appear if a postorder traversal of the tree were used to print the names?

   A. Doc, Dopey, Happy, Grumpy, Sleepy, Sneezy
   B. Doc, Grumpy, Happy, Sleepy, Sneezy, Dopey
   C. Sneezy, Sleepy, Happy, Grumpy, Dopey, Doc
   D. Doc, Grumpy, Sleepy, Sneezy, Happy, Dopey
   E. Sleepy, Sneezy, Grumpy, Happy, Doc, Dopey

5. An industrious student decides to use TreeNodes and a binary search tree to implement the Set interface for an application that will store only Strings in the set. The new class will be called TreeNodeSet. The binary search tree will use the standard algorithms for insertion and deletion. Which of the following statements is true about the implementation?

   A. In the worst case, TreeNodeSet will run faster than TreeSet for add and remove operations.
   B. In the worst case, TreeSet will run faster than TreeNodeSet for add and remove operations.
   C. In the worst case, TreeSet and TreeNodeSet will take approximately the same amount of time for add and remove operations.
   D. The student cannot use TreeNodes to implement the Set interface because the data in TreeNodes are not necessarily Comparable.
   E. The student cannot use TreeNodes to implement the Set interface because one cannot put a TreeNode into a Set.

Questions 6 and 7 refer to the incomplete code below which is meant to find the largest object in a nonempty binary search tree which is less than or equal to the target object. If there is no element in the tree that is less than or equal to the target object, then null is to be returned.

```
public Object search (TreeNode root, Comparable target)
{
  if (root == null)
  {
    return null;
  }
  if (target.compareTo( root.getData() ) < 0)
  {
    return search(root.getLeft(), target);
  }
  else if ( /* MISSING CODE */ )
  {
    return root.getData();
  }
  else
  {
    Object ret = search(root.getRight(), target);
    if (ret == null)
    {
      return root.getData();
    }
    else
    {
      return ret;
    }
  }
}
```

6. Which of the following *cannot* be used to replace the missing code without potentially introducing errors?

```
A. target.compareTo( root.getData() ) == 0
B. target.compareTo( root.getData() ) <= 0
C. target.equals( root.getData() )
D. target == root.getData()
E. root.getData().equals( target )
```

7. If there are N nodes in the tree, what is the worst-case running time of this method?

A. O(1)
B. O(logN)
C. O(N)
D. O(NlogN)
E. O(N^2)

8. What is the result of running the following code?

```
ListNode data = null;
for (int i=0; i<7; i++)
{
   data = new ListNode(new Integer(i*i), data);
}
int total = 0;
ListNode p = data;
while (p != null)
{
  if (total < 20)
  {
    Integer piece = (Integer) p.getData();
    total += piece.intValue();
    p = p.getNext();
    data.setNext(null);
  }
}
System.out.println("Total is" + total);
```

A. Prints "Total is 14"
B. Prints "Total is 21"
C. Prints "Total is 36"
D. Machine is caught in an infinite loop.
E. A `NullPointerException` is thrown.

SOLUTIONS TO THE PRACTICE PROBLEMS

1. D. Circular linked lists are not terminated by a null reference; there are no restrictions on the contents or names of items in a linked list; and there is no restriction on other use of data that are stored in a linked list. The answer is D.

2. B. The last two items are "lost" when q's next field is reset. The other items are reversed. The answer is B.

3. B. Any node in the tree must be inserted before its children. Therefore Dopey must be inserted before Doc, and Sleepy must be inserted before Sneezy. This rules out the first and third sequences. The second sequence produces the desired tree. The answer is B.

4. **D.** The last item printed in a postorder traversal will be the root itself. This rules out the first and third choices. The second item printed will be the right child of the root (assuming that such a child exists.) This rules out the third and fifth choices. The answer is D.

5. **B.** Any item may be placed in a `Set`, so the last choice is incorrect. Similarly, the restriction on the data in `TreeNodes` is no different from the restriction on data placed in a `TreeSet`, so the fourth choice is incorrect. Since `TreeSets` use a balanced tree to hold the data and since `TreeNodeSets` use the standard (nonbalancing) algorithms, `TreeSets` will be more efficient in the worst case. The answer is B.

6. **D.** Using the == operator introduces the possibility of errors if two objects are clones of each other. Notice that it is permissible to use the <= operator in the second choice because the previous `if` test has already screened out all the negative return values. The answer is D.

7. **C.** This method could require visiting the deepest node in the tree. If the tree were built out of data received in increasing order, it would essentially be a linked list and this depth would be N. The answer is C.

8. **C.** The first loop builds a seven-element list whose data are the squares of the numbers from six to zero. The second loop sums those values, stopping when the total exceeds 20. Although all elements of the list are disconnected after the code has finished executing, no exceptions are thrown. The answer is C.

Elementary Data Structures: Stacks, Queues, and Priority Queues

LISTS—GENERAL AND SPECIAL PURPOSE

! The AP Computer Science syllabus includes both the `ArrayList` and `LinkedList` classes covered earlier. If you were to examine the documentation for these classes carefully, you would learn that both implement the `List` interface. In a general sense, what these classes—and this interface—do is enable the client to add (and remove) items from arbitrary locations within a list. This is clearly very general, and is often useful—particularly if the items are arranged in some specific order, e.g., sorted order, within the list. These operations also come with a cost, however. The ability to perform arbitrary modifications to the list means that some of the operations will take O(N) time on average. There are times when a client may wish to achieve faster performance and may not need the ability to perform arbitrary modifications to the list. In this chapter, we discuss three data structures that offer alternatives to the general `ArrayList` and `LinkedList` classes: **stacks, queues,** and **priority queues**.

STACKS

! There are times when all that is needed is a "one-ended" structure. This is, in fact, how the computer keeps track of which method is executing at any given time. Suppose that we start our program by executing method A (often, but not always "main"). This method invokes B, which in turn invokes C, which in turn invokes D. When D terminates, the computer resumes one of the previous methods. The decision about which of the previous methods to resume is made quite simply: the most recently suspended method is the one that is resumed—in our example, that would be C. This situation can be modeled physically as follows: every time a method is invoked, a slip of paper corresponding to that method is placed on the top of a pile on a desk; and every time a method terminates, its slip of paper is removed from the top of the pile and the method corresponding to the new top slip is resumed at the place it left off. The pile of slips gives us

---

Chapters 9–12 contain material that falls only within the AB curriculum. Students studying for the A examination may safely skip these four chapters.

the ability to quickly determine which method to resume. The slips of paper can be thought of as comprising a list, but in this case, we add or remove items from only one end of the list. This means that we don't need all the "power" of a general list—we could implement a data structure for this "list" more simply and more efficiently.

The key property of such a one-ended "list" is the **LIFO property**—last in, first out. The LIFO property states that we don't actually care where the items are stored, just as long as things are set up so that when we remove an item, the item removed is the one that was most recently (or "last") added. LIFO structures have many applications in the field of computer science—enough that the concept has been formalized. An object that implements the LIFO protocol is called a *stack,* and it has particular operations associated with it. Within the context of the AP Computer Science exam, these operations are expressed through an interface. This interface is fairly standard, but is not actually part of the Java library. An abbreviated form of the interface is shown below. (Note that a more complete version of this interface would be provided with the exam; you will save time, however, if you are familiar with it before you begin the test itself.)

```
public interface Stack
{
  boolean isEmpty();      // returns true if stack is empty
  void push(Object x);    // adds x to the stack
  Object pop();           // removes top item from the
                          // stack and returns it
  Object peekTop();       // returns top item of the
                          // stack without removing it
}
```

The more extensive documentation for these methods explains that they implement the LIFO protocol described above. The names push, pop, and isEmpty are universal; the peekTop method is simply called top in some textbooks. As with any interface, there is no code, so one cannot make statements about the running time of the methods. However, the standard ways of implementing these methods result in O(1) time being taken (on average) for each of them. An implementation of stacks using ArrayLists is shown below:

```
public class ArrayListStack implements Stack
{
  private ArrayList data;
  public ArrayListStack()
    { data = new ArrayList(); }
  public boolean isEmpty()
    { return data.size()==0; }
  public void push(Object x)
    { data.add(x); }
  public Object pop()
    { return data.remove(data.size()-1); }
  public Object peekTop();
    { return data.get(data.size()-1); }
}
```

The documentation provided with the interface includes one subtlety not directly addressed by this code: both the pop and peekTop methods are supposed to throw an unchecked exception if the stack is empty. (After all, how can you take an item out of an empty stack?) Note that if the stack is empty, the size of data is zero. In such a case the code will attempt to remove or get item number –1 from the ArrayList. This will result in an IndexOutOfBoundsException being thrown. This fulfills that term of the contract.

Applications of Stacks

Stacks are typically used at the assembly-language level to ensure that method invocation works as desired. Each time a new method is invoked, an item is added to the systems "call stack." If you invoke methods continually without stopping—perhaps because of an error in the coding of a recursive method—then the call stack will fill up and a `StackOverflowError` will occur. The point at which this error occurs depends upon the number of parameters the method has, the amount of memory available to the Java Virtual Machine, and other criteria; the specifics are not important, but a student should understand that the overflow will occur. The name of this error is not tested on the exam, but the general concept might be.

Stacks are also used by compilers to help translate high-level languages into assembly code. They are used to help the compiler match else clauses with if statements (i.e., an else is matched with the last if statement seen so far). They are also used to control the order in which operations are performed. Consider the expression 3+4*5; it evaluates to 23, but a different order of operations would cause the value to be 35. These two interpretations of the expression are shown in trees in the figure below. Underneath each tree is the result of a postorder traversal of that tree.

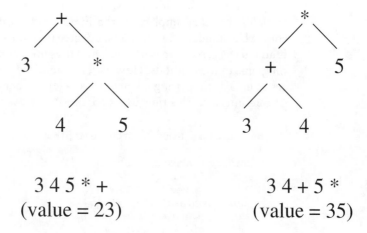

$$3\ 4\ 5\ *\ +$$
$$(\text{value} = 23)$$

$$3\ 4\ +\ 5\ *$$
$$(\text{value} = 35)$$

The two expressions (3 4 5 * +) and (3 4 + 5 *) are called *postfix expressions* because the multiplication and addition operators come after (*post*) the data. Typical expressions such as 3 + 4 are called *in-fix expressions* because the operator is in the middle of the data. When the compiler encounters an arithmetic expression, it often converts that expression to its postfix form. It then uses the following algorithm to code that form:

> *For each token (e.g., number or operator)*
> *If that token is a number, push it onto the stack.*
> *If that token is an operator, pop the top two numbers off the stack, apply the*
> *operator, and push the result back onto the stack.*
> *When all the data have been processed, the answer is on top of the stack (and is*
> *the only value in the stack)*

All this happens internally either during the compilation of the program (if-else matching) or during the execution (method invocation, expression evaluation). Although the stack is "out of sight," it is nonetheless a fundamental part of the execution of any program.

In less technical contexts, stacks are also used to model situations where data access is limited to only one "end," such as a pile of objects that grows upward, or parking cars in a dead-end alley.

QUEUES

Queues are very similar to stacks. They differ in that they implement the **FIFO,** or first in, first out, **protocol.** This is the protocol that most (polite) people use when waiting in line. The first person to arrive in line is the first person to be "served." After that person has been served, the next person to be served will be the one who arrived first—of those remaining in the queue.

As with stacks, AP Computer Science students will be provided with an interface for queues. The abbreviated version of that interface is given below:

```
public interface Queue
{
  boolean isEmpty();          // returns true if queue is empty
  void enqueue(Object x);     // adds x to the queue
  Object dequeue();           // removes front item from the
                              // queue and returns it
  Object peekFront();         // returns front item of the
                              // queue without removing it
}
```

Similar to the case with stacks, the more extensive documentation for these methods explains that they implement the FIFO protocol described above. These names are somewhat standard, but to a lesser degree than the stack method names. Again, Queue is an interface, so there is no code, and thus one cannot make statements about the running time of the methods. However, the standard ways of implementing these methods result in O(1) time being taken (on average) for each of them. An implementation of the Queue interface, this time using LinkedLists, is shown below:

```
public class LinkedListQueue implements Queue
{
  private LinkedList data;
  public LinkedListQueue()
    { data = new LinkedList(); }
  public boolean isEmpty()
    { return data.size()==0; }
  public void enqueue(Object x)
    { data.addLast(x); }
  public Object dequeue()
    { return data.removeFirst(); }
  public Object peekFront();
    { return data.getFirst(); }
}
```

Again, as with the Stack interface, the documentation for the Queue interface states that an exception must be thrown if we invoke either the dequeue or peekFront methods on an empty queue. The LinkedList class does this for us, throwing the NoSuchElementException in these cases. Note that this is not the same exception as in the stack example, but that does not matter. The contract did not specify a particular exception to throw.

Applications of Queues

Queues are probably most commonly used in simulations where objects (people, cars, etc.) must "line up"; in fact, there is an entire branch of mathematics called *queuing theory* which studies the performances of queues under a variety of assumptions. They are also used by operating systems for various tasks, including managing network traffic and print jobs; you may have had occasion to look at the list of jobs in a printer queue at some point. They are also sometimes used by the operating system to schedule the various processes that are running "simultaneously" on a computer.

A queue is also an excellent data structure for printing out the data in a tree in a "top to bottom" or level ordering. For instance, the level ordering of the tree below is mercury, mars, venus, saturn, neptune, jupiter, earth.

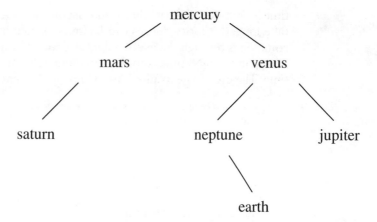

A level-order traversal of the tree can be performed with the following algorithm:

Insert the root into an empty queue
As long as the queue is not empty
   Remove an item from the queue.
   If the item has a left child, insert that child into the queue.
   If the item has a right child, insert that child into the queue.
   Process the item (possibly just print it).

PRIORITY QUEUES

Consider a worker who is swamped with tasks. When she finishes what she is working on, she starts on a new task. Which one should she start? Why, the most important one, of course! There is another kind of specialized list that models this process, namely the *priority queue*. The idea of the priority queue is that items are gathered in whatever order works, but that each item has a priority. When it is time to remove (start) an item, it is the item with the highest priority that is removed, not the most recently added item (as with stacks) or the least recently added item (as with queues.) In the case of our worker, the priority of a task is the same as the importance of that task.

Once again, the test may make use of an interface that can be used to implement priority queues. An abbreviated version of that interface follows:

```
public interface PriorityQueue
{
  boolean isEmpty();    // returns true if queue is empty
  void add(Object x);   // adds x to the priority queue
  Object removeMin();   // removes the lowest priority
                        // item from queue and returns it
  Object peekMin();     // returns the lowest priority
                        // without removing it
}
```

The more extensive documentation for these methods provides the exact conditions of the contract. Note that in the world of priority queues, having a lower priority means that an object is "closer to the front of the line," similar to the way that a low score is good in sports such as golf and some card games, such as hearts. (The relative priorities of an object are determined through the use of the `compareTo` method.) These method names—`removeMin`, `peekMin`, and `isEmpty`—are clear, but there is no particularly standard name for them. `PriorityQueue` is an interface, so again there is no code, and thus one cannot make statements about the running time of the methods. Unlike implementations of `Stack` and `Queue`, however, it is not possible to attain O(1) time bounds for all the methods. At least one of the `add` and `removeMin` methods must take longer. Priority queues can be implemented in many ways, but one of the most common is through the use of a data structure known as a **heap.** Items can be added to a heap in O(logN) time, and the minimum item can also be removed in that amount of time. The use of a heap allows us to implement a particularly elegant sorting algorithm:

```
// to sort the items in an array named data
Heap h = new Heap();
for (i=0; i<data.length; i++)
{
  h.add(data[i]);
}
for (j=0; j<data.length; j++)
{
  data[j] = h.removeMin();
}
```

The body of the first loop takes O(logN) time to execute. It is executed N times, so the total cost of the first loop is O(NlogN). The second loop is the same, so the total time to sort the list is O(NlogN). This algorithm is named **Heapsort** and is one of the fastest sorting algorithms from a worst-case point of view.

Tip

If the exam only makes use of the interfaces for stacks, queues, and priority queues, how will questions be asked? It depends upon the question. It would be straightforward to ask for a class that implemented the interface. On the other hand, if the exam is to make use of such a class, it will be phrased similarly to this:

```
Stack s = new ArrayStack();
       // ArrayStack implements the Stack interface
```

HEAPS

Heaps are a special kind of binary tree. Rather than store the items in "comparison order" so that searches can be performed quickly, heaps store the items so that the minimum data item can be found easily. If a binary tree has the property that all of it is as full as possible (with any gaps coming in the bottom row on the right-hand side) and the root has the minimum value of all items in the tree *and* if this condition applies to all subtrees, then that binary tree is a heap.

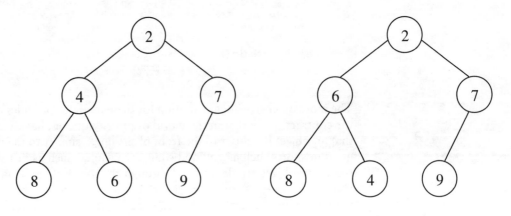

A Heap   Not a Heap (6>4)

To add an item to a heap, we put it in the "next" spot, i.e., the left-most available spot on the bottom row. If the new item is larger than its parent, we are done; if not, we swap it with its parent and continue to do so until the item is larger than its parent (or we reach the root).

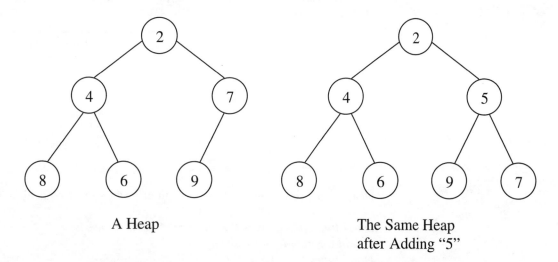

A Heap

The Same Heap
after Adding "5"

Removing the minimum item is similarly easy. We know that the minimum is at the root, so we simply take it out and hold it in a temporary variable. Then we copy up the last node to the root, and we slide it down the heap until it is smaller than both its children as in the figure below:

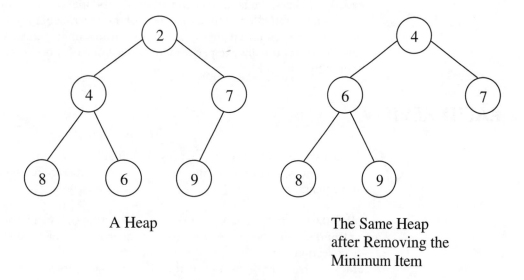

A Heap

The Same Heap
after Removing the
Minimum Item

An array can be used to mimic a binary tree in the following manner: the root is placed in cell number 1 (cell number 0 is unused); the left child of the node in cell j is put in cell 2*j; the right child of the node in cell j is put in cell 2*j+1. This makes it easy for a given node to find its children (or its parent), but there is one large drawback; if the tree is similar to a linked list, the size of the array that is needed is *much* larger than the number of elements in the tree. This waste of memory is so enormous that trees are virtually never implemented via arrays. Most rules have exceptions, however, and this one does, too. Since the heap guarantees that the tree will always be as full as possible, it also guarantees that the array will waste no space. Thus, most implementations of heaps use arrays rather than dynamically linked structures because the array is simpler and won't waste any memory.

Heaps are a particularly good data structure to use when implementing a priority queue. Adding/removing items to/from the priority queue is accomplished by adding/removing them to/from the heap. The minimum element is found at the root, and testing for emptiness is likewise simple. The running times for a priority queue implemented via an array-based heap are given in the following table.

Operation	Worst-Case Running Time
add(Object x)	O(logN)
removeMin()	O(logN)
peekMin()	O(1)
isEmpty()	O(1)

Heaps can also be used in a simple, but efficient sorting algorithm:

Do N times (where N is the number of items to be sorted)
    Add the next item to a heap.
Do N times
    Remove the minimum element from the heap.

The items will be removed in sorted order. The body of the first loop takes O(logN) time to execute and is executed N times. Thus the first loop contributes O(N*logN) time. The body of the second loop also takes O(logN) time to execute and is executed exactly N times. Thus, it also contributes O(N*logN) time. Thus, the entire sorting process takes O(N*logN) time regardless of the ordering of the data. (Although not part of the AP curriculum, many texts discuss various improvements that can be made to this algorithm to enhance performance, but none of those improvements change the overall time bound.)

RAPID REVIEW

While lists are useful for general programming, it is often the case that problems can be solved using specialized lists that restrict the set of operations, but permit more efficient implementations.

LIFO (last in, first out): A protocol for a collection that can be added to or removed from. It requires that the item to be removed be the one most recently added to the collection.

Stack: A structure that supports the LIFO protocol. Stacks are usually implemented in such a manner that all methods run, on average, in O(1) time.

FIFO (first in, first out): A protocol for a collection that can be added to or removed from. It requires that the item to be removed be the one least recently added to the collection.

Queue: A structure that supports the FIFO protocol. Queues are usually implemented in such a manner that all methods run in O(1) time.

Priority Queue: A structure that supports a protocol wherein the item to be removed from the collection is the one with the lowest associated priority. Priority queues are usually implemented in such a manner that no method takes longer than O(logN) time to complete.

Heap: A complete-as-possible binary tree where the root's value is smaller than any other value in the tree and all subtrees share the same property.

PRACTICE PROBLEMS

1. What is printed by the following block of code?

```
Stack s = new ArrayStack();
    // ArrayStack implements the Stack interface
s.push("Pow");
System.out.print(s.pop() + " ");
s.push("Bam");
s.push("Oof");
s.push("Boink");
System.out.print(s.pop() + " ");
s.push("Slam");
System.out.print(s.pop() + " ");
System.out.print(s.pop() + " ");
```

A. Pow Bam Oof Boink
B. Pow Boink Slam Slam
C. Slam Boink Oof Bam
D. Pow Boink Slam Oof
E. Pow Boink Oof Bam

2. What is printed by the following block of code?

```
Queue q = new LinkedListQueue();
    // LinkedListQueue implements the Queue interface
q.enqueue("Pow");
System.out.print(q.dequeue() + " ");
q.enqueue("Bam");
q.enqueue("Oof");
q.enqueue("Boink");
System.out.print(q.peekFront() + " ");
q.enqueue("Slam");
System.out.print(q.dequeue() + " ");
System.out.print(q.dequeue() + " ");
```

A. Pow Bam Oof Boink
B. Pow Bam Bam Oof
C. Slam Boink Oof Bam
D. Pow Boink Bam Oof
E. Bam Boink Slam

3. What is printed by the following block of code?

```
PriorityQueue pq = new ImpPriorityQueue();
    // ImpPriorityQueue implements the PriorityQueue interface
pq.add("Pow");
System.out.print(pq.peekMin() + " ");
pq.add("Bam");
pq.add("Oof");
pq.add("Boink");
System.out.print(pq.removeMin() + " ");
pq.add("Slam");
System.out.print(pq.peekMin() + " ");
System.out.print(pq.removeMin() + " ");
```

A. Bam Bam Boink Boink
B. Bam Boink Oof Pow
C. Pow Pow Bam Bam
D. Pow Bam Boink Bam
E. Pow Bam Boink Boink

4. Suppose that one has a priority queue available but wishes to have it behave in a FIFO manner, i.e., as a queue. Which of the following strategies will work?

   I. Assign the first item priority 0 and increase the priority for each subsequent item as it is enqueued.

  II. Assign the first item priority 0 and decrease the priority for each subsequent item as it is enqueued.

 III. Assign each item a priority number that is equal to the number of items currently in the queue plus one.

  A. I only
  B. II only
  C. III only
  D. II and III only
  E. None of the three schemes will work

5. The following block of code is intended to print the contents of a nonempty queue named myData leaving the items in the same order as they were originally. Which of the statements following the code is true?

```
Stack s = new SomeStack();
      // SomeStack implements the Stack interface

while (! myData.isEmpty() )
{
  s.push( myData.peekFront() );
  if (! myData.isEmpty() )
  {
    System.out.println( myData.dequeue() );
  }
}
while (! s.isEmpty() )
{
  myData.enqueue( s.pop() );
}
```

  A. The code works as intended.
  B. An unchecked exception may be thrown for some input sets.
  C. All the items from the queue will be printed in the proper order, but all the data from the queue will now be in reverse order.
  D. Almost all the items from the queue will be printed in the proper order, but some data from the queue will be lost.
  E. All the items from the queue will be printed, but in reverse order; the data from the queue will be in the correct order, however.

6. One approach to implementing the PriorityQueue interface is to use an ArrayList. The add method is implemented by invoking the ArrayList's add method. The removeMin method uses a sequential search to find the smallest item and then invokes the ArrayList's remove method on the index found. Which of the following indicate the worst-case bounds on the running times of the add and removeMin methods, respectively?

  A. O(1); O(1)
  B. O(1); O(N)
  C. O(logN); O(logN)
  D. O(N); O(N)
  E. None of the above

7. Joe's Parking Garage actually parks all its cars in a long line in an alley accessible from either end of the block, but only from those ends. What data structure would most naturally keep track of the cars in the alley?

   A. A stack
   B. A queue
   C. A priority queue
   D. A one-dimensional array
   E. None of the above

SOLUTIONS TO THE PRACTICE PROBLEMS

1. **D.** Remember that stacks are LIFO. Each print statement pops off the top item. The stack holds the single `String` "Bam" after execution of this block of code. The answer is D.

2. **B.** The second print only peeks at the front of the queue, so the item is not removed as part of that operation. The queue holds the single `String` "Boink" ahead of the `String` "Boink" after execution of this block of code. The answer is B.

3. **E.** The addition of the new items changes the minimum value between the first two print statements, but the last two items printed must be the same regardless of the data in the list. (Remember that `String`s are always compared lexicographically, i.e., in alphabetical order, but where all uppercase letters precede all lowercase letters.) The answer is E.

4. **A.** The first strategy works. The second one imitates a stack instead of a queue. The third plan will imitate no easily described structure. The third plan could also result in two or more items having the same priority, which should not happen with a queue as one of the two items would always have been inserted before the other. The answer is I only or A.

5. **C.** The items are indeed printed as they come out of the queue, but the use of the stack for temporary storage means that they will be placed back in the queue in reverse order. The answer is C.

6. **D.** The sequential search used by the `removeMin` method will take O(N) time. Completing the removal involves invoking the `remove` method on the `ArrayList` which takes an additional O(N) time. The total cost of a `removeMin` operation is thus O(N). The `add` method involves simply invoking the method of the same name on the `ArrayList`. Although the `add` method on an `ArrayList` takes O(1) time on average, its worst-case time is O(N). Thus, adding to the priority queue will take O(N) time in the word case. The answer is D.

7. **E.** Cars can be removed from both ends of the alley, but not from the middle. Stacks, queues, and priority queues offer no choice as to which item is removed; therefore, they are inappropriate. An array could store the data for the cars, but there is no natural way to add data at both ends of an array. The answer is E, none of the above.

CODE PRACTICE

The AP Computer Science curriculum states that it is expected that students will know how to implement various interfaces using "appropriate data structures." Although the format would vary, the following question contains many elements that might be present in a free-response question:

Implement the Queue interface using a linked list of ListNodes. For each of your methods, give the best possible big-oh bound on the worst-case running time for that method assuming that there are N items in the queue.

ANSWER TO CODE PRACTICE

```java
public class LinkedListQueue implements Queue
{
  private ListNode front;
  private ListNode rear;
  public LinkedListQueue ()
  {
    front = null;
    rear = null;
  }

  public boolean isEmpty()
  {
    return (front == null);
  }

  public void enqueue(Object x)
  {
    rear = new ListNode(x,rear);
    if (front == null) front = rear;
  }

  public Object dequeue()
  {
    if (front == null)
    {
      throw new NoSuchElementException();
    }
    Object toReturn = front.getValue();
    front = front.getNext();
    if (front == null) rear = null;
    return toReturn;
  }

  public Object peekFront()
  {
    if (front == null)
    {
      throw new NoSuchElementException();
    }
    return front.getValue();
  }
}
// Each of the methods runs in O(1) time
```

Other answers are possible, but the running times will almost certainly be O(1) in all cases. Note, however, that it is possible that the running time is O(N) for any of the last three methods if a loop is used to set the front or rear pointers.

PART IV

PRACTICE EXAMS
AND SOLUTIONS

Computer Science A Practice Exam A1

Answer Sheet for Multiple-Choice Questions

1. _____	11. _____	21. _____	31. _____
2. _____	12. _____	22. _____	32. _____
3. _____	13. _____	23. _____	33. _____
4. _____	14. _____	24. _____	34. _____
5. _____	15. _____	25. _____	35. _____
6. _____	16. _____	26. _____	36. _____
7. _____	17. _____	27. _____	37. _____
8. _____	18. _____	28. _____	38. _____
9. _____	19. _____	29. _____	39. _____
10. _____	20. _____	30. _____	40. _____

PRACTICE EXAM A1

Section I

Time: 1 hour and 15 minutes; number of questions, 40; percentage of grade, 50

Directions: Determine the answer to each of the following questions or incomplete statements. Using the available space for any necessary scratch work. Then fill in the space on the answer sheet corresponding to the best choice given. No credit will be given for anything written in the examination booklet. Do not spend too much time on any one problem.

Note: Assume the Java Standard Libraries and the AP Java Subset are included in any programs that use the code segments provided in individual questions. You may refer to the College Board document (Copyright © 2004 by College Entrance Examination Board), "A Quick Reference," while taking this practice exam. This document is available at www.collegeboard.com/student/testing/ap/sub_compscia.html.

1. Consider the following method:

```
public static double solve(int n)
{
  double answer = 1.0;
  for(int k = 1; k < n; k++)
    answer *= (double)k/(k + 1);
  return answer;
}
```

What value is returned by a call to method `solve`?

A. 0.0
B. the kth root of n
C. 1/n
D. 1/(n – 1)
E. $(1/2)^n$

2. Consider the following incomplete class declaration:

```
public class SeatLocation
{
  private String row; // "A", "B", ..., "Z", "AA", "BB", ..., "ZZ"
  private int seatNumber;

  public String getRow() {...}
  public int getSeatNumber() {...}
  // constructor and other methods not shown
}
public class Ticket
{
  private double price;
  private SeatLocation loc;

  public void setPrice(double p) {price = p;}
  public void setSeatLocation(SeatLocation s) {loc = s;}
  public double getPrice() {return price;}
  public SeatLocation getSeatLocation() {return loc;}
  // constructor and other methods not shown
}
```

Assume the following valid declarations have been made:

```
SeatLocation s = new SeatLocation("Q", 107);
Ticket t = new Ticket(85.00, s);
double totalCost = 0.0;
```

Which of the following statements in a client program is valid?

A. `if(s.row > "M") System.out.println("Too far back.");`
B. `t.setSeatLocation("E", 19);`
C. `System.out.println(t.getSeatLocation(s.getRow(), s.getSeatNumber()));`
D. `t.setPrice(0.5 * t.getPrice());`
E. `for(String row = "A"; row.compareTo("Z") < 0; row++)`
     `totalCost += t.getPrice(row, loc.getSeatNumber());`

3. Consider the following code segment:

```
int x = 2
int y = 4;
x += y;
y += x;
System.out.println("x = " + x + ", y = " + y);
```

What output is produced by executing this code?

A. `x = 2, y = 4`
B. `x = 6, y = 6`
C. `x = 6, y = 10`
D. `x = 6, y = 12`
E. `x = 24, y = 42`

4. Consider the following method:

```
public boolean evaluate(boolean p, boolean q)
{
  return ((p && q) || !(p || q));
}
```

What is returned by `evaluate`?

A. `evaluate` always returns `false`.
B. `evaluate` returns `true` when p and q are both true or both false.
C. `evaluate` returns `true` only when p and q are both true.
D. `evaluate` returns `true` only when p and q are both false.
E. `evaluate` returns `true` when either p or q is true and the other is false.

5. Consider the following method, which is intended to count the number of times a value is doubled before it is at least as large as a target value:

```
// precondition: d > 0
public void doubleUp(double d)
{
  static final double TARGET = 100.0;
  int count;
  while(d < TARGET)
  {
    count = 0;
    d *= 2;
    count++;
  }
  System.out.println(count);
}
```

Of the following, which best describes the error in doubleUp?

A. The static modifier cannot be used with a constant.
B. A variable is used without being initialized.
C. A double cannot be multiplied by an int.
D. The counter is incremented in the wrong place.
E. A variable is initialized in the wrong place.

6. Consider the following method:

```
public static void fun(String msg)
{
  System.out.print(msg);
  if(msg.length() < 2)
    return;
  else
    fun(msg.substring(0, msg.length()/2));
  System.out.print(msg);
}
```

What would be printed by the call fun("tickleme")?

A. ticklemeticklemeticklemeticklemeticklemetickleme
B. ticklemetickti
C. titicktickleme
D. ticklemeticktititicktickleme
E. ticklemeticktiiitititicktickle

For questions 7 and 8, consider the inheritance hierarchy shown below:

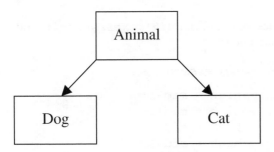

7. Suppose that we wish to add the class Snake to this hierarchy. Suppose further that the set of operations that Snakes can perform is a superset of the operations that Cats can perform. Which of the two implementation schemes below is more appropriate and why?

I.   The class Snake should extend the class Animal
II. The class Snake should extend the class Cat

A. Implementation I is a better choice because it is the case that a Snake IS-A Animal, but it is not the case that a Snake IS-A Cat.
B. Implementation I is a better choice because the code will be shorter and easier to understand.
C. Implementation II is a better choice because the Snake class can inherit most of its operations from the Cat class.
D. Implementation II is a better choice because it leads to a deeper inheritance hierarchy.
E. The two implementations are approximately equivalent.

8. Which of the following is *not* true about the data and methods in the various classes?

   A. A Dog object may use public instance variables declared in the Animal class.
   B. An Animal object may use public instance variables associated with a separate Dog object.
   C. A Cat object may use private instance variables declared in the Animal class.
   D. A Cat object may invoke public methods declared in the Animal class.
   E. A Cat object may use private instance variables associated with a separate Dog object whenever appropriate access methods are provided.

9. Consider the following incomplete method that is intended to return the position in array nums where target is found or −1 if target is not in the array.

```
// Precondition: nums is arranged in increasing order
public static int binsrch(Comparable[] nums, Comparable target)
{
  int low = 0;
  int high = nums.length - 1;
  int mid;
  while( <expression1> )
  {
    mid = (low + high)/2;

    if(nums[mid].compareTo(target) == 0)
      return mid;
    else
      if(nums[mid].compareTo(target) < 0)
        <expression2>;
      else
        <expression3>;
  }
  return -1;
}
```

Which of the following could be used to replace *<expression1>*, *<expression2>*, and *<expression3>* so that the code works as intended?

	<expression 1>	*<expression 2>*	*<expression 3>*
A.	low < high	low = mid+1	high = mid-1
B.	low <= high	low = mid-1	high = mid+1
C.	low <= high	low = mid+1	high = mid-1
D.	low >= high	low = mid+1	high = mid-1
E.	low >= high	low = mid+1	high = mid-1

Questions 10 and 11 refer to the following method.

```
private int n;

public static boolean check(int[] arr)
{
  boolean theCheck = true;
  for(int k = 0; k < n - 1; k++)
  {
    if(arr[k] >= arr[k + 1])
      theCheck = !theCheck;
  }
  return theCheck;
}
```

10. Which of the following is the best precondition for method `check` assuming that we do not wish to generate an exception?

    A. `0 <= n < arr.length`
    B. `n < arr.length`
    C. `n <= arr.length`
    D. `n >= 0`
    E. No precondition is necessary.

11. Which of the following is the best postcondition for method `check`?

    A. returns `true` if there are no duplicates in the first n elements of `arr`; otherwise, returns `false`
    B. returns `true` if the (n - 1)th element of `arr` is less than the nth element; otherwise returns `false`
    C. returns `true` if the first n elements of `arr` are all the same value; otherwise, returns `false`
    D. returns `true` if the first n elements of `arr` are in strictly increasing order; otherwise, returns `false`
    E. returns `true` if there are an even number of times when an element is at least as large as its successor among the first n elements of `arr`; otherwise, returns `false`

12. A programmer has mistakenly placed a semicolon at the end of the `while` statement in the following code fragment. What will be the result of executing the code?

```
while ( j < n );    // Mistaken semicolon
{
  System.out.println("in loop");
  j++;
}
```

    A. The code will behave in the same manner as if the semicolon were not included.
    B. The machine will get caught in an infinite loop, appearing to do nothing.
    C. The machine will get caught in an infinite loop, repeatedly printing the message, "in loop."
    D. Depending upon the code that precedes this loop within the program, either an infinite loop will result or the "in loop" message will be printed a single time.
    E. The code will not compile because of the presence of the semicolon.

13. Consider the following recursive method:

```
public static int seq(int x)
{
  if(x <= 1 || x == 3)
    return x;
  else
    return (seq(x - 1) + seq(x - 2));
}
```

    What value will be printed by the call `seq(5)`?

    A. 1
    B. 3
    C. 4
    D. 7
    E. 11

14. Consider the following incomplete method:

```
// precondition: vals1.length = vals2.length
// postcondtion: returns true if for all k, 0 <= k < n,
//                vals1[k] = vals2[k]
public boolean match(String[] vals1, String[] vals2)
{
  int n = vals1.length;
  < missing code >
}
```

Which of the following is a valid replacement for < missing code >?

A. ```
    for(int k = 0; k < n; k++)
       return vals1[k].equals(vals2[k]);
    ```
B.  ```
    for(int k = 0; k < n; k++)
       if(vals1[k].equals(vals2[k]))
          return true;
    return false;
    ```
C. ```
    boolean same = true;
    for(int k = 0; k < n; k++)
      if(! vals1[k].equals(vals2[k]))
        same = false;
      else
        same = true;
    return same;
    ```
D.  ```
    boolean same = true;
    int k = 0;
    while(same && k < n)
      k++;
    return same;
    ```
E. ```
    int k = 0;
    while(k < n && vals1[k].equals(vals2[k]))
      k++;
    return k == n;
    ```

Questions 15–20 refer to the Marine Biology Simulation case study.

**15.** Which statement about the Simulation step method is false?

A.  step casts the elements of allObjects to Fish because act is a Fish method.
B.  The only requirement for the elements returned to step from allObjects is that they contain a Location attribute.
C.  The order in which fish are processed is controlled in part by step and in part by the implementation of allObjects.
D.  The environment is accessed once during each call to step.
E.  step could be modified such that the order in which fish are processed is different from the order in which they are displayed.

**16.** Which of the following classes is responsible for knowing what behavior is required in the simulation?

A.  Fish only
B.  Environment only
C.  Fish and Environment
D.  Fish and Simulation
E.  Fish, Environment, and Simulation
    ```

17. Which statement about the `Environment` and `EnvDisplay` interfaces is true?

    A. `Environment` and `EnvDisplay` were designed as interfaces in order to specify necessary methods but not impose implementation.
    B. A program that includes `Environment` and `EnvDisplay` must also include a `Simulation` object.
    C. `Environment` and `EnvDisplay` cannot be implemented by the same class.
    D. If text display is intended, `Environment` and `EnvDisplay` must both include the signature for a `toString` method.
    E. `Environment` and `EnvDisplay` need not be implemented in order for `step` to work.

18. What will happen if the `breed` method replaces the call to `generateChild` with the following code for adding a fish? (Assume `env`, `row`, and `column` are valid values.)

    ```
    env.add(new Fish(env, new Location(row, column)));
    ```

    A. An `IllegalArgumentException` will be thrown stating that the location is not a valid empty location.
    B. The code will not compile because it is an error to nest `new` operators.
    C. A `Fish` will be added at location (`row`, `column`), and normal execution will continue.
    D. Two `Fish` will be added, but the second `Fish` is a duplicate and will be ignored.
    E. The wrong species of fish will be added to the environment.

19. Which of the following is not a black box test case?

    A. Test for fish moving to a valid location.
    B. Test for fish movement in an environment with multiple nonempty locations.
    C. Test for a valid data file.
    D. Test for a fish, selecting each path through a conditional statement.
    E. Test for multiple fish assigned to the same location.

20. Consider a `Fish` in the center of a 3 × 3 grid as shown below.

After one step in the simulation, which of the following *cannot* be a valid configuration?

A.

B.

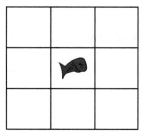

C.

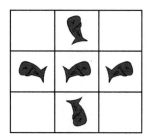

D.

E.

21. Assuming that b is a `boolean` variable, what will be the result of executing the code?

```
b = (b != b);
```

   A. Sets b to `false`.
   B. Sets b to `true`.
   C. Changes the value of b to its negation.
   D. Leaves the value of b unchanged.
   E. The code will not compile.

22. Consider the following method:

```
public static int mystery(int n)
{
  int a, b, c = 0;
  while(n > 0)
  {
    a = n/10;
    b = n%10;
    c *= 10;
    c += b;
    n = a;
  }
  return c;
}
```

Which statement best describes the value that is returned by `mystery`?

   A. Ten to the nth power is returned.
   B. The number of digits in n is returned.
   C. The number of times 10 is a factor of n is returned.
   D. The number whose digits are the reverse of n is returned.
   E. The sum of the digits in n is returned.

Questions 23 and 24 refer to the following code.

Consider the following class declarations that represent information about school supplies and a catalog that lists school supplies for sale.

```
public class SchoolItem
{
  // private data, constructor, and implementations not shown

  public String getItemName() { }
  public double getItemPrice() { }
  public String getItemStockNumber() { }
}

public class SchoolCatalog
{
  private SchoolItem [] myCatalog;
  private int numCatalogItems;

  public double findPrice(String stockNo)
  {
    double price = 0.0;
    <missing code>
    return price;
  }

    // other methods not shown
}
```

23. The findPrice method is intended to search myCatalog for the price of a school item with a particular stock number. If the stock number isn't found, the method should return 0.0. Which of the following can be used to replace <missing code> in findPrice?

    A. ```
       int k = 0;
       while(!myCatalog[k].getItemStockNumber().equals(stockNo))
         k++;
       price = myCatalog[k-1].getItemPrice();
       ```
    B. ```
       for(int k = 0; k < myCatalog.length(); k++)
         if(SchoolCatalog[k].getItemStockNumber.equals(stockNo))
           price = SchoolCatalog[k].getItemPrice();
       ```
    C. ```
       for(int k = 0; k < numCatalogItems; k++)
         if(myCatalog[k].getItemStockNumber.equals(stockNo))
           price = myCatalog[k].getItemPrice();
       ```
    D. ```
       if(SchoolItem.getItemStockNumber.equals(stockNo))
         price = SchoolItem.getItemPrice();
       ```
    E. ```
       if(myCatalog.getItemStockNumber.equals(stockNo))
         price = myCatalog.getItemPrice();
       ```

24. A new method is needed, printNamesAndPrice, that will print the names and prices of all the items in the catalog. Which of the following is the best design decision?

    A. Make printNamesAndPrice a private method of the SchoolItem class.
    B. Make printNamesAndPrice a public method of the SchoolItem class.
    C. Make printNamesAndPrice a private method of the SchoolCatalog class.
    D. Make printNamesAndPrice a public method of the SchoolCatalog class.
    E. Make printNamesAndPrice a static method of the client program.
       ```

25. Consider the following recursive method:

```
// precondition: 0 <= n < s.length
public static int puzzle(String[] s, int n, String wd)
{
  if(n < 0)
    return -1;
  else if(s[n].equals(wd))
    return n;
  else
    return puzzle(s, n - 1, wd);
}
```

Which of the following code segments is the iterative equivalent of the body of `puzzle`?

A.
```
for(int n = 0; n < s.length; n++)
  {
    if(n == 0)
      return n;
    if(wd.equals(s[n]))
      return 1;
  }
  return -1;
```

B.
```
for(int j = 0; j < n; j++)
  {
    if(wd.equals(s[j]))
      return j;
  }
  return -1;
```

C.
```
for(int n = 0; n < s.length; n++)
  {
    if(wd.equals(s[n]))
      return s[n];
  }
```

D.
```
for(int j = s.length - 1; j >= 0; j--)
  {
    if(wd.equals(s[j]))
      return s[j];
  }
  return -1;
```

E.
```
for(int j = n; j >= 0; j--)
  {
    if(wd.equals(s[j]))
      return j;
  }
  return -1;
```

26. Consider the following class declaration:

```
public class SimpleInt
{
  private int myInt;

  public void setVal(int v)
  {
    myInt = v;
  }

  public int getVal()
  {
    return myInt;
  }
}
```

Assuming that x is a properly constructed SimpleInt, which of the following statements will compile in a program that uses SimpleInt?

I.   System.out.println(x.getVal());
II. System.out.println(x.myInt);
III. System.out.println(x.setVal(10));

A. I only
B. II only
C. I and II only
D. I and III only
E. All three will compile

27. Which expression below is equivalent to the following? (Assume x, y, and z are objects whose public instance variables info implement the Comparable interface.)

```
((x != null) && (x.info.compareTo(z.info) > 0))
```

A. ((x.equals(null)) || (x.info.compareTo(z.info) > 0))
B. ((x.equals(null)) && (x.info.compareTo(z.info) == 0)
C. !((x != null) || (x.info.compareTo(z.info) >= 0))
D. !((x == null) && (x.info.compareTo(z.info) < 0))
E. !((x == null) || (x.info.compareTo(z.info) <= 0))

Questions 28 and 29 refer to the following class hierarchy:

```
public class Alpha
{
  public void eeny( int a, int b )
  { System.out.print("alpha eeny "); }
  /* Other methods not shown */
}

public class Beta extends Alpha
{
  public void miny( int x )
  { System.out.print("miny "); }
  /* Other methods not shown */
}

public class Gamma extends Beta
{
  public void eeny( int a, int b )
  { System.out.print("gamma eeny "); }
  /* Other methods not shown */
}
```

```
public class Delta extends Alpha
{
  public void eeny( int x )
  { System.out.print("delta eeny "); }
  /* Other methods not shown */
}
```

28. What is printed as a result of executing the following code? (Assume that all the classes have parameterless constructors.)

```
Beta b = new Beta();
Alpha a = new Gamma();

b.eeny(1, 1);
a.eeny(0, 1);
```

    A. Nothing; the code does not compile
    B. `alpha eeny`
    C. `alpha eeny alpha eeny`
    D. `alpha eeny gamma eeny`
    E. `miny gamma eeny`

29. What is printed as a result of executing the following code? (Assume that all the classes have parameterless constructors.)

```
Delta d = new Delta();

d.eeny(2);
d.eeny(0, 1);
```

    A. Nothing; the code does not compile
    B. `alpha eeny alpha eeny`
    C. `delta eeny`
    D. `delta eeny alpha eeny`
    E. `delta eeny delta eeny alpha eeny`

30. Which of the following cannot always be checked by a compiler?

    A. The version of a method being invoked.
    B. The spelling of keywords.
    C. Possible missing punctuation within code.
    D. Return values matching method return types.
    E. Invocation of a private method from outside the class.

31. In the statement

```
if ((x != null) && (x.performanceRating() > THRESHOLD))
{
  <do something>
}
```

what prevents a `NullPointerException` from being thrown?

    A. Method overloading
    B. Polymorphism
    C. Inheritance
    D. Short-circuiting
    E. Dynamic allocation

32. Assume that the `ArrayList names` holds the following values:

Alyce, Barbara, Chris, Denny, Ed, Fran, Gene, Henry, Ian, Julie

What values does this `ArrayList` hold after executing the following code?

```
for (int i=1; i<=4; i++)
{
  names.remove(i);
}
```

A. Alyce, Barbara, Chris, Denny, Ed, Fran
B. Alyce, Fran, Gene, Henry, Ian, Julie
C. Alyce, Chris, Ed, Gene, Ian, Julie
D. Barbara, Denny, Fran, Henry, Ian, Julie
E. Ed, Fran, Gene, Henry, Ian, Julie

33. Suppose data items are entered into an array in ascending order as each item is read. Which statement below best characterizes this process?

A. This process is more efficient than any sorting algorithm.
B. This process is less efficient than any sorting algorithm.
C. This process is more efficient than Selection or Insertion sort.
D. This process is as efficient as Selection or Insertion sort.
E. This process is as efficient as Merge sort.

For questions 34 and 35, consider the following class:

```
public class Doohickey
{
  private String myID;
  private double myMass;

  public Doohickey ()
  /* Implementation not shown */

  public String getID() { return myID; }

  public double getMass() { return mass; }

  public String toString()
  { /* Missing code */ }
}
```

34. Which of the following would *not* be acceptable as the body for the `toString` method?

A. `return myID + " " + myMass;`
B. `return (String) myID + " " + myMass;`
C. `return getID()+ " " + myMass;`
D. `return getID() + " " + getMass();`
E. `return getID().getMass();`

35. Suppose that `glop` is an `ArrayList` of `Doohickeys`. Consider the following code fragment that is meant to print out the ID numbers of all `Doohickeys` whose mass is greater than zero.

```
for (int num=0; num<glop.size(); num++)
{
  if (/* missing code */)
  {
    System.out.println(glop[num].getID());
  }
}
```

Which of the following expressions will complete the code fragment correctly?

A. `(glop) Doohickey.get(num).getMass() > 0`
B. `((Doohickey) getNum(glop)).getMass()> 0`
C. `glop.get((Doohickey) num).getMass() > 0`
D. `((Doohickey) glop.get(num)).getMass() > 0`
E. `glop.get( glop.getMass(num) ) > 0`

36. A programmer has mistakenly typed a 2 instead of a 1 in the recursive call in the following search method. What will be the result of starting a search at position 0?

```
// postcondition:  returns first index of key within a at or after position start
//                  returns -1 if key is not present
public static int recSearch(Object[] a, Object key, int start)
{
  if (start == a.length)
  {
    return -1;
  }
  else if (a[start].equals(key))
  {
    return start;
  }
  else
  {
    return recSearch(a, key, start+2);
    // should have been start+1;
  }
}
```

A. The search will still work, but less efficiently than with the "+1."
B. The correct value will be returned only when the key is found in an even numbered location.
C. The correct value will be returned only when the length of the array is even.
D. An `IndexOutOfBoundsException` will be thrown whenever the length of the array is odd.
E. None of these explanations correctly describes when the code will work.

Questions 37 and 38 refer to the following method that is intended to remove all duplicates of the first value in an `ArrayList`. For example, if the `ArrayList` contains 2 3 2 4 4 2 2 2 3, `removeDupsOfFirst` should return 2 3 4 4 3. The method does not always work as intended.

```
public static void removeDupsOfFirst(ArrayList a)
{
  int k = 1;
  while(k < a.size())
  {
  if(((Integer)a.get(k)).compareTo(((Integer)a.get(0)))==0)
    a.remove(k);
  k++;
  }
}
```

37. Which of the following sets of test data would cause `removeDupsOfFirst` to fail?

    A. 2 1 0
    B. 2 2 2
    C. 2 3 4 5 6
    D. 2 3 4 5 2
    E. 2 2 3 2 4 2 5

38. Which of the following best describes how to correct `removeDupsOfFirst` so that it always works as intended?

    A. Initialize a variable to count the number of duplicates to be removed.
    B. Initialize k to 0.
    C. Change the `while` loop to a `for` loop.
    D. Insert `else` before k++.
    E. Make the return type `ArrayList` and return a.

39. Consider the following declarations and definitions:

```
public class Sample
{
  public void noReason(Sample1 x1, Sample2 x2)
  { /* Implementation not shown */ }
}

public class Sample1 extends Sample
{ /* Implementation not shown */ }

public class Sample2 extends Sample1
{ /* Implementation not shown */ }

Sample s = new Sample();
Sample1 s1 = new Sample1();
Sample2 s2 = new Sample2();
```

Which of the following is a correct invocation of the method `noReason`?

    A. s.noReason(s, s);
    B. s1.noReason(s1, s1);
    C. s1.noReason(s2, s1);
    D. s2.noReason(s, s);
    E. s2.noReason(s2, s2);

40. Consider the recursive method `minVal` that is intended to return the smallest value among the first n values in array a.

```
public static int minVal(int[] a, n)
{
  if(n==1)
    return <missing code 1>;
  int min = minVal(a, n-1);
  if(min<a[n-1])
    return <missing code 2>;
  else
    return <missing code 3>;
}
```

Which of the following should be used to complete the three return statements?

	<missing code 1>	<missing code 2>	<missing code 3>
A.	a[0]	min	a[n]
B.	a[0]	a[n]	min
C.	a[1]	a[min]	a[n-1]
D.	a[1]	a[min]	a[min-1]
E.	a[0]	min	a[n-1]

Section II

Time: 1 hour and 45 minutes; number of questions: 4; percentage of grade: 50

Directions: Show all your work. Remember that program segments are to be written in Java. In writing your solutions to a part of the problem, you may assume that code from previous parts works correctly regardless of what you wrote in those parts. In such cases, it is expected that you will invoke the appropriate method; reimplementing a solution from an earlier part of a question will result in a less than perfect score being awarded for that problem.

1. Consider the following declarations for maintaining an inventory list of toys at a toy store. Information about each toy includes the name, price, appropriate age range (in years), and appropriate gender ("girl," "boy," "either"). The inventory is ordered by age range. For example, a very abbreviated inventory might be the following:

Name	Price	Lower Bound	Upper Bound	Gender
Canopy tricycle	$29.99	3	5	either
Beach ball	$ 1.29	3	80	either
Guess Who	$14.99	6	9	either
Skateboard	$24.99	6	12	boy
Fashion doll	$11.99	6	14	girl
Monopoly	$11.99	8	100	either
Easy Bake Oven	$19.99	8	12	girl
Trivial Pursuit	$34.99	12	100	either

```java
public class Toy
{
  private String name;
  private double price;
  private int lBound;        // lower bound of age range
  private int uBound;        // upper bound of age range
  private String gender;

  public String getName() {return name;}
  public double getPrice() {return price;}
  public String getGender() {return gender;}

  // returns true if a toy is appropriate for age;
  // otherwise, returns false
  public boolean isAgeAppropriate(int age)
  {
    // missing code
  }
  // other methods not shown
}
```

A. Write the `Toy` method `isAgeAppropriate` that returns `true` if a toy is recommended for a child of a particular age; otherwise, returns `false`.

```
// Postcondition: returns true if a toy is appropriate for age;
// Postcondition: otherwise, returns false
public boolean isAgeAppropriate(int age)
```

B. Suppose a high school service club is looking for a list of toys that are age and gender appropriate for a group of needy children. The club asks the toy store manager for suggestions.

```
public class ToyInventory
{
  private ArrayList toyList;

  // Prints the name and price of each toy in the
  // inventory that is appropriate for anAge and aGender
  public ArrayList toySelection(int anAge, String aGender)

  {
  //missing code
  }

  //other data and methods not shown
}
```

Write the `ToyInventory` method `toySelection` that prints the name and price of each toy in its inventory that is age and gender appropriate for a particular child. For example, for a 10-year-old girl, the abbreviated list in the example above should return an `ArrayList` containing fashion doll, beach ball, Monopoly, and Easy Bake Oven.

```
// Builds a list containing each toy in the
// inventory that is appropriate for anAge and aGender
public ArrayList toySelection(int anAge, String aGender)
```

2. RearView Motors, Inc., manufactures three different models of car (coupe, sedan, or wagon). Each car has one of five exterior colors (black, white, red, blue, or silver) and one of three interior colors (tan, gray, or burgundy). In addition there is a list of options that buyers may purchase. Some of the options are heated seats, surround-sound system, and steel wheels, but there are many others. Cars are assembled at various plants throughout the country. Each plant is responsible for keeping track of the cars it has produced each month. Executives at corporate headquarters are likely to ask for such information as the total number of cars produced, a description of the car most recently produced, and the number of cars with any given feature (e.g., "cars with steel wheels" or "cars with heated seats.") The company keeps track of all this via an `AssemblyPlant` class, part of which is shown below:

```
public class AssemblyPlant
{
  private String plantName;
  private ArrayList carsProduced;
  // Holds one Car object for each car produced

  public int totalCarsProduced() { ... }
  public String mostRecentCarProduced() { ... }
  public int carsProducedWith( String feature ) { ... }
  // Other methods and/or constructors not shown
}
```

A. Write a class definition for the `Car` class (note: NOT the `AssemblyPlant` class) that will keep track of the information and provide the services for the class, putting only "{ ... }" in for the bodies of the constructor(s) and method(s). In writing this definition you must:

  • Choose appropriate names for all identifiers.
  • Provide (at least) the functionality specified above.
  • Make data representation decisions consistent with the specification above.
  • Make design decisions that are consistent with the principles of object-oriented design.

  Comments are not required, but may be included to explain your intent.

  Do not write the implementations of the constructors or the methods of the **Car** class.

B. Write the method `carsProducedWith` from the `AssemblyPlant` class. The header is given below.

```
// precondition:  feature is a valid feature
// postcondition: returns the number of cars with the specified feature that have
//                been produced at this plant
public int carsProducedWith( String feature )
```

C. Write the implementation(s) for any methods in the `Car` class that were used in your answer to Part B.

3. This question involves reasoning about the code from the Marine Biology Simulation case study. (For the actual exam, a copy of the visible code and interfaces for the black box classes will be provided.)

Consider defining a new type of fish, called `ZigZagFish`, that always prefers to move in a zigzag pattern as illustrated below. The new class extends `Fish`.

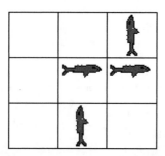

On each time step, regardless of orientation, a `ZigZagFish` attempts to move forward one cell in the grid, turns right, moves forward again, turns left, and moves forward one more time. A `ZigZagFish` checks ahead to be sure the entire path is valid and empty before making its move. If a `ZigZagFish` cannot zigzag, it simply turns right or left with equal probability, and its turn in the time step is finished.

A `ZigZagFish` does one more thing. When it successfully completes a zigzag move on three consecutive time steps, it executes a little victory dance by turning in a circle in place.

All `ZigZagFish` are blue.

You will be asked to write a constructor for the `ZigZagFish` class and redefine the `move` and `nextLocation` methods. You may assume the `ZigZagFish` class already contains a private method `victoryDance`. You will not write `victoryDance`, but you may use the method.

A. Write a partial class declaration for `ZigZagFish` that includes the heading for the class, any instance variables necessary for the class, and a two-parameter constructor that takes the environment and initial location of the `ZigZagFish` as parameters. Do not write any other constructors and do not specify any other methods.

B. Write the `nextLocation` method for a `ZigZagFish` that overrides `nextLocation` in the `Fish` class. Recall that on each time step, regardless of orientation, a `ZigZagFish` attempts to move to a location that is two cells forward and one cell to the right of its current location. It must complete this move by going forward one cell in the grid, turning right, moving forward again, turning left, and moving forward one more time. The entire path must be valid and empty in order for a `ZigZagFish` to select the location. Otherwise, it turns right or left with equal probability and its location does not change.

Complete the `ZigZagFish` method `nextLocation` below the header.

```
protected Location nextLocation()
```

C. Write the `ZigZagFish` method `move` that overrides `Fish` `move`. Recall that a `ZigZagFish` moves if the path and location it needs are valid and empty. Otherwise, it simply turns left or right with equal probability. In addition, if it has successfully completed a zigzag move on three or more consecutive time steps, it does its victory dance.

Complete the `ZigZagFish` method `move` below.

```
protected void move()
```

4. Every substance in the world can be expressed via a chemical formula. The formula for water is H_2O, meaning that water is made up of two atoms of hydrogen (symbol H) and one atom of oxygen (symbol O.) The formula for table salt is NaCl, meaning that salt is made up of one atom of sodium (symbol Na) and one atom of chlorine (symbol Cl.) Elements can be modeled via the following class.

```
public class Element
{
  // return full name of this element, e.g. "Hydrogen"
  public String getFullName()
  { /* Implementation not shown */ }

  // return the atomic symbol for this element, e.g. "H"
  public String getSymbol()
  { /* Implementation not shown */ }

  // return the mass of this element
  public double getMass()
  { /* Implementation not shown */ }

  // Constructors, other methods, and instance variables are not shown
}
```

The data for all known elements are stored in a `PeriodicTable` which is represented as shown below.

```
public class PeriodicTable
{
  // Stores one Element for each element known
  private Element[] knownElements;
  // Returns the element whose symbol matches the given symbol;
  // returns null if no such element exists
  public Element getElement(String symbol)
  { /* Implementation not shown */ }

  // Constructors, other methods, and instance variables are not shown
}
```

A. Complete the following method to implement the `getElement` method of the `PeriodicTable` class. Be sure to handle the case when the symbol is not known.

```
public Element getElement( String symbol )
```

Elements are then grouped into compounds by including them with frequencies. For instance, water and sulfuric acid (H_2SO_4) would be represented, respectively, as:

Hydrogen	Oxygen
2	1

Hydrogen	Sulfur	Oxygen
2	1	4

Each column of this table can be modeled via the following class:

```
public class CompoundComponent
{
  // return the atomic symbol of this piece of the compound
  public String getElementSymbol()
  { /* Implementation not shown */ }

  // return the frequency of this element within a compound
  public int getFrequency()
  { /* Implementation not shown */ }

  // Constructors, other methods, and instance variables are not shown
}
```

A complete compound, as represented in the two tables above, is modeled via the following class:

```
public class Compound
{
  private ArrayList components;
  private PeriodicTable table;

  // return the molecular mass for this compound
  public double getMolecularMass()
  { /* Implementation not shown */ }

  // Constructors, other methods, and instance variables are not shown
}
```

B. The molecular mass of a compound is determined by multiplying the mass of each element in the compound by the number of times that element appears in the compound and summing all those results. For instance, if the masses of hydrogen, sulfur, and oxygen are as given in the tables below, then the molecular masses of the compounds are also as given below:

Element	Mass
Hydrogen	1.1
Sulfur	32.3
Oxygen	16.0

Compound		Molecular Mass
Water	H_2O	18.2
Sulfuric acid	H_2SO_4	98.5

Complete the following method to implement the getMolecularMass method of the Compound class.

```
// precondition: the instance variable table contains
//               all known elements, and components contains
//               only valid elements with positive frequencies
public double getMolecularMass()
{
```

ANSWERS TO PRACTICE EXAM A1, SECTION I

1.	C	11.	E	21.	A	31.	D
2.	D	12.	D	22.	D	32.	C
3.	C	13.	D	23.	C	33.	D
4.	B	14.	E	24.	D	34.	E
5.	E	15.	B	25.	E	35.	D
6.	D	16.	D	26.	A	36.	E
7.	A	17.	A	27.	E	37.	B
8.	C	18.	A	28.	D	38.	D
9.	C	19.	D	29.	D	39.	E
10.	C	20.	B	30.	A	40.	E

✓ SOLUTIONS TO PRACTICE EXAM A1, SECTION I

1. The correct answer is C. This code keeps a running product, $(1/2)(2/3)(3/4)$ . . . $[n/(n+1)]$. The result of this multiplication is $1/n$. Note that without the cast to a `double`, the result is `0.0`.

2. The correct answer is D. `setPrice` is correctly called, sending in a `double`. Answer A is incorrect for two reasons: using private data and string comparison. B, C, and E misuse parameters.

3. The correct answer is C. In the third line of code, $x = 2 + 4 = 6$; in the fourth line, the new value of x is added to y, $y = 4 + 6 = 10$.

4. The correct answer is B. If p and q are different, then the first part of the expression is always false. If p and q are different, then $p||q$ is true; the second clause is the negation of this. So, the expression is false whenever p and q are different. Viewed conversely, the expression is true whenever p and q have the same value.

p	q	p&&q	p||q	!(p||q)	(p&&q)||!(p||q)
T	T	T	T	F	T
T	F	F	T	F	F
F	T	F	T	F	F
F	F	F	F	T	T

5. The correct answer is E. `count` is reinitialized to 0 on each pass through the loop.

6. The correct answer is D. The method prints the message twice, before and after the recursive call. Each recursive call sends a message that starts in position 0 but is half as long as the previous call. Remember, with recursion you have to back out of each recursive call level by level.

`"tickleme"` printed (length of msg = 8)

`"tickleme"` printed

   `"tick"` printed (length of msg = 4)

  `"tick"` printed

     `"ti"` printed (length of msg = 2)

    `"ti"` printed

       (length of msg = 1)

7. The correct answer is A. Inheritance should always reflect the IS-A relationship between classes. The claims of choices B and C may or may not be true, but they would be less important than the IS-A relationship in any case. Choice D implies that deeper inheritance hierarchies are somehow better than shallow ones, which is not necessarily true.

8. The correct answer is C. Subclasses do not have direct access to private information in the superclass. An accessor method must be used. On the other hand, public variables and methods are always available for other objects to use.

9. The correct answer is C. If `low` and `high` cross over, that is, the value of `low` is greater than the value of `high`, the target value is not in the array and -1 is returned. If the target is less than the value in the middle, search from `low` to the `(mid-1)`; otherwise, search from `(mid+1)` to `high`.

10. The correct answer is C. To avoid an exception, we must know that only valid subscripts are used to index the array. Each time through the loop, we access the $(k+1)$th cell, so we must be sure that `k < arr.length-1`. The loop condition guarantees that $k<n-1$. Thus, n can be no larger than `arr.length`.

11. The correct answer is E. Each time a value is found that is not less than its successor, the `boolean` variable `theCheck` is set to its negation. If this happens an even number of times, `theCheck` will be true; otherwise it will be false.

12. The correct answer is D. If $j < n$ is true, the code will get caught in an infinite loop; if $j >= n$, the `while`, in essence, is skipped, but the body of the loop will be treated as the next statement to be executed, and the "in loop" message will be printed a single time.

13. The correct answer is D. The base case returns the value of x sent to that particular recursive call, while the general case sums pairs returned from recursive calls. `seq(5) = seq(4) + seq(3)`, but `seq(3) = 3`. Once you have calculated the return value of lower-level calls, you can substitute those into some of the higher-

level calls. This can be a real time-saver on the exam.

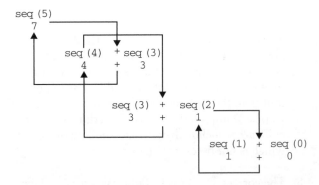

14. The correct answer is E. Answer A returns the truth value of the first two elements. B returns true if one pair of elements match. C returns the truth value of the last pair. D always returns true. E returns true if the loop counter (array index) traverses the entire list; otherwise, there is an early exit, and false is returned.

15. The answer is B. The only requirement is that the objects be Locatable, not that they contain a Location. Of course, it is expected that an object will have a location because the location method must be implemented. The other four statements are true. The objects must be cast to Fish because Fish know how to act. The order in which fish are processed depends upon how the environment put them into allObjects and on what the loop in step does. That means fish could be processed in row-major order, column-major order, the reverse of either, or even randomly as long as each fish has an opportunity to act.

16. The answer is D. The simulation represents the behavior that happens in every time step, and the fish have to know how to do whatever the simulation tells them to do. The environment models the grid, keeping track of the objects in the grid, but it does not care what the behavior is except when the behavior changes the number of objects in the grid or their locations.

17. The correct answer is A. This is what an interface does. It specifies methods that should be included in classes that implement the interface but leaves room for different classes to implement the methods in different ways. Environment and EnvDisplay are not dependent upon having a Simulation class, so answer B is false. Answer C is false; a class can extend only one class but it can implement many. D is incorrect because Environment

doesn't display itself, so toString is never needed for Environment; the display method in EnvDisplay takes care of displaying the environment, whatever form that takes. The exact opposite of answer E is true. step uses both Environment and EnvDisplay, so there must be classes that implement them.

18. The correct answer is A. A new fish is *constructed* in the parameter to add. This fish has already added itself to the environment, so when env.add is invoked, the location is no longer empty.

19. The correct answer is D. Black box test cases test preconditions, not the paths through the code.

20. The correct answer is B. A Fish breeds or moves and may die, but it does not remain in the same place if there is an open space into which it can move. The Fish could die, as in answer A; it could breed, as in answer C, or breed and then die as in D; or it could fail to breed and move to a valid empty location as in E.

21. The correct answer is A. The test for b not being equal to itself must be false in all cases.

22. The correct answer is D. Helper variables a and b hold the integer quotient of n divided by 10, and the remainder, respectively. To reverse n, variable c is multiplied by 10, and the new remainder is added. The process continues, multiplying by 10 to move the current value over one place value, until the integer quotient is 0.

23. The correct answer is C. Answer A fails to check for the end of the array. B uses the class name rather than the instance of the class. D and E fail to traverse the array.

24. The correct answer is D. Answers A and C are incorrect because the method should be public. B and E are incorrect because the method should be a member of the SchoolCatalog class.

25. The correct answer is E. A and C "lose" the parameter n by declaring a local variable of the same name. B searches for a match in the array with increasing order of index, but the recursive routine searches in decreasing order of index. D returns a String instead of an int.

26. The correct answer is A. println cannot access private data from outside a class, so the second option won't compile. setVal is a void method, so its value can't be used as an argument.

27. The correct answer is E. This illustrates DeMorgan's Law for the negation of a conjunction.

28. The correct answer is D. Beta extends Alpha. Beta does not have a method eeny so b.eeny invokes eeny from the superclass. The second invocation is made on a Gamma object, so *that* code generates the second portion of the output. Note that a is defined as a new Gamma, and a Gamma IS-A Alpha. Look first to the subclass, Gamma, to see if it has overridden method eeny before looking to the superclass, Alpha.

29. The correct answer is D. When methods are overloaded, the parameters determine which version of the method will be invoked.

30. The correct answer is A. If a subclass and its superclass both contain a method with the same signature, the version invoked is determined at runtime by the class of the instance variable calling the method.

31. The correct answer is D. In a conjunction ("and" statement) both parts must be true for the entire condition to be true. If the first part is false, there is no need to test the second part. Therefore, if x is a null reference, its info field is never dereferenced and the exception is avoided. The program can continue execution. The implementation of this process in a programming language such as Java is called *short-circuiting*.

32. The correct answer is C. When the element in position 1 is removed, all remaining elements shift "down" one position. The element that was in position 2 fills in for the removed element and, therefore, is now in position 1. The loop counter moves to position 2, resulting in a skipped name. In fact, because the list shrinks with each iteration, every other name is skipped.

33. The correct answer is D. The process is essentially the same as Insertion sort.

34. The correct answer is E. Methods are invoked by instances of a class, not by other methods. The toString method may use the private instance variables directly or access them through class methods.

35. The correct answer is D. Access the object in position num and cast it to a DooHickey so that the getMass method can be called. The other answers are incorrect for multiple reasons; we point out at least one reason for each. Answer A is wrong because the get method must be called on the ArrayList glop, not on the class DooHickey. B is wrong because there is no getNum method. C is incorrect because num is an integer, not the DooHickey in the attempt to cast num. E is wrong because glop.getMass(num) is an improper invocation of a parameterless method; if the method call was correct, the return value is a double, which is an incorrect type for the get method.

36. The correct answer is E. Answer A is incorrect because half the array elements are skipped. B is incorrect because the method will return −1 correctly if the key is not present in an array whose length is even. C and D are incorrect because the key may be found regardless of the length of the array, and if the key is found, the out of bounds check will not be tested.

37. The correct answer is B. If there are two or more consecutive copies of the first element of the ArrayList, the code will miss every other one of them.

38. The correct answer is D. Increment k only if a duplicate was not found at the kth index. Otherwise, check the same position again because the next element will have shifted to that position and it, too, might be a duplicate.

39. The correct answer is E. This is an example of the IS-A relationship. noReason expects a Sample1 and a Sample2 object. A Sample2 object IS-A Sample1 and IS-A Sample.

40. The correct answer is E. n is the number of elements in the array. When n is 1, the only element is a[0], so it is returned and stored as min. Otherwise, the method is called until n is 1. When this happens, the minimum value is the lesser of the current min and the nth element farther along in the array, found in position (n − 1).

✓ ANSWERS TO PRACTICE EXAM A1, SECTION II

Problem 1A

```
public boolean isAgeAppropriate(int age)
{
  return ((age >= lBound) && (age <= uBound));
}
```

Problem 1B

```
public ArrayList toySelection(int anAge, String aGender)
{
  ArrayList suggestions = new ArrayList();
  for (int k=0; k<toyList.size(); k++)
  {
    Toy t = (Toy) toyList.get(k);
    String gender = t.getGender();
    if ( (t.isAgeAppropriate(anAge) &&
        (gender.equals("either") || gender.equals(aGender)))
    {
      suggestions.add(t);
    }
  }
  return suggestions;
}
```

Problem 2A

```
public class Car
{
  private String exteriorColor;
  private String interiorColor;
  private String model;
  private ArrayList options;

  public Car(String outColor, String inColor,
            String type, ArrayList optionalEquipment) { ... }
  public String getExteriorColor() { ... }
  public String getInteriorColor() { ... }
  public String getModel() { ... }
  public boolean hasOption( String feature ) { ... }
  public String toString() { ... }
}
```

Problem 2B

```
public int carsProducedWith( String feature )
{
  int carsWithFeature = 0;
  for (int k=0; k<carsProduced.size(); k++)
  {
    Car auto = (Car) carsProduced.get(k);
    if (auto.hasFeature(feature))
    {
      carsWithFeature++;
    }
  }
  return carsWithFeature;
}
```

Problem 2C

```
public boolean hasOption( String feature )
{
  for (int k=0; k<options.size(); k++)
  {
    if (feature.equals( options.get(k) )
      return true;
  }
  return false;
}
```

Problem 3A

```
public class ZigZagFish extends Fish
{
  protected int consecutiveZigsMade;
  public ZigZagFish(Environment env, Location loc)
  {
    super(env, loc, env.randomDirection(), Color.blue);
    consecutiveZigsMade = 0;
  }
}
```

Problem 3B

```
protected Location nextLocation()
{
  Environment env = environment();
  Location oneInFront = env.getNeighbor(location(), direction());
  Location twoInFront = env.getNeighbor(oneInFront, direction().toRight);
  Location threeInFront = env.getNeighbor(twoInFront, direction());
  if ( env.isEmpty(oneInFront) && env.isEmpty(twoInFront)
       && env.isEmpty(threeInFront) )
    return threeInFront;
  else
    return location();
}
```

Problem 3C

```
protected void move()
{
  Location nextLoc = nextLocation();
  if ( ! nextLoc.equals(location()) )
  {
    changeLocation(nextLoc);
    consecutiveZigsMade++;
    if (consecutiveZigsMade >= 3)
    {
      victoryDance();
    }
  }
  else
  {
    consecutiveZigsMade = 0;
    Random randNumGen = RandNumGenerator.getInstance();
    if (randNumGen.nextDouble() < 0.5)
      changeDirection(direction().toLeft());
    else
      changeDirection(direction().toRight());
  }
}
```

Problem 4A

```
public Element getElement(String symbol)
{
  for (int k=0; k<knownElements.length; k++)
  {
    if (knownElements[k].getSymbol().equals(symbol))
        return knownElements[k];
  }
  return null;
}
```

Problem 4B

```
public double getMolecularMass()
{
  double mass = 0.0;
  for (int k=0; k<components.size(); k++)
  {
    CompoundComponent c = (CompoundComponent) components.get(k);
    Element e = table.getElement( c.getElementSymbol() );
    mass += (e.getMass()*c.getFrequency());
  }
  return mass;
}
```

✓ RUBRICS AND COMMENTARY FOR PRACTICE EXAM A1, SECTION II

Note: In many cases where a rubric says "+1," it may be possible to earn a half point for a nearly correct solution.

Problem 1 (9 points)

Part A (2 points)

+1 for a comparison involving parameter and one of the age bounding variables

+1 for a completely correct answer, including the boundary cases

Part B (7 points)

+1 for construction of a list to be returned and for returning it at the end

+1 for a loop that traverses the entire inventory (`toyList`)

+1 for correctly extracting a toy from the inventory (`get` method)

+1 for identifying the gender for which the toy is used (`getGender` method)

+1 for a test that checks both gender and age appropriateness

+1 for a completely correct test, including the either case (could be the toy's gender, could be the parameter)

+1 for properly adding the toy to the "answer" list

Commentary

Solutions to Part A that use if tests would be acceptable as well.

Variations exist for the Part B solution that invoke `getGender` twice and do not store a separate `String`. It is also possible to make use of nested if statements to simplify the conditional.

The first point for Part B will not be awarded if there is no code involving the inventory.

A solution that checks the age bounds directly instead of using the `isAgeAppropriate` method would not receive full credit for the tests. It is now

expected that students will *not* reimplement code in subsequent parts of an AP exam.

Problem 2 (9 points)

Part A (4 points)

+1 for proper class format, including a proper list of private instance variables

+1 for a constructor that enables the various fields to be set

+1 for accessor methods for each instance variable

+1 for including a composite type (array or `ArrayList`) for options with appropriate accessor

Part B (4 points)

+1 for initializing a counter and for returning it at the end

+1 for a loop that traverses the entire list of options

+1 for determining whether or not the option is on the car

+1 for updating the counter appropriately

Part C (1 point)

+1 for properly implementing the appropriate accessor method

Deductions

Points could be deducted for poorly chosen variable or method names, but experience shows that this happens rarely—usually when single-letter names are used. In general, if a good-faith effort has been put into naming the variable, that is acceptable.

Commentary

It is equally valid to use an array instead of an `ArrayList` to hold the options. It is also permissible to have an accessor that returns the entire option list rather than the `boolean` method shown. Some method analogous to the `toString` method should be present as the narrative mentions the need for "a description of the car."

It is imperative that the solution to Part B use the methods as outlined in Part A. The variations described in the previous paragraph will lead to variations in the solution to Part B.

The first point for Part B will not be awarded if there is no code involving the list of options.

Solutions that use the `contains` method (assuming an `ArrayList` implementation) are completely acceptable.

Problem 3 (9 points)

Part A (2 points)

+1 for proper invocation of constructor for superclass, including parameters

+1 for proper declaration and initialization of consecutive move counter

Part B (3 points)

+1 for identifying each of the three critical locations (through which the fish must move)

+1 for determining whether or not the move can take place

+1 for returning the correct value

Part C (4 points)

+1 for determining whether to move or change direction (includes both determining the next location and checking that it is not the current location)

+1 for moving correctly when the location changes

+1 for changing direction when the location does not change

+1 for handling victory dance, including update of state variable in both cases

Commentary

The best approach to this problem is to model the solution after the code in the `DarterFish` class. If

necessary, an example of the use of the random number generator can be found in the `SlowFish` class. The listings provided with the case study make great references for these problems!

In Part A it is possible to initialize the state variable at the time of declaration rather than in the constructor.

A solution to Part B that nests the if tests is also possible, but the logic may be more difficult to follow.

Problem 4 (9 points)

Part A (3 points)

+1 for traversing the `knownElements` array as necessary

+1 for identifying and returning the correct element based upon its symbol

+1 for handling the case when the symbol is unknown (returning `null`)

Part B (6 points)

+1 for initializing and returning a `double` containing the mass

+1 for looping through the entire compound

+1 for accessing the correct element from the periodic table

+1 for attempting to determine both the mass and the frequency of the element

+1 for getting the correct value for both the mass and the frequency of the element

+1 for properly updating the mass (includes proper multiplication and addition)

Commentary

Many acceptable solutions to Part A will simply initialize a value to `null` before the loop and assign that value within the conditional statement. Since nothing was stated about duplicate elements, this is entirely acceptable.

The first point for Part B will not be awarded if there is no code involving the compound.

Computer Science A Practice Exam A2

Answer Sheet for Multiple-Choice Questions

1. _____	11. _____	21. _____	31. _____
2. _____	12. _____	22. _____	32. _____
3. _____	13. _____	23. _____	33. _____
4. _____	14. _____	24. _____	34. _____
5. _____	15. _____	25. _____	35. _____
6. _____	16. _____	26. _____	36. _____
7. _____	17. _____	27. _____	37. _____
8. _____	18. _____	28. _____	38. _____
9. _____	19. _____	29. _____	39. _____
10. _____	20. _____	30. _____	40. _____

PRACTICE EXAM A2

Section I

Time: 1 hour and 15 minutes; number of questions: 40; percentage of grade: 50

Directions: Determine the answer to each of the following questions or incomplete statements, using the available space for any necessary scratch work. Then fill in the space on the answer sheet corresponding to the best choice given. No credit will be given for anything written in the examination booklet. Do not spend too much time on any one problem.

Note: Assume the Java Standard Libraries and the AP Java Subset are included in any programs that use the code segments provided in individual questions. You may refer to the College Board document (Copyright © 2004 by College Entrance Examination Board), "A Quick Reference," while taking this practice exam. This document is available at www.collegeboard.com/student/testing/ap/sub_compscia.html.

1. Consider the following code segment:

```
public static int calculate(int x)
{
  x = x + x;
  x = x * x;
  return x;
}
```

What is the result of a call to compute?

A. Returns $2x$
B. Returns x^4
C. Returns $2x^2$
D. Returns $4x^2$
E. Returns the original value of x, since the method is static

2. Which of the following is the negation of the expression: a && !b?

A. !a || b
B. !(!a || b)
C. !a && b
D. !(!a && b)
E. a && b || !b

3. Consider method `doubleUp` that is intended to return the number of times `value` must be doubled before it is greater than `target`. `doubleUp` does not work as intended.

```
public static int doubleUp(int value, double target)
{
  int value = 1;
  int count = 0;
  while(value < target)
  {
    count++;
    value *= 2;
  }
  return count;
}
```

Of the following, which best describes the error in `doubleUp`?

A. An extra variable is used.
B. An uninitialized variable is used.
C. An `int` cannot be compared to a `double`.
D. A variable is incremented in the wrong place.
E. The loop test is incorrect.

4. Consider the following method:

```
// precondition: num >= 0
public static void mystery(int num)
{
  if (num > 1)
    mystery(num/2);
  System.out.print(num%2);
}
```

What is the best postcondition for `mystery`?

A. Reverses the digits of num.
B. Prints the remainder when num is divided by 2.
C. Prints one-half num.
D. Prints the square root of num.
E. Prints the binary representation of num.

5. Consider the following code segment:

```
for(int j = 0; j <= <some value>; j += 2)
  System.out.println(j);
```

Which replacement for `<some value>` will result in exactly five lines of output being produced?

A. 4
B. 5
C. 9
D. 10
E. 11

Questions 6 and 7 refer to the following class declarations and definitions:

```
public class Uno
{
  public void doSomething(Uno a, Dos b, Tres c)
  {
    <code not shown>
  }
}
public class Dos extends Uno
{
  public void doSomethingElse(Dos d, Tres e)
  {
    <code not shown>
  }
}
public class Tres extends Dos
{
  public void doOneThingMore(Dos f, Tres g)
  {
    <code not shown>
  }
}
```

6. Which of the following is a valid relationship?

   I. Tres IS-A Uno
  II. Uno HAS-A Tres
 III. Dos IS-A Tres

   A. I only
   B. II only
   C. I and II only
   D. II and III only
   E. I, II, and III

Suppose the following declarations have been made in the client program.

```
Uno first = new Uno();
Dos second = new Dos();
Tres third = new Tres():
```

7. Which of the following is a correct method call?

   A. first.doSomething(first, first, first);
   B. second.doSomething (first, second, second);
   C. third.doOneThingMore(third, third);
   D. second.doSomethingElse(third, second);
   E. first.doOneThingMore(second, third);

For questions 8 and 9, consider the following class:

```
public class Widget
{
  private String name;
  private double cost;

  public Widget(String n, double c)
  /* Implementation not shown */

  public String getName() { return name; }

  public double getCost() { return cost; }

  public boolean isOnSale()
  /* Implementation not shown */
}
```

8. Suppose that a `Widget` named w has been properly constructed. Which of the following expressions will compile and execute as intended without error?

A. `System.out.println(name + " " + cost);`
B. `System.out.println(w.name + " " + w.cost);`
C. `System.out.println(w.name + " " + (String) w.cost);`
D. `System.out.println(w.getName()+ " " + w.getCost());`
E. `System.out.println(w.getName()+ " " + (String) w.getCost());`

9. Suppose that `inventory` is an array of `Widgets`. Consider the following code fragment that is meant to print out the list of all `Widgets` that are on sale:

```
for (int num=0; num<inventory.length; num++)
{
  if ( /* missing code */ )
  {
    System.out.println(inventory[num].getName());
  }
}
```

Which of the following expressions will complete the code fragment?

A. `inventory[num].isOnSale()`
B. `inventory.get(num).isOnSale()`
C. `inventory.isOnSale(num)`
D. `inventory.num.isOnSale()`
E. `isOnSale(inventory[num])`

Questions 10 and 11 refer to the information below.

The initial content of an array of integers is shown below.

9   7   3   6   5   8   1   4

After three passes of a particular algorithm, the contents contain the following.

1   3   4   6   5   8   9   7

10. Which algorithm has been applied to the array?

A. Insertion sort
B. Merge sort
C. Binary search
D. Selection sort
E. Sequential search

11. Which of the following is the best loop invariant for the algorithm demonstrated above? Assume the array name is `arr` and the loop is controlled by variable `j`.

    A. `arr[0]` through `arr[j]` are the `j` smallest elements and are in order; `arr[j+1]` through `arr[arr.length()-1]` are unexamined.
    B. `arr[0]` through `arr[j-1]` are the `j` smallest elements and are in order; `arr[j]` through `arr[arr.length()-1]` are in no particular order.
    C. `arr[0]` through `arr[j-1]` are in order with respect to each other; `arr[j]` through `arr[arr.length()-1]` are unexamined.
    D. The value in `arr[j]` is in its correct final position; elements to the left of `arr[j]` are less than `arr[j]`; elements to the right are greater than or equal to `arr[j]`.
    E. Successive pairs of elements are in order with respect to each other.

12. Consider the following code segment with operations on an `ArrayList`:

```
ArrayList items = new ArrayList();
for(int count = 1; count <= 10; count++)
  items.add(new Integer(count));
for(int count = 10; count >= 1; count-=2)
  items.remove(count);
System.out.println(items);
```

    Which of the following best represents the result of executing this code?

    A. 1 3 5 7 9
    B. 2 4 6 8 10
    C. 1 2 3 4 5
    D. An `ArrayIndexOutOfBounds` exception will be thrown
    E. A compile time error will occur

Questions 13 and 14 refer to the following information.

Consider the following code segment that is intended to output a message describing a student's academic status.

```
if(grade >= 90)
  System.out.println("Excellent");
if(grade >= 80)
  System.out.println("Good");
if(grade >= 70)
  System.out.println("Passing");
if(grade >= 60)
  System.out.println("Borderline");
if(grade < 60)
  System.out.println("Failing");
```

13. If the above code is executed with a grade of 80, what will be printed?

    A. `ExcellentGood`
    B. `Good`
    C. `GoodPassingBorderline`
    D. `GoodPassingBorderlineFailing`
    E. `PassingBorderline`

14. The code segment is flawed. If the code is rewritten, which set of values below is best for testing its correctness?

    A. {95, 85, 75, 65, 55}
    B. {90, 89, 80, 79, 70, 69, 60, 59}
    C. {100, 90, 80, 70, 60, 50, 0}
    D. Ten values chosen randomly from 0 to 100 should be tested
    E. {99, 89, 79, 69, 59, 49} plus several random values

Questions 15 through 20 refer to the Marine Biology Simulation case study.

15. A new species `StepperFish` is designed to move diagonally forward and to its right, if possible, and otherwise to simply turn right. Which methods need to be redefined to reflect this movement pattern?

    A. `act`
    B. `move`
    C. `nextLocation`
    D. `changeDirection`
    E. More than one of the above methods must be redefined

16. Which method ensures that a `Fish` will not move backward?

    A. `Fish` method `move`
    B. `Fish` method `emptyNeighbors`
    C. `Fish` method `nextLocation`
    D. `Environment` method `isValid`
    E. `Environment` method `neighborsOf`

17. Consider the grid below that contains two Fish , a SlowFish , and a DarterFish  .

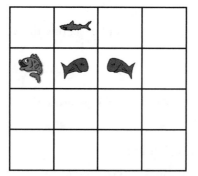

If the fish are processed in column-major order and on its turn each fish breeds and dies, which configuration below represents `EnvDisplay display` after one time step?

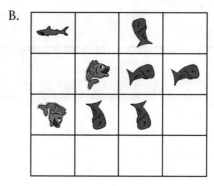

C.

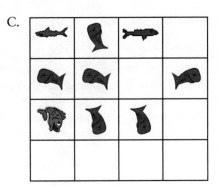

D.

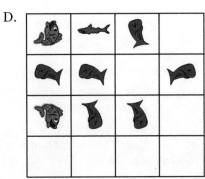

E.

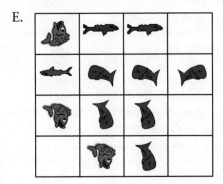

18. The biologists want to create a new subclass, Guppie, with its own private data, age. A Guppie moves like a SlowFish at age 1 but moves like a DarterFish at age 2. After that it behaves like a Fish. Until it behaves like a Fish, a Guppie cannot breed, but it may die. Which is a true statement about the Guppie class?

A. Because a Guppie does not breed until it is old enough to behave like a Fish, there is no need to overwrite generateChild in the Guppie class.
B. The Guppie class can inherit all the methods it needs by extending SlowFish and DarterFish.
C. The Guppie class can inherit all the methods it needs by extending SlowFish and implementing DarterFish.
D. In designing the Guppie class, the programmer should answer the question, "Does a Fish, a SlowFish, a DarterFish, or none of these HAS-A Guppie?"
E. In designing the Guppie class, the programmer should answer the question, "IS-A Guppie a Fish, a SlowFish, a DarterFish, or none of these classes?"

19. A test is being designed to determine whether fish facing east are dying with a specified probability. Three test designs are being considered.

    I.   Seed the random number generator so that the same sequence of pseudorandom numbers is generated every time the program is run. The number of east-facing fish that die in the first time step should be consistent.
    II. Run the program many times without seeding the random number generator. Count the number of east-facing fish that die on each time step, and accumulate the findings to determine whether they approach the specified probability.
    III. Run the program many times with different data files in which all of the fish are facing east. The number of fish that die on the first time step of each run should approximate the expected probability.

    Which test design would specifically aid in determining if the probability is working as expected?

    A. I only
    B. II only
    C. III only
    D. II and III only
    E. I, II, and III

20. Suppose the biologists wish to include a fish's length and weight among its private data. Of the following, which is the best way to initialize these variables?

    A. Add a new constructor with parameters for the environment, the fish's location, its length, and its weight. No other changes to the class are necessary.
    B. Add a new constructor with parameters for the environment, the fish's location, its length, and its weight and initialize the instance variables before calling `initialize`. All other constructors are modified to initialize length and weight to default values before calling the `initialize` method.
    C. Add a new constructor with parameters for the environment, the fish's location, its length, and its weight. Include the additional variables in the parameter list for `initialize`. For the new constructor, send the length and weight parameters to `initialize`; for all other constructors, send randomly generated values within a reasonable range for length and weight.
    D. Assign the new instance variables default values. Add public `setLength` and `setWidth` methods to the `Fish` class, allowing the client code to provide different values if desired.
    E. Generate random values within a reasonable range for length and weight of each fish in the `initialize` method.

21. Consider the following method:

```
public int strange(int[] arr)
{
  int s = 0;
  for(int k = 0; k < arr.length; k++)
  {
    if(arr[k] % 2 != 0)
      s += arr[k];
  }
  return s;
}
```

    Which of the following best describes the value returned by `strange`?

    A. The sum of the odd numbers in `arr`
    B. The sum of the even numbers in `arr`
    C. The sum of the positive numbers in `arr`
    D. The sum of the negative numbers in `arr`
    E. The sum of the nonzero numbers in `arr`

22. What is always true when a `while` loop terminates (in the absence of a `break` statement)?

    A. The loop test condition is true.
    B. The loop test condition is false.
    C. The variables used in the loop are undefined.
    D. The variables used in the loop are redefined as 0 or null.
    E. The body of the loop has been executed.

23. Under what circumstances will Insertion sort run at least as fast as Merge sort on a given list?

    A. When there are fewer than ten data items.
    B. When the data are already in order.
    C. When the data are in reverse order.
    D. When the data are randomly distributed.
    E. Insertion sort is never more efficient than Merge sort.

24. Which of the following statements about interfaces in Java is true?

    A. Since interfaces have no instance variables, the classes that implement them must also have no instance variables.
    B. Interfaces may, but do not usually, have static variables.
    C. If a class implements an interface, it must do so exactly; it may not have any methods whose names match the names of methods in the interface unless the parameter sequences also match.
    D. A class may not implement two different interfaces if they contain the same method signature.
    E. Because it has no code, an interface is never instantiated.

25. Consider the unsorted contents of an array of `Strings` shown below.

    "Sun" "Mon" "Tues" "Wed" "Thurs" "Fri" "Sat"

    Suppose a programmer executes a binary search on the array. For which elements will the correct position in the array be returned?

    A. "Sun" "Mon" "Tues" "Wed" "Thurs" "Fri" "Sat"
    B. "Mon" "Tues" "Wed"
    C. "Wed"
    D. The code will execute, but the correct position will not be returned for any of the elements
    E. The code will not execute; a compiler error will be generated

26. Suppose the contents of an array have been separated by successive recursive calls into N individual subarrays (still housed in a single array), where N is the number of elements in the original array.

    Using the Merge sort algorithm, how many calls to merge are necessary to rebuild the original array in ascending order?

    A. log(N)
    B. N − 1
    C. N
    D. N logN
    E. N^2

27. Consider the code segment below that is intended to determine if two arrays, `alpha` and `beta`, of `Integer` type are equal. The arrays are equal if they are the same length and contain the same values in parallel positions.

```
int k = 0;
while((k<alpha.length)&&(k<beta.length)&&(alpha[k].equals(beta[k])))
  k++;
```

Which of the following is true when the loop terminates?

A. `k >= alpha.length && k >= beta.length`
B. `k >= alpha.length || k >= beta.length`
C. `!(alpha[k].equals(beta[k]))`
D. `k >= alpha.length && k >= beta.length && !(alpha[k].equals(beta[k]))`
E. `k >= alpha.length || k >= beta.length || !(alpha[k].equals(beta[k]))`

28. Consider the following method that is meant to search for a given value within an array:

```
// precondition: a is an array with at least one element
// postcondition: returns the location of key within the array a;
//                returns -1 if key is not present
public int srch(int[] a, int key)
{
  int n = a.length;
  int j = 1;
  while(j <= n && a[j-1] != key)
    j++;
  if(j > n)
    return -1;
  else
    return j;
}
```

Which of the following most accurately characterizes the behavior of this code?

A. It does not compile.
B. It sometimes generates an exception.
C. It always returns an incorrect value.
D. It always returns a value, but that value is not always correct.
E. It runs as specified.

29. Consider the following class structure:

```
public class A
{
  private B someData;
  /* Other parts of class not shown */
}

public class B
{
  private A otherData;
  /* Other parts of class not shown */
}
```

Which of the following statements is true?

A. Objects of these classes can exist with no other changes needed to the class structure.
B. For objects of these classes to exist, either A or B must extend the other class.
C. For objects of these classes to exist, at least one of `someData` and `otherData` must be made public.
D. For objects of these classes to exist, there must a recursive method in either A or B.
E. There is no way that two classes can share instance variables in this manner.

30. Which of the following statements about recursive algorithms are true?

    I.   Recursive algorithms must feature a number as one of their inputs.
    II. Recursion is best used when there is an identifiable general case and an identifiable simplest case.
    III. Some algorithms, such as binary search, require the use of recursion.

    A. I only
    B. II only
    C. III only
    D. Exactly two of the statements are true
    E. All three of the statements are true

31. An interface is designed to represent an athlete. An athlete has a name and a sport. The class heading is as follows.

    ```
    public interface Athlete
    ```

    Which of the following will result in a compiler error if included in the `Athlete` interface?

    I.   ```
         private String myName;
         private String mySport;
         ```
    II.  ```
         public Athlete(String name, String sport)
         {
            myName = name;
            mySport = sport;
         }
         ```
    III. ```
         public String getName();
         public String getSport();
         ```

    A. I only
    B. II only
    C. I and II only
    D. I, II, and III
    E. None of I, II, or III would result in an error message

32. Consider the following code segment:

    ```
    String w = <some word>;
    int j = 0;
    int k = w.length() - 1;
    // <loop invariant>
    while(j<k && w.substring(j,j+1).equals(w.substring(k,k+1)))
    {
      j++;
      k--;
    }
    ```

    Which of the following should replace `<loop invariant>`?

    A. `w[k] through w[w.length()-1] is the reverse of w[0] through w[j]`
    B. `w[k] through w[w.length()-1] is equivalent to w[0] through w[j]`
    C. `w[k+1] through w[w.length()-1] is the reverse of w[0] through w[j-1]`
    D. `w[k+1] through w[w.length()-1] is equivalent to w[0] through w[j-1]`
    E. `w[k-1] through w[w.length()-1] is in alphabetical order with respect to w[0] through w[j+1]`
    ```

33. Consider the following code segment that is intended to toggle variable x between 1 and −1. Assume x initially contains either the value 1 or −1.

```
if(x == 1)
  x = -1;
else
  x = 1;
```

Which of the following can replace this code so that the program still works as intended?

A. `x += -x;`
B. `x -= -x;`
C. `x *= -x;`
D. `x /= -x;`
E. `x = -x;`

34. Assume that an Internet browser keeps track of each successive site visited and, on command, offers the user the opportunity to return to the most recent site by clicking the "back" button. Of the following, which is the best way to store the addresses of the return sites?

A. Create an array of site addresses in which the sites are added to the front of the array, allowing easy access to the most recently visited site; return by reading each array element in order.
B. Create an array of site addresses and maintain the array in sorted order.
C. Create an `ArrayList` of site addresses in which the sites are added to the end of the `ArrayList`.
D. Create a sorted `ArrayList` in which each site visited is inserted into its correct position by location address.
E. Create a class `Sites` in which each instance of the class is the address of site. The instances are named `site1`, `site2`, etc., and can easily be accessed by their number.

35. Classes `Snacks` and `GoodSnacks` are defined as follows:

```
public class Snacks
{
  public void test1()
  { System.out.print("potato chips "); }

  public void test2()
  { System.out.print("candy bar "); }
}

public class GoodSnacks extends Snacks
{
  public void test1()
  { System.out.print("apple ");
    super.test1();
  }
}
```

What is output by the following code segment?

```
GoodSnacks g = new GoodSnacks();
g.test1();
g.test2();
```

A. `potato chips apple`
B. `apple potato chips`
C. `potato chips apple candy bar`
D. `apple potato chips candy bar`
E. `apple candy bar`

Use the following class definitions in answering questions 36 and 37.

```
public class Date implements Comparable
{
  private int theDay;
  private int theMonth;
  private int theYear;

  public int getDay()   {<implementation not shown>}
  public int getMonth() {<implementation not shown>}
  public int getYear()  {<implementation not shown>}
  public int compareTo(Date d)
  { < missing code > }

  //other methods not shown
}

public class Person
{
  private String name;
  private Date birthdate;

  public Date getDate()
  { return birthdate; }
  //other data and methods not shown
}
```

36. Consider the following implementations of the body of `compareTo` in the `Date` class. (To simplify the problem, assume there are no leap years and all months have 30 days.)

    I. `return ((theDay<d.getDay())&&(theMonth<d.getMonth())&&(theYear<d.getYear()));`
    II. `return ((365*theYear + 30*theMonth + theDay) -`
    `        (365*d.getYear() + 30*d.getMonth() + d.getDay()));`
    III. `if ((theYear>d.getYear()) || (theYear==d.getYear() && theMonth>d.getMonth())`
    `    || (theYear==d.getYear() && theMonth==d.getMonth() && theDay>d.getDay()))`
    `        return 1;`
    `else`
    `        return -1;`

    A. I only
    B. II only
    C. III only
    D. I and II only
    E. II and III only

37. Suppose more than one student in the problem above has a birthday today. Which of the following, from a programmer's point of view, is the best way for the teacher to obtain a copy of the names of all such students so that further processing may be done?

    A. Search the entire `ArrayList` and print the name of each student whose birthday is today as the match is found.
    B. Create an array the same length as the `ArrayList` and as each matching birthday is found, store the name in the array, keeping track of the current number of valid elements. Return the array.
    C. Create an `ArrayList` of `Strings` and, as each match is found, add the name to the `ArrayList`. Return the `ArrayList`.
    D. Create a second `ArrayList` of `Person` and, as each match is found, remove the `Person` from the first `ArrayList` and add the `Person` to the new `ArrayList`.
    E. Create an array where each element is an `ArrayList` of all students whose birthdays fall on the same day. Use the `compareTo` method to sort the array by date of birth so the teacher can easily access all students whose birthdays fall on any day of the year.

38. Below are three assertions about arrays or `ArrayLists`:

I. Many operations on `ArrayLists` can be performed using substantially less code than the equivalent operation on an array.
II. The keyword `new` is used to create both arrays and `ArrayLists`.
III. Both arrays and `ArrayLists` implement the `List` interface.

Which of the preceding statements is true?

A. I only
B. II only
C. I and II only
D. II and III only
E. All three assertions are true

39. Consider the following incomplete class declarations:

```
public interface Quadrilateral
{
  public double area(double dimension1, double dimension2);
}

public abstract class Parallelogram implements Quadrilateral
{
  < data and methods not shown>
}

public class Rectangle extends Parallelogram
{
  < data and methods not shown >
}
```

Which statement below is true?

A. `Parallelogram` is required to implement `area`.
B. `Rectangle` may implement `area` even if it was already implemented in `Parallelogram`.
C. `Rectangle` may have more than one area method as long as the methods differ in return type.
D. `Rectangle` may have more than one area method as long as the methods have the same number and type of parameters in the same order.
E. `Rectangle` may contain an abstract method.

40. Which assignment statement is legal?

A. `String s = 40;`
B. `Integer i = 40;`
C. `String s = new String(40);`
D. `Integer i = new Integer(40);`
E. All the above are legal

Section II

Time: 1 hour and 45 minutes; number of questions: 4; percent of total grade: 50

Directions: Show all your work. Remember that program segments are to be written in Java. In writing your solutions to a part of the problem, you may assume that code from previous parts works correctly regardless of what you wrote in those parts. In such cases, it is expected that you will invoke the appropriate method; reimplementing a solution from an earlier part of a question will result in a less than perfect score being awarded for that problem.

1. The meteorologists at Channel 5 report the conditions not only from their base of operations, but also from various "weather watchers" in surrounding towns. These weather watchers report the high, low, and current temperatures for the day as well as current conditions (e.g., "clear," "snowing," "mostly cloudy," etc.), the daily precipitation total, and the current wind speed and direction (so as to announce reports such as, "the wind is currently 5 miles per hour out of the northeast"). These conditions are stored in the computer as Weather objects.

   A. Write a class definition for the Weather class that will keep track of the information and provide the services for the class, putting only "{ . . . }" in for the bodies of the constructor(s) and method(s). In writing this definition you must:

      - Choose appropriate names for all identifiers.
      - Provide (at least) the functionality specified above.
      - Make data representation decisions consistent with the specification above.
      - Make design decisions that are consistent with the principles of object-oriented design.

   Comments are not required, but they may be included to explain your intent.

   Do not write the implementations of the constructors or the methods of the Weather class.

   B. As the various weather watchers e-mail their information, Channel 5 stores each item in an unordered list of Weather objects. This list is stored in an array named watcherReports. The array is large enough to hold all reports; if some reports do not arrive, then there are an associated number of null cells at the end of the array. The meteorologists are fond of saying things like, ". . . and the warmest area in the region is Johnstown." Write the method warmestSpot that will provide the name of the location reporting with the highest temperature. The header for this method is given below:

```
// precondition:  the array watcherReports contains at least one actual report
// postcondition: returns the name of the location reporting the highest current
//                temperature; if more than one such location exists,
//                any such name may be returned
public String warmestSpot()
```

   C. During the winter, the meteorologists also like to announce whether or not it is snowing somewhere in the viewing area. Write the method isSnowingSomewhere that will help them with this. Its header is given below:

```
// precondition:   the array watcherReports contains at least one actual report
// postcondition:  returns true if at least one location is reporting that it is
//                 currently snowing; otherwise returns false
public boolean isSnowingSomewhere()
```

2. Golf is scored by keeping a running total of the strokes a player takes on each of 18 holes. Players also sometimes keep count of the number of putts (a subset of the total number of strokes taken), i.e., those strokes taken on the green, or area closest to the hole. In a tournament, the player with the *lowest* score wins.

This question concerns classes involved with the game of golf. The Hole class keeps track of the number of strokes and the number of those strokes that were putts for a single hole of golf. The Round class keeps track of a player's score on each of the 18 holes. The Player class holds the name and four-round tournament score for one player. The Tournament class contains four round scores for each player in a tournament.

```
public class Hole
{
  // returns the total number of strokes this hole
  public int getStrokes() {/* implementation not shown */ }
  public int getPutts()   {/* implementation not shown */ }

  //other data and methods not shown
}
public class Round
{
  private Hole[] oneRound = new Hole[18];

  // returns the total number of strokes taken during one round of golf
  public int getRoundTotal()
  {
    // implementation not shown
  }

  // returns the number of holes during one round for which exactly 0 or 1 putts were taken
  public int numZeroOrOnePutts()
  {
    < missing code >
  }

  // other data and methods not shown
}
public class Player
{
  private String name;
  private Round[] myRounds = new Round[4];

  // returns a player's total score after four rounds
  public int getTournamentScore()
  {
    < missing code >
  }

  public String getName() {return name;}
}
public class Tournament
{
  private ArrayList competitors;

  // returns the name of the player with the lowest score;
  // in the event of a tie, returns the String "playoff"
  public String findWinner()
  {
    < missing code >
  }
}
```

A. Write the Round method numZeroOrOnePutts as started below. numZeroOrOnePutts returns the number of holes in an 18-hole round of golf in which exactly 0 or 1 putting stroke was needed.

```
// returns the number of holes during one round
// for which exactly 0 or 1 putts were taken
public int numZeroOrOnePutts()
```

B. Write the `Player` method `getTournamentScore` that determines the total score for a player after four rounds of golf.

```
// returns a player's total score after four rounds
public int getTournamentScore()
```

C. Write the `Tournament` method `findWinner` that returns the name of the player with the lowest score. If more than one player has the same lowest score, `findWinner` returns the message "playoff."

```
// returns the name of the player with the lowest score;
// in the event of a tie, returns the String "playoff"
public String findWinner()
```

3. This question involves reasoning about the code from the Marine Biology Simulation case study. (For the actual exam, a copy of the visible code and interfaces for the black box classes will be provided.)

In this question, we add the element of disease to the simulation. Any fish in the simulation may be infected with a disease. A fish that is infected has twice the probability of dying than an uninfected fish has. In addition, any living, infected fish may spread its infection to neighboring fish at the end of its action phase.

To accommodate these changes, modifications must be made to the `Fish` class. The first is the addition of two new instance variables. The first variable is a `boolean` named `infected`; it is set to `false` in the `initialize` method when the fish is created, and it is set to `true` when a fish becomes infected. (Once infected, a fish is infected for life.) The second variable is named `probOfInfecting` and represents the probability that an infected fish will spread its infection to a given neighbor. Similar to the variables `probOfBreeding` and `probOfDying`, this variable is set to a constant value in the `initialize` method.

Two additional methods will be added to the `Fish` class to support these changes as well.

A. The first additional method is an accessor method which is used to determine the `Fish`'s infection status. Complete the method below:

```
// Returns this fish's infection status.
public boolean isInfected()
```

B. The second additional method is a helper method similar to the `breed` method. Instead of producing new `Fish`, however, this method is used to expose all the neighboring `Fish` to the infection (if this `Fish` is indeed infected). As a result of invoking this method, each `Fish` that is in a neighboring cell is exposed to the infection of this `Fish`. An exposed `Fish` has a `probOfInfecting` chance of catching the infection from such an exposure. (During any given step of the simulation, it is possible that some of an infected `Fish`'s neighbors will catch the infection while others will not.) Complete this method whose header is given below:

```
// precondition:    this Fish is infected
// postcondition:   Fish that are neighbors of this Fish are
//                  exposed to an infection
protected void exposeNeighborsToInfection()
```

C. Exposing of the neighboring `Fish` requires that the `act` method be changed to permit infected `Fish` to spread that infection to other `Fish`. Modify the `act` method to reflect the changes in behavior described at the beginning of this problem. In doing so, you are to make appropriate use of the newly defined methods.

```
// Acts for one step in the simulation.
public void act()
```

4. Pete's Party Emporium sells all kinds of party supplies, e.g., hats, noise makers, and balloons. The store keeps track of its items using a `PartyItem` class, shown below:

```
public class PartyItem
{
  private String name;
  private double price;

  public String getName() { return name; }
  public double getPrice() { return price; }

  /* Constructors and other methods not shown */
}
```

As a customer purchases an item, it, along with the quantity purchased, is entered onto a `SalesSlip`. A `SalesSlip` consists of an array of `ReceiptItems`. The `ReceiptItem` class is shown below:

```
public class ReceiptItem
{
  private Item purchasedItem;
  private int quantity;

  public Item getItem()     { return purchasedItem; }
  public int getQuantity() { return quantity; }

  /* Constructors and other methods not shown */
}
```

An outline of the `SalesSlip` class is shown below:

```
public class SalesSlip
{
  public static final int MAX_ITEMS = 30;
  public static final double TAX_RATE = <some number>;
  private ReceiptItem[] purchases;
  private int numItemsPurchased;

  public double totalDue()
  { /* Implementation not shown */ }

  public int quantityPurchased(String itemName)
  { /* Implementation not shown */ }
}
```

No `SalesSlip` is ever used for more than the stated maximum number of items. Also, the tax rate is given as a double, not as a percentage, so 0.04 represents a tax rate of 4 percent.

A. The `totalDue` method determines the total amount that the customer owes to Pete's Party Emporium. All the items that Pete sells are taxable, so this amount includes the tax due. The tax due is computed by multiplying the tax rate by the total cost of all of the goods that are being sold. For example, if the tax rate is 0.10 (10 percent), balloons cost $1.00 and hats cost $0.50, then a purchase of six balloons and four hats would return a value of $8.80 (eight dollars for the goods, plus eighty cents in tax.) You are to implement the `totalDue` method below:

```
public double totalDue()
```

B. The `quantityPurchased` method counts how many items of a given type are purchased on a given `SalesSlip`. If a `SalesSlip` had three entries for balloons with 3, 4, and 9 balloons being purchased each time, then the quantity of balloons purchased would be 16. You are to implement the `quantityPurchased` method below:

```
public int quantityPurchased(String itemName)
```

ANSWERS TO PRACTICE EXAM A2, SECTION I

1. D	11. B	21. A	31. C
2. B	12. D	22. B	32. C
3. A	13. C	23. B	33. E
4. E	14. B	24. E	34. C
5. C	15. C	25. B	35. D
6. A	16. C	26. B	36. B
7. C	17. A	27. E	37. C
8. D	18. E	28. D	38. C
9. A	19. D	29. A	39. B
10. D	20. C	30. B	40. D

✓ SOLUTIONS TO PRACTICE EXAM A2, SECTION I

1. The correct answer is D. x is doubled, and that quantity is squared.

2. The correct answer is B. This is an example of DeMorgan's Law.

3. The correct answer is A. The inclusion of the word int in the first statement creates a new variable named value; the value sent in through the parameter is lost.

4. The correct answer is E. The remainders of successive division by 2 are printed in reverse order. This is the binary representation of a decimal value.

Suppose num = 6   Output: 110

Successive calls:

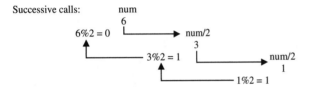

5. The correct answer is C. The numbers 0, 2, 4, 6, and 8 are printed.

6. The correct answer is A. The question tests classic inheritance relationships. A subclass IS-A specialized version of its superclass. That means a Tres IS-A Dos IS-A Uno. But the IS-A relationship doesn't work in the other direction, so a Dos is not a Tres. The HAS-A relationship means that an instance of a class has, as part of its instance data, an instance (or object) of another class. IS-A is about classes; HAS-A is about objects.

7. The correct answer is C. A subclass is an instance of its parent classes and, therefore, can be substituted where a parent class is specified, but the reverse is not the case. Answers A and D are incorrect because the actual parameters don't match the formal parameters. While a Dos can invoke doSomething, answer B is also incorrect because of the parameters. E is wrong because an Uno can't invoke doOneThingMore.

8. The correct answer is D. Private data can only be invoked through accessor methods. There is a toString method for doubles, so there is no need to cast the cost to a String.

9. The correct answer is A. Using array terminology, inventory[num] is a Widget and can, therefore, invoke the isOnSale method. Answer B uses ArrayList terminology. Answers C and E attempt to send a parameter to a method that does not expect a parameter. Answer D treats num as a Widget object, but num is the integer index into the array.

10. The correct answer is D. Selection sort chooses the smallest element and swaps it with the first element, then the second smallest is swapped, and so on. After three passes the three smallest elements have been moved to the first three positions in the array and are in the correct order.

11. The correct answer is B. Before execution begins, at the start of each iteration, and when the algorithm ends, it is true that the j-1 smallest elements have been swapped to the j-1 positions in the list and are in order. Elements from the jth through the end are unordered. Note that the entire list is examined each time during each pass in order to find the minimal (remaining) element.

12. The correct answer is D. The numbers 1 through 10 are stored in positions 0 through 9; therefore, the reference to cell 10 will cause an exception to be thrown.

13. The correct answer is C. Because 80 is greater than or equal to 80, 70, and 60, output is produced for each of these ranges. The code can be corrected by inserting else before each if after the first or by changing the conditions to test both ends of each range.

14. The correct answer is B. If the boundary cases work correctly, values between the boundary cases will be correct. Testing grades greater than 100 and less than 0 should be done, but this question is about a set of values that will test this code segment.

15. The correct answer is C. The way a StepperFish selects its next location is different from that of a Fish. Otherwise, they behave in the same way.

16. The correct answer is C. The `nextLocation` method determines the location in the reverse direction from the direction this fish is facing and removes it from the list of empty neighbors.

17. The correct answer is A. Column major order processes objects column by column, top to bottom, left to right.

18. The correct answer is E. To determine how a class fits into a hierarchy, ask if it IS-A member of the superclass. A `Guppie` would need its own `generateChild` if it were to propagate its own species. A class can extend only one other class; it can implement more than one interface or abstract class but `SlowFish` and `DarterFish` are neither.

19. The correct answer is D. Seeding the random number generator will result in the same series of random numbers and the same probability every time the program is run. While there are valid times to use a consistent seed number, in this case we wish to calculate the probability under varying test conditions and determine how closely the results approximate the expected probability.

20. The correct answer is C. This answer is consistent with the initialization of other instance variables in the simulation.

21. The correct answer is A. If the remainder is not zero, the value is not even.

22. The correct answer is B. The one thing we know is that the loop is not exited unless the condition being tested is false. We cannot say anything about the variables without additional information, and a `while` loop may never be executed at all if the test condition is false in the first place.

23. The correct answer is B. If the data are in order, Insertion sort requires one pass through the n data items. Merge sort follows its "divide and conquer" algorithm regardless of how the data are arranged, and that requires more work than a straightforward pass through the data.

24. The correct answer is E. Interfaces contain no code, but the classes that implement them do. This rules out answers A and B. Also, an interface promises only that the methods described therein exist, not what they do. Thus, all that matters is that the method with the correct signature exists; what it does is unimportant, as is

what any other method does. This rules out answers C and D.

25. The correct answer is B. If the target is "Wed," it will be found because it is in the middle of the array and is the first element examined. "Mon" and "Tues" will be found because they are in order with respect to "Wed"; for all the other elements the algorithm will return a value that indicates "not found." A value is returned for each of the elements, but the correct value is returned only for those in answer B.

26. The correct answer is B. Try this with arrays of different sizes, such as 1, 2, 7, 8, or 9. Actually, you should only need to try it on one or two of these. For the more mathematically inclined, each call to `merge` reduces the number of subarrays by one (i.e., two subarrays become one subarray.) Since we begin with N subarrays and finish with one subarray, there must have been N-1 calls to merge.

27. The correct answer is E. At least one of the three conditions is false. Answers A, B, and C check only part of the conditions. D tests for all three false but that need not be the case.

28. The correct answer is D. In the event that `key` is not in the list, −1 will be properly returned. In the event that `key` is in the list, however, a value that is one too large will be returned.

29. The correct answer is A. There is nothing wrong with this. For example, class `A` might be an `Employee` class, while class `B` is a `Manager`. Each `Employee` has a supervising `Manager`, and each `Manager` has a "key" `Employee`. None of the criteria in the other answers needs to be applied.

30. The correct answer is B. There are recursive algorithms that take only `Strings` as parameters, e.g., to reverse a `String`, so option I is not true. Also, any recursive algorithm can be converted to a nonrecursive algorithm, so option III is not true. (Even without knowing this latter fact, the question could be answered by remembering that binary search can be written either way.)

31. The correct answer is C. An interface declares appropriate methods for an object type but does not specify how those methods should be implemented. Private data and a constructor define implementation and do not belong in an interface.

32. The correct answer is C. The code is clearly doing something in reverse order because as one counter increases, the other decreases. The truth of the invariant is with respect to the positions in the string already examined, the previous values of `j` and `k`.

33. The correct answer is E. `x` is assigned its opposite. This code can be used to control which of two items (e.g., players in a game or items being printed) is active.

34. The correct answer is C. An `ArrayList` is a dynamic structure; it can grow and shrink as the user traverses and returns from site paths. The only access needed is to the end of the `ArrayList` which is also very efficient.

35. The correct answer is D. `g` calls its own method `test1`, and that method invokes `test1` in the `Snacks` class. `GoodSnacks` doesn't have a `test2` method, so it looks to the parent class and executes the `test2` it finds there.

36. The correct answer is B. Choice I returns a `boolean` rather than an integer. Choice III fails to return 0 if the dates are equal.

37. The correct answer is C. The problem did not say to print the student names, so choice A is incorrect. Choice D will change the original `ArrayList`, and choice E builds an entirely new (and unnecessary) structure. Choice B would work, but requires maintaining a second variable to keep track of the number of students with the given birthday, while choice C does not require the additional variable. Given two acceptable options, the simpler is to be preferred.

38. The correct answer is C. The various `ArrayList` methods permit some operations (such as insertion of an item at an arbitrary location) to be performed with a single method call, whereas the same operation with an array is much more complex; therefore, assertion I is true. Assertion II is true even though arrays are not in the classic `Object` hierarchy. Assertion III is false because arrays do not extend any class or implement any interfaces.

39. The correct answer is B. A subclass may override a method of the parent class. Answer A is false because an abstract class can declare a method abstract and just pass it along to subclasses to implement. That simply tells the programmer that this method should be implemented in each subclass. Answers C and D are false because it is differences in the parameter list that distinguish which of two or more overloaded methods is invoked, not the return type. Answer E is false because `Rectangle` is not an abstract class and, therefore, cannot have any abstract methods.

40. The correct answer is D. It is legal to initialize an `Integer` with an anonymous constant value.

ANSWERS TO PRACTICE EXAM A2, SECTION II

Problem 1A

```
public class Weather
{
  private String location;
  private int lowTemp;
  private int highTemp;
  private int currentTemp;
  private String conditions;
  private double precipitation;
  private int windSpeed;
  private String windDirection;

  public Weather(String name, int temp, String conditions,
    int speed, String direction) { ... }

  public String getSiteName() { ... }
  public int getLowTemp() { ... }
  public int getHighTemp() { ... }
  public int getCurrentTemp() { ... }
  public String getConditions() { ... }
  public double getPrecipitation() { ... }
  public int getWindSpeed() { ... }
  public String getWindDirection() { ... }

  public void setTemp(int temp) { ... }
  public void setConditions(String sky) { ... }
  public void setPrecipitation(int fallAmount) { ... }
  public void setWind(int speed, String direction) { ... }
}
```

Problem 1B

```
public String warmestSpot()
{
  int hotTemp = watcherReports[0].getHighTemp();
  int hotLocation = 0;
  for (int k=0; k<watcherReports.length; k++)
  {
    if (watcherReports[k].getHighTemp() > hotTemp())
    {
      hotTemp = watcherReports[k].getHighTemp();
      hotLocation = k;
    }
  }
  return watcherReports[hotLocation].getSiteName();
}
```

Problem 1C

```
public boolean isSnowingSomewhere()
{
  for (int k=0; k<watcherReports.length; k++)
  {
    if (watcherReports[k].getConditions().equals("snowing"))
    {
      return true;
    }
  }
  return false;
}
```

Problem 2A

```
public int numZeroOrOnePutts()
{
  int numGoodHoles = 0;
  for (int k=0; k<18; k++)
  {
    if (oneRound[k].getPutts() < 2)
    {
      numGoodHoles++;
    }
  }
  return numGoodHoles;
}
```

Problem 2B

```
public int getTournamentScore()
{
  return myRounds[0].getRoundTotal()
       + myRounds[1].getRoundTotal()
       + myRounds[2].getRoundTotal()
       + myRounds[3].getRoundTotal();
}
```

Problem 2C

```
public String findWinner()
{
  Player lowScorer = (Player) competitors.get(0);
  boolean tieForLead = false;
  for (int k=1; k<player.size(); k++)
  {
    Player p = (Player) competitors.get(k);
    if (p.getTournamentScore() == lowScorer.getTournamentScore())
      tieForLead = true;
    if (p.getTournamentScore() < lowScorer.getTournamentScore())
    {
      lowScorer = p;
      tieForLead = false;
    }
  }
  if (tieForLead)
    return "playoff";
  else
    return lowScorer.getName();
}
```

Problem 3A

```
public boolean isInfected()
{
  return infected;
}
```

Problem 3B

```
protected void exposeNeighborsToInfection()
{
  Random randomNumGen = RandNumGenerator.getInstance();
  ArrayList nbrs = environment().neighborsOf( location() );
  for (int index=0; index<nbrs.size(); index++)
  {
    Location loc = (Location) nbrs.get(index);
    if ( ! environment().isEmpty(loc) )
    {
      if (randomNumGen.nextDouble() < probOfInfecting)
      {
        Fish f = (Fish) environment().objectAt(loc);
        f.infected = true;
        f.probOfDying *= 2;
      }
    }
  }
}
```

Problem 3C

```
public void act()
{
  if ( ! isInEnv() )
    return;

  if ( ! breed() )
    move();

  Random randomNumGen = RandNumGenerator.getInstance();
  if (randomNumGen.nextDouble() < probOfDying)
    die();

  if ( isInfected() )
    exposeNeighborsToInfection();
}
```

278 • Practice Exams and Solutions

Problem 4A

```
public double totalDue()
{
  double total = 0.0;

  for (int item=0; item<numItems; item++)
  {
    total += purchases[item].getItem().getPrice()
      * purchases[item].getQuantity();
  }

  total *= (1 + TAX_RATE);
  return total;
}
```

Problem 4B

```
public int quantityPurchased(String itemName)
{
  int count = 0;

  for (int item=0; item<numItems; item++)
  {
    if (purchases[item].getItem().getName().equals(itemName))
    {
      count += purchases[item].getQuantity();
    }
  }
  return count;
}
```

✓ RUBRICS AND COMMENTARY FOR PRACTICE EXAM A2, SECTION II

Note: In many cases where a rubric says "+1," it may be possible to earn half a point for a nearly correct solution.

Problem 1 (9 points)

Part A (4 points)

+1 for proper class format, including a proper list of private instance variables

+1 for a constructor that enables the various fields to be set

+1 for accessor methods for each instance variable

+1 for methods allowing variable instance data to be set (**Note:** does not include site name)

Part B (3 points)

+1 initializes and updates a variable keeping track of the bestSiteSoFar

+1 checks each Weather site in the list

+1 for correctly extracting the necessary data from the data set (includes both array indexing and use of appropriate get methods)

Part C (2 points)

+1 checks each Weather site in the list (at least until a snowy site is found); includes both indexing and extraction of conditions data

+1 for returning the correct value based upon data extracted

Deductions

Points could be deducted for poorly chosen variable or method names, but experience shows that this happens rarely—usually when single letter names are used. In general, if a good-faith effort has been put into naming the variable, this is acceptable.

Commentary

Slightly different sets of instance variables would be acceptable. Alternative solutions might use more or fewer methods to set the data depending upon the

parameters in those methods. Likewise, the parameter sequence on the constructor might be different.

It is imperative that the solution to Part B use the methods as outlined in part A.

The first point for Part B will not be awarded if there is no code involving the weatherReports array.

If the data in Part A are public, it is possible that directly accessing them in Parts B and/or C would result in an additional deduction.

Problem 2 (9 points)

Part A (3 points)

+1 initializes, maintains, and returns variable that counts certain rounds

+1 checks 18 scores

+1 properly determines which holes qualify for zero or one putts

Part B (2 points)

+1 adds four quantities from a list of round scores

+1 returns correct sum, including proper use of methods calls

Part C (4 points)

+1 initializes and maintains low scoring golfer, including returning name

+1 checks all competitors

+1 properly determines when a new low scoring golfer is found

+1 detects and returns correct value ("playoff") in the case of a tie

Commentary

Each of Parts A and B can be done either with or without a loop, although Part A would require 18 lines of code without a loop versus the 4 that are required with no loop in Part B.

If the solution to Part C uses a return inside the loop to determine ties, it is probably incorrect; a lower score may appear later in the list.

Problem 3 (9 points)

Part A (1 point)

+1 for returning the instance variable as it was named in the problem

Part B (4 points)

+1 for checking each potential location for a fish

+1 for exposing every fish (and no empty locations)

+1 for correctly determining which infection has taken place

+1 for updating the instance variables properly

Part C (4 points)

+1 for checking whether or not the fish is infected before exposing neighbors

+1 for exposing the neighbors

+1 for dying according to the correct probability

+1 for otherwise acting in the proper manner (including order of all actions)

Commentary

The solution for Part B is best modeled after the `emptyNeighbors` method although there is no need to return the list of fish in this case.

It is not necessary to adjust the probability of dying during the exposure. If this is not done, however, then such must be accounted for in the `act` method. Either solution is acceptable, but it is necessary to be consistent.

Problem 4 (9 points)

Part A (4 points)

+1 for initializing and returning a `double` for the total

+1 for looping through the entire `purchases` array

+1 for correctly determining the price and quantity of each item purchased

+1 for updating the total correctly (includes computation of tax)

Part B (5 points)

+1 for initializing and returning an `int` for the count

+1 for looping through the entire `purchases` array

+1 for correctly determining the name and quantity of the item

+1 for correctly determining whether to count the item or not

+1 updating the count correctly

Commentary

In Part A, solutions which get the item and store it in a variable and then get the price for the item are perfectly acceptable. The same applies to Part B concerning the item name. On the other hand, solutions which attempt to get the price or name without first getting the item would not receive credit for this task.

In Part B, the `equals` method must be used to compare `Strings`, not the `==` operator.

Computer Science AB
Practice Exam AB1

Answer Sheet for Multiple-Choice Questions

1. _____	11. _____	21. _____	31. _____
2. _____	12. _____	22. _____	32. _____
3. _____	13. _____	23. _____	33. _____
4. _____	14. _____	24. _____	34. _____
5. _____	15. _____	25. _____	35. _____
6. _____	16. _____	26. _____	36. _____
7. _____	17. _____	27. _____	37. _____
8. _____	18. _____	28. _____	38. _____
9. _____	19. _____	29. _____	39. _____
10. _____	20. _____	30. _____	40. _____

PRACTICE EXAM AB1

Section I

Time: 1 hour and 15 minutes; number of questions: 40; percentage of grade: 50

Directions: Determine the answer to each of the following questions or incomplete statements, using the available space for any necessary scratch work. Then fill in the space on the answer sheet corresponding to the best choice given. No credit will be given for anything written in the examination booklet. Do not spend too much time on any one problem.

Note: Assume the Java Standard Libraries and the AP Java Subset are included in any programs that use the code segments provided in individual questions. You may refer to the College Board document (Copyright © 2004 by College Entrance Examination Board), "A Quick Reference," while taking this practice exam. This document is available at www.collegeboard.com/student/testing/ap/sub_compsciab.html.

1. Consider the following loop:

```java
for (int n=0; n<1000; n=n+3)
{
  if (n%2 == 0)
    System.out.println(n);
}
```

Which of the following most precisely describes the numbers that are printed when this loop is executed?

A. Nonnegative even numbers less than 1000.
B. Nonnegative even numbers less than 1000 that are not multiples of 3.
C. Nonnegative odd numbers less than 1000 that are multiples of 3.
D. Nonnegative numbers less than 1000 that are multiples of 6.
E. No numbers are printed.

Questions 2 and 3 concern the following three methods found within a class.

```
public void method1(int n)
{
  if (n>1)
  {
    for (int i=0; i<n; i++)
    {
      method2(i);
    }
    method2(n/2);
  }
}
public void method2(int n)
{
  for (int j=0; j<n*n; j++)
  {
    method3(j*j);
  }
}
public void method3(int n)
{
    // Implementation not shown
}
```

2. Which of the following expressions best describes the number of times that `method2` will be invoked as result of executing the statement:

`method1(n);`

assuming that n is at least 100?

A. O(1)
B. O(logn)
C. O(n)
D. O(n²)
E. `method2` will not be invoked

3. Which of the following expressions best describes the number of times that `method3` will be invoked as result of executing the statement:

`method2(n);`

assuming that n is at least 100?

A. O(n)
B. O(n*logn)
C. O(n²)
D. O(n³)
E. `method3` will not be invoked

4. Suppose that x, y, and z are `boolean` variables. x contains the value `true`; y contains the value `false`; the value of z is unknown. For which of the following is the value of the expression known?

A. `x && !y && (y||z)`
B. `z||(y && !z)||! (y||z)`
C. `!x||z||(y && x)`
D. `(x && z)||(y||z)`
E. `z && (y||x) && !(y && x)`

5. Treesort works as follows:

   I. For each piece of data in the initial list, insert it into a binary search tree.
   II. Perform an in-order traversal of the binary search tree, placing each item into the sorted list in the order in which it is traversed.

   In terms of data ordering and running time, Treesort most resembles what sorting algorithm?

   A. Selection sort
   B. Insertion sort
   C. Merge sort
   D. Quicksort
   E. Heapsort

6. Given a square n × n matrix of integers, the code segment below is intended to assign 0 to all the elements on both diagonals.

```
for(int row = 0; row < n; row++)
{
   <missing code>
}
```

   Of the following, which is the best replacement for `<missing code>`?

   A. `mat[row][row] = 0; mat[row][n - row] = 0;`
   B. `mat[row][row] = 0; mat[row][n - row - 1] = 0;`
   C. `mat[n - row - 1][row] = 0; mat[row][n - row - 1] = 0;`
   D. `mat[row][row - n] = 0; mat[n - row + 1][row] = 0;`
   E. `mat[row - n][n - row] = 0; mat[n - row][row - n];`

Questions 7 and 8 make use of the classes below:

```
public abstract class Shape
{
   private String name;
   public String getName() { return name; }
   public int getArea() { return 0; }
   abstract public void draw();
   /* other methods/instance variables not shown */
}
public class Rectangle extends Shape
{
   private int length;
   private int width;
   public Rectangle() {}
   public void draw()
   { /* Implementation not shown */ }
}
```

7. Which of the following is true about the class `Rectangle`?

   A. It will not compile because it never makes use of the instance variables `length` and `width`.
   B. It will not compile because it does not include code for the method `getArea`.
   C. It will not compile because it extends an abstract class, but it is not declared abstract itself.
   D. It will compile, but some methods will be likely to give incorrect answers.
   E. Assuming that the `draw` method is properly implemented, the class will function properly.

8. It is desired to implement a new concrete class that represents a type of `Shape`, namely an `Oval`. Which of the following statements is false?

   A. It is better design to have `Oval` extend `Shape` than to have it extend `Rectangle`.
   B. If `Oval` extends `Rectangle`, it will not be required to define a `getArea` method.
   C. If `Oval` extends `Shape`, it will not be required to define a `getArea` method.
   D. If `Oval` extends `Rectangle`, it will not be required to define a `draw` method.
   E. If `Oval` extends `Shape`, it will not be required to define a `draw` method.

For questions 9, 10, and 11, consider the BankAccount class below. The class is meant to implement a simple account at a bank to which customers can make deposits and withdrawals to adjust their balance. At this bank, no customer ever has more than one account.

```
public class BankAccount
{
  private String ownerID;
  private double balance;

  public String getOwner()   { return ownerID; }
  public double getBalance() { return balance; }

  public void deposit( double amt )
  { /* Implementation not shown */ }

  public void withdraw( double amt )
  { /* Implementation not shown */ }

  /* Other methods not shown */
}
```

9. A bank needs to keep track of a large number of accounts. Which of the following data structures would give the best average performance for an operation that involves searching for various customers' accounts?

   A. An ArrayList of BankAccounts sorted by ownerID
   B. A LinkedList of BankAccounts sorted by ownerID
   C. An ArrayList of BankAccounts sorted by balance
   D. A LinkedList of BankAccounts sorted by balance
   E. A TreeSet of BankAccounts

10. Suppose that we wished to implement the hashCode method for BankAccounts. Which of the following implementations will generate the best behavior if a large number of BankAccounts are to be inserted into a hash table?

    A. return balance.hashCode();
    B. return ownerID.hashCode();
    C. return (ownerID+balance).hashCode();
    D. return "BankAccount".hashCode();
    E. return Math.round(balance);

11. Consider the code below which is meant to find the ownerID of any account whose balance is at least as large as all the others in a nonempty collection.

```
Collection c = <some initialized collection of BankAccounts>;
double bestBalance = 0;
String bestID = null;
Iterator it = c.iterator();
while (it.hasNext())
{
  BankAccount ba = (BankAccount) it.next();
  if ( ba.getBalance() > bestBalance )
  {
    bestBalance = ba.getBalance();
    bestID = ba.getOwnerID();
  }
}
return bestID;
```

Which of the following best describes the circumstances under which the code works properly?

A. It always works correctly.
B. It works correctly for any Collection as long as at least one account has a positive balance.
C. It works correctly for any List, but not if the Collection is a Set.
D. It works correctly for an ordered List and for a TreeSet, but not for other Collections.
E. It works correctly only if all accounts have the same balance.

12. Which of the following is a good reason for keeping instance variables private?

    A. Doing so may make future modifications to the class easier to implement.
    B. Doing so makes it easier to change other methods in the class.
    C. Doing so makes the methods in the class run more efficiently.
    D. Doing so allows subclasses to access the data.
    E. Failing to do so means that subclasses of this class cannot be created.

Questions 13 and 14 involve the following code:

```
public static int minMax(int a[], int n)
{
  if (n==1)
    return a[0];
  else
  {
    int x = maxMin(a,n-1);
    if (x < a[n-1])
      return x;
    else
      return a[n-1];
  }
}
public static int maxMin(int a[], int n)
{
  if (n==1)
    return a[0];
  else
  {
    int x = minMax(a,n-1);
    if (x > a[n-1])
      return x;
    else
      return a[n-1];
  }
}
```

13. What value is printed by the following code?

```
int a[] = {7, 8, 1, 4, 6, 9};
System.out.println(minMax(a, a.length));
```

    A. 1
    B. 6
    C. 7
    D. 9
    E. None of the above

14. If b is an array containing an odd number of integers, how many times (including the initial call) is the method maxMin invoked as a result of the code below?

```
minMax(b, b.length)
```

    A. 0
    B. `(b.length-1)/2`
    C. `(b.length+1)/2`
    D. `b.length`
    E. Some other number of times

Questions 15–20 involve the Marine Biology Simulation (MBS) case study. Some information about the MBS can be found in the Quick Reference guide provided with this exam.

15. Two plans are suggested for implementing islands in the environment:

Plan A: Maintain parallel data structures, one that tracks fish locations and one that maintains locations that are islands.

Plan B: Add a `boolean` instance variable to the `Fish` class, it is true if the fish is an island and false otherwise. "Islands" do nothing when they `act`.

Consider code modifications to the `allObjects` method that returns a list of all fish and to the `isEmpty` method invoked by `emptyNeighbors` to allow for islands using these plans. Which of the following statements best describes the complexity of the code modifications?

  A. Changes to both methods are more difficult with Plan A.
  B. Changes to both methods are more difficult with Plan B.
  C. `isEmpty` is more difficult to modify using Plan A.
  D. `allObjects` is more difficult to modify using Plan B.
  E. The plans do not differ in the complexity of code modifications.

16. Below are three ways in which the `Environment` interface *might* be implemented. Which of these could be used without changing the behavior of the simulation?

  I. Use a two-dimensional array whose coordinates represent `Fish` locations; each cell in the array will store a `List` of `Fish` located at that location.
  II. Model the entire `Environment` as a single `List`, storing `Fish/Location` pairs.
  III. Model the entire `Environment` as a single `List`, storing only `Fish` objects in each cell, but storing them in the order in which they would be processed by a single step of the simulation.

  A. None of these would work as described
  B. I only
  C. I and II only
  D. II and III only
  E. All three ways of modeling would work

17. The biologists wish to study fish living in a bounded environment that die *only* when they move into a cell along the edge of the environment, i.e., the "top" or "bottom" row, or the "left" or "right" column. Which of the following configurations of fish guarantees that at least one `Fish` will die during the next step within an `Environment` with ten rows and ten columns? (Do not worry about how the `Fish` got to their current positions.)

  A. (1,1) North, (2,2) North
  B. (1,1) North, (1,3) East, (1,4) West, (2,3) West
  C. (1,1) South, (2,1) North, (2,2)West, (3,1) North
  D. (1,1) North, (1,8) South, (8,1) East, (8,8) North
  E. (7,1) South, (8,1) East, (8,2) West

18. Which of the following *cannot* be tested via a black box test case?

  A. Test whether a `DarterFish` reverses direction when it cannot move forward.
  B. Test to see that a fish whose only adjacent empty cell is directly behind it does not move.
  C. Test whether a file with two or more fish at the same location generates an error.
  D. Test whether a fish goes left, right, or forward approximately the same percent of the time.
  E. Test whether a fish that has been removed from the environment is asked to act.

19. Suppose that the BoundedEnv class could not, for some reason, maintain an instance variable to hold the object count. It is proposed to have numObjects invoke allObjects and then return the size of the array.

    What would be the result of making this change?

    A. numObjects would no longer run correctly.
    B. numObjects would run correctly, but more slowly than before the change was made.
    C. numObjects would need to be declared as a private method in order for the class to compile.
    D. allObjects would now run more slowly than before the change was made.
    E. There would be no perceptible difference.

20. Suppose that one were to implement a new type of Fish, ExamFish. What would be the consequence of neglecting to implement the generateChild method in the ExamFish class?

    A. The class would not compile.
    B. ExamFish would not be able to breed, but the simulation would otherwise proceed normally.
    C. An exception would be raised the first time an ExamFish tried to breed.
    D. ExamFish would breed, but would not give birth to ExamFish.
    E. The simulation would behave as before, but the colors of the ExamFish would be random.

21. Which of the following statements is false?

    A. Computer security concerns are (or should be) greater when one is using a network than when one is using a standalone system.
    B. Passwords can be a security measure, but only if they are well chosen.
    C. Documents posted on the Internet are public and therefore may be distributed freely as long as appropriate authorship credit is given.
    D. Computer viruses can be propagated through the use of programs such as compilers even though those programs do not directly access a network.
    E. Even network hardware such as routers and bridges can be affected by a computer virus.

22. A certain application requires that a series of insertions and deletions will be performed on a given data structure. Whenever an item is removed from the data structure, it is printed on the console. The structure is initially empty and will also be empty upon completion. Two data structures under consideration for this application are a stack and a queue. Under what circumstances would they cause the same data to be printed in the same order?

    A. Only if no data are ever inserted, and hence nothing is ever printed.
    B. Only if at most one item is ever inserted.
    C. Only if the insertions and deletions alternate.
    D. Only if the data are inserted in increasing order.
    E. As long as all of the data are removed, both structures will behave the same way.

23. Which of the following statements about the Java Collections classes is false?

    A. All Collections classes support an add method.
    B. Lists are the only classes that support a get method.
    C. A HashMap is not a Collection.
    D. An ArrayList can be used to store data in an ordered fashion.
    E. A ListIterator is the best way to iterate through a Collection.

Questions 24 and 25 refer to the following binary tree:

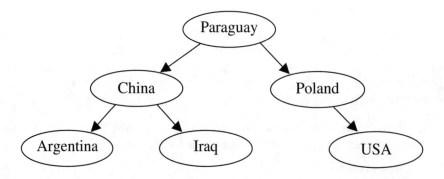

24. Which of the following represents the order in which the elements would be traversed by a preorder traversal of this tree?

    A. Argentina, China, Iraq, Paraguay, Poland, USA
    B. Argentina, Iraq, China, USA, Poland, Paraguay
    C. Paraguay, Argentina, China, Iraq, Poland, USA
    D. Paraguay, China, Argentina, Iraq, Poland, USA
    E. Paraguay, Poland, USA, China, Argentina, Iraq

25. In which of the following three orders could the data have been inserted into this tree?

    I.   Argentina, China, Iraq, Paraguay, Poland, USA
    II. Paraguay, China, Argentina, Iraq, Poland, USA
    III. Paraguay, China, Poland, Argentina, Iraq, USA

    A. I only
    B. II only
    C. III only
    D. Exactly two of the three orders would produce the desired tree
    E. All three orders would produce the desired tree

26. Class Foo processes data. Class CountingFoo is meant to help keep track of the number of times that data have been processed on a given object of type Foo.

```
public class Foo
{
  public void process()
  {
    /* Implementation not shown */
  }
  /* constructors/other methods/instance variables not shown */
}
public class CountingFoo extends Foo
{
  private int counter;
  public CountingFoo() { counter = 0; }
  public void process()
  {
    counter++;
    process();
  }
  public int processCount() { return counter; }
}
```

Which of the following is true about this implementation?

A. It will accomplish its stated purpose as written.
B. It cannot work because the instance variable `counter` needs to be declared in the class `Foo`.
C. The method `process` in the class `CountingFoo` is an example of improper recursion.
D. It will work only if the two statements in `CountingFoo`'s `process` method are reversed.
E. It will only work if the class `Foo` is declared abstract.

27. The following method is intended to return the index where the data item `key` is found within the linked list (of `ListNodes`) starting at `head`. (An index representing a value outside of the list is to be returned if `key` is not found within the list.)

```
public static int search(ListNode head, Object key)
{
  int index = 0;
  while (! key.equals(head.getData()) )
  {
    head = head.getNext();
    index++;
  }
  return index;
}
```

Which of the following statements about `search` is most accurate?

A. The method will not compile unless the type of `key` is changed to `Comparable`.
B. The method will work correctly at all times.
C. The method will work correctly one time, but will destroy the integrity of the list as it searches.
D. The method will work correctly if `key` is in the list, but it will return the wrong value if it is not.
E. The method will work correctly if `key` is in the list, but it will cause an exception to be generated if it is not.

28. What are the contents of the `ArrayList` a after the following code fragment is executed?

```
ArrayList a = new ArrayList();
for( int i=1; i<=8; i++)
{
  a.add( new Integer(i) );
}
for (int j=1; j<4; j++)
{
  a.remove(j);
}
```

A. [1, 2, 3, 4, 5]
B. [1, 3, 5, 7]
C. [1, 3, 5, 7, 8]
D. [1, 5, 6, 7, 8]
E. [4, 5, 6, 7, 8]

Questions 29 and 30 use the code below:

```
public abstract class A
{
  public abstract int z();
  public String y(int n) { return "stop"; }
  /* Remainder of class definition not shown */
}
public abstract class B extends A
{
  public void x( String s )
  {
    System.out.println( s + "now" );
  }
  /* Remainder of class definition not shown */
}
public class C extends B
{
  public C() { /* Implementation not shown */ }
  public int z() { return 23; }
  public int y() { return 17; }
  public int x() { return 49; }
}
```

29. The compiler will generate an error resulting from which of the following?

    A. Class B needs to implement method z or declare it abstract.
    B. Method x cannot be void in class B and return an int in class C.
    C. Class A may not implement method y since A is an abstract class.
    D. Since it extends an abstract class, class C must also be declared abstract.
    E. There are no compiler errors generated.

30. Assuming that any errors in the above code have been corrected, what is printed by the following code fragment?

```
C obj = new C();
System.out.print( obj.x() + obj.z() );
System.out.print( obj.y(2) );
```

    A. 72stop
    B. 4923stop
    C. 492317
    D. 7217
    E. 89

31. Which of the following are advantages of using an ArrayList rather than a LinkedList?

    I.   An ArrayList uses less memory than a LinkedList.
    II. The get method is more efficient with an ArrayList than with a LinkedList.
    III. It is easier to traverse the list backwards with an ArrayList than with a LinkedList.

    A. I only
    B. I and II only
    C. II only
    D. II and III only
    E. I, II, and III

32. The contents of matrix `mat` are as follows:

```
1     2     3     4
5     6     7     8
9    10    11    12
```

The contents as shown may be output using the code segment below:

```
for(int a = 0; a < mat.length; a++)
{
  for(int b = 0; b < mat[0].length; b++)
  {
    System.out.print(mat[a][b] + " ");
  }
  System.out.println();
}
```

How will the output appear if the two `for` statements are swapped and no other change is made in the code?

A.
```
1     5     9
2     6    10
3     7    11
4     8    12
```

B.
```
4     3     2     1
8     7     6     5
12   11    10     9
```

C.
```
9    10    11    12
5     6     7     8
1     2     3     4
```

D.
```
12   11    10     9
8     7     6     5
4     3     2     1
```

E.
```
4     8    12
3     7    11
2     6    10
1     5     9
```

33. Consider the following inheritance hierarchy:

```
public abstract class Animal
{
  /* Implementation not shown */
}
public class Dog extends Animal
{
  /* Implementation not shown */
}
public class Cat extends Animal
{
  /* Implementation not shown */
}
```

Assuming that each class has a parameterless constructor, which of the following statements will compile without error?

I.   `Animal a = new Animal();`
II. `Dog d = new Animal();`
III. `Animal a = new Cat();`

A. I only
B. I and II only
C. I and III only
D. II only
E. III only

34. The code below may sometimes generate a `NoSuchElementException`.

```
LinkedList data = <filled with data via some method>;
Iterator it = data.iterator();
for (int pos = 0; pos < data.size()-1; pos++ )
{
  Object thisItem = it.next();
  if (thisItem.equals(it.next())
  {
    System.out.println(it.next() + "was found in" +
            "consecutive positions.");
  }
}
```

Which of the following best describes when that will occur?

A. The exception will always be generated.
B. The exception will be generated whenever the list is nonempty.
C. The exception will be generated whenever the list size is a multiple of three.
D. When the exception will be generated depends upon the actual data contained in the `LinkedList`.
E. The exception will never be generated.

35. Consider the following block of code which operates on a previously initialized `List` named `list` that contains N elements.

```
Iterator it = list.iterator();
while ( it.hasNext() )
{
  update( it.next() );
}
```

Assuming that the `update` method runs in O(1) time, how long will it take to execute the block of code if `list` is an `ArrayList` or a `LinkedList`?

	ArrayList	LinkedList
A.	O(1)	O(N)
B.	O(N)	O(N)
C.	O(NlogN)	O(N²)
D.	O(N)	O(N²)
E.	O(N²)	O(NlogN)

36. A student has constructed a conglomeration of `ListNodes` that interconnect. Which of the following must be true about the structure?

A. The `next` field of some `ListNode` must be null.
B. There must be a unique "first" item for the structure.
C. No data item can be linked to more than one other item.
D. There must be at least two `ListNodes` present.
E. None of the above.

37. Consider the following method that is intended to determine if the values in an `ArrayList` are in strictly increasing order; that is, if each item is greater than (and not equal to) its predecessor. It does not work properly.

```
public static boolean isInIncreasingOrder(ArrayList a)
{
  boolean upwards = true;
  for (int k=0; k<a.size()-1; k++)
  {
    if((a.get(k)).compareTo(a.get(k+1))<0)
      upwards = true;
    else
      upwards = false;
  }
  return upwards;
}
```

For which of the following `ArrayLists` would `isInIncreasingOrder` return an incorrect value?

A. [] (an empty `ArrayList`)
B. ["bat"]
C. ["ant," "cat," "dog"]
D. ["cat," "ant," "dog"]
E. ["dog," "cat," "ant"]

38. What is the effect of attempting to execute the following block of code?

```
ListNode p = new ListNode( new String("Exam"), null);
p.setNext(p);
```

A. A compiler error will result.
B. A `NullPointerException` will result.
C. The effect is the same as if the second line read, `p.setNext(null);`
D. A circular linked list of size 1 will result.
E. A `ListNode` will be created, but it will eventually be removed from memory by Java's runtime garbage collection even if no other changes are made to any of these values.

39. Which of the following statements is true regarding the Merge sort algorithm?

A. In its normal implementation, it requires more storage than does the Quicksort algorithm.
B. It always runs faster than Insertion sort.
C. It always runs slower than Quicksort.
D. It runs most efficiently (in a "big-oh" sense) on a randomly arranged list.
E. None of the above.

40. The code below implements the `Queue` interface using an `ArrayList`. What is the best approximation to the average running times of the `enqueue` and `dequeue` methods when there are N items in the queue?

```
public class ArrayListQueue implements Queue
{
  private ArrayList myData;
  public ArrayListQueue() { myData = new ArrayList(); }

  public void enqueue(Object x) { myData.add(x); }

  public Object dequeue() { return myData.remove(0); }

  // Other methods not shown
}
```

	enqueue	dequeue
A.	O(1)	O(1)
B.	O(1)	O(N)
C.	O(N)	O(1)
D.	O(N)	O(N)
E.	None of the above	

Section II

Time: 1 hour and 45 minutes; number of questions: 4; percent of total grade: 50

Directions: Show all your work. Remember that program segments are to be written in Java. In writing your solutions to a part of the problem, you may assume that code from previous parts works correctly regardless of what you wrote on those parts. In such cases, it is expected that you will invoke the appropriate method; reimplementing a solution from an earlier part of a question will result in a less than perfect score being awarded for that problem.

1. A certain organization has a variety of people who perform work. Some of these people are volunteers (and do not get paid for their work); others are known as employees (and do get paid for their work.) The worker information is kept in the following class:

```java
public class Worker
{
  private String name;
  private String companyID;
  private int hoursWorked;

  public Worker (String nm, String ID)
  { name = nm; companyID = ID; hoursWorked = 0; }

  public String getName() { return name; }

  public String getID() { return ID; }

  public void work(int hours) { hoursWorked += hours; }

  public void resetHours() { hoursWorked = 0; }

  public int getHours() { return hoursWorked; }
}
```

Employees must get paid and therefore must implement the following interface:

```
public interface Employee
{
  public String getName();
  public int calculateEarnings();
}
```

Employees get paid according to two schemes: SalariedEmployees receive 1/26th of their annual salary (rounded down) for each pay period. HourlyEmployees receive a certain wage for each hour that they have worked. A separate class is used to handle each of these categories of worker.

A. You are to write the SalariedEmployee class. Your code should include any needed instance variables, constructors, and methods. In writing your class, you are to use appropriate identifiers and your style should be consistent with the principles of good design.

B. The payroll office needs to generate paychecks for all employees. The workers are stored in a linked list of ListNodes, each of which contains a single employee. (Volunteers are not stored in this list.) The following method will cause an appropriate paycheck to be printed:

```
// Prints an appropriate paycheck for amount dollars, payable to name
public void printCheck(String name, int amount)
{ /* Implementation not shown */ }
```

You are to implement the method generateAllPayChecks described below:

```
// precondition:    head is a reference to the front of a linked
//                  list of Employees who need to be paid
// postcondition:   a paycheck has been generated for each
//                  Employee in the list referred to by head
public void generateAllPayChecks(ListNode head)
```

2. This problem concerns the maintenance of student grades. (For purposes of this problem, each Student may be assumed to have a unique name.) The data for a given Student are to be stored in an object. Students may take any number of courses; for each course they receive a single grade. Courses are identified by a single (unique) String indicating the name of the course. Grades are also Strings. Among the other tasks supported by this class, it is expected that a transcript (report card) can be printed for a given student.

Two classes are to be used to help understand all the data being maintained. One class, called the Curriculum, keeps track of all the courses, and for each course, the students enrolled in that course. Among the other tasks supported by this class, it is expected that a roster of all enrolled students, including grades, can be produced.

The other class, called the StudentBody, keeps track of the all of the Students. It is assumed that a StudentBody can supply the Student record associated with any given name through the findStudent method.

A. You are to design the data organization for this system. For each of the classes, Student and StudentBody, you are to list and explain with a comment the private instance data (individual items or collections of items) you would include to facilitate (at least) the two tasks described above. Be sure to give both a name and a type for each item. If your type is a collection of items, be sure to explain what items are in the collection (e.g., "a Set of Students," or "a List of Strings containing grades.") You do not need to specify any constructors or methods while completing this portion of the problem

```
public class Student
{
  // Postcondition: returns the name of this student
  public String getName()
  { /* Implementation not shown */ }

  // Precondition:    this student is enrolled in course
  // Postcondition:   returns grade this student attained in course
  public String getGrade(String course)
  { /* Implementation not shown */ }

  public void printTranscript()
  { /* Implementation not shown */ }

  // Constructor and other methods not shown
}

public class StudentBody
{
  // Precondition:  student named 'name' exists
  // Postcondition: returns Student object whose name is 'name'
  public Student findStudent(String name)
  { /* Implementation not shown */ }

  // Constructor and other methods not shown
}
```

B. The Student class needs a method to print the transcript (report card) for a given student. Implement the printTranscript method of the Student class that is described below:

```
// postcondition: all of this student's courses are
//   printed, one to a line with the grade following
//   the course name on the same line, separated by
//   some constant number of spaces, e.g.:
//     Calculus B+
//     History C
//     Spanish A-
//     Gym B-
// The order in which the courses appear is unimportant
public void printTranscript()
```

C. The `Curriculum` class is partially described below:

```
public class Curriculum
{
  private HashMap courseList;
    // keys in this map are course names
    // values in this map are Sets of Students enrolled
    // in the associated course

  public void printGrades(String courseName)
  { /* Implementation not shown */ }

  // Constructors and other methods not shown
}
```

Implement the `printGrades` method of the `Curriculum` class that is described below:

```
// precondition: none
// postcondition: a listing of all Students enrolled in this
// course is printed, one to a line with the grade following
// the student's name on the same line, separated by
// some constant number of spaces, e.g.:
//    Jennifer A
//    George C-
//    Fred B
// The order in which the Students appear is unimportant.
public void printGrades(String courseName)
```

3. This question involves reasoning about the code from the Marine Biology Simulation case study. (For the actual exam, a copy of the visible code and interfaces for the black box classes will be provided.)

This question concerns an alternative representation for the `UnboundedEnv` class. In this implementation, the fish will be stored in a `HashMap` rather than in an `ArrayList`. The `Location` of a `Fish` will be the key, and the `Fish` object itself will be the value. Implementing this schema will require changes to several methods. Throughout this problem, you may assume that the proper changes have been made to all methods other than the one you are writing, regardless of anything you may have written in a previous section. (Note: the `Location` class has a `hashCode` method, and you may assume that it is properly implemented as well.)

The private data and constructor for this new implementation are shown below:

```
public class UnboundedEnv
{
  private HashTable objects;

  public UnboundedEnv()
  {
    objects = new HashMap();
  }
  /* Other methods not shown */
}
```

A. Show the implementation of the `add` method.

```
public void add(Locatable obj)
```

B. Show the implementation of the `allObjects` method.

```
public Locatable[] allObjects()
```

C. The `recordMove` method is more complex. Since the `Fish` has updated its location and since that location is used as a hash value for the `Fish`, it is very unlikely that the `Fish` is in the correct spot in the `HashTable`. The `recordMove` method must reestablish the integrity of the `HashTable`. Show the implementation of the `recordMove` method.

```
public void recordMove(Locatable obj, Location oldLoc)
```

4. A `VideoCatalog` contains information about a variety of `Movies`. Users may search the catalog for information about `Movies` including the reviewer ratings assigned to the `Movie` by various users. The catalog may be searched by a user to learn about movies she or he might wish to view. An *incomplete* class declaration of the `Movie` class is shown below:

```
public class Movie implements Comparable
{
  private String myName;
  private String myRating;
    // MPAA Rating, "G", "PG", "PG-13", etc.
  private ArrayList myReviews;
    // Contains the reviewer scores (Integers: 0-10)

  public getName() { return myName; }

  public getRating() { return myRating; }

  // precondition: 0 <= reviewScore <= 10
  // postcondition: myReviews has one additional review whose value is reviewScore
  public void addReviewScore(int reviewScore)
  { /* implementation not shown */ }

  // postcondition: returns the average review score
  public double averageReview()
  { /* implementation not shown */ }

  public int compareTo(Object other)
  { /* implementation not shown */ }
}
```

A `VideoCatalog` organizes `Movies` as a binary search tree, using the name of the movie as the search key. (Movie names may be assumed to be unique.) A partial listing of the `VideoCatalog` class is shown below:

```
public class VideoCatalog
{
  private TreeNode  root;

  // precondition:  the movie corresponding to movieName
  //                is represented in the binary search tree
  // postcondition: the list of reviewScores for
  //                movieName has had one rating of
  //                reviewScore added to it
  public void addReview(String movieName, int reviewScore)
  { /* to be implemented in part (a) */ }
  // postcondition: returns the movie title whose MPAA
  //                rating matches the parameter, and which has
  //                the highest average review score. If no
  //                movie has the appropriate rating, the
  //                String "<not found>" is returned.
  public String bestMovie(String rating)
  { /* Implementation shown in part(b) */ }

  private Movie bestMovieHelper(TreeNode rt, String rating)
  { /* to be implemented in part (b) */ }

  // ... constructor and other methods not shown
}
```

A. Write the `VideoCatalog` method `addReview`. The `addReview` method adds the given review score to the list of review scores stored for the associated `Movie`.

```
// precondition:    movieName is represented in
//                  the binary search tree
// postcondition:   the list of reviewScores for
//                  movieName has had one rating of
//                  reviewScore added to it
public void addReview(String movieName, int reviewScore)
```

B. As shown below, the `bestMovie` method uses the private method `bestMovieHelper` to aid in its computation.

```
// postcondition:   returns the movie title whose MPAA
//                  rating matches the parameter, and which has
//                  the highest average review score. If no
//                  movie has the appropriate rating, the
//                  String "<not found>" is returned.
public String bestMovie(String rating)
{
  Movie m = bestMovieHelper(root, rating);
  if (m==null)
  {
    return "<not found>";
  }
  else
  {
    return m.getName();
  }
}
```

Write the `VideoCatalog` method `bestMovieHelper`. The `bestMovieHelper` method returns the name of the movie with the highest average review score among those movies in the catalog whose rating matches the parameter.

```
// postcondition:   returns the Movie whose MPAA
//                  rating matches the parameter, and which has
//                  the highest average review score. If no
//                  movie has the appropriate rating, a null
//                  value is returned.
public Movie bestMovieHelper(TreeNode rt, String rating)
```

ANSWERS TO PRACTICE EXAM AB1, SECTION I

1.	D	11.	B	21.	C	31.	C
2.	C	12.	A	22.	C	32.	A
3.	C	13.	B	23.	E	33.	C
4.	B	14.	B	24.	D	34.	D
5.	D	15.	C	25.	D	35.	B
6.	B	16.	E	26.	C	36.	C
7.	D	17.	B	27.	E	37.	D
8.	E	18.	E	28.	C	38.	D
9.	A	19.	A	29.	E	39.	A
10.	B	20.	D	30.	A	40.	B

✓ SOLUTIONS TO PRACTICE EXAM AB1, SECTION I

1. The correct answer is D. The `if` statement guarantees that only even numbers are printed. The n=n+3 portion of the `for` loop causes n to assume only values that are multiples of three. Even numbers that are multiples of three are multiples of six.

2. The correct answer is C. The `for` loop is executed n times, invoking `method2` once per execution. After the loop is over, `method2` is invoked one last time, so the total number of executions is n+1 which is O(n).

3. The correct answer is C. The `for` loop in this case is executed n^2 times, invoking `method3` once per execution. The parameter used in the call is irrelevant when counting the number of executions.

4. The correct answer is B. Given that x is known to be true and y is known to be false, choice B evaluates to true regardless of the value of z. Each of the other choices can be simplified until its truth value is seen to be the same as z.

x	y	z	y&&!z	!(y||z)	z||(y&&!z)||!(y||z)
T	F	F	F	T	T
T	F	T	F	F	T

5. The correct answer is D. The first element inserted in the tree will partition the remaining elements into "smaller than root" and "larger than root" portions. The data in each of these portions will be treated in the same manner as was the whole data set; in other words, the sections are handled recursively. Partitioning data into small and large portions that are then sorted recursively is the signature of Quicksort.

6. The correct answer is B. The cells on the main diagonal have the same index for the row and column. For cells on the other diagonal, the sum of the indexes must be n−1. The only choice that has this property is choice B. When confronted with a matrix problem that involves indexes, it pays to make sure that the values work on the first and last rows. (Note that

choices D and E will have negative indexes when row is equal to zero.)

7. The correct answer is D. The code will compile, but since the `Rectangle` class does not override the `getArea` method, the inherited code will be used. Unless all `Rectangles` have an area of zero, the implementation for `getArea` in the `Shape` class will not give the correct answers.

8. The correct answer is E. Since it is not true that an `Oval` IS-A `Rectangle`, it should not extend that class. As with the `Rectangle` class in question 7, implementing the `getArea` method is advisable, but not required; and if `Oval` did extend `Rectangle`, then it could inherit the `draw` method from that class and so would not be required to implement its own version.

9. The correct answer is A. Since we are searching by customer, it can be assumed that we know the `ownerID`, but not necessarily the balance. If we know the `ownerID`, we can use binary search on an `ArrayList` sorted by `ownerID` to achieve an O(logN) time bound. We could also use binary search on a `LinkedList` sorted by `ownerID`, but the time bound would be much higher. If our list is sorted by balance, then we may use only sequential search in any event. Finally, a `TreeSet` requires that `BankAccounts` be `Comparable` and the class did not implement that interface.

10. The correct answer is B. The `hashCode` value for a given `BankAccount` may not change over time. The balance in a `BankAccount` may reasonably be expected to change over time. Thus, any option that involves the balance will not function correctly as a hash function. Choice D would work but would cause all `BankAccounts` to be hashed to the same location in the table and would thus be incredibly inefficient.

11. The correct answer is B. If all accounts have a balance of zero (or lower, if that is permitted), then `bestID` will never be reset from its original value of null. Nonetheless, some account qualifies to be returned, so an error results. If at least one account has a positive balance, then `bestID` will be reset and a proper answer will be returned.

12. The correct answer is A. Making the variable private ensures that no client code uses that variable; thus any changes involving that variable are within this class and will be easier to find and implement. None of the other choices is even true and therefore cannot represent good reasons.

13. The correct answer is B. The table below shows how certain values are computed. The left column indicates the initial function call; the middle column indicates how it is computed, and the right column indicates the actual value. Note that the first two columns are constructed from top to bottom while the values in the right column are computed from "bottom up," i.e., each uses the value below as part of its computation. Creating a table like this one can be a handy exam technique.

would be stored instead of Fish objects. There would be a very small efficiency difference, but no other effect. Option II would work fine and is a good way to implement an UnboundedEnv; if the order in which the Fish act is important, then the allObjects method would need to perform a sort before returning its array. Option III also works; whenever a Fish's location is needed, it can be asked to provide it; recording the move with this option would become an O(N) operation, but the simulation would work as before.

17. The correct answer is B. The first Fish may move north, east, or west. (It cannot move backwards.) If it moves north or west, it dies. If it moves east, the second Fish will be trapped and will be forced to move north and will die. Thus, one Fish is guaranteed to die.

minMax({7,8,1,4,6,9}, 6)	smaller of 9 and maxMin({7,8,1,4,6}, 5)	6
maxMin({7,8,1,4,6}, 5)	larger of 6 and minMax({7,8,1,4}, 4)	6
minMax({7,8,1,4}, 4)	smaller of 4 and maxMin({7,8,1}, 3)	4
maxMin({7,8,1}, 3)	larger of 1 and minMax({7,8}, 2)	7
minMax({7,8}, 2)	smaller of 8 and maxMin({7}, 1)	7
maxMin({7}, 1)	7	7

14. The correct answer is B. The invocations alternate between minMax and maxMin with the second parameter decreasing until it has the value 1. The *total* number of invocations made will be b.length, but only every other one is made to maxMin. Since the initial invocation is made to minMax, maxMin will be invoked one time fewer than minMax. The table above illustrates this if you ignore the first row and swap the names of the methods.

15. The correct answer is C. If islands are not considered objects, then allObjects is unchanged in either plan. Since a cell with an island is not empty, and since a Fish cannot move to an island, in Plan A, isEmpty will require checking both structures, while in Plan B, the code is unchanged. [Note, if islands are indeed considered objects, then the modification to allObjects is more difficult in Plan A, but that does not affect the answer.]

16. The answer is E. Option I is really just the same as the classic BoundedEnv; Lists of size 1

18. The correct answer is E. Black box testing can test only situations that can arise during the proper execution of a program. Note that it *is* possible to have a data file that has two Fish in the same location. It would *not* be possible to use black box techniques to test for such a situation after the simulation began.

19. The correct answer is A. The array size in allObjects is set to the return value of numObjects. This change would cause an unending chain of mutually recursive calls to be created any time either method was invoked. A StackOverflowError would occur as a result.

20. The correct answer is D. When an ExamFish breeds, it invokes its generateChild method. Since the method is not present in the ExamFish class, the method from the parent (Fish) class would be used instead. Thus, all the children would be Fish rather than ExamFish.

21. The correct answer is C. Copyright can be, and usually is, retained when documents, images,

songs, etc., are posted on the Internet. Such material may not be freely distributed without permission of the copyright holder, usually the creator. The other four statements are all true.

22. The correct answer is C. The conditions suggested by choices A and B will result in similar behavior, but they are not the only such situations and thus are not correct answers. The problem does not even state that the data are orderable, and thus choice D cannot be correct. The case of two insertions followed by two deletions shows that choice E is incorrect.

23. The correct answer is E. Lists support a ListIterator, but Sets do not; therefore, a ListIterator is *not* the best way to go through all collections. The other choices all represent true statements. (Note: a question such as this is a good time to be referencing the Quick Reference guide which contains the answer—provided that you are familiar enough with the guide to find it!)

24. The correct answer is D. A preorder visits the root first, then the left subtree, then the right subtree. Only choices C and D do this. In addition, however, the root of the left subtree must be visited second. Only choice D does this.

25. The correct answer is D. To generate this tree, Paraguay must be inserted first; China must be inserted before Argentina and Iraq; and Poland must be inserted before USA. Only options II and III have this property.

26. The correct answer is C. Without a prefix of super., the invocation of the process method within the class CountingFoo will cause the same method to be invoked again (recursively)—a process that will only end with a StackOverflowError.

27. The correct answer is E. The while loop will terminate only if key is found. If key does not exist within the list, then head will eventually become null and a NullPointerException will be raised. Note that in this case, no value is returned, so choice D is not accurate. Choice A is simply not true, as the code invokes only the equals method, not the compareTo method. And, since no link fields are reset, the list maintains its integrity, and because of the pass-by-value parameter passing mechanism, the reference in the invoking method will be unchanged; hence choice C is not correct.

28. The correct answer is C. The Integers representing one through eight are inserted by the first for loop. The items in positions 1, 2, and 3 are removed by the second for loop, but it is important to remember that as part of each removal (and therefore before the subsequent one) the remaining objects are shifted to the left.

29. The correct answer is E. An abstract class may, or may not, implement any of its methods. Class A is permitted to implement the y method, so choice C is incorrect; likewise, class B does not have to implement the z method, so choice A is incorrect. In a similar vein, methods in inherited classes can have different return types as long as they have different signatures, so choice B is not correct. Also, if choice D were correct, then abstract classes would have no purpose because one could never design a concrete class below them in the inheritance hierarchy.

30. The correct answer is A. The first two calls return 49 and 23, respectively, but these values are added before being printed. The invocation, y(2) invokes the method within class A rather than C because of the presence of the parameter. Note that had the first print statement started by printing " " and the concatenating the calls to x and z, then answer B would have been correct.

31. The correct answer is C. Depending upon how close it is to capacity, an ArrayList may or may not use less memory than a LinkedList, so option I is false. A ListIterator may traverse either kind of list backwards with the same code (and same efficiency), so option III is also false.

32. The correct answer is A. The columns and rows are swapped, so the output will now have four lines. This eliminates all but choices A and E. A hand trace shows that the first number printed will be the [0][0] cell, so choice A is the correct answer. This is a case in which starting a hand trace will lead immediately to the correct answer.

33. The correct answer is C. An Animal IS-A Animal, so the first assignment works. It is not the case that an Animal IS-A Dog, so the second assignment does not work. A Cat IS-A Animal, so the third assignment works.

34. The correct answer is D. The basic problem is that the next method is called on the iterator more than once per iteration of the loop, and

hence is not guarded. The number of calls per iteration is either two or three depending upon whether or not the values of the first two items are equal. An even-sized list of distinct items will *not* cause the exception to be raised, but if only the last two items are equal, then the exception will be raised. This observation can be used to invalidate each of the other choices.

35. The correct answer is B. Every method present runs in O(1) time regardless of the data structure used. The loop executes N times regardless of the data structure used. Therefore, the total time is O(N) for either structure.

36. The correct answer is C. A `ListNode` has only one field that can be used to link to another node.

37. The correct answer is D. Because of an improper use of an `else` clause in the loop, the value of the last comparison is used to state whether the entire `ArrayList` is in order. The only case in which the last two items are in order, but the entire `ArrayList` is not, is choice D.

38. The correct answer is D. The first line creates a single `ListNode`. The second line sets its `next` field to point to that very node, creating one item that points to itself, i.e., a circular list with one item in it.

39. The correct answer is A. Choice A is true. On the other hand, Insertion sort is faster than Merge sort on a list that is already in order; Quicksort is slower than Merge sort on such a list; and, in a big-oh sense, Merge sort always runs in O(N*logN) time.

40. The correct answer is B. Adding at the end of an `ArrayList` is an O(1) operation, but removing the first item requires all remaining items to be "shifted left" one position and thus requires O(N) time.

ANSWERS TO PRACTICE EXAM AB1, SECTION II

Problem 1A

```java
public class SalariedEmployee extends Worker implements Employee
{
  private int annualSalary;

  public SalariedEmployee(String name, String ID, int salary)
  {
    super(name, ID);
    annualSalary = salary;
  }

  public int calculateEarnings()
  { return annualSalary/26; }
}
```

Problem 1B

```java
public void generateAllPayChecks(ListNode head)
{
  while (head != null)
  {
    Employee e = (Employee) head.getValue();
    printCheck(e.getName(), e.calculateEarnings());
    head = head.getNext();
  }
}
```

Problem 2A

```java
public class Student
{
  // Information from problem statement omitted here

  private String name; // Name of this student
  private HashMap coursesTaken;
          // keys in this map are courseNames
          // values in this map are the grades attained in the associated courses
}
public class StudentBody
{
  // Information from problem statement omitted here

  private HashSet enrolledStudents;
          // Set of Students
}
```

Problem 2B

```java
public void printTranscript()
{
  Iterator it = coursesTaken.iterator();
  while (it.hasNext())
  {
    String course = (String) it.next();
    System.out.println (course + " " + coursesTaken.get(course));
  }
}
```

Problem 2C

```
public void printGrades(String courseName)
{
  Set s = courseList.get(courseName);
  if (s != null)
  {
    Iterator it = s.iterator();
    while (it.hasNext())
    {
      Student pupil = (Student) it.next();
      System.out.println( pupil.getName() + " " + pupil.getGrade(courseName) );
    }
  }
}
```

Problem 3A

```
public void add(Locatable obj)
{
  Location loc = obj.location();
  if ( ! isEmpty(loc) )
    throw new IllegalArgumentException("Location " + loc + " is not a valid empty location");

  objects.put(loc, obj);  // Add object to the environment.
}
```

Problem 3B

```
public Locatable[] allObjects()
{
  Locatable[] objectArray = new Locatable[objects.size()];

  Iterator it = objects.keySet().iterator();
  while (it.hasNext())
  {
    objectArray[index] = (Locatable) it.next();
  }
  return objectArray;
}
```

Problem 3C

```
public void recordMove(Locatable obj, Location oldLoc)
{
  Object objectAtNewLoc = objects.get(obj.location())
  if ( ! ( objectAtNewLoc == null)||objectAtNewLoc.equals(obj))
  {
    throw new IllegalArgumentException("Recording illegal move of " + obj + " from " + oldLoc);
  }
  objects.remove(oldLoc);
  objects.put(obj.location(), obj);
}
```

Problem 4A

```
public void addReview(String movieName, int reviewScore)
{
  TreeNode movie = root;
  while (! (Movie)movie.getValue().getName().equals(movieName))
  {
    String thisName = movie.getValue().getName();
    if (thisName.compareTo(movieName) > 0)
    {
      movie = movie.getLeft();
    }
    else
    {
      movie = movie.getRight();
    }
  }
  Movie m = (Movie)movie.getValue();
  m.addReviewScore(reviewScore);
}
```

Problem 4B

```
public Movie bestMovieHelper(TreeNode rt, String rating)
{
  double bestReview = -1.0;
  Movie bestMovie = null;

  if (rt != null)
  {
    Movie m = (Movie) rt.getValue();
    if (m.getRating().equals(rating))
    {
      bestReview = m.averageReview();
      bestMovie = m;
    }
    Movie bestL = bestMovieHelper(rt.getLeft(), rating);
    if ((bestL != null) &&
                  (bestL.averageReview() > bestReview))
    {
      bestReview = bestL.averageReview();
      bestMovie = bestL;
    }
    Movie bestR = bestMovieHelper(rt.getRight(), rating);
    if ((bestR != null) &&
                  (bestR.averageReview() > bestReview))
    {
      bestReview = bestR.averageReview();
      bestMovie = bestR;
    }
  }
  return bestMovie;
}
```

✓ RUBRICS AND COMMENTARY FOR PRACTICE EXAM AB1, SECTION II

Note: In many cases where a rubric says "+1," it may be possible to earn a half point for a nearly correct solution.

Problem 1 (9 points)

Part A (6 points)

+1 for extending `Worker` and implementing `Employee`

+1 for storing the salary information privately

+1 for a constructor that accepts the proper parameters

+1 for properly initializing the data in the superclass

+1 for implementing the `calculateSalary` method

+1 for computing the amount correctly

Part B (3 points)

+1 for properly traversing the linked list

+1 for extracting the appropriate data (includes casting to `Employee`)

+1 for properly printing the paycheck

Commentary

Several variations in Part A are possible. Using a `double` to hold the salary is acceptable, but this must calculate earnings and must return a double. A `setSalary` method might be included as well as a `getSalary` method.

Reimplementing `getName` is a poor idea as the only correct way to do so is via a direct call to the method in the superclass. Doing so might well result in a deduction.

In Part B, the cast to `Employee` must be made. It is inappropriate to cast to a particular type of `Employee` (e.g., `SalariedEmployee`) the list may (and probably does) contain both kinds of employees.

Note that a local variable in Part B is *not* needed. The code as presented in the solution does not destroy the list.

Problem 2 (9 points)

Part A (2 points)

+1 for an adequately explained and feasible solution for `Student` class

+1 for an adequately explained and feasible solution for `StudentBody` class

Part B (3 points)

+1 for going through more than a constant number of courses for student

+1 for processing every course that student takes exactly once

+1 for printing name and properly obtained grade for each course taken

Part C (4 points)

+1 for determining if the course exists and, if so, which `Students` are enrolled

+1 for processing more than a constant number of `Students`

+1 for processing each enrolled `Student` exactly once

+1 for printing name and properly obtained grade for each student enrolled

Commentary

Many other solutions are possible in Part A. The key idea is that an unlimited number of `Students` must be kept in the `StudentBody` and that each `Student` must be able to keep an unlimited number of courses. One feasible alternative for the student is to keep parallel `Lists` of courses and grades. Doing so would require more careful work in Parts B and C, however. Note that `TreeSets` and `TreeMaps` are perfectly fine if the data are known to be `Comparable`. `Strings` are `Comparable`, but

Students are not (unless the appropriate additions were made as part of the answer).

In Parts B and C, the same instance variables (name and type) must be used as were given by the student in Part A.

In Parts B and C, if Lists were used, then an iterator may not be needed; the get method might serve equally well.

In Part C, the precondition did *not* guarantee that the course existed and this condition may (or may not) need to be guarded, depending upon the data structures used in Part A.

Problem 3 (9 points)

Part A (1 point)

+1 for correctly adding the Fish

Part B (4 points)

+1 for building and returning the array properly

+1 for initializing an iterator that will find all the Fish

+1 for using the iterator to visit each Fish exactly once

+1 for placing the Fish properly in the array

Part C (4 points)

+1 for some check that involves attempting to guarantee that the move is legal

+1 for that check being correct

+1 for removing the old entry for the Fish from the Map (must not use remove method of UnboundedEnv class—won't work!)

+1 for adding the Fish back in

Commentary

In Part B, it is possible (and acceptable) to avoid using an iterator, but such a solution would involve making use of the toArray method, which is not part of the AP curriculum.

It is incorrect in Part C to use the remove method from the UnboundedEnv class to take the entry out of the Map. Since the location of the Fish has already been updated, the remove method from the

UnboundedEnv class will not work properly. One can, however, use the add method of the UnboundedEnv class to add the Fish back into the environment.

Problem 4 (9 points)

Part A (4 points)

+1 for comparing the parameter to the name at a given location in the tree

+1 for identifying when the correct Movie object is found

+1 for searching the correct portion of the tree when the name is not found

+1 for properly adding the review score to the Movie object

Part B (5 points)

+1 for initializing and returning the Movie with the best review and its review score

+1 for handling the empty tree case

+1 for updating "best so far" only when the rating of the movie matches the parameter at the root

+1 for properly searching the subtrees

+1 for properly incorporating the best results of each subtree

Commentary

It would be acceptable to solve Part A using a (possibly recursive) private helper method, but a recursive solution is unlikely to work without such a method.

It is not necessary to keep a "best review score" variable in this part; instead this value may be recomputed [using "bestMovie.averageReview()"] when needed. In addition, it is possible to initialize this value to any negative number, or even to zero if >= is used in the compareTo expression.

Also, the root value, the right subtree value, and the left subtree value may be checked in any order. No matter in which order they are checked, the first one (and only the first one) does not need to check that its review score is the best so far.

Note that it would be unacceptable to rewrite bestMovie in any way—even, or especially—to avoid the need for the helper method.

Computer Science AB
Practice Exam AB2

Answer Sheet for Multiple-Choice Questions

1. _____	11. _____	21. _____	31. _____
2. _____	12. _____	22. _____	32. _____
3. _____	13. _____	23. _____	33. _____
4. _____	14. _____	24. _____	34. _____
5. _____	15. _____	25. _____	35. _____
6. _____	16. _____	26. _____	36. _____
7. _____	17. _____	27. _____	37. _____
8. _____	18. _____	28. _____	38. _____
9. _____	19. _____	29. _____	39. _____
10. _____	20. _____	30. _____	40. _____

PRACTICE EXAM AB2

Section I

Time: 1 hour and 15 minutes; number of questions: 40; percentage of grade: 50

Directions: Determine the answer to each of the following questions or incomplete statements, using the available space for any necessary scratch work. Then fill in the space on the answer sheet corresponding to the best choice given. No credit will be given for anything written in the examination booklet. Do not spend too much time on any one problem.

Note: Assume the Java Standard Libraries and the AP Java Subset are included in any programs that use the code segments provided in individual questions. You may refer to the College Board document (Copyright © 2004 by College Entrance Examination Board), "A Quick Reference," while taking this practice exam. This document is available at www.collegeboard.com/student/testing/ap/sub_compsciab.html.

1. Suppose that s is an `ArrayList` that initially contains `Integers` [1, 2, 3]. Consider the following code:

```
for (int n=1; n<8; n++)
{
  s.add(n,new Integer(n));
  s.remove(n);
}
```

Which of the following most precisely describes the result of executing that code?

A. The list will be empty.
B. The list will contain the `Integers` [1, 2, 3].
C. The list will contain the `Integers` [5, 6, 7].
D. An exception will prevent the loop from completing.
E. The code will not execute because of syntax errors.

2. Which sequence represents the order in which nodes would be visited during a postorder traversal of the tree below?

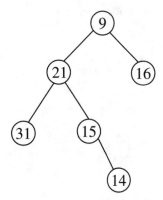

A. 9, 14, 15, 16, 21, 31
B. 9, 21, 16, 31, 15, 14
C. 31, 21, 15, 14, 9, 16
D. 14, 31, 15, 21, 16, 9
E. 31, 14, 15, 21, 16, 9

3. Which of the following statements about abstract classes is true?

    A. An abstract class must declare an abstract method.
    B. An abstract class cannot declare instance data.
    C. An abstract class cannot declare public static data elements such as constants.
    D. A pure abstract class is the same thing as an interface.
    E. An abstract class cannot be instantiated.

4. Suppose that x, y, and z are boolean variables. x contains the value false; y contains the value true. Which values of z will cause the following expression to be true?

    ```
    (((!z && y) || x) != ((z || y) && (x == z))
    ```

    A. No value of z will make the expression true.
    B. Any value of z will make the expression true.
    C. z must be true for the expression to be true.
    D. z must be false for the expression to be true.
    E. It cannot be determined from the given information.

5. Which of the following best describes the result of trying to use an Iterator on an empty Collection?

    A. A syntax error will result.
    B. An exception will occur when the Iterator method is called on the Collection object for the initial assignment.
    C. The Iterator will be constructed, but an exception will occur as soon as any method is invoked upon it.
    D. The Iterator will be constructed, but an exception will occur as soon as the next method is invoked upon it.
    E. No errors or exceptions will occur, but the behavior of the Iterator is unpredictable.

6. Consider the following code segment:

    ```
    int[][] table = new int[3][4];
    for(int r = 0; r < table.length; r++)
    {
      for(int c = 0; c < table[0].length; c++)
      {
        if(c < r)
          table[r][c] = c;
        else
          table[r][c] = r;
      }
    }
    ```

    What are the contents of table after this code is executed?

    A. 0   0   0   0
       0   1   1   1
       0   1   2   2

    B. 0   1   2   3
       1   1   2   3
       2   2   2   3

    C. 0   1   2   3
       1   2   3   0
       2   3   0   1

    D. 0   1   2   3
       1   2   3   4
       2   3   4   5

    E. 0   0   0   0
       1   1   1   1
       2   2   2   2

7. Consider the following generalized code fragments:

Fragment 1

```
if(<test1>)
  if(<test2>)
    <do thingOne>
```

Fragment 2

```
if(<test1>)
    <do thingOne>
else if(test2)
      <do thingOne>
```

Which statement about the above code fragments is true?

A. For both code fragments, thingOne will be executed at least once.
B. The two if statements in Fragment 1 can be simplified using an "and" operation, and those in Fragment 2 can be simplified using an "or" operation.
C. The two if statements in Fragment 1 can be simplified using an "or" operation, and those in Fragment 2 can be simplified using an "and" operation.
D. The second "if" in Fragment 1 is unnecessary.
E. The second "if" in Fragment 2 is unnecessary.

8. Consider the following recursive method:

```
public int mystery(int a, int b)
{
  if(a == b)
    return a;
  if(a < b)
    return mystery(a, b-a);
  else
    return mystery(b, a-b);
}
```

What is returned by a call to mystery?

A. The greatest common factor of a and b is returned.
B. The least common multiple of a and b is returned.
C. The value a to the b power is returned.
D. The quotient of a divided by b is returned.
E. The remainder of a divided by b is returned.

For questions 9 and 10 consider the class `Widget` below:

```
public class Widget
{
  public void doSomething(String arg)
  { /* Implementation not shown */ }

  public int doSomethingElse()
  { /* Implementation not shown */ }

  /* Constructor and private data not shown */
}
```

9. A programmer wishes to create a `Set` of `Widgets`. Which of the following is a valid reason for choosing between a `TreeSet` and a `HashSet`?

   A. A `TreeSet` must be used because there is no `hashCode` method defined in the class.
   B. A `HashSet` must be used because there is no `compareTo` method defined in the class.
   C. A `TreeSet` should be used to guarantee that accesses are performed in O(logN) time as is required.
   D. A `HashSet` should be used to guarantee that accesses are performed in O(1) time as is required.
   E. Based upon the information given, there is no reason to choose one over the other.

10. Which of the following statements about the use of `Widgets` in a `HashMap` is false?

    A. `Widgets` can be used as values within a `HashMap` without changes.
    B. `Widgets` can be used as keys within a `HashMap`, but problems may arise if it is possible for two distinct `Widget` objects to be considered equal.
    C. `Widgets` can be used either as keys or as values within a `HashMap`.
    D. `Widgets` can be used only as keys within a `HashMap` if the class is modified to implement the `Comparable` interface.
    E. `Widgets` can be used as keys within a `HashMap` only if `Widgets` respond to the `equals` method.

11. If head initially points to the first item in a nonempty singly linked list of `ListNodes`, how will the structure of that list change as a result of executing the following block of code?

```
ListNode q = head;
ListNode p = head;
while (p.getNext() != null)
{
  q = p;
  p = p.getNext();
}
p.setNext(head);
q.setNext(null);
```

    A. The list has been turned into a circularly linked list.
    B. The first item in the list will have been moved to the end of the list and head will no longer point to the first item.
    C. The last item in the list will have been moved to the front of the list and head will no longer point to the first item.
    D. The list will have been broken up into lists of size one, most of which will eventually be reclaimed by the garbage collector.
    E. The structure of the list is unchanged.

12. Consider the following block of code that operates on a previously initialized List named `list` that contains N elements.

```
for (int k=0; k<list.size(); k++)
{
  update( list.get(k) );
}
```

Assuming that the `update` method runs in O(1) time, which of these expressions represent the most accurate bounds for the amount of time it will take to execute the block of code if `list` is an `ArrayList` or a `LinkedList`?

	ArrayList	LinkedList
A.	O(1)	O(N)
B.	O(N)	O(N)
C.	O(N)	O(N²)
D.	O(NlogN)	O(N²)
E.	O(N²)	O(NlogN)

13. What is the best possible big-oh bound for the number of times "Wow" is printed by the following code fragment?

```
for (int j=0; j<n; j++)
{
  for (int k=0; k<j; k++)
  {
    System.out.println("Wow");
  }
}
for (m=n; m>0; m--)
{
  System.out.println("Wow");
}
```

A. O(1)
B. O(n)
C. O(n*j)
D. O(n²)
E. O(n³)

14. Reflecting a tree involves taking any node that was a right child and making it a left child, and vice versa. The figure below shows a small tree and its reflection.

The following is the header for a method that reflects a tree:

```
public static void reflect (TreeNode root)
```

Which of the blocks of code shown below can be used to correctly implement `reflect`?

I.
```
if (root != null)
{
   TreeNode left = root.getLeft();
   TreeNode right = root.getRight();
   TreeNode t = left;
   left = right;
   right = t;
   reflect(root.getLeft());
   reflect(root.getRight());
}
```

II.
```
TreeNode t = root.getLeft();
Root.setLeft( root.getRight() );
Root.setRight( t );
if (root.getLeft() != null)
  reflect(root.getLeft());
if (root.getRight() != null)
  reflect(root.getRight());
```

III.
```
if (root != null)
{
   root.setLeft( root.getRight() );
   root.setRight( root.getLeft() );
   reflect(root.getLeft());
   reflect(root.getRight());
}
```

A. None of the code fragments is correct.
B. I only.
C. II only.
D. III only.
E. More than one of the code fragments work.

Questions 15–20 involve the Marine Biology Simulation (MBS). Some information about the MBS can be found in the Quick Reference guide provided with this exam.

15. The biologists are going to continue to work with a bounded environment, but they are considering using the data structure from the unbounded environment implementation (the list of objects with locations) instead of the matrix of objects. Which of the following would be the most compelling reason why they should *not* do this?

A. The extra overhead of having the class structure (as opposed to the matrix structure) will create memory inefficiencies.
B. Finding immediate neighbors for a given `Fish` will be less efficient than with the matrix implementation.
C. The code in the `Fish` class is simpler with the list implementation.
D. Making this change will require a change in the file structure used to initialize the simulation.
E. The list data structure requires that `Fish` be allowed to move anywhere; it is intrinsically unbounded.

16. Consider the bounded environment shown below containing a `SlowFish` and a `DarterFish` .

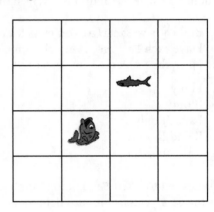

If the fish are processed in column-major order and on its turn each fish neither breeds nor dies, which configuration below could be where these `Fish` were two moves ago?

A.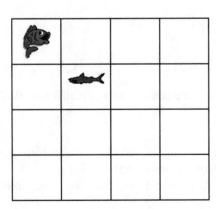

D.

B.

E.

C.

17. Suppose we wish to add a new subclass, JumpingFish. During each time step, when a JumpingFish moves, it can jump out of the environment and land in any valid empty location within five spaces of its original location in any direction, except directly behind itself. Which of the following methods should be reimplemented in JumpingFish?

I. move
II. emptyNeighbors
III. nextLocation

A. I and II only
B. II only
C. III only
D. II and III only
E. I, II, and III

18. The biologists want to examine a variety of movement patterns common to all fish in the environment. (For instance, the Fish might move in random order, or all DarterFish might move before any other fish, etc.) To do this, Pat decides to replace the Simulation class with an interface named Steppable that contains a single method step. Which of the following is a reasonable way to implement the interface?

I. Build a new Simulation class for each new movement pattern, implementing Steppable.
II. Have each Environment class implement Steppable.
III. Have the Fish class implement Steppable.

A. I only
B. II only
C. I and II only
D. II and III only
E. I, II, and III

19. It is desired to insert Fish into a HashTable. Doing so requires that we define the hashCode method for the Fish class. One such definition is below:

```
public int hashCode()
{
  return toString().hashCode();
}
```

This is a poor choice of implementation. Which of the following reasons best explains why this is so?

A. The method will not compile as written.
B. There is no toString method in the Fish class.
C. It is never a good idea to use toString as part of an implementation of the hashCode method.
D. If this implementation is used, the Fish will not disperse throughout the table.
E. If this implementation is used, it may be impossible to retrieve a given Fish from the table.

20. In a whimsical mood, the biologists request having one location that behaves like a "black hole" or tunnel, such that a fish that selects that location is transported into another environment where it continues to act. Which of the following is an *unnecessary* test case to be sure the new code works as intended and that the old code is not broken?

   A. The location of the black hole in the alternate environment is valid.
   B. A fish cannot enter the black hole if there is a `Fish` in the alternate environment at the location of the black hole in that alternate environment.
   C. A fish that enters the black hole emerges into the alternate environment.
   D. A fish that enters the black hole is no longer in the array returned by the original environment's `allObjects`.
   E. A `Fish` does not enter the black hole if the hole is behind the `Fish`.

21. Which of the following statements about testing is true?

   A. Black box testing can be used to test every line of code, but not every possible path through the code.
   B. Defining test suites in advance is a good practice no matter what type of testing is being done.
   C. Black box testing cannot be used to test the generation of exceptions.
   D. Both integration testing and black box testing are useful techniques, but they must be used separately.
   E. Once a set of black box tests has been passed, those tests may be removed from the test suite so that future testing can complete more effectively.

22. Swimmers at a swimming pool arrive one at a time, join the others in the pool, swim for a while, and then leave. Different swimmers may stay in the pool for different amounts of time. Which of the following data structures would store `Swimmer` objects in a manner that most closely mimics the real world situation?

   A. `ArrayList`
   B. `Map`
   C. `Queue`
   D. `Set`
   E. `Stack`

23. Which of the following is the best reason why one should not use the `get` method with a `LinkedList`?

   A. The `LinkedList` class does not support the `get` method.
   B. The `get` method will not work with an empty `LinkedList`.
   C. The `get` method will work, but is inefficient in terms of time.
   D. The `get` method will work, but uses excessive memory.
   E. The premise is incorrect. It is perfectly fine to use the `get` method with a `LinkedList`.

Questions 24 and 25 refer to the following classes which use a priority queue to implement the `Stack` interface. Since the most recently added item will have the lowest priority, it will be the first item out of the stack.

```
public class PriorityItem implements Comparable
{
  private Object data;
  private Comparable priority;
  public PriorityItem( Object o, Comparable c )
  { data = o; priority = c; }

  public Object getData() { return data; }
  public int compareTo(Object other)
  { return priority.compareTo(other.priority); }
}

public class PQStack implements Stack
{
  private ExamPriorityQueue theData;
  // Class ExamPriorityQueue implements exactly the
  //   PriorityQueue interface using a standard heap structure

  private int itemsInserted; // Initialize to a large number

  public void push(Object item)
  {
    itemsInserted--;
    Integer priority = new Integer(itemsInserted);
    theData.add(new PriorityItem(item,priority));
  }
  // Other methods not shown
}
```

24. Which of the following blocks of code correctly implements the `pop` method?

I. `Object item = theData.peekMin();`
    `theData.removeMin();`
    `return item;`
II. `return theData.removeMin().getData();`
III. `theData.removeMin();`
     `theData.getData();`

A. I only
B. II only
C. I and II only
D. II and III only
E. I, II, and III

25. Which of the following best approximates the running time of the `pop` method in this implementation?

A. O(1)
B. O(logN)
C. O(N)
D. O(N²)
E. None of the above

26. A programmer is attempting to search a list for a target item. Unfortunately, the programmer has used a binary search algorithm even though the list may not be sorted. Which of the following statements is most accurate?

    A. The search algorithm will never find the item.
    B. The search algorithm won't find the item unless the list is sorted.
    C. The only item that will always be found is the smallest in the list.
    D. The search algorithm will behave correctly when the item is not in the list.
    E. The search algorithm may cause an exception to be raised if the list is not sorted.

27. In which of the following situations is it more appropriate for a new construct to implement an interface than to extend a parent class?

    I.   The new construct needs to repeat this operation (implementing or extending) with multiple existing constructs.
    II. Data from the preexisting construct is needed by the new construct.
    III. The preexisting construct is declared abstract.

    A. I only
    B. II only
    C. I and II
    D. I and III
    E. II and III

28. Consider the following method:

```
public static void mystery(int[] a)
{
  int k = a.length - 1;
  while(k >= a.length/2)
  {
    a[a.length - 1 - k] = a[k];
    k--;
  }
}
```

    If a contains the values {1, 2, 3, 4, 5, 6}, what will a contain after a call to mystery(a)?

    A. {1, 2, 3, 3, 2, 1}
    B. {1, 2, 3, 4, 5, 6}
    C. {6, 5, 4, 3, 2, 1}
    D. {6, 5, 4, 4, 5, 6}
    E. {6, 6, 6, 6, 6, 6}

Questions 29 and 30 refer to the following incomplete class definitions:

```
public class Point
{
  private int x;
  private int y;
  public Point(int xVal, int yVal) { setPoint(xVal,yVal); }

  public void setPoint(int xVal, int yVal)
  { x = xVal; y = yVal; }

  public int getX() { return x; }
  public int getY() { return y; }

  // constructors and other methods not shown
}

public class Circle
{

  private Point center;
  private double radius;

  public void setCircle(Point p, double r)
  { center = p; radius = r; }

  // constructors and other methods not shown
}
```

29. Which of the following blocks of code can be used as the body of a constructor for the `Circle` class whose signature is `public Circle(Point p, double r)`?

```
I.    { center = new Point(p.getX(),p.getY()); radius = r; }
II.   { center.setPoint(p.getX(), p.getY()); radius = r; }
III.  { center = p; radius = r; }
```

A. I only
B. II only
C. I and II only
D. I and III only
E. II and III only

30. Consider the following code segment.

```
Point p1 = new Point(1, 3);
Point p2 = new Point(-4, -2);
Circle one = new Circle(p1, 5.0);
Circle two = new Circle(p2, 2.5);
two = one;
two.setCircle(new Point(0, 0), 1.0);
one.setCircle(new Point(-1, 5), 4.0);
```

After the above code segment is executed, what circles will be represented by one and two?

	one	two
A.	(−1, 5), 4.0	(−1, 5), 4.0
B.	(−1, 5), 4.0	(0, 0), 1.0
C.	(0, 0), 1.0	(0, 0), 1.0
D.	(1, 3), 5.0	(−4, −2), 2.5
E.	(1, 3), 5.0	(1, 3), 5.0

31. Consider the code below, which operates on a linked list of ListNodes named p. What would be the best description of the effect of this code on the list, prior to Java's garbage collector being invoked?

```
ListNode extra = p;

while (p != null)
{
  extra = extra.getNext();
  if (extra != null)
  {
    extra = extra.getNext();
    p.getNext().setNext(p);
  }
  p = extra;
}
```

A. The list is unchanged.
B. The first two elements of the list have been made into a circular list, and the rest are unchanged.
C. Each pair of elements of the list has been made into a circular list of size 2; any leftover node is unchanged.
D. The list has been split into two separate lists of nearly equal (within one) size.
E. A NullPointerException has been thrown.

32. Consider the incomplete class declaration MatrixManip given below. MatrixManip includes methods used to manipulate a matrix.

```
public class MatrixManip
{
  private Object[][] myMat;

  public void reverseRow(int row)
  { /* Implementation not shown */ }
  public void reverseCol(int col)
  { /* Implementation not shown */ }
  public void reverseMat()
  { /* Implementation not shown */ }

  // constructor and other methods not shown
}
```

If myMat initially held

   1   2   3
   4   5   6

after the reverseMat method had been invoked, it would hold

   6   5   4
   3   2   1

Which code segment below could serve as the body for reverseMat? (You may assume that the other methods in the class work correctly.)

A. `for( int r = 0; r<myMat.length; r++)`
        `reverseRow(r);`

B. `for( int r = 0; r<myMat.length/2; r++)`
        `reverseRow(r);`

C. `for( int r = 0; r<myMat.length; r++)`
        `reverseRow(r);`
    `for( int c = 0; c<myMat[0].length; c++)`
        `reverseCol(c);`

D. `for( int r = 0; r<myMat.length; r++)`
        `reverseCol(r);`
    `for( int c = 0; c<myMat[0].length; c++)`
        `reverseRow(c);`

E. `for( int r = 0; r<myMat.length; r++)`
        `for( int c = 0; c<myMat[0].length; c++)`
        `{`
          `reverseRow(r);`
          `reverseCol(c);`
        `}`

Questions 33 and 34 refer to the following class hierarchy:

```
public abstract class Alpha
{
  public void eeny( int a, int b )
    { System.out.print("alpha eeny "); }
  public abstract void miny( int x );
  // Other methods not shown
}


public class Beta extends Alpha
{
  public void miny( int x )
    { eeny(x, x); }
  // Other methods not shown
}


public class Gamma extends Beta
{
  public void eeny( int a, int b )
    { System.out.print("gamma eeny "); }
  // Other methods not shown
}
```

33. What is printed as a result of executing the following code? (Assume that all the classes have parameter-less constructors.)

```
Beta b = new Beta();
Alpha a = new Gamma();

b.miny(2);
a.miny(0);
```

   A. Nothing; the code does not compile
   B. alpha eeny
   C. alpha eeny alpha eeny
   D. alpha eeny gamma eeny
   E. beta eeny gamma eeny

34. A new class, Delta, is added to the hierarchy. It is specified below:

```
public class Delta extends Alpha
{
  public void eeny( int x )
    { System.out.print("delta eeny "); }
  public void miny()
    { System.out.print("delta miny "); }
  // Other methods not shown
}
```

What is printed as a result of executing the following code? (Assume that all the classes have parameter-less constructors.)

```
Delta d = new Delta();

d.eeny(2);
d.miny();
```

   A. Nothing; the code does not compile
   B. alpha eeny alpha eeny
   C. alpha eeny delta miny
   D. delta eeny alpha eeny
   E. delta eeny delta miny

35. Which of the following represents a worst-case data set for Merge sort?

    A. A list that is already in order.
    B. A list that is in reverse order.
    C. A list in which all the items in the first N/2 positions are the largest N/2 items.
    D. A random list.
    E. All, or none, of these; Merge sort works approximately equally well in all cases.

36. Suppose that the class `Quandary` is known to contain no static data and that the class is written obeying all standard conventions. Suppose further that the following code is executed:

```
Quandary one = new Quandary();
Quandary two = new Quandary();
Quandary three = one;

if (one.equals(two)) System.out.print("copper ");
if (one == two) System.out.print("silver ");
if (three.equals(one)) System.out.print("nickel ");
if (one == three) System.out.print("gold ");
```

    Consider the three possible output sequences below. Depending upon the code in the class `Quandary`, which of the three might actually be printed?

    I.   copper silver nickel gold
    II. copper nickel gold
    III. copper silver gold

    A. While II and III might be the output, I is an impossible result.
    B. While I and III might be the output, II is an impossible result.
    C. While I and II might be the output, III is an impossible result.
    D. II is the only possible output.
    E. Any of the three might be printed.

37. The following code works on a binary tree composed of `TreeNodes`. What value is being returned?

```
public static int treeMystery(TreeNode root)
{
  int answer = 0;
  if (root != null)
  {
    int left = treeMystery( root.getLeft() );
    answer = left + 1;
    int right = treeMystery( root.getRight() );
    if (right >= answer)
    {
      answer += (right-left);
    }
  }
  return answer;
}
```

A. The total number of nodes in the tree
B. The total number of nodes in the tree that have two children
C. The total number of paths from the root to a leaf in the tree
D. The number of nodes along the shortest path from the root to a leaf in the tree
E. The number of nodes along the longest path from the root to a leaf in the tree

38. Which of these tasks is not carried out by the compiler in an object-oriented language such as Java?

A. Verification of syntax within expressions
B. Verification that the types of data passed as parameters to methods are compatible with the intended types
C. Determination of which block of code executes when a method is invoked
D. Verification of the feasibility of a casting operation
E. Verification that private data are not accessed from outside a class

39. Which of the following most accurately describes when the preorder and postorder traversals of a binary tree will visit the data in the same order.

A. Never
B. Only on empty trees
C. Only on trees with at most one node
D. Only on trees all of whose children on one side (left or right) are null
E. Only on trees without leaves

40. In the code below, ExamQueue implements the Queue interface, and ExamStack implements the Stack interface. What are the contents of the q, and the s after executing the code?

```
Queue q = new ExamQueue();
Stack s = new ExamStack();

for (int i=0; i<8; i++)
{
  Integer data = new Integer(i);
  if (i%2 == 0)
  {
    q.enqueue(data);
    q.enqueue(data);
  }
  else
  {
    q.dequeue();
  }
  if (i%3 == 0)
  {
    s.push(data);
    s.push(data);
  }
  else
  {
    s.pop();
  }
}
```

	q	s
	front is at right	top is at right
A.	\<empty\>	\<empty\>
B.	6, 4, 2, 0	\<empty\>
C.	\<empty\>	6, 3, 0
D.	6, 6, 4, 4	6

E. An exception will occur before the code completes execution

Section II

Time: 1 hour and 45 minutes; number of questions: 4; Percent of total grade: 50

Directions: Show all your work. Remember that program segments are to be written in Java. In writing your solutions to a part of the problem, you may assume that code from previous parts works correctly regardless of what you wrote in those parts. In such cases, it is expected that you will invoke the appropriate method; reimplementing a solution from an earlier part of a question will result in a less than perfect score being awarded for that problem.

1. Appropriate People, Inc., is a company that manages nonanonymous surveys. Each question in its survey is answered by a simple integer. Some sample questions are given below:

   A. What is your gender? (0) male; (1) female
   B. What is you political affiliation? (0) Democrat; (1) Republican; (2) Independent
   C. How much is your annual income? (0) Under $15,000; (1) $15,001–35,000; (2) $35,001–60,000; (3) $60,001–100,000; (4) $100,001–200,000; (5) Over $200,000
   D. What was the highest level of education you reached? (0) Did not graduate from high school; (1) High school graduate; (2) Associate's degree; (3) Bachelor's degree; (4) Master's degree; (5) Doctorate
   E. How many foreign countries have you visited? (0) 0; (1) 1–5; (2) More than 5

   The survey is not anonymous. The respondent's name is retained along with his or her answers.

   The company produces lists of all respondents who answered a given question in the same way, i.e., a list of all females, a list of all Independents, or a list of all respondents who earn between $35,001 and $60,000. More complicated cross-referencing is not done at this time.

   Suppose that five people took the survey above and responded as follows:

Anderson	1	1	2	4	0
Capecci	1	2	3	2	1
Carter	0	0	5	4	1
Brusca	1	1	4	3	1
Rosas	0	1	3	3	2

   A list of all females would contain: Anderson, Capecci, Brusca
   A list of all Democrats would contain: Carter
   A list of all without a high school diploma would be empty (null)

   A `Survey` class, as started below, is designed to oversee processing of the survey. Its key instance variable is a matrix of `ListNodes` named `table`. Each row of `table` corresponds to a question in the survey; each column corresponds to an answer to the given question. A given cell of the matrix contains either `null` (if no one gave that answer to that question) or a linked list of `ListNodes`, each of whose value field refers to a respondent who gave that answer to that question. Respondents are stored in a `Respondent` class whose details are unimportant for this problem, but you may assume that it properly implements the `toString` method.

```
public class Survey
{
  private ListNode[][] table;

  // default constructor sets all elements of table to null

  public Survey(int numQuestions, int maxNumChoices)
  { /* Implementation to be provided in part (a) */ }

  //  Precondition: aPerson contains a respondent;
  //    questAns contains the respondent's answers to each
  //    of the questions; all of the questions are always
  //    answered in the correct order
  //  Postcondition: the appropriate lists in the table have
  //    been updated to include aPerson
  public void add(Respondent aPerson, int[] questAns)
  { /* Implementation to be provided in part (b) */ }

  //  Precondition: aQuest contains a valid question
  //    number; anAns contains a valid response number
  //  Postcondition: the list of respondents who
  //    responded to question aQuest with answer anAns
  //    has been printed one to a line; "<no respondents>"
  //    is printed if no one answered that question with
  //    that answer.
  public void printList(int aQuest, int anAns)
  { /* Implementation to be provided in part (c) */}

  // other methods not shown
}
```

A. Complete the Survey constructor as started below:

```
    // default constructor sets all elements of table to null
    public Survey(int numQuestions, int maxNumChoices)
    {
```

B. The lists of respondents are not maintained in any particular order. Complete the Survey class method add as started below:

```
    //  Precondition: aPerson contains a respondent;
    //    questAns contains the respondent's answers to each
    //    of the questions; all of the questions are always
    //    answered in the correct order
    //  Postcondition: the appropriate lists in the table have
    //    been updated to include aPerson
    //
    public void add(Respondent aPerson, int[] questAns)
    {
```

C. Complete the Survey class method printList as started below:

```
    //  Precondition: aQuest contains a valid question
    //    number; anAns contains a valid response number
    //  Postcondition: the list of respondents who responded
    //    to question aQuest with answer anAns has been
    //    printed one to a line; "<no respondents>" is printed
    //    if no one answered that question with that answer.
    public void printList(int aQuest, int anAns)
    {
```

2. Atlas Publishing keeps track of distances (via road) between cities as part of the data that it maintains and publishes. For each city, A, the company is aware of cities that are directly accessible from A. These cities, and their distances are stored in a Map, roughly as follows:

CityADistancesMap

Adjacent City (key, stored as **String**)	Distance to that City (value, stored as **Integer**)
R	200
D	150
L	375

Since there are many cities in a given atlas, they are all also stored in a Map, roughly as follows:

DistanceInformation

City Name (key, stored as **String**)	Data for that City (value, stored as **Map** described above)
A	CityADistancesMap
L	CityLDistancesMap
D	CityDDistancesMap
R	CityRDistancesMap

All information is symmetric and redundant. If a distance is stored for City B in City A's Map, then the same distance is stored for City A in City B's Map.

For a given atlas, this map is encapsulated in a class as shown below:

```
public class DistanceMap
{
  private Map distanceInformation;

  public void update(String cityA, String cityB, int distance)
  { /* To be implemented in part (a) */ }

  public int routeDistance( ArrayList itinerary )
  { /* To be implemented in part (b) */ }

  public String midCity(String cityA, String cityB)
  { /* To be implemented in part (c) */ }
}
```

A. As new roads are built, the distances (via road) between cities may change. The company updates its information via the update method. Complete this method, in accordance with the description below:

```
//  Updates or adds, if necessary, the information about the distance
//    between the two cities. The new information replaces the
//    old information regardless of the relative values.
//
//    precondition: cityA and cityB are both in the
//        distanceInformation Map
public void update(String cityA, String cityB, int distance)
{
```

B. In addition to traveling directly to a city, it is sometimes useful to know the distance traveled along an entire route. Implement the method routeDistance described below:

```
//  Computes the total distance along a route of cities, each
//    specified as a String in the ArrayList
//
//    precondition: each successive pair of cities in the list
//        has a direct route recorded in the Map
public void routeDistance(ArrayList itinerary)
{
```

C. If one is traveling from one city to another, it often pays to make a single stop in a third (middle) city. The method midCity is designed to discover the name of such a city. Implement that method as specified in its documentation below:

```
//  Determines the city between cityA and cityB that is directly
//    accessible to each and which minimizes the distance traveled
//    along the route cityA->result->cityB. In the event of a
//    tie, any such city may be returned. If no city is accessible
//    to both cities, then the string "<no city>" is returned.
//
//    precondition: cityA and cityB are both valid cities
public String midCity(String cityA, String cityB)
{
```

3. This question involves the Marine Biology Simulation case study. A copy of the code for the simulation is among the materials available with the exam.

In this question, we add the notion of a "lure" that attracts fish to the simulation. While most fish will move as before, some fish will be "lured" to a given location. To accommodate this change, modifications must be made to the Fish class. The first is the addition of a new instance variable. This variable will hold a Location, named desiredLoc, to which a Fish is attracted. If this variable is null, then the Fish is not being lured anywhere and will move as before. Two methods are added to access and/or modify this variable. These are shown below:

```
private Location desiredLoc;

/** Returns the location toward which this Fish is moving
 *  @return the location to which this Fish is moving
 *          or null if this Fish is moving randomly
 */
public Location getDesiredLocation()
{ return desiredLoc; }

/** Sets the location to which this Fish would like to move
 *  @param newTarget the new desired location
 *          (null if random, i.e. non-lured, movement is desired)
 */
public void setDesiredLocation(Location newTarget)
{ desiredLoc = newTarget; }
```

In addition, the nextLocation method is modified to invoke a private method nextLuredLocation to determine where this Fish would like to move. (Note: This implementation means that DarterFish will not necessarily move toward the location of the lure; this is entirely acceptable.)

```
/** Returns a location to which this fish can move so as to
 *  be closer to its desired location
 *  @return any location to which this fish can move so as to
 *          be closer to its desired location; returns the
 *          current location if all possibilities are blocked
 *          and null if this fish is moving randomly.
 */
private Location nextLuredLocation()
{   /* To be implemented in part (a) */ }

/** Finds this fish's next location.
 *  A fish may move to any empty adjacent locations except the
 *  one behind it (fish do not move backward). If this fish
 *  cannot move, the method returns its current
 *  location.
 *  @return  the next location for this fish
 **/
protected Location nextLocation()
{
  Location desired = nextLuredLocation();
  if (desired != null)
    return desired;

  // Get list of neighboring empty locations.
  ArrayList emptyNbrs = emptyNeighbors();
  // Remove the location behind, since fish do not move backward.
  Direction oppositeDir = direction().reverse();
  Location locationBehind = environment().getNeighbor(location(), oppositeDir);
  emptyNbrs.remove(locationBehind);
  Debug.print("Possible new locations are: " + emptyNbrs.toString());

  // If there are no valid empty neighboring locations, then we're done.
  if ( emptyNbrs.size() == 0 )
    return location();

  // Return a randomly chosen neighboring empty location.
  Random randNumGen = RandNumGenerator.getInstance();
  int randNum = randNumGen.nextInt(emptyNbrs.size());
  return (Location) emptyNbrs.get(randNum);
}
```

In writing `nextLuredLocation`, you may make use of the following four new methods in the `Location` class.

```
/** Determines whether this location is south of the given
 * location. (The amount, if any, that the other location
 * is east or west of this location is irrelevant.)
 * @param loc  the location to test
 * @return     true if this location is south (by any amount)
 *             the given location; false otherwise
 */
public boolean isSouthOf(Location loc)
{ /* Implementation not shown */ }

/** Similar to isSouthOf, but the key direction is north.
 */
public boolean isNorthOf(Location loc)
{ /* Implementation not shown */ }

/** Similar to isSouthOf, but the key direction is east.
 */
public boolean isSouthOf(Location loc)
{ /* Implementation not shown */ }

/** Similar to isSouthOf, but the key direction is west.
 */
public boolean isWestOf(Location loc)
{ /* Implementation not shown */ }
```

A. Complete the `nextLuredLocation` method below:

```
/** Returns a location to which this fish can move so as to
 *     be closer to its desired location
 *     @return any location to which this fish can move so as to
 *             be closer to its desired location; returns the
 *             current location if all possibilities are blocked
 *             and null if this fish is moving randomly.
 */
private Location nextLuredLocation()
{
```

When a lure is placed in the environment, it attracts the nearest fish, and only the nearest fish. (In the event of a tie, any nearest fish—but only one—would be attracted to the lure.) To aid this, the following method is added to the `Environment` interface:

```
/** Causes the Fish nearest to the specified location to desire to
 *     move toward that location. (If a number of fish are the same,
 *     minimal distance from the location, only one is affected.)
 *     precondition: isValid(loc) && there is at least one fish in
 *        the environment
 **/
protected void attractFish(Location loc)
{    /* To be implemented in part(b) */ }
```

The biologists are insisting that a particular algorithm be used to determine the fish to be attracted. That algorithm is specified below:

Create an empty queue and an empty set.
Put the given location into each of these collections.
Repeat the following until a fish has been found or until the queue is empty:
Remove a current location from the queue.
If any of its neighbors contains a fish, then that fish may be selected.
If none of its neighbors contains a fish, then each neighbor that is not already in the set should be added to both the set and the queue.

B. Complete the `attractFish` method below using the biologists' algorithm. Any solution that implements a different algorithm will not receive full credit even if the alternate algorithm is correct. In writing your solution, you may make use of the class `MBSQueue` shown below:

```
public class MBSQueue implements Queue
{ /* Implementation not shown */ }

/**  Causes the Fish nearest to the specified location to desire to
 *    move toward that location. (If a number of fish are the same,
 *    minimal distance from the location, only one is affected.)
 *    precondition: isValid(loc) && there is at least one fish in
 *      the environment
 **/
protected void attractFish(Location lureLoc)
{
```

4. At Educational Technology School, students enroll in courses, some of which have prerequisites. A student must pass all the prerequisites for a course before she may enroll in that course. A given course may have zero, one, or two prerequisites. The prerequisite structure is maintained in a binary tree format. If a given course has no prerequisites, it is a leaf in the tree; if it has a single prerequisite, the prerequisite is the left child of the course; if it has two prerequisites, they are the children of that node. One possible tree is shown below:

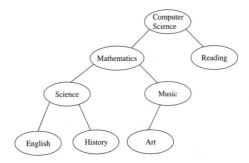

In this curriculum, a student must complete both English and History before taking Science. Similarly, she must complete both Mathematics and Reading before taking Computer Science. Before taking Music, however, she need complete only Art. Reading, English, History, and Art may be taken at any time.

A partial description of the `Course` class is shown below:

```
public class Course
{
  // Postcondition: No student has passed this course
  public Course()
  { /* Implementation not shown */ }

  public String getName()
  { /* Implementation not shown */ }

  // Postcondition: returns true if the specified student
  //   has passed the course; returns false otherwise.
  public boolean wasPassedBy(Student s)
  { /* Implementation not shown */ }

  // Postcondition: in the future, wasPassedBy(s)
  //   will return true;
  public void markAsFinishedBy(Student s)
  { /* implementation not shown */ }

  // ... constructor and other methods not shown
}
```

A `Curriculum` organizes `Courses` as a binary tree, with courses as the data objects in the `TreeNodes`. The prerequisite structure of the courses is as described above. A partial listing of the `Curriculum` class follows:

```
public class Curriculum
{
  private TreeNode root;

  //  Postcondition: returns the set of courses that
  //    can be taken by the specified Student
  public Set canBeTakenBy(Student s)
  { /* Implementation not shown */ }

  //  Precondition: the specified course exists
  //    somewhere in the binary tree of prerequisites
  //  Postcondition: the specified student will be
  //    given credit for passing the course and will
  //    therefore (potentially) be able to take other
  //    courses now that prerequisites have been met
  public void passes(Student s, Course c)
  { /* Implementation not shown */ }

  // . . . constructor and other methods not shown
}
```

A. The Curriculum method canBeTakenBy makes use of a (private) helper method. canBeTakenBy returns a Set of Courses that the specified student may take. This set is constructed first and then passed to the helper method along with the root of the tree.

```
// Postcondition: returns the set of courses that
//    can be taken by the specified Student
public Set canBeTakenBy(Student s)
{
  HashSet courseSet = new HashSet();
  canBeTakenByHelper(s, root, courseSet);
  return courseSet;
}
```

You are to implement the helper method, as described in its documentation:

```
// Precondition: root != null, courses != null
// Postcondition: all of the courses that lie below
//    root in the prerequisite tree that
//    can be taken by the specified Student
//    have been added to set of courses
public void canBeTakenByHelper(Student s,
            TreeNode root, Set courses)
{
```

B. The Curriculum method passes is also written using a helper method. Invoking this method should update the specified course in the prerequisite tree to reflect that the given student has passed the course.

```
// Precondition: the specified course exists
//    somewhere in the binary tree of prerequisites
// Postcondition: the specified student will be
//    given credit for passing the course and will
//    therefore (potentially) be able to take other
//    courses now that prerequisites have been met
public void passes(Student s, Course c)
{
  passesHelper(s,c,root);
}
```

Again, you are to implement the helper method as described in its documentation:

```
// Precondition: the specified course exists
//    somewhere in the binary tree of prerequisites
// Postcondition: the specified student will be
//    given credit for passing the course and will
//    therefore (potentially) be able to take other
//    courses now that prerequisites have been met
public void passesHelper(Student s, Course c, TreeNode root)
{
```

ANSWERS TO PRACTICE EXAM AB2, SECTION I

1.	D	11.	C	21.	B	31.	C
2.	E	12.	C	22.	D	32.	C
3.	E	13.	D	23.	C	33.	D
4.	A	14.	A	24.	B	34.	A
5.	D	15.	B	25.	B	35.	E
6.	A	16.	A	26.	D	36.	D
7.	B	17.	C	27.	A	37.	E
8.	A	18.	A	28.	D	38.	C
9.	B	19.	E	29.	D	39.	C
10.	D	20.	E	30.	A	40.	D

✓ SOLUTIONS TO PRACTICE EXAM AB2, SECTION I

1. The correct answer is D. Without worrying about index values, it can be seen that the list grows by one and shrinks by one each time through the loop. Thus, there are never more than four items in the list. Attempting to remove the fifth element from such a list will cause an `IndexOutOfBoundsException` to be raised.

2. The correct answer is E. A postorder traversal will start with the left-most item and end with the root. The only choice that does this is choice E.

3. The correct answer is E. Abstract classes are like nonabstract classes, but are permitted to have incomplete methods. Thus, the first three choices are incorrect. Furthermore, they are classes and can be extended, unlike interfaces, which are implemented.

4. The correct answer is A. If z is true, then the left side of the inequality is `false` as is the right side. Thus, the expression will be false. If z is `false`, the left side of the inequality is `true`, as is the right side. Thus, the expression is `false`. Since these are the only possibilities, the expression must always be `false`. (See table below.)

cause `thingOne` to be executed even though the two tests are on different lines.

8. The correct answer is A. `mystery(7,7)` returns 7, so only the first two choices are possible. `mystery(1,2)` returns `mystery(1,1)` which returns 1, so the second choice does not work either.

9. The correct answer is B. Only objects that are `Comparable` may be placed in a `TreeSet`. The statements about big-oh bounds are valid concerns, but relevant only if the code would actually execute.

10. The correct answer is D. No `Map` places any restriction on values (other than that the values must be objects.) Keys in a `HashMap` must implement both the `equals` and `hashCode` methods, but all classes inherit these from the `Object` class, so there is no issue there. By contrast, `HashMaps` do not in any way require that an object be `Comparable`.

11. The correct answer is C. The loop proceeds until p refers to the last element in the list and q refers to the second to last. After the loop

x	y	z	!z&&y	(!z&&y)||x	z||y	x==z	(z||y)&&(x==z)	((!z&&y)||x != ((z||y)&&(x == z))
F	T	T	F	F	T	F	F	F
F	T	F	T	T	T	T	T	F

5. The correct answer is D. It is perfectly acceptable to create an `Iterator` for an empty `Collection`. An exception is raised with any `Iterator` when the `next` method is invoked and there are no remaining items in the `Collection`. In this case, that will occur the first time the `next` method is invoked.

6. The correct answer is A. The body of the inner loop sets the cell to the smaller of its row and column indexes.

7. The correct answer is B. It requires both tests to be true to execute `thingOne` in Fragment 1, whereas either test being true in Fragment 2 will

executes, p's `next` field is set to refer to the beginning of the list and the list is terminated at q.

12. The correct answer is C. The `get` method takes O(1) time for an `ArrayList`, but O(N) time for a `LinkedList`. Since the loop executes N times, the overall times are O(N) and O(N2), respectively.

13. The correct answer is D. There is a classic doubly nested loop (similar to Insertion sort) that executes $O(N^2)$ times, followed by a loop that executes exactly N times. The latter has no effect on the big-oh bound.

14. The correct answer is A. Code fragment I does not work because it never resets any of the references in any of the TreeNodes. Code fragment II does not work if the tree is empty. Code fragment III tries to swap the sides, but the left side is lost because it is not being saved in a temporary variable.

15. The answer is B. The matrix method is the one that uses more memory, so the first choice is incorrect. Furthermore, the list data structure is not intrinsically unbounded; one need only adjust the numRows and numCols methods to return the limits, so the last choice is wrong, too. Choice D is not true; if it were, then we would have needed a different file structure for unbounded data sets already, and choice C is actually an argument in favor of the switch.

16. The answer is A. The SlowFish can be anywhere within two cells of its current location (including in its current location.) The DarterFish must have been at either (1,0)-East, (1,1)-East, or (1,2)-West last move. The last is not possible because it would have required a Fish to be at (1,1) and the SlowFish would already have moved away to end up in its current location. The only way that the DarterFish could be at (1,1)-East is if a Fish had been at (1,0) the step before. The SlowFish could not have been there and still ended at (0,1). So, the DarterFish was at (1,0)-East the step before. The only previous position for the DarterFish in that case is (1,0)-West. The only overall configuration meeting these qualifications is Choice A.

17. The correct answer is C. Jumping to a valid empty location could be accomplished by modifying move, but doing so would result in a lot of duplicated code, and in reality, the movement isn't changing, only the method of choosing the next place to move. It could also be accomplished by modifying emptyNeighbors, now effectively defining a neighbor to be any cell within five units; this is undesirable because it changes the definition of neighbor. To mimic the current architecture most closely, one should modify nextLocation, as was done with the DarterFish class.

18. The correct answer is A. The step method controls each of the Fish in the Environment. This is not a responsibility that an individual Fish should have. Similarly, it is not a responsibility that an Environment should have; if it were, there would not have been a Simulation class in the original design.

19. The correct answer is E. The method hashes a given Fish based upon the hash value returned by its toString method. As a Fish moves, however, the value returned by toString will change, and thus the Fish will have different hash values at different points in time. [Note that using the toString method as a first step in determining a hash value is a fine idea provided that the value returned by toString never changes.]

20. The correct answer is E. Not moving backward is a property of the Fish, not of the Environment. In fact, one could hypothesize a RetreatingFish class that did sometimes move backward. Making the test described in choice E would not only be unnecessary, but it would be wrong if such a class existed.

21. The correct answer is B. Black box testing does not test lines of code; rather it tests whether or not code meets external specifications, including the generation of exceptions. It is completely compatible with regression testing, one of the tenets of which is that software must be subjected to all tests after a change is made.

22. The correct answer is D. Swimmers can arrive and depart in any order, and they have no intrinsic order while they are in the pool. Furthermore, the same swimmer cannot be in the pool twice. This is a near perfect description of a Set.

23. The correct answer is C. The get method is supported by the LinkedList class, but unlike the version in the ArrayList class, this version takes O(N) time rather than O(1).

24. The correct answer is B. The second block works. The first block uses an extra variable, but the flaw is that it returns the PriorityItem, not just the data object contained therein. The third block generates a syntax error because there is no getData method for an ExamPriorityQueue.

25. The correct answer is B. removeMin is an O(logN) operation on a standard heap structure. peekMin and getData are O(1), so any of the blocks of code yield the same answer.

26. The correct answer is D. If the item being searched is the median item, it will be found whether or not the list is sorted. This rules out the first three choices. On a nonsorted list, the binary search algorithm may fail to find an item that is in the list, but it will not raise an exception. No searching algorithm, however, will find an item that is not on the list.

27. The correct answer is A. A class may implement many interfaces, but may extend only one parent class, so if the operation is to be repeated, an interface is preferred in case I. If the existing construct contains data or is declared abstract, then it cannot be an interface, so extending is the only option. This covers cases II and III.

28. The correct answer is D. In the first iteration of the loop, the initial cell of the array receives a copy of the value in the last cell. This rules out the first two choices. In the next iteration, the second cell receives a copy of the second to last cell. After three iterations, the array contains {6, 5, 4, 4, 5, 6}. The last three iterations end up copying values into cells that already hold those values.

29. The correct answer is D. The first code fragment creates a new `Point` and stores its reference in `center` while the third code fragment simply sets `center` to refer to the original `Point`. The second fragment, however, invokes the `setPoint` method on `center` even though no `Point` has been allocated; this will cause a `NullPointerException` to be raised.

30. The correct answer is A. After the assignment on the fifth line, both `one` and `two` refer to the same `Circle`; thus only the last `setCircle` operation is relevant.

31. The correct answer is C. At the beginning of each loop, `extra` and `p` refer to the same `ListNode`. If there are not at least two nodes, `p` will be set to `null` and the loop will terminate on the next pass. If there are at least two nodes, `extra` is set to the next field of the second, and then the second is set to refer to the first. `p` is then set to refer to the same node as `extra`.

32. The correct answer is C. Each row must be reversed once, and each column must be reversed once. The only choices that do this are choice C and choice D. Choice D, however, uses the row index to reverse the columns and vice versa. Unless the matrix is square, this will not work.

33. The correct answer is D. A `Beta` uses the `eeny` method from its parent class and thus prints "alpha eeny." A `Gamma` uses the `miny` method from its parent and invokes `eeny`. It then uses its own `eeny` method to print "gamma eeny."

34. The correct answer is A. `Delta` has a method named `miny`, but it does not have the same sig-

nature as the abstract method in its parent class, so `Delta` must also be an abstract class or a compiler error will result.

35. The correct answer is E. In an asymptotic sense, Merge sort is $O(N*logN)$ on all data sets.

36. The correct answer is D. Because `one` and `three` refer to the same object, both "nickel" and "gold" must appear in the output. Because `one` and `two` refer to different objects, "silver" cannot appear in the output. Of the three sequences shown, only II is a possibility.

37. The correct answer is E. The function returns 0 on an empty tree and one more than the larger of the left subtree and the value of the right subtree. Since only one subtree is being considered, the first three choices are eliminated. Since we are returning the larger value, the fourth choice is eliminated as well.

38. The correct answer is C. When inheritance is involved, which block of code is to be executed is determined through runtime polymorphism, i.e., the method to be invoked is determined by the actual type of the object; thus the compiler cannot perform this function. It does perform the others. (The compiler does check that a casting operation is *feasible*; for instance, one cannot cast a known `String` as an `ArrayList`. This check does not protect against all poor castings; that's why there is a `ClassCastException`.)

39. The correct answer is C. If the tree has no root, no data are visited by either traversal, so the traversals are trivially the same. If the root has no children, then both traversals visit only the root and thus they are again the same. If the root has any child, then a preorder traversal will visit the root first, then the child; whereas a postorder traversal will visit the child before the root. Hence, the traversals will differ when the tree has more than one node. (The only tree with no leaves is the empty tree.)

40. The correct answer is D. Every two loops, the queue grows by one; every three loops, the stack returns to empty. Thus, after six iterations, the stack is empty and the queue contains two elements. After two more iterations, the stack will have pushed two elements and popped one, so it will have only one item. The queue will have enqueued two elements and dequeued one, so it will have four items. The only answer matching this pattern is choice D.

ANSWERS TO PRACTICE EXAM AB2, SECTION II

Problem 1A

```java
public Survey(int numQuestions, int maxNumChoices)
{
  table = new ListNode[numQuestions][maxNumChoices];

  for(int r=0; r<numQuestions; r++)
  {
    for(int c=0; c<maxNumChoices; c++)
    {
      table[r][c] = null;
    }
  }
}
```

Problem 1B

```java
public void add(Respondent aPerson, int[] questAns)
{
  for (int q=0; q<questAns.length; q++)
  {
    int reply = questAns[q];
    table[q][reply] = new ListNode(aPerson,table[q][reply]);
  }
}
```

Problem 1C

```java
public void printList(int aQuest, int anAns)
{
  ListNode resp = table[aQuest][anAns];
  if (resp == null)
    System.out.println("<no respondents>");
  else
  {
    while (resp != null)
    {
      System.out.println(resp.getValue());
      resp = resp.getNext();
    }
  }
}
```

Problem 2A

```java
public void update(String cityA, String cityB, int distance)
{
  Map m = (Map) distanceInformation.get(cityA);
  m.put(cityB, new Integer(distance));

  m = (Map) distanceInformation.get(cityB);
  m.put(cityA, new Integer(distance));
}
```

Problem 2B

```
public int routeDistance(ArrayList itinerary)
{
  int totalDistance = 0;
  for (int i=0; i<itinerary.size()-1; i++)
  {
    String startCity = (String) itinerary.get(i);
    String endCity = (String) itinerary.get(i+1);
    Map m = (Map) distanceInformation.get(startCity);
    Integer distance = m.get(endCity);
    totalDistance += distance.intValue();
  }
  return totalDistance;
}
```

Problem 2C

```
public String midCity(String cityA, String cityB)
{
  String bestCity = "<no city>";
  int bestDistance = -1;
  Map cityAMap = (Map) distanceInformation.get(cityA);
  Set candidates = cityAMap.keySet();
  Iterator it = candidates.iterator();
  while (it.hasNext())
  {
    String toTest = (String) it.next();
    Map m = distanceInformation.get(toTest);
    Integer d1 = m.get(cityA);
    Integer d2 = m.get(cityB);
    if ((d1 != null) && (d2 != null))
    {
      int thisDist = d1.intValue() + d2.intValue();
      if ( bestCity.equals("<no city>") || (thisDist<bestDistance) )
      {
        bestCity = toTest;
        bestDistance = thisDist;
      }
    }
  }
  return bestCity;
}
```

Problem 3A

```
private Location nextLuredLocation()
{
  if (desiredLoc == null)
        return null;

  Location southOfMe = environment().getNeighbor(location(), Direction.SOUTH);
  if (environment().isEmpty(southOfMe)) && desiredLoc.isSouthOf(location())
     return southOfMe;

  Location northOfMe = environment().getNeighbor(location(), Direction.NORTH);
  if (environment().isEmpty(northOfMe)) && desiredLoc.isNorthOf(location())
     return northOfMe;

  Location eastOfMe = environment().getNeighbor(location(), Direction.EAST);
  if (environment().isEmpty(eastOfMe)) && desiredLoc.isEastOf(location())
     return eastOfMe;

  Location westOfMe = environment().getNeighbor(location(), Direction.WEST);
  if (environment().isEmpty(westOfMe)) && desiredLoc.isWestOf(location())
     return westOfMe;

  return location();
}
```

Problem 3B

```
protected void attractFish(Location lureLoc)
{
  Location selected = null;
  Queue q = new MBSQueue();
  if (! isEmpty(lureLoc))
    selected = lureLoc;
  q.enqueue(lureLoc);
  HashSet beenChecked = new HashSet();
  beenChecked.add(lureLoc);
  while (selected == null)
  {
    Location toCheck = (Location) q.dequeue();
    ArrayList nbrs = neighborsOf(toCheck);
    Iterator it = nbrs.iterator();
    while (it.hasNext())
    {
      nextNbr = (Location) it.next();
      if (isEmpty(nextNbr))
      {
        if (! beenChecked.contains(nextNbr))
        {
          q.enqueue(nextNbr);
          beenChecked.add(nextNbr);
        }
      }
      else
        selected = nextNbr;
    }
  }
  Fish f = (Fish) objectAt(selected);
  f.setDesiredLocation(lureLoc);
}
```

Problem 4A

```
public void canBeTakenByHelper(Student s, TreeNode root, Set courses)
{
  Course c = (Course) root.getData();
  if (! c.wasPassedBy(s) )
  {
    boolean passedLeft = true;
    boolean passedRight = true;
    if (root.getLeft() != null)
    {
      Course left = (Course) root.getLeft().getData();
      passedLeft = left.wasPassedBy(s);
      canBeTakenByHelper(s, root.getLeft(), courses);
    }
    if (root.getRight() != null)
    {
      Course right = (Course) root.getRight().getData();
      passedRight = right.wasPassedBy(s);
      canBeTakenByHelper(s, root.getRight(), courses);
    }
    if (passedLeft && passedRight)
    {
      courses.add(c);
    }
  }
}
```

Problem 4B

```
public void passesHelper(Student s, Course c, TreeNode root)
{
  if (root.getData().equals(c))
  {
    Course found = (Course) root.getData();
    found.markAsFinishedBy(s);
  }
  else
  {
    if (root.getLeft() != null)
      passesHelper( s, c, root.getLeft() );
    if (root.getRight() != null)
      passesHelper( s, c, root.getRight() );
  }
}
```

RUBRICS AND COMMENTARY
FOR PRACTICE EXAM AB2, SECION II

Note: In many cases where a rubric says "+1," it may be possible to earn a half point for a nearly correct solution.

Problem 1 (9 points)

Part A (1 point)

+1 for constructing the matrix (no initialization is necessary)

Part B (4 points)

+1 for handling each answer in the array

+1 for creating a new `ListNode` for this respondent

+1 for properly linking that `ListNode` into the correct list when that list is nonempty

+1 for properly dealing with the first respondent to a question (empty list case)

Part C (4 points)

+1 for properly finding the list within the table

+1 for handling the empty list case correctly

+1 for attempting to print each respondent's information

+1 for properly printing each respondent's information exactly once

Commentary

In Part A, no initialization is required, but if it is present (as in the sample solution), it must be correct or a deduction will be made.

In Part B, the easiest thing to do is to place the new respondent at the front of the list, but it is permissible to place that respondent anywhere in the list.

In Part C, the use of `toString` is optional. It is incorrect to use `table[aQuest][anAns]` as the loop control variable, because this will destroy the integrity of the table.

Problem 2 (9 points)

Part A (2 points)

+1 for correctly accessing at least one of the two appropriate city `Maps`

+1 for correctly placing the updated value into both `Maps`

Part B (2 points)

+1 for correctly scanning each pair of cities

+1 for correctly totaling the individual distances and returning that total

Part C (5 points)

+1 for identifying and doing some work with each of the pairs of cities

+1 for extracting some form of distance information from the `Map`

+1 for correctly computing the distance via an intermediate city

+1 for correctly comparing and updating the value other than in the initial case

+1 for handling all initialization, updating, and returning correctly

Commentary

In Part A, the order of the updates is unimportant. Also, because of the way that the `put` method works, it is unnecessary to worry about a value that is already present.

It is incorrect to assume that either a `HashMap` or a `TreeMap` is stored in the `distanceInformation` structure. Thus, the type of m must be a `Map`.

In Part B, it is possible to use an iterator to traverse the `ArrayList`, but the need to loop "one less time" makes the logic a bit more cumbersome. It is also possible to use only one "`get`" per loop. (In fact, doing so is necessary with the `Iterator` solution.) It is also possible to use `Objects` rather than `Strings` for the `startCity` and `endCity` variables.

In Part C, it is not necessary to test `d1` to see if it is `null`; the integrity of the data structure ensures this, but it is necessary to test `d2`.

It is incorrect to assume that either a `HashMap` or a `TreeMap` is stored in the `distanceInformation` structure. Thus, the type of `m` must be a `Map`, and the type of `candidates` must be a `Set`.

Problem 3 (9 points)

Part A (3 points)

+1 for correctly returning `null` when there is no desired location and the current location when a move cannot be made

+1 for a proper test of movement in a particular direction

+1 for correctly moving in each of the four directions

Part B (6 points)

+1 for proper initialization [including construction of queue and set as well as initializing the loop control variable (`selected` in the sample solution)]

+1 for properly processing each test location

+1 for properly handling the case when a fish is actually found

+1 for properly dealing with all the neighbors of a given location

+1 for properly processing each of those neighbors

+1 for properly causing the selected fish to be attracted to the lure location

Commentary

In Part A, the order of the directional tests is unimportant. It is also possible to use an `ArrayList` returned by `emptyNeighbors` to shorten the code. (This technique was used in the answer to Part B.)

It is incorrect to make any assumption about whether row/column numbers increase or decrease as one moves north/west.

In Part B, a `TreeSet` may be used as the `Location` class implements the `Comparable` interface.

There are several other alternative means of terminating the outer loop.

The inner loop (to process the empty neighbors) may be controlled without an `Iterator` if the `ArrayList`'s `get` method is used. The entire loop may be removed if each neighbor is checked by hand. (This technique was used in the answer to Part A.)

Problem 4 (9 points)

Part A (6 points)

+1 for handling the case when the course at the root has been passed

+1 for properly determining if a student passed a given course

+1 for adding some of the correct courses to the course set

+1 for adding all the correct courses (among those that are checked) to the course set

+1 for searching all the correct locations within the tree

+1 for adding the course to the set when appropriate

Part B (3 points)

+1 for correctly marking the course as passed once it is found

+1 for attempting to search both sides of the tree looking for the course

+1 for finding the course correctly in all cases (includes `null` checks, if necessary)

Commentary

It is permissible to make recursive calls even when the course at the root has been passed, but it is incorrect for such calls to ever result in any courses being added to the set of available courses.

A more naïve (and longer, but still correct) solution explicitly checks for the cases of zero, one, and two prerequisites.

A slightly more efficient solution recurses only when the given course was not passed.

The given solution is essentially a preorder traversal of the tree. The `else` clause effectively prevents the search from descending below the desired course (but does not prevent other inefficiencies). The `else` clause can be omitted without affecting correctness. If that is done, then in-order and postorder traversals of the tree are also effective.

Note that `passesHelper` has an implicit precondition stating that `root` is not `null`. If this prerequisite is assumed, as in the sample solution, then subsequent invocations of the method must ensure that `root` is not `null`. If the method body guards against this case, then such checks are not required.

PART V

APPENDIXES

Glossary

Note: If an item is indicated as being discussed in Chapter 9 or later, students taking only the A exam need not have mastered that concept. If a concept discussed in an earlier chapter will be tested exclusively on the AB exam, that is indicated when the concept is discussed.

Second Note: Concepts introduced through the case study (Marine Biology Simulation) are defined in this glossary, but the specific class implementations are discussed only in Chapter 7.

abstract class A class in which some of the methods, either named locally, or inherited, have not been defined. Such methods, and indeed the class itself, are labeled with the keyword `abstract`. (Chapter 4, pp. 101, 102; Chapter 7, p. 148)

accessor method A method that returns some aspect of the state of an object. (Chapter 1, p. 53)

actual parameters The values supplied by the client in the parameter list of a method call. In the method call,

```
int sum = nums.sumUp(start, end);
```

the actual parameters are `start` and `end`. (Chapter 1, p. 54)

algorithm Step-by-step process for solving a problem. (Chapter 6, p. 124)

AP subset The subset of the Java language that is tested. While you are in no way limited to how much Java you may learn, the test developers are limited to this subset in writing questions. (Chapter 3, p. 77)

AP Computer Science Quick Reference Guide A document provided with the exam to which students may refer while taking the exam. It is available at www.collegeboard.com/student/testing/ap/comp scia.html or . . ./compsciab.html. (Chapter 3, p. 74)

arithmetic operator Any of the operators that are used to compute numeric values in Java. AP students are expected to know the addition, subtraction, multiplication, division, and modulus operators. (Chapter 3, p. 72)

array A one-dimensional collection of data of a given type. The individual items in the collection are called *elements* and are accessed through subscripting. (Chapter 5, p. 110)

ArrayList A Java class that stores data in a one-dimensional `Collection`. Its performance is the same as if the data were stored in an array. AB students are expected to know that this means that access is O(1). (Chapter 10, p. 173)

assignment operator A Java operator (indicated by =) that gives value to a variable. (Chapter 3, p. 71)

asymptotic behavior A description of the performance of a system as its size increases. In the context of AP Computer Science, the behavior of a program as the amount of data it processes increases. (Chapter 9, p. 161)

asymptotic running time A description of the amount of time that a program (or program fragment) will need to complete execution as the amount of data increases. (Chapter 9, p. 161)

asymptotic space analysis A description of the amount of memory that a program (or program fragment) will need to complete execution as the amount of data increases. Sometimes this analysis includes the memory used to hold the original data; sometimes only "additional" memory is counted; it should always be clear from the context of the question. (Chapter 9, p. 165)

big-oh notation A way of expressing an overestimate for an asymptotic behavior of a system, usually either the running time or the memory usage of a program (or program fragment). For example, traversing an array or array list is linear, so it is usually O(N), where N is the number of elements. Traversing a two-dimensional array, which requires nested loops, is usually O(N^2). (Chapter 9, p. 161)

binary Any two-valued system, but most often the base two computation system. (Chapter 8, p. 157)

binary search A search algorithm that works by successively eliminating half the data to be searched. The precondition for binary search is that the data be ordered (ascending or descending). Note that this implies that the items to be searched are comparable. AB students should know binary search is an O(logN) algorithm. (Chapter 6, p. 125)

binary search tree A specialized type of binary tree that stores objects that are comparable to each other in some way. In a binary search tree, all the objects referenceable via the left child of a given node are no greater than the object at that node and all the objects referenceable via the right child of that node are at least as large as the object at that node. (Chapter 11, p. 195)

binary tree A group of objects arranged such that each object can reference up to two additional objects with no object being referenced more than once. `null`, or missing, references indicate the end of a particular path. (Chapter 11, p. 193)

black box testing Testing performed by examining (and verifying) pre- and postconditions, but without viewing the code itself. (Chapter 7, p. 151)

boolean A data type in Java that can assume one of only two values: `true` or `false`. (Chapter 3, p. 74)

cast A programming technique used to cause a data item to be treated as a different type; often used when an `Object` must be treated as a particular type in order to invoke a method on that type. Casting is indicated by placing the type name within parentheses immediately preceding the expression to be cast. (Chapter 3, p. 72; Chapter 4, p. 97)

central processing unit (CPU) The control unit reads and processes program instructions; registers are small amount of memory space needed to keep track of instructions and some data; the arithmetic-logic unit performs arithmetic. (Chapter 8, p. 155)

circularly linked list A linked list whose last node refers to the first node in the list. Note that this means that the list is not terminated via a null reference. (Chapter 11, p. 197)

class A programming unit that captures abstraction. A class maintains the state or attributes of (nouns that describe) an object (the abstraction) and encapsulates its behavior, the services or tasks it can perform (often described as verbs), in its methods. (Chapter 1, p. 50; Chapter 2, p. 61)

class heading The line of code that names the class and defines its relationship, if any, to another class or to interfaces. (Chapter 1, p. 50)

class variable A variable that is shared by all instances of a given class. The keyword `static` is used to define a class variable. It may be refer-

enced using the class name but more importantly, if changed by one instance of the class, its value is changed for all instances. (Chapter 1, p. 50)

ClassCastException An `exception` raised by the Java environment when a line is executed applying a cast operation to an object whose type is *not* as promised by the cast operation. (Chapter 4, p. 97)

client User of a class; may be the main method or the method of another class. (Chapter 1, p. 49)

code-based testing Testing that is done with the idea of testing specific paths of execution through the program. (Chapter 7, p. 151)

code model A set of code provided as a good model to follow when writing code; the Marine Biology Simulation (MBS) is an example. (Chapter 7, p. 138)

cohesion The degree to which a portion of a program (i.e., a class) can be viewed as an independent entity that performs a single task. Cohesion in program units is highly desirable. (Chapter 2, p. 63)

collection (general) A way of grouping data together into a single object so that it is possible to compute using methods of the `Collection` interface. (Chapter 3, p. 76)

Collection interface A Java interface that defines a common set of operations on large amounts of data that are gathered into one object. Since `Collection` is an interface, a `Collection` is never constructed, but several specific classes, including `ArrayList` and `TreeSet`, implement this interface. (Chapter 10, p. 182)

Comparable interface A Java interface that contains a single method, `compareTo`, which must be implemented by any class that implements the interface. (Chapter 3, p. 75)

compiler A program that translates a program from one language into another. Typically compilers translate so-called high level languages to the machine code of a particular computer. The standard Java compiler translates Java into a more universal Java byte code language. (Chapter 8, p. 156)

concatenate Attach the beginning of one string to the end of another to form a new string. (Chapter 3, p. 77)

concrete class A class that has definitions for all its methods, including those that were inherited. Only concrete classes can be instantiated to create objects. (Chapter 4, p. 102)

conditional statement A decision statement that controls program flow based upon a condition (an expression that can be evaluated to true or false). The form of this statement in Java is
`if(< test condition >) . . .` and may

include an `else`. . . . A conditional statement is executed exactly once. Conditional statements may be nested. Compound conditional expressions combine simple conditions using "and" and "or." (Chapter 3, p. 79)

constant A value that, once set, cannot be changed during program execution. The purpose of constants is to make programs more readable (by substituting names for numbers) and to make it easier for the programmer to change a value that is used repeatedly throughout the program, for example, a tax rate. Constants are specified with the keyword `final`. (Chapter 1, p. 51; Chapter 3, p. 74)

constant behavior Also described as O(1). The behavior is independent of the amount of data. (Chapter 9, p. 167)

constructor A method whose task is to instantiate (create or build) an object, accomplished by initializing the instance variables. A constructor is easily identified because its name must be the same name as the class name and there is no return type. There may be more than one constructor for a given class, distinguished by a difference in number or types of arguments in the parameter list. (Chapter 1, p. 53)

coupling The degree to which one portion of a program depends upon how another portion of the program does its job. Since high degrees of coupling make it difficult to maintain large programs, high degrees of coupling are to be avoided if possible. (Chapter 2, p. 63)

cubic behavior Also described as O(N³). The behavior is proportional to the cube of the parameter. In terms of running time, this means that doubling the amount of data will cause the running time to increase by a factor of eight. (Chapter 9, p. 167)

default A value that will be used instead of a programmer-specified parameter, often for a constructor. A constructor that uses no parameters at all, instead substituting predefined values, is often called a *default constructor*. (Chapter 1, p. 53)

DeMorgan's Laws Two mathematical equalities involving Boolean expressions. AP students are expected to understand the equivalences represented in these equalities. (Chapter 3, p. 85)

design cycle An iterative process consisting of analysis, design, implementation, and testing throughout the development of a program; illustrated throughout the Marine Biology Simulation. (Chapter 7, p. 138)

doubly linked list A linked list in which each item refers not only to its successor, but also to its predecessor. (Chapter 11, p. 197)

elements The individual pieces of data within an array (or sometimes a `Collection`). (Chapter 5, p. 111)

encapsulation The process by which one portion of a program is isolated from other portions with access limited to a (generally small) number of methods. (Chapter 2, p. 61)

`equals` The method used to compare two objects for equality. (Chapter 3, p. 75)

escape sequences Characters beginning with a backslash character, \, used in `String` literals to format output. AP students are expected to know the following sequences: "\n" (new line), "\t" (tab), and "\"" (printed double quotation marks). (Chapter 3, p. 77)

exception An error or unusual situation arising in a program. In Java, this situation is represented by an `Exception` object of a specific type, such as `ArithmeticErrorException`. (Chapter 5, p. 117)

explicit parameter A piece of information passed in the parameter list. (Chapter 1, p. 54)

`extends` The Java keyword that is used to express the inheritance (IS-A) relationship between classes. (Chapter 4, p. 95)

field Another name for an instance variable. (Chapter 1, p. 51)

FIFO (first in, first out) A protocol for a collection that can be added to or removed from. It requires that the item to be removed be the one least recently added to the collection. (Chapter 12, p. 205)

`for` loop Counting loop; generally used when there is a definite number of iterations; for example, `for(int k = 0; k < 10; k++)`. (Chapter 3, p. 81)

formal parameters The parameters listed in a method signature. For example, in the method signature

```
public int sumUp(int first, int last)
```

`first` and `last` are formal parameters. (Chapter 1, p. 54)

hardware The physical components of a computer. (Chapter 8, p. 155)

HAS-A A relationship between two classes; we say that X HAS-A Y if any object of type X would necessarily contain an object of type Y. This is *not* an inheritance relationship. (Chapter 4, p. 94)

`hashCode` A method in the `Object` class (and hence in all classes) that converts the object to an integer. It must always convert the same object to the same integer (to work at all) and should convert different objects to different integers as often as possible to attain the best possible performance of hash tables. (Chapter 10, p. 176)

HashMap A Java class that implements the `Map` interface using a hash table to hold the keys. When the `hashCode` method (on the keys) is well implemented, most operations run in O(1) time, but the worst-case behavior will be O(N). (Chapter 10, p. 181)

HashSet A Java class that implements the `Set` interface using a hash table to hold the objects. When the `hashCode` method is well implemented, most operations run in O(1) time, but the worst-case behavior will be O(N). (Chapter 10, p. 176)

head (of a list) A reference to the initial object in a linked list. (Chapter 11, p. 190)

heap A binary tree whose leaves are as close to the root as possible and where the value of any object is no greater than the value of any object reachable from that object's node. (Note that this is a description of a "min-heap." If the phrase "no less" is substituted for the phrase "no greater" in the definition, then a "max-heap" results.) (Chapter 11, p. 196; Chapter 12, p. 210)

Heapsort A sorting algorithm that involves first inserting the items into a heap and then removing them in sorted order. Students should know that the running time of this algorithm is O(N*log N). (Chapter 12, p. 210)

helper method A private method used within a class. A helper method may avoid repetition of code or may aid in breaking down a complicated method into simpler tasks. (Chapter 1, p. 52)

hexadecimal The base sixteen computational system. (Chapter 8, p. 157)

implementation Code that defines a construct. (Chapter 1, p. 49)

implements The Java keyword that indicates that a class will provide all the capabilities specified by the given interface. (Chapter 4, p. 99)

implicit parameter The object upon which a method is called. (Chapter 1, p. 54)

infinite loop An iterative process that fails to end. (Chapter 3, p. 82)

inheritance A component of object-oriented design that permits data, methods, and/or algorithms to be shared among different data types that are related. (Chapter 2, p. 64; Chapter 4, p. 93)

inheriting a method A subclass inherits a method from a superclass when it fails to (re)define that method in its own class definition. In such a case the code from the superclass is used when the method is invoked on any object of the subclass's type. (Chapter 4, p. 95)

in-order traversal A traversal of a tree in which the data to the left of the root are traversed first, followed by the data in the root itself, and finally by the data to the right of the root, where left and right are determined by the linking structure. (Chapter 11, p. 194)

Insertion sort A sorting algorithm that works by traversing the array from left to right; with each new element, the array is scanned backward until the position for this element is discovered and it is inserted in its correct order with respect to the data already examined. AB students should know that the best, worst, and average running times are O(N), O(N^2), and O(N^2), respectively. (Chapter 6, p. 127)

instance An object of a specified class type. More than one object of a given class may be instantiated at any given time. (Chapter 1, p. 49)

instance variable A variable that must be referenced through an instance of the class. Instance variables embody the attributes of a particular object and are generally private to the class. (Chapter 1, p. 51)

interface (English usage) The collection of all methods provided by a construct for use by entities outside that construct. (Chapter 2, p. 61)

interface (Java keyword) A Java construct that consists of a list of method signatures that are required of classes that implement the interface of this name. (Chapter 4, p. 99)

interpreter A program that reads and executes code one line at a time on a particular machine. (Chapter 8, p. 156)

IS-A A relationship between two objects; X IS-A Y if the objects that X models are *always* also considered to be objects of type Y. This means that it must be the case that any method that can be invoked on an object of type Y can also be invoked on an object of type X. (Chapter 4, p. 94)

iteration The act of repeating a task through looping; a statement that controls the flow of a program through repetition. (Chapter 3, p. 81)

iterator A Java class whose objects can be used to range through a `Collection` in such a way that each item that has been inserted into that `Collection` is visited once and only once. The order of visits is not controllable by the programmer. (Chapter 10, p. 178)

leaf An object in a binary tree that references no other objects. (Chapter 11, p. 193)

left (right) child The name of one (or the other) of the two references from an object in a binary tree. The adjective usually applies to the relative position on the page if the data structure is drawn out. (Chapter 11, p. 193)

LIFO (last in, first out) A protocol for a collection that can be added to or removed from. It requires that the item to be removed be the one most recently added to the collection. (Chapter 12, p. 204)

linear behavior [also described as O(N)] The behavior is proportional to the parameter. In terms of running time, this means that doubling the amount of data will double the running time. (Chapter 9, p. 162)

linked list (general term) Any of a number of list structures in which each item references an adjacent item or adjacent items. Examples include singly, doubly, and circularly linked lists. (Chapter 11, p. 189)

LinkedList (class) A Java class that implements the List interface using a doubly linked list of objects. This permits relatively easy modification of the data structure, but randomly accessing elements of the list using the get method may be inefficient. (Chapter 10, p. 174)

List A Java interface that extends the Collection interface. The interface defines additional methods that take advantage of the fact that items in a list are inherently ordered by position, even if the list is not kept in sorted order. (Chapter 10, p. 173)

ListIterator A Java class that extends Iterator to include additional methods to set and add elements during a traversal of a List. (It also contains methods to reverse the traversal process although these are not tested on the AP exam.) (Chapter 10, p. 179)

ListNode A simple class that contains a reference to an Object as well as a reference to one ListNode. This class will be used by exam designers to create questions about singly linked lists. (Chapter 11, p. 188)

local variable Variable declared (and usable only) within a method. (Chapter 1, p. 55)

logarithmic behavior [also described as O(logN)] The behavior is proportional to the number of digits in the parameter. As to running time, this means that the program will run *very* quickly. (Chapter 9, p. 164)

logical operator Any of the three operators used exclusively on Boolean values. AP students are expected to know all three operators: logical and, logical or, and logical negation. (Chapter 3, p. 84)

loop invariant (AB topic) A statement about the loop that is true before a loop executes, at the beginning of each iteration, and at the end of each iteration. (Chapter 3, p. 83)

loop statement A statement that causes a block of code (possibly a single statement) to be executed some number of times, repeating the entire block each time. Both for and while statements are examples of loop statements. Loop statements may be nested and/or combined with conditional statements. (Chapter 3, p. 81)

main diagonal The collection of elements of a square matrix that extends from the upper left-hand corner to the lower right. (Chapter 5, p. 115)

main method The method in an application where execution begins. (Chapter 1, p. 57)

Map A Java interface for large numbers of objects that does *not* extend the Collection interface. Rather Maps store key-value pairs of objects. The key values are used to "look up" the value portions of the pairs. The keys in a Map are distinct by definition, but values may be duplicated. (Chapter 10, p. 181)

Marine Biology Simulation (MBS) An extensive program and accompanying narrative that will serve as the basis for up to 25 percent of the questions on the exam. (Chapter 7, p. 138)

Math class A class that includes a variety of useful mathematical functions. AP students are expected to be able to use those methods of the Math class listed in the AP subset. (Chapter 3, p. 78)

matrix A two-dimensional array. Elements may be accessed through two subscripts, e.g., M[i][j]. (Chapter 5, p. 114)

Merge sort A recursive sorting algorithm that works by repeatedly dividing the array in half, then in half again, etc., until the subarrays are of size 1; then the subarrays are merged in ascending (or descending) order until all are merged back together. Merge sort typically uses an auxiliary array, thus doubling the amount of memory required. AB students should know that the running time of this algorithm is O(N*logN). (Chapter 6, p. 129)

method A specific (named) task that an instance of a class can perform. (Chapter 1, p. 51)

modifier or **mutator method** A method that changes the state of an object. Modifier methods are usually, but not always, void, meaning they do not return a value. (Chapter 1, pp. 51, 54)

network Two or more connected computers that can share data or other resources. (Chapter 8, p. 157)

NullPointerException A particular Exception thrown by the Java Virtual Machine when a method is invoked upon a null Object. Since the Object does not exist, the method cannot be invoked. (Chapter 11, p. 195)

O(NlogN) behavior The behavior is proportional to a function slightly larger than the parameter itself. Although clumsy to pronounce, this behavior is seen fairly often, particularly in sorting algorithms. (Chapter 9, p. 164)

object (English usage) A specific instance of a class. (Chapter 1, p. 49)

Object (Java keyword) The parent of all other classes. All other classes extend (inherit from) this class, even though the class declaration may not explicitly say so. Methods include equals and toString. (Chapter 3, p. 75; Chapter 4, p. 99)

object code Low-level code, often directly machine executable. It is generally not in human readable form. (Chapter 8, p. 156)

object diagrams A visualization of the classes within a program, helpful in understanding individual classes and coupling; object diagrams are available for the Marine Biology Simulation—they are not tested but are a good study aid. (Chapter 7, p. 138)

octal The base eight computation system. (Chapter 8, p. 157)

operating system A collection of programs that manages and prioritizes computer resources such as the user interface, loading and saving files, program execution, printing, memory allocation, and the central processing unit. (Chapter 8, p. 156)

overloading The idea that two methods may have the same name as long as they have different signatures. (A consequence of this is that the system can distinguish which method is to be used based upon the parameter sequence.) (Chapter 1, p. 53)

override A subclass overrides a method from a superclass if it (re)defines a method with the same signature as one in the superclass. In such a case, the redefined method will be invoked on any object of the subclass's type. (Chapter 4, p. 96)

parameter A piece of required information passed to a method so that it may accomplish its task. (Chapter 1, p. 54)

peripheral device A piece of hardware other than the central processing unit. Examples include internal drives, external drives, keyboard, monitor, and printer. (Chapter 8, p. 156)

postcondition An assertion that specifies what will be true when a method terminates—provided that the associated preconditions were met; usually written in terms of the return value or change of state. (Chapter 1, p. 52; Chapter 2, p. 62)

postorder traversal A traversal of a tree in which the data to the left of the root are traversed first, followed by the data to the right of the root, and finally by the data in the root itself, where left and right are determined by the linking structure. (Chapter 11, p. 194)

precedence rules The rules that govern the order in which the components of an expression are evaluated. (Chapter 3, p. 83)

precondition An assertion (precisely worded comment) that specifies what must be true for a method to succeed in its task; usually written in terms of the parameters. Unless these stipulations are met, the programmer of the method is under no obligation to do anything. (Chapter 1, p. 52; Chapter 2, p. 62)

preorder traversal A traversal of a tree in which the data in the root are traversed first, followed by the data to the left of the root, and finally by the data to the right of the root, where left and right are determined by the linking structure. (Chapter 11, p. 194)

primary memory The active part of memory where a program runs. (Chapter 8, p. 155)

primitive A data type that is not an object. The primitive data types in the AP subset are `int`, `double`, and `boolean`. (Chapter 3, p. 71)

priority queue (AB topic) A structure that supports a protocol wherein the item to be removed from the collection is the one with the lowest associated priority. Priority queues are usually implemented in such a manner that no method takes longer than $O(logN)$ time to complete. (Chapter 12, p. 207)

private A visibility modifier that states that this construct is usable only within its class. (Chapter 2, p. 62; Chapter 4, p. 97)

programming by contract The idea that interfaces are specified in terms of contracts wherein a class that provides a service (or more precisely the programmer of such a class) agrees to provide particular services for clients provided that the client first provides certain data. The contract is often expressed through the use of pre- and postconditions. (Chapter 2, p. 61)

protected (not covered on the AP exam, except in the context of the case study) A visibility modifier that states that this construct is usable only within its class and any subclasses of its class.(Chapter 4, p. 97)

public A visibility modifier that states that this construct is usable by all users of the class. (Chapter 2, p. 62; Chapter 4, p. 97)

quadratic behavior [also described as $O(N^2)$]. The behavior is proportional to square of the parameter. In terms of running time, this means that doubling the amount of data will quadruple the running time. (Chapter 9, p. 162)

queue A structure that supports the FIFO protocol. Queues are usually implemented in such a manner that all methods run in $O(1)$ time. (Chapter 12, p. 205)

Quicksort (AB topic) A recursive sorting algorithm that works by selecting a splitting value, often called a pivot point, and separating the array into two sides. The left side contains all values less than the splitting value; the right side, all values greater than or equal to the splitting value. The process is applied recursively to each side and continues until the two sides, or segments, are of size one, at which time the array is sorted. The arrangement of the data and the choice of the pivot are critical factors. The more random the distribution and the closer the pivot is to the mean data value, the better Quicksort will work. The best, worst, and average running times are O(N*logN), O(N²), and O(N*logN), respectively. (Chapter 6, p. 130)

random access memory (RAM) Main memory; read and write; volatile, i.e., cleared when the computer is turned off. (Chapter 8, p. 155)

Random class A class that supports the generation of pseudorandom numbers. AP students are expected to be able to use those methods of the Random class listed in the AP subset. (Chapter 3, p. 78)

recursion Name given to an algorithmic process (in Java, usually a method) that invokes itself. (Chapter 3, p. 85; Chapter 5, p. 116; Chapter 11, p. 194)

regression testing The set of "older" tests that are performed on existing code when changes have been made to a program. The goal is to verify that the new changes did not cause any unintended changes in the existing code. (Chapter 7, p. 151)

relational operator Any of the six operators used to compare values in Java. AP students are expected to know about all six relational operators: less than, less than or equal, greater than, greater than or equal, equals, and not equal. (Chapter 3, p. 73)

right (left) child The name of one (or the other) of the two references from an object in a binary tree. The adjective usually applies to the relative position on the page if the data structure is drawn out. (Chapter 11, p. 193)

root A reference to the initial object in a binary tree. (Chapter 11, p. 193)

runtime polymorphism A component of object-oriented design that causes each object in a system to behave in a specialized manner even when its properties are otherwise known only in a general way. (Chapter 2, p. 64)

scope of a variable The block of code in which a variable is defined. (Chapter 3, p. 74)

secondary diagonal The collection of elements of a square matrix that extends from the upper right-hand corner to the lower left. (Chapter 5, p. 115)

secondary memory Nonvolatile, long-term memory; includes hard drive, floppy drive, CD, DVD, memory stick, external drive, tape. (Chapter 8, p. 155)

Selection sort A sorting algorithm that works by repeatedly selecting the next smallest (or largest) value and swapping it with the item in the first, then the second, then the third, and so on, position in the data list. There is no best or worst case; Selection sort does the same amount of work regardless of the original arrangement of the data. AB students should know that it runs in O(N²) time. (Chapter 6, p. 126)

sequential search An algorithm that loops through the data from beginning to end, or until the target item is found. Data need not be in any particular order. Sequential search looks at each item, one by one. AB students need to know that it is an O(N) algorithm, where N is the number of items to be searched. (Chapter 6, p. 124)

Set A Java interface that extends the Collection interface. This interface defines additional methods that are appropriate for an unordered collection of distinct elements. (Chapter 10, p. 176)

short-circuit evaluation A method of evaluation of logical expressions wherein the later portions of an expression are not evaluated once the final value can be determined. (Chapter 3, p. 84)

signature The heading of a method. This defines the method as public, private, or protected, specifies its return type, lists the method name, and specifies its parameters. The name is not important to the definition of the signature but, if the method is well named, the name tells another programmer what the method does. (Chapter 2, p. 65)

singly linked list Sometimes simply referred to as *linked list*, this data structure consists of a series of objects, each of which can reference the next item in the series. A null, or missing, object usually terminates the list. (Chapter 11, p. 189)

software The instructions and data stored in the computer. (Chapter 8, p. 186)

source code Code written in a high-level language such as Java. It is generally in a human readable form. (Chapter 8, p. 186)

stack (AB topic) A structure that supports the LIFO protocol. Stacks are usually implemented in such a manner that all methods run, on average, in O(1) time. (Chapter 12, p. 203)

String class A class that represents a sequence of characters. String constants are enclosed in double quotation marks. AP students are expected to be able to use those methods of the String class listed in the AP subset. (Chapter 3, p. 76)

subclass The more specialized of two classes in an inheritance relationship. Also sometimes called the *derived class* or the *child class*. (Chapter 4, p. 93)

super The Java keyword used to indicate that the method or data being referred to should come from the superclass rather than from the class that is making the reference. (Chapter 4, p. 98)

superclass The more general of two classes in an inheritance relationship. Also sometimes called the *base class* or the *parent class*. (Chapter 4, p. 93)

test data Set of values used to test a method or program; the purpose is to try to expose and correct errors; should include a general case, boundary cases, and each path through the code. (Chapter 3, p. 86; Chapter 7, p. 151)

this A reserved word for the implicit parameter; used within a class when a reference to the implicit parameter is needed. (Chapter 4, p. 93)

traversal An algorithm that visits each element of a linked structure. If the structure is a tree, the algorithm is often called a *tree traversal*. (Chapter 11, p. 194)

TreeMap A Java class that implements the Map interface using a balanced binary tree to hold the keys. Most operations run in O(logN) time, but the objects used as keys must be Comparable. (Chapter 10, p. 181)

TreeNode A simple class that contains a reference to an object as well as two references to TreeNodes. This class will be used by exam designers to create questions about binary trees. (Chapter 11, p. 189)

TreeSet A Java class that implements the Set interface using a balanced binary tree to hold the objects. Most operations run in O(logN) time, but the objects inserted into the set must be Comparable. (Chapter 10, p. 176)

visibility modifier Defines which components of a Java program can access a given Java construct; public, private, and protected are all visibility modifiers. (Chapter 1, p. 52)

while loop Iterative process based on a condition, while the condition is true. (Chapter 3, p. 81)

wrapper class One of the classes used in Java to encapsulate a primitive value into an object. AP students are expected to be familiar with the Integer and Double wrapper classes. (Chapter 3, p. 76)

Webliography: An Annotated List of Web Sites of Interest to the AP Student

The College Board maintains a Web site with all sorts of materials of interest to the AP student or teacher. In addition, a large number of AP teachers and their friends have set up independent Web sites with a variety of materials of interest to the AP Computer Science student. In true Web fashion, many of these sites reference one another.

Beware: URLs for Web sites change and usually without notice. If you can't find one of these sites, go to some of the others and check the cross-referencing links. This will almost always lead you to the material you desire.

College Board Sites

www.collegeboard.com/student/testing/ap/sub_compscia.html
www.collegeboard.com/student/testing/ap/sub_compsciab.html
> These are the starting pages for the A and AB curricula, respectively. From here you may download the Course Description documents as well as be apprised of any errata therein.

www.collegeboard.com/student/testing/ap/compsci_a/samp.html
www.collegeboard.com/student/testing/ap/compsci_ab/samp.html
> This page links to free-response questions from recent exams as well as to documents explaining how those questions were graded.

www.collegeboard.com/student/testing/ap/compsci_a/case.html
> This is the starting page for the Marine Biology Simulation (MBS) case study discussed in Chapter 7. From here, you can download both the narrative and the code for the simulation.

apcentral.collegeboard.com
> This is the landing page for AP Central, a Web site maintained by the College Board for use by AP teachers. It links to many valuable resources, but your teacher will need to register to gain access.

Independent Web Sites

Chris Nevision's Site (cs.colgate.edu/APCS/index.html)

Chris was in charge of grading the AP Computer Science exam from 2000–2004. Prior to that, he had served on the (test) development committee for AP Computer Science. His site contains complete code for solutions to old exam problems, links to materials on using Java (including specific development environments), and links to the sites of many other educators.

Alyce Brady's Site (max.cs.kzoo.edu/AP/)

Alyce is a former member of the (test) development committee for AP Computer Science and the primary author of the Marine Biology Simulation. Her site contains links to a variety of materials, particularly materials related to the Marine Biology Simulation. The object diagrams referenced in Chapter 7 may be found at this site. The site also contains several other worthwhile projects.

Owen Astrachan's Site (www.cs.duke.edu/csed/ap/)

Owen was in charge of grading the AP Computer Science exam back in the days when the course was taught in Pascal. He is also the author of one of the most popular introductory C++ textbooks. He has created a smaller version of the Java API which is restricted to the classes and methods that AP Computer Science students must understand. His site also contains solutions to some questions on past exams.

Maria and Gary Litvin's Site (www.skylit.com/resource.html#java)

Maria and Gary have written some of the most popular AP Computer Science texts. Their site is designed to promote their books, but it contains many interesting papers, projects, and advice.

Joe Bergin's Site (csis.pace.edu/~bergin/)

Joe is a leading computer science educator and the developer of the Karel J. Robot software. Joe's site is less about AP Computer Science than it is about the concepts of object-oriented programming (and learning) in general. The articles here may be of interest to the AP Computer Science student with some extra time.

Dave Wittry's Site (www.apcomputerscience.com/)

Dave is a high school teacher and faculty consultant for the College Board. His site features a variety of materials, including worksheets, information about development environments, and general AP news.